CENSUS OF INDIA 1901

Census of India 1871-1951, 9 Sets In 384 Bindings (9788121258876) Rs. 700000

Census of India 1901, 21 Vols. In 64 Bindings (9788121271356) Rs. 130000

1. India - Report (9788121279192) Rs. 3220 (Vol. I, Pt. 1)
2. India - Tables (9788121279178) Rs. 3000 (Vol. I-A, Pt. 2)
3. India - Administrative volume with appendices (9788121279239) Rs. 2220 (Vol. I, Pt. 3)
4. India - Ethnographic appendices : being the data upon which the caste chapter of the report is based (9788121279215) Rs. 1370 (Vol. I, Pt. 4)
5. Ajmer-Merwara - Report (9788121279147) Rs. 890 (Vol. II, Part 1)
6. Ajmer-Merwara - Tables (9788121279130) Rs. 1090 (Vol. II-A, Part 2)
7. The Andaman and Nicobar Islands : Report on the census (9788121279116) Rs. 2475 (Vol. III)
8. Assam - Report (9788121279086) Rs. 1130 (Vol. IV, Part 1)
9. Assam - Tables (9788121279079) Rs. 1630 (Vol. IV, Part 2)
10. Baluchistan - Report & Imperial Tables (9788121279031) Rs. 1440 (Vol. V and V-A, Part 1,2)
11. Baluchistan - Provincial Tables (9788121279017) Rs. 1970 (Vol. V-B, Part 3)
12. The Lower Provinces of Bengal Their Feudatories - Report (9788121278959) Rs. 3000 (Vol. VI, Pt. 1)
13. The Lower Provinces of Bengal And Their Feudatories - The Imperial Tables (9788121278942) Rs. 2630 (Vol. VI-A, Pt. 2)
14. The Lower Provinces of Bengal And Their Feudatories - Provincial Tables (9788121278935) Rs. 940 (Vol. VI-B, Pt. 3)
15. Report on the Census of Bengal - Administrative volume (9788121278966) Rs. 940 (Vol. VI-C, Pt. 4)
16. Calcutta : town and suburbs - A short history of Calcutta and Report (Administrative) (9788121278881) Rs. 1150 (Vol. VII, Pt. 1, 2)
17. Calcutta : town and suburbs - Tabular statistics (9788121278867) Rs. 3625 (Vol. VII, Pt. 3)
18. Calcutta : town and suburbs - Report (statistical) (9788121278850) Rs. 1000 (Vol. VII, Pt. 4)
19. Berar - Report (9788121278812) Rs. 1440 (Vol. VIII, Pt. 1)
20. Berar - Imperial Tables (9788121278805) Rs. 1075 (Vol. VIII-A, Pt. 2)
21. Berar - Provincial Tables (9788121278799) Rs. 650 (Vol. VIII-B, Pt. 3)
22. Bombay - Report (9788121278720) Rs. 1450 (Vol. IX, Pt. 1)
23. Bombay - Imperial Tables (9788121278713) Rs. 3425 (Vol. IX-A, Pt. 2)
24. Bombay - Provincial Tables (9788121278706) Rs. 1455 (Vol. IX-B, Pt. 3)
25. Bombay (Town & Island) - History (9788121278690) Rs. 820 (Vol. X. Pt. 4)
26. Bombay (Town & Island) - Report (9788121278683) Rs. 1005 (Vol. XI. Pt. 5)
27. Bombay (Town & Island) - Tables (9788121278676) Rs. 1670 (Vol. XI-A, Pt. 6)
28. Burma - Report (9788121278621) Rs. 1370 (Vol. XII. Pt. 1)
29. Burma - Imperial Tables (9788121278614) Rs. 2175 (Vol. XII-A, Pt. 2)
30. Burma - Provincial Tables : Lower Burma (9788121278607) Rs. 2570 (Vol. XII-B, Pt. 3)
31. Burma - Provincial Tables : Upper Burma, the Shan States and the Chin Hills (9788121278591) Rs. 3560 (Vol. XII-C, Pt. 4)
32. Central Provinces - Report (9788121278553) Rs. 1775 (Vol. XIII. Pt. 1)
33. Central Provinces - Tables (9788121278546) Rs. 3000 (Vol. XIII-A, Pt. 2)
34. Central Provinces - Provincial Tables (9788121278539) Rs. 800 (Vol. XIII. Pt. 3)
35. Coorg - Report and Tables and Madras - Report (9788121278478) Rs. 1860 (Vol. XIV, Vol. XV, Pt. 1)
36. Madras - Imperial Tables (9788121278461) Rs. 1950 (Vol. XV-A, Pt. 2)
37. Madras - Provincial Tables (9788121278454) Rs. 1220 (Vol. XV-B, Pt. 3)
38. N.-W. Provinces And Oudh - Report (9788121278416) Rs. 1590 (Vol. XVI. Pt. 1)
39. N.-W. Provinces And Oudh - Imperial Tables (9788121278409) Rs. 2640 (Vol. XVI-A, Pt. 2)
40. N.-W. Provinces And Oudh - Provincial Tables And Appendices (9788121278393) Rs. 525 (Vol. XVI-B, Pt. 3)
41. The Punjab, its feudatories and the North-west Frontier Province - The report on the census. (9788121278362) Rs. 2425 (Vol. XVII. Pt. 1)
42. Imperial Tables, I-VIII, X-XV, XVII and XVIII for the Punjab, with the native states under the political control of the Punjab Government, and for the North-west Frontier Province (9788121278355) Rs. 3075 (Vol. XVII-A. Pt. 2)
43. Baroda - Report (9788121278317) Rs. 3800 (Vol. XVIII, Pt. 1)
44. Baroda -Tables and Provincial Tables (9788121278300) Rs. 1570 (Vol. XVIII-A, Pt. 2, B, Pt. 3)
45. Central India - Report (9788121278256) Rs. 1540 (Vol. XIX. Pt. 1)
46. Central India - Tables (9788121278249) Rs. 1590 (Vol. XIX-A, Pt. 2)
47. Central India - Provincial Tables (9788121278232) Rs. 1450 (Vol. XIX-B, Pt. 3)
48. Cochin - Report and Imperial Tables (9788121278201) Rs. 2040 (Vol. XX. Pt. 1, XX- A, Pt. 2)
49. Gwalior - Report (9788121278164) Rs. 670 (Vol. XXI, Pt. 1)
50. Gwalior - Tables (9788121278157) Rs. 3045 (Vol. XXI-A, Pt. 2)
51. Hyderabad - Report (9788121278126) Rs. 2615 (Vol. XXII, Pt. 1)
52. Hyderabad -Tables (9788121278119) Rs. 1120 (Vol. XXII-A, Pt. 2)
53. Kashmir - Report (9788121278089) Rs. 645 (Vol. XXIII, Pt. 1)
54. Kashmir - Tables (9788121278072) Rs. 1800 (Vol. XXIII-A, Pt. 2)
55. Mysore - Report (9788121278027) Rs. 5275 (Vol. XXIV, Pt. 1)
56. Mysore - Tables (9788121278010) Rs. 4500 (Vol. XXIV-A, Pt. 2)
57. Mysore - Tables (9788121278003) Rs. 4200 (Vol. XXIV-B, Pt. 3)
58. Mysore - Tables (9788121277990) Rs. 4950 (Vol. XXIV-C, Pt. 4)
59. Rajputana - Report (9788121277952) Rs. 1300 (Vol. XXV, Pt. 1)
60. Rajputana - Imperial Tables (9788121277945) Rs. 4000 (Vol. XXV-A, Pt. 2)
61. Rajputana - Provincial Tables (9788121277938) Rs. 1920 (Vol. XXV-B, Pt. 3)
62. Travancore - Report (9788121277891) Rs. 2840 (Vol. XXVI. Pt. 1)
63. Travancore - Imperial Tables (9788121277884) Rs. 1920 (Vol. XXVI-A, Pt. 2)
64. Travancore - Provincial Tables (9788121277877) Rs. 3500 (Vol. XXVI-B, Pt. 3)

Owing to the antiquity and rarity of this book, certain pages are regrettably absent, and readability is compromised due to the blurring of the original text. If you possess any insights regarding the availability of these missing sections, kindly inform us. Your assistance is crucial in ensuring the completion of this significant work for the benefit of future generations.

CENSUS OF INDIA, 1901

BOOK - 54: VOLUME XXIII-A

KASHMIR

Part - II

TABLES

By

KHAN BAHADUR MUNSHI GHULAM AHMED KHAN

GYAN

Published by

Gyan Publishing House
5, Ansari Road
Daryaganj, New Delhi-110002
Phone: 011-47034999, 9811692060
E-mail: books@gyanbooks.com

Distribution Network
gyanbooks.com
India, USA, Canada, UK, Australia

ISBN: 978-81-212-7135-6 (Set) 21 Vols. In 64 Bindings
978-81-212-7807-2 (PB) Book-54, Vol. XXIII-A, Pt. II

First Published, 1902

2nd Impression 2024

Printed at: Gyan Press, Delhi.

CENSUS OF INDIA 1901

Author: KHAN BAHADUR MUNSHI GHULAM AHMED KHAN

CENSUS OF INDIA, 1901.

VOLUME XXIII-A.

KASHMIR.

PART II.

TABLES.

BY

KHAN BAHADUR MUNSHI GHULAM AHMED KHAN.
REVENUE MEMBER STATE COUNCIL,
AND
SUPERINTENDENT OF CENSUS OPERATIONS, JAMMU AND KASHMIR STATE.

Lahore:
THE "CIVIL AND MILITARY GAZETTE" PRESS,
Sole Contractors for Printing to the Punjab Government.
1902.

TABLE I.

JAMMU AND KASHMIR STATE.

Area, houses and population.

TABLE I.

JAMMU AND KASHMIR STATE

AREA, HOUSES AND POPULATION.

Province.	Area in square miles.	Towns.	Villages.	OCCUPIED HOUSES.			POPULATION.								
							PERSONS.			MALES.			FEMALES.		
				Total.	In towns.	In villages	Total.	Urban.	Rural.	Total.	Urban.	Rural	Total.	Urban.	Rural.
1	2	3	4	5	6	7	8	9	10	11	12	13	14	15	16
Total State ...	**80,900**	**2**	**8,946**	**464,635**	**25,055**	**439,580**	**2,905,578**	**158,748**	**2,746,830**	**1,542,057**	**87,763**	**1,454,294**	**1,363,521**	**70,985**	**1,292,536**
Jammu including Jagirs ...	5,223 (a)	1	4,472	271,887	6,816	265,071	1,521,307	36,130	1,485,177	807,792	22,221	785,571	713,515	13,909	699,606
Kashmir including Jagirs ...	7,022 (b)	1	3,740	153,136	18,239	134,897	1,157,394	122,018	1,034,776	616,887	65,542	551,345	540,507	57,076	483,431
Frontier Districts ...	443 (c)	...	725	39,612	...	39,612	226,877	...	226,877	117,378	...	117,378	109,499	...	109,499

(a)—Of these 2,266 are assessed square miles and 2,957 estimated, while the areas of Bhadarwah and Poonch Jagirs are not available

(b)—The whole is the assessed area.

(c)—The whole is the assessed area, while the areas of agency Ilaqas are not available

TABLE II.

JAMMU AND KASHMIR STATE.

Variation in Population since 1872.

TABLE

JAMMU AND

VARIATION IN

Province.	Persons. 1901	1891	1881.	1872.
1	2	3	4	5
JAMMU PROVINCE				
Jammu	344,016	307,970	..	..
Udhampur	284,048	323,515	...	..
Bhimber	400,229	355,499		..
Jasrota	154,213	151,518	...	...
Jogirs { *Punch*	304,488	268,609	...	...
Jogirs { *Bhadarwah*	34,311	32,433	...	...
Total Jammu Province	1,521,307	1,439,543	.	...
KASHMIR PROVINCE.				
Khas	989,196	814,241	...	...
Mozaffarabad	168,198	134,900	...	.
Total Kashmir Province	1,157,394	949,041		...
FRONTIER DISTRICTS.				
Ladakh	165,992	138,599	..	...
Gilgit	60,885	16,769	...	...
Total Frontier Districts	226,877	155,368	...	...
TOTAL STATE	2,905,578	2,543,952	...	..

KASHMIR STATE.

POPULATION SINCE 1872.

Variation Increase (+) or Decrease (−)			Net variation in period 1872–1901 Increase (+) or Decrease (−).	Males.				Females.			
1891 to 1901.	1881 to 1891.	1872 to 1881.		1901.	1891.	1881.	1872.	1901.	1891.	1881.	1872.
6	7	8	9	10	11	12	13	14	15	16	17
+36,048	...	...	...	185,722	169,413	...	...	158,296	138,557	...	...
−39,467	...	..	.	151,425	172,421	..	.	132,623	151,094	...	...
+41,730	...	...	...	210,075	188,253	...	...	190,154	167,246	...	...
+2,695	...	...	...	82,301	81,434	...	...	71,822	70,084	...	...
+35,880	.	...	...	160,679	141,945	..	...	143,809	126,663	...	...
+1,878	...	...	...	17,590	16,775		..	16,811	15,658	...	...
+81,764	..	..	...	**807,792**	**770,241**	.	..	**713,515**	**669,302**	...	...
+174,955	...	...	...	526,158	429,464	...		463,038	384,777	..	..
+33,398	...	...	..	90,729	72,881	...	...	77,469	61,910	.	...
+208,353	...	...	..	**616,887**	**502,345**		–	**540,507**	**446,696**	...	...
+27,393	...	..		83,600	70,448	...	.	82,392	68,151	...	...
+44,116	...	...	...	33,778	10,195	...	...	27,107	6,574	...	...
+71,509	...	...	...	**117,378**	**80,643**	.	–	**109,499**	**74,725**	...	...
+361,626	...	...	...	**1,542,057**	**1,353,229**	...	...	**1,363,521**	**1,190,723**	...	...

TABLE III.

JAMMU AND KASHMIR STATE.

Towns and Villages classified by Population

JAMMU AND

TOWNS AND VILLAGES

Province.	Total number of inhabited towns and villages.	Population.	Under 500.		500 – 1,000.		1,000—2,000.	
			Number.	Population.	Number.	Population.	Number.	Population.
1	2	3	4	5	6	7	8	9
JAMMU PROVINCE.								
JAMMU	1,101	344,018	1,064	188,585	86	59,141	32	40,025
UDHAMPUR	1,055	284,048	913	165,378	106	71,870	31	38,147
BHIMBER	1,019	400,229	789	168,919	158	101,217	54	75,328
JASROTA	584	154,213	506	83,887	63	41,822	11	14,840
Jagirs { *Punch*	491	304,488	279	67,474	122	87,654	73	101,691
Jagirs { *Bhadarwah* . ..	133	34,311	129	29,394	3	2,263	...	...
TOTAL JUMMOO PROVINCE ...	4,473	1,521,307	3,656	703,696	540	363,967	201	270,040
KASHMIR PROVINCE.								
KHAS	2,920	989,196	2,475	482,375	343	214,491	87	1,16,616
MUZAFFERABAD	827	168,198	773	124,084	41	26,172	12	14,530
TOTAL KASHMIR PROVINCE ...	3,747	1,157,394	3,243	606,459	384	240,663	99	131,045
FRONTIER DISTRICTS								
LADAKH	461	165,992	374	78,000	62	42,541	22	30,559
GILGIT	264	60,885	238	37,102	22	14,534	2	3,074
TOTAL FRONTIER DISTRICTS ...	728	226,877	612	115,201	84	57,075	24	33,633
TOTAL STATE ...	8,948	2,905,578	7,540	1,425,256	1,008	661,705	324	434,718

KASHMIR STATE.

CLASSIFIED BY POPULATION

2,000 – 5,000.		5,000 – 10,000.		10,000 – 20,000.		20,000 – 50,000.		50,000 – 100,000.		Over 100,000.	
Number.	Population.	Number.	Population.	Number.	Population.	Number.	Population.	Number.	Population.	Number.	Population.
10	11	12	13	14	15	16	17	18	19	20	21
8	20,137		...	-	...	1	36,150	...	...	..	...
3	8,053	...	...	...	...	...	...	...	...	...	...
17	47,736	1	7 030	...	...	...	..	...	...	...	...
3	7,8[illegible]4	1	5,801	...	...	...	...	...	...	...	...
16	39,454	1	8,215	...	...	...	...	...	...	...	...
1	2,654	...	...	..	...	...	...	...	...	...	...
48	126 488	3	21.046	...	...	1	36.130	...	...	...	...
11	29,318	3	23,579	...	...	...	...	...	...	1	122,618
1	3,412	...	...	...	...	...	...	...	...	...	...
12	32.730	3	23.579	...	...	...	...	...	...	1	122.318
6	14,793	...		...	...	...	...	...	...	...	...
2	6,175	..		...	...	...	.	...	...	...	...
8	20.963		..				..		..	...	...
63	180.186	6	44.925	...		1	36 130	.	...	1	122.618

TABLE IV.

JAMMU AND KASHMIR STATE.

Towns classified by population with variation since 1872.

TABLE IV.

JAMMU AND KASHMIR STATE.

TOWNS CLASSIFIED BY POPULATION WITH VARIATION SINCE 1872.

Town.	District or State.	Municipality, Suburbs, Cantonments, Civil Lines, etc.	Population.				Variation Increase (+) or Decrease (-)			Net Variation in period 1872 to 1901. Increase (+) or Decrease (-).	Males.				Females.			
			1901.	1891.	1881.	1872.	1891 to 1901.	1881 to 1891	1872 to 1881		1901.	1891.	1881.	1872	1901.	1891.	1881	1872
1	2	3	4	5	6	7	8	9	10	11	12	13	14	15	16	17	18	19
Total State ...	...	...	158,748	153,502	...	...	+ 5,246	...	...	...	87,763	85,265	...	...	70,985	68,237	...	...
Jammu ...	Jammu ...	Municipality ...	34,879	34,542	...	...	+ 337	...	...	...	21,079	22,545	...	...	13,800	11,897	...	...
		Cantonment ...	1,251	...	...	...	+ 1,251	...	...	...	1,142	...	...	...	109	...	...	...
		Total ...	36,130	34,542	...	...	+ 1,588	...	...	...	22,221	22,545	...	...	13,909	11,897	...	...
Srinagar ...	Khas (Kashmir) ...	Municipality ...	122,618	118,960	...	...	+ 3,658	...	...	—	65,542	62,720	...	...	57,076	56,340	...	...

TABLE V.

JAMMU AND KASHMIR STATE.

Towns arranged Territorially with Population by Religions.

TABLE

JAMMU AND

TOWNS ARRANGED TERRITORIALLY

INDO

Province.	Town.	Population.			Hindu.								
					Total			Sanatan.			Arya.		
		Persons.	Males.	Females.	Persons.	Males.	Females.	Persons.	Males.	Females.	Persons.	Males.	Females.
1	2	3	4	5	6	7	8	9	10	11	12	13	14
Total ...	...	158-748	87.783	70.965	48.985	28.141	20.844	48.906	28.091	20.815	79	50	29
Jammu	Jammu ...	36,130	22,221	13,909	21,112	12,881	8,231	21,063	12,831	8,202	79	50	29
Kashmir	Srinagar ...	1,22,618	65,542	57,076	27,873	15,260	12,613	27,873	15,260	12,613	...	..	...

NOTE.—The above are the only.

KASHMIR STATE.

WITH POPULATION BY RELIGIONS.

ARYAN.						IRANIAN			SEMITIC.														
Sikh.			Jain			Zoroastrian.			Musalman.									Christian			Minor.		
									Total			Other than Ahmadias			Ahmadias.								
Persons.	Males.	Females.	Persons	Males.	Females.	Persons.	Males.	Females	Persons.	Males.	Females	Persons	Males	Females.	Persons	Males.	Females.	Persons.	Males	Females.	Persons.	Males.	Females.
15	16	17	18	19	20	21	22	23	24	25	26	27	28	29	30	31	32	33	34	35	36	37	38
1.379	903	478	433	251	167	11	8	3	107.648	58.307	49.341	107 605	58.285	49.320	43	22	21	253	132	121	34	21	13
885	548	337	437	251	180	...	...	...	13.627	8.501	5,126	13.584	8.479	5.105	45	22	21	69	40	29	...	...	...
494	355	139	1	...	1	11	8	3	94.021	49.806	44.215	94.021	49.806	44.215	...	...	...	184	92	92	34	21	13

religions returned in the cities.

TABLE VI.

JAMMU AND KASHMIR STATE.

Religion

TABLE

JAMMU AND

RELI

District.	Total Population.			INDO Hindu Total			Sanatan		
	Persons.	Males.	Females.	Persons	Males	Females.	Persons.	Males.	Females.
1	2	3	4	5	6	7	8	9	10
TOTAL STATE ...	2,905.578	1,542.057	1,363.521	689.073	370.801	318.272	688.994	370.751	318.243
TOTAL JAMMU PROVINCE INCLUDING JAGIRS.	1,521,307	807,792	713,515	626.177	334,418	291,759	626.098	334,368	291,730
JAMMU	344,018	185,722	158,296	207,412	111,757	95,656	207,333	111,707	95,626
UDHAMPUR	284,048	151,425	132,623	171,470	91,050	80,420	171,470	91,050	80,420
BHIMBER	400,220	210,075	190,154	83,051	44,450	38,592	83,051	44,459	38, 59[illegible]
JASROTA	154,213	82,391	71,822	121,779	64,674	57,105	121,779	64,674	57,105
Jagirs.{ Punch ... Bhadarwah ... }	338,799	178,179	160,620	42,465	22,478	19,987	42,465	22,478	19,987

VI.

KASHMIR STATE.

GION.

ARYAN.

Arya.			Sikh.			Jain.			Buddhist.		
Persons.	Males.	Females.	Persons.	Males.	Females.	Persons.	Males.	Females.	Persons.	Males.	Females.
11	12	13	14	15	16	17	18	19	20	21	22
79	50	29	25.828	14.342	11.486	442	254	188	35.047	17.566	17.481
79	50	29	13,113	7.418	5,695	439	252	187	4,831	2,431	2,400
79	50	29	2.257	1,333	924	437	251	186	...	...	...
...	...	...	155	102	53	2	1	1	4,831	2,431	2.400
...	...	...	2,638	1,537	1,101	...	...	...	...	...	...
...	...	...	179	123	56	...	...	...	...	...	...
...	...	...	7,554	4.323	3,561	...	...	...	...	...	...

TABLE

JAMMU AND

RELI

District.	IRANIAN.			SEMI			
	Zoroastrian.			Muham			
				Total.			Other
	Persons.	Males.	Females.	Persons.	Males.	Females.	Persons.
1	23	24	25	26	27	28	29
TOTAL STATE ...	11	8	3	2,154,695	1,138,814	1,015,881	2,154,652
TOTAL JAMMU PROVINCE INCLUDING JAGIRS.	...	...	...	876,599	463,186	413,413	876,536
JAMMU	...	...	...	133,775	72,301	61,474	133,732
UDHAMPUR	...	...	...	107,588	57,839	49,749	107,588
BHIMBER	...	...	...	314,539	164,078	150,461	314,539
JASROTA	...	...	...	32,255	17,594	14,661	32,255
Jagirs. { Punch ... / Bhadarwah ... }	...	...	...	288,442	151,374	137,068	288,442

KASHMIR STATE.

GION—concluded.

TIC.								Minor.		
MADAN.					Christian.					
than Ahamdia.		Ahamdia.								
Males.	Females.	Persons.	Males.	Females.	Persons.	Males.	Females.	Persons.	Males.	Females.
30	31	32	33	34	35	36	37	38	39	40
1,138,793	1,015,880	43	22	21	422	236	186	60	36	24
463,164	413,392	43	22	21	145	87	58	3	...	3
72,279	61,453	43	22	21	134	80	54	3	...	3
57,839	49,749	...	...	...	2	2	...	...	...	...
161,075	150,461	...	...	...	1	1	...	...	...	...
17,594	14,661	...	...	...	...	...	...	...	...	...
151,374	137,065	...	...	...	5	4	4	...	...	...

TABLE VI.

JAMMU AND KASHMIR STATE.

Religion

TABLE

JAMMU AND

RELI

District.	Total Population.			INDO-: Hindu: Total			Sanatan.		
	Persons.	Males.	Females.	Persons.	Males.	Females.	Persons.	Males.	Females.
1	2	3	4	5	6	7	8	9	10
Kashmir Province ...	1,157,394	616,887	540,507	60,682	34,261	26,421	60,682	34,261	26,421
Srinagar	969,196	520,158	463,038	56,317	31,718	24,799	56,317	31,718	24,799
Muzaffarabad ...	168,189	90,729	77,460	4,165	2,543	1,622	4,165	2,543	1,022
Frontier District ...	226,877	117,378	109,490	2,214	2,122	92	2,214	2,122	92
Ladakh	165,992	83,600	82,392	213	189	24	213	189	24
Gilgit	60,885	33,778	27,107	2,001	1,933	68	2,001	1,933	68

KASHMIR STATE.

GION.

ARYAN.

Arya.			Sikh.			Jain.			Buddhist.		
Persons.	Males.	Females.	Persons.	Males.	Females.	Persons.	Males.	Females.	Persons.	Males.	Females.
11	12	13	14	15	16	17	18	19	20	21	22
...	...	...	12,637	6,860	5,777	2	1	1	...	...	...
...	...	...	6,027	3,283	2,744	2	1	1	...	...	...
...	...	...	6,610	3,577	3,033	...	...	...	...	...	...
...	...	...	75	64	11	1	1	...	30,216	15,135	15,081
...	...	...	4	3	1	...	...	...	30,216	15,135	15,081
...	...	...	74	61	13	1	1	...	...	...	...

TABLE

JAMMU AND

RELI

District.	IRANIAN.			SEMI			
				MOHAM			
	ZOROASTRIAN.			Total.			Other
	Persons.	Males.	Females.	Persons.	Males.	Females.	Persons.
1	23	24	25	26	27	28	29
KASHMIR PROVINCE ...	11	8	3	1,083,766	575,598	508,168	1,083,766
SRINAGAR	11	8	3	926,360	491,000	435,360	926,360
MUZAFFARABAD	...	...	...	157,406	84,598	72,808	157,406
FRONTIER DISTRICT ...	...	...	...	194,330	100,030	94,300	194,330
LADAKH	...	...	...	135,551	68,268	67,283	135,551
GILGIT ...	...	...	...	58,779	31,762	27,017	58,779

VI.

KASHMIR STATE.

GION—concluded.

TIC.

MADAN.					CHRISTIAN.			MINOR.		
than Aramdis.		Aramdis.								
Males.	Females.	Persons.	Males.	Females.	Persons.	Males.	Females.	Persons.	Males.	Females.
30	31	32	33	34	35	36	37	38	39	40
575,598	508,168	—	...	...	244	128	116	52	31	21
491,000	435,[illegible]	...	...	...	235	122	113	44	26	18
84,598	72,508	...	...	...	9	6	3	8	5	3
[illegible]	94,[illegible]	...	...	...	33	21	12	5	5	...
68,265	67,2[illegible]8	...	...	...	5	2	3	3	3	...
3[illegible],762	27,017	...	...	...	28	19	9	2	2	...

TABLE VII.

JAMMU AND KASHMIR STATE.

Age, Sex and Civil Condition by Religion.

TABLE VII.

JAMMU AND KASHMIR STATE.

AGE, SEX AND CIVIL CONDITION BY RELIGION.

Age.	Population.			Unmarried.			Married.			Widowed.		
	Persons.	Males.	Females.	Persons.	Males.	Females.	Persons.	Males.	Females.	Persons.	Males.	Females.
1	2	3	4	5	6	7	8	9	10	11	12	13
TOTAL STATE ...	**2,905,578**	**1,542,057**	**1,363,521**	**1,362,410**	**824,112**	**538,298**	**1,308,548**	**647,745**	**660,803**	**234,620**	**70,200**	**164,420**
I.—All Religions.												
0 and under 1 ...	107,900	54,454	53,506	107,876	54,419	53,457	83	35	48	1	...	1
1 " " 2 ...	45,282	23,783	21,499	45,216	23,758	21,458	64	25	39	2	.	
2 " " 3 ...	87,259	43,509	43,750	86,980	43,430	43,550	272	70	103	7	...	7
3 " " 4 ...	93,835	46,373	47,462	93,241	46,145	47,096	503	219	344	31	9	22
4 " " 5 ...	88,081	45,306	43,015	88,306	45,136	43,170	641	217	427	31	13	18
Total 0 and under 5 ...	**423,217**	**213,485**	**209,832**	**421,619**	**212,888**	**208,731**	**1,626**	**575**	**1,051**	**72**	**22**	**50**
5 and under 10 ...	428,708	223,551	205,217	416,428	221,044	195,384	11,881	2,300	9,491	489	117	372
10 " " 15 ...	341,555	189,531	152,024	272,842	174,770	98,063	66,980	14,368	52,618	1,727	384	1,313
15 " " 20 ...	239,670	128,389	111,287	111,536	91,933	19,603	123,401	35,093	88,458	4,079	1,153	3,226
20 " " 25 ...	222,035	109,245	113,300	52,213	47,280	4,933	102,912	50,404	103,418	7,510	2,471	5,039
25 " " 30 ...	220,147	117,065	111,482	36,071	30,023	6,048	180,071	82,557	98,114	11,705	4,185	7,830
30 " " 35 ...	246,013	132,735	113,278	19,231	16,870	2,356	207,105	100,120	97,070	10,077	6,730	12,047
35 " " 40 ...	165,048	92,511	72,537	10,823	9,600	1,157	138,003	77,651	61,040	15,022	5,201	10,881

40 and under 45	188,680	100,886	87,702	7,068	7,337	651	149,273	84,772	64,501	31,410	8,779	22,640
45 " " 50	92,067	51,110	40,957	3,667	3,411	256	70,252	42,483	27,769	18,148	5,210	12,032
50 " " 55	121,042	69,299	52,343	3,616	3,307	309	83,632	56,597	27,035	34,391	9,395	24,999
55 " " 60	36,685	20,283	16,462	1,697	1,618	79	24,344	16,027	8,317	11,244	3,238	8,006
60 " over	170,315	93,365	76,950	4,679	3,950	729	87,502	66,496	21,006	78,134	22,919	55,215
Total Hindus	689,073	370,801	318,272	289,049	193,679	95,370	307,792	152,443	155,349	92,232	24,679	67,553
0 and under 1	18,355	9,676	8,679	18,347	9,676	8,671	11	3	8	...	...	...
1 " " 2	9,591	6,100	4,491	9,583	5,098	4,485	8	2	6	...	...	...
2 " " 3	15,856	7,815	8,041	15,824	7,805	8,019	29	10	19	...	...	...
3 " " 4	17,027	8,954	8,073	17,544	8,635	8,909	73	18	55	3	...	3
4 " " 5	16,768	8,282	8,476	16,617	8,237	8,380	135	44	91	10	1	9
										6	1	5
Total 0 and under 5	78,190	39,530	38,660	77,915	39,451	38,464	256	77	179	19	2	17
II.—Hindus. 5 and under 10	80,143	43,985	42,158	81,901	43,417	38,484	4,043	528	3,515	199	40	159
10 " " 15	74,782	43,284	31,498	55,421	39,071	16,450	18,633	3,197	15,436	728	116	612
15 " " 20	56,365	30,467	25,898	23,737	21,961	1,776	30,951	8,195	22,756	1,677	311	1,366
20 " " 25	57,201	28,888	28,313	15,470	14,995	475	38,744	13,197	25,547	2,987	696	2,291
25 " " 30	63,657	34,215	29,442	11,751	11,467	284	46,703	21,371	25,332	5,203	1,377	3,826
30 " " 35	63,649	34,908	28,741	7,941	7,752	189	47,323	25,071	22,252	8,385	2,085	6,300
35 " " 40	40,259	22,965	17,294	4,046	3,986	60	29,591	17,290	12,301	6,622	1,779	4,843
40 " " 45	49,410	27,084	22,326	3,938	3,863	75	32,705	20,244	12,461	12,767	2,077	9,790
45 " " 50	25,254	11,450	10,804	2,062	1,981	21	15,508	10,268	5,240	7,744	2,201	5,543
50 " " 55	32,983	18,707	14,186	1,979	1,935	44	18,512	13,528	4,984	12,492	3,334	9,158
55 " " 60	11,299	6,640	4,750	664	655	9	6,072	4,509	1,563	4,563	1,376	3,187
60 " over	49,881	25,658	24,193	2,254	2,215	39	18,751	15,058	3,693	28,846	8,385	20,461

TABLE VII.

JAMMU AND KASHMIR STATE.

AGE, SEX AND CIVIL CONDITION BY RELIGION.—continued.

Age.	Population.			Unmarried.			Married.			Widowed.		
	Persons.	Males.	Females.	Persons.	Males.	Females.	Persons.	Males.	Females.	Persons.	Males.	Females.
1	2	3	4	5	6	7	8	9	10	11	12	13
Total Sikhs	25.828	14.342	11.486	12.410	7.848	4.562	11.577	5.913	5.664	1.841	521	1.280
III.—Sikhs. 0 and under 1	1.085	526	559	1.085	526	559	...	...	...	...	...	...
1 " " 2	330	176	154	330	176	154	...	...	...	...	...	...
2 " " 3	831	445	386	831	445	386	...	...	...	...	...	...
3 " " 4	785	408	379	781	404	377	3	1	2	1	1	...
4 " " 5	810	427	383	806	426	380	3	1	2	...	...	...
Total 0 and under 5	3.850	1.980	1.870	3.843	1.977	1.866	6	2	4	1	1	...
5 and under 10	3,810	2,097	1,723	3,755	2,082	1,073	59	14	45	5	1	
10 " " 15	2,945	1,730	1,215	2,534	1,066	868	400	63	337	11	1	10
15 " " 20	2,286	1,270	1,016	1,069	968	101	1,100	207	893	27	5	22
20 " " 25	2,091	1,060	932	488	465	23	1,463	583	880	50	21	29
25 " " 30	2,085	1.119	966	316	304	12	1,096	788	808	63	27	56
30 " " 35	2,101	1.166	935	166	158	8*	1,810	966	844	125	42	83
35 " " 40	1,380	704	676	54	52	2	1,190	702	455	125	40	85

40 „ „ 45 ...	1,089	906	783	75	68	7	1,305	771	594	240	67	152
45 „ „ 50 ...	723	469	254	30	29	1	530	407	173	113	33	80
50 „ „ 55 ...	1,134	665	409	29	29	...	781	511	210	324	95	229
55 „ „ 60 ...	292	187	105	6	6	...	207	119	58	79	32	47
60 „ over ...	1,534	500	641	45	11	1	840	630	210	649	216	433
Total Jains ...	442	254	188	191	125	66	196	103	93	55	28	29
IV.—Jains. 0 and under 1 ...	3	2	1	3	2	1	...	...	...	...	...	...
1 „ „ 2 ...	6	3	3	6	3	3	...	...	...	...	...	...
2 „ „ 3 ...	14	11	3	14	11	3	...	...	...	...	...	...
3 „ „ 4 ...	9	4	5	9	4	5	...	...	...	...	...	...
4 „ „ 5 ...	15	9	6	15	9	6	...	...	...	...	...	...
Total 0 and under 5 ...	47	29	18	47	29	18	...	...	...	...	...	...
5 and under 10 ...	45	22	23	43	21	22	2	1	1	...	...	...
10 „ „ 15 ...	50	24	26	45	23	22	4	...	4	1	1	...
15 „ „ 20 ...	41	26	15	13	11	2	27	11	13	1	1	...
20 „ „ 25 ...	40	24	16	10	9	1	29	11	15	1	1	...
25 „ „ 30 ...	41	33	8	10	10	...	27	19	8	4	4	...
30 „ „ 35 ...	35	18	17	5	5	...	23	9	11	7	4	3
35 „ „ 40 ...	23	12	11	3	3	...	17	8	9	3	1	2
40 „ „ 45 ...	41	20	21	3	3	...	30	15	15	8	2	6
45 „ „ 50 ...	20	13	7	3	3	...	14	8	6	3	2	1
50 „ „ 55 ...	25	16	9	4	4	...	14	8	6	7	4	3
55 „ „ 60 ...	8	5	3	1	1	...	3	2	1	4	3	2
60 „ over ...	26	12	14	4	3	1	6	5	1	16	4	12

TABLE VII.

JAMMU AND KASHMIR STATE.

AGE, SEX AND CIVIL CONDITION BY RELIGION,—continued.

V.—Buddhists.

Age.	Population.			Unmarried.			Married.			Widowed.		
	Persons.	Males.	Females.	Persons.	Males.	Females.	Persons.	Males.	Females.	Persons.	Males.	Females.
1	2	3	4	5	6	7	8	9	10	11	12	13
Total Budhists	35.047	17.566	17.481	14.532	7.539	6.993	16.911	8 773	8.138	3.604	1 254	2.350
0 and under 1	720	354	366	720	354	366	...	...	...		...	...
1 " " 2	213	95	118	213	95	118	...	..	...	...	...	...
2 " " 3	474	232	242	472	232	240	1	...	1	1	...	1
3 " " 4	695	343	352	683	335	348	12	8	4	...	...	
4 " " 5	673	336	337	661	330	331	11	5	6	1	1	...
Total 0 and under 5	2.775	1.360	1.415	2.749	1.346	1.403	24	13	11	2	1	1
5 and under 10	3.821	1.951	1.873	3,663	1,871	1,792	150	70	80	2	1	1
10 " " 15	3,213	1,632	1,581	2,745	1,340	1,405	416	260	157	22	3	19
15 " " 20	2,961	1,531	1,130	1,932	977	955	987	531	456	42	23	19

20 „ „ 25	2,532	1,234	1,298	938	454	484	1,400	701	709	125	70	46
25 „ „ 30	2,809	1,467	1,342	550	322	228	1,082	927	1,055	277	218	59
30 „ „ 35	2,716	1,520	1,187	339	329	110	2,142	1,091	1,051	335	200	26
35 „ „ 40	2,524	1,361	1,163	281	200	81	1,972	1,022	950	271	139	132
40 „ „ 45	2,256	1,186	1,070	244	167	77	1,708	865	843	304	154	150
45 „ „ 50	1,921	986	935	151	102	49	1,474	778	696	296	106	190
50 „ „ 55	1,726	841	885	206	143	63	1,250	658	592	270	40	230
55 „ „ 60	1,057	526	531	93	66	27	794	436	358	170	24	146
60 „ over	4,733	1,902	2,771	641	322	319	2,504	1,383	1,121	1,588	257	1,331
Total Zoroastrians ...	11	8	3	3	3	...	8	5	3	...	...	...
VI.—Zoroastrians												
0 and under 1	2	2		2	2	...	...	...	...	...	.	...
Total 0 and under 5 ...	2	2	.	2	2	...	...		...	...		...
5 and under 10	1	1	.	1	1	...		...	...	...	...	...
20 „ „ 25	2	...	2	...	...	...	2	..	2		...	...
25 „ „ 30	1	1	...	...	...	...	1	1	...	...	...	...
30 „ „ 35	2	2	...	...	...	...	2	2	...		...	..
40 „ „ 45	2	1	1	...	...	...	2	1	1	...	...	...
45 „ „ 50	1	1	...	...	...	...	1	1	...	...	...	...

TABLE VII.

JAMMU AND KASHMIR STATE.

AGE, SEX AND CIVIL CONDITION BY RELIGION.—continued.

VI.—Musalmans.

Age.	Population.			Unmarried.			Married.			Widowed.		
	Persons.	Males.	Females.	Persons.	Males.	Females.	Persons.	Males.	Females.	Persons.	Males.	Females.
1	2	3	4	5	6	7	8	9	10	11	12	13
Total Musalmans ...	**2,154,695**	**1,138,814**	**1,015,881**	**1,045,952**	**614,764**	**431,188**	**971,884**	**480,403**	**491,481**	**136,859**	**43,647**	**93,212**
0 and under 1	87,773	43,883	43,890	87,700	43,851	43,840	72	32	40	1	...	1
1 " " 2	35,133	18,404	16,729	35,075	18,381	16,094	56	23	33	2	...	2
2 " " 3	70,070	35,001	35,069	69,535	34,932	34,893	243	69	173	3	...	3
3 " " 4	74,700	36,953	37,747	74,205	36,754	37,451	475	102	283	20	7	13
4 " " 5	70,707	36,311	34,396	70,188	36,133	34,055	495	107	328	24	11	13
Total 0 and under 5 ...	**338,383**	**170,552**	**167,831**	**336,393**	**170,051**	**166,942**	**1,340**	**483**	**857**	**50**	**18**	**32**
5 and under 10	334,015	175,172	159,143	327,015	173,629	153,386	7,017	1,768	5,840	283	75	208
10 " " 15	260,336	142,645	117,691	212,089	131,783	80,306	47,303	10,810	36,684	964	263	701
15 " " 20	177,996	95,081	82,915	84,763	68,004	16,759	90,301	25,904	64,337	2,932	1,113	1,819
20 " " 25	169,592	77,090	92,503	35,274	31,335	3,939	121,181	44,990	76,191	4,347	1,674	2,673
25 " " 30	160,492	90,794	70,098	24,011	18,499	5,512	130,546	59,738	70,808	5,935	2,557	3,378
30 " " 35	177,450	95,076	82,374	10,761	8,718	2,043	155,760	81,969	73,800	10,920	4,350	6,331
35 " " 40	120,836	67,355	53,481	6,432	5,421	1,011	105,806	58,604	47,202	8,598	3,330	5,268

40 and under 45 ...	135,257	71,674	63,583	3,723	3,231	402	113,445	63,865	50,580	15,089	5,078	12,511
45 " " 50 ...	64,137	35,181	28,953	1,470	1,294	185	52,608	31,017	21,651	9,000	2,873	7,117
50 " " 55 ...	85,760	48,973	36,787	1,397	1,106	201	63,064	41,855	21,200	21,298	5,021	15,377
55 " " 60 ...	24,032	13,023	11,000	383	200	43	17,203	10,920	6,334	6,426	1,903	4,023
60 " over ...	114,110	64,788	40,322	1,702	1,333	309	65,381	49,402	15,979	47,027	14,053	32,974
Total Christians ...	**422**	**236**	**186**	**236**	**131**	**105**	**162**	**95**	**67**	**24**	**10**	**14**
0 and under 1 ...	14	7	7	14	7	7	...	...	...	...	...	...
1 " " 2 ...	7	4	3	7	4	3	...	...	...	...	...	...
2 " " 3 ...	13	5	7	12	5	7	...		...	...	...	...
3 " " 4 ...	16	11	5	16	11	5	...	...	...	...	...	...
4 " " 5 ...	9	1	8	9	1	8	...	...	...	...	...	...
Total 0 and under 5 ...	**58**	**28**	**30**	**58**	**28**	**30**		...	...			...
5 and under 10 ...	43	20	23	42	20	22	1		1	...	...	...
10 " " 15 ...	25	13	12	25	13	12			...	...	...	...
15 " " 20 ...	24	13	12	10	10	9	5	2	3	...	...	...
20 " " 25 ...	46	22	24	20	15	11	20	7	13	...	...	...
25 " " 30 ...	67	32	25	30	18	12	24	12	12	5	2	1
30 " " 35 ...	57	35	22	19	14	5	33	20	13	5	1	4
35 " " 40 ...	35	23	12	7	4	3	25	17	8	3	2	1
40 " " 45 ...	24	16	8	5	5	...	17	10	7	2	1	1
45 " " 50 ...	11	7	4	2	2	...	7	4	3	2	1	1
50 " " 55 ...	13	6	7	1	...	1	10	6	4	2	...	2
55 " " 60 ...	6	2	4	...	...	...	5	2	3	1	...	1
60 " over ...	28	20	3	3	2	...	15	15	...	6	3	3

VIII.—CHRISTIANS.

TABLE VII.

JAMMU AND KASHMIR STATE.

AGE, SEX AND CIVIL CONDITION BY RELIGION.—concluded.

Age.	Population.			Unmarried.			Married.			Widowed.		
	Persons.	Males.	Females.	Persons.	Males.	Females.	Persons.	Males.	Females.	Persons.	Males.	Females.
1	2	3	4	5	6	7	8	9	10	11	12	13
Total Unspecified	60	36	24	37	23	14	18	10	8	5	3	2
IX.—Unspecified. 0 and under 1	5	1	4	5	1	4	...	...	...	...	...	...
1 " " 2	2	1	1	2	1	1	...	...	...	...	...	...
2 " " 3	2	...	2	2	...	2	...	...	...	...	...	...
3 " " 4	3	2	1	3	2	1	...	...	...	...	...	...
Total 0 and under 5	12	4	8	12	4	8	...	...	—	...	...	...
5 and under 10	8	3	5	8	3	5	...	...	...	...	...	...
10 " " 15	4	3	1	3	3	...	...	...	...	1	...	1
15 " " 20	3	2	1	3	2	1	...	...	...	...	...	...
20 " " 25	11	9	2	7	7	...	4	2	2	...	...	...

25 „ „ 30	5	4	1	8	8	...	3	1	1	...	...	...
30 „ „ 35	3	1	2	...	...	...	8	1	8	...	...	...
35 „ „ 40	2	1	1	...	...	...	2	1	1	...	...	...
40 „ „ 45	1	1	...	...	...	...	1	1	...	...	...	...
50 „ „ 55	2	2	...	...	...	...	1	1	...	1	1	...
55 „ „ 60	1	1	...	...	...	...	...	...	...	1	1	...
60 „ over	8	5	3	1	1	...	5	3	2	2	1	1

TABLE VII.

JAMMU AND KASHMIR STATE.

JAMMU PROVINCE.

Age, Sex and Civil Condition by Religion.

TABLE VII.

JAMMU AND KASHMIR STATE.

JAMMU PROVINCE.

AGE, SEX AND CIVIL CONDITION BY RELIGION.

Age.	Population.			Unmarried.			Married.			Widowed.		
	Persons.	Males.	Females.	Persons.	Males.	Females.	Persons.	Males.	Females.	Persons.	Males.	Females.
1	2	3	4	5	6	7	8	9	10	11	12	13
I—Hindus. Total Hindus	**626.177**	**334.418**	**291.759**	**259.284**	**173.243**	**86.041**	**281.705**	**138.556**	**143.149**	**85.188**	**22.619**	**62.569**
0 and under 1	10,235	8,596	7,630	10,227	8,595	7,632	8	1	7	...		...
1 " " 2	8,885	4,737	4,148	8,878	4,736	4,142	7	1	6	...	...	...
2 " " 3	14,308	7,046	7,262	14,280	7,036	7,244	27	10	17	1	...	1
3 " " 4	15,899	7,848	8,051	15,828	7,833	7,995	64	14	50	7	1	6
4 " " 5	15,315	7,538	7,777	15,179	7,496	7,683	131	42	89	5	...	5
Total 0 and under 5	**70.642**	**35.765**	**34.877**	**70.332**	**35.696**	**34.696**	**237**	**68**	**169**	**13**	**1**	**12**
5 and under 10	78,433	40,053	38,380	74,294	39,515	34,779	3,955	504	3,451	184	34	150
10 " " 15	68,578	39,606	28,973	60,273	39,518	13,755	17,500	2,973	14,617	715	114	601
15 " " 20	51,090	27,324	23,766	21,133	19,454	1,679	28,357	7,675	20,782	1,600	295	1,305
20 " " 25	51,134	25,270	25,864	13,257	12,846	411	35,115	11,781	23,337	2,729	643	2,086
25 " " 30	57,385	30,280	27,105	10,227	9,951	276	43,361	19,052	23,309	4,797	1,277	3,520
30 " " 35	58,075	31,533	26,542	6,983	6,799	184	43,226	22,781	20,445	7,866	1,053	5,813
35 " " 40	36,430	20,521	15,909	3,623	3,464	59	26,800	15,423	11,377	6,107	1,634	4,473

40 " " 45	45,171	24,685	20,486	3,361	3,293	68	30,141	18,744	11,397	11,669	2,648	9,021
45 " " 50	22,575	12,795	9,780	1,700	1,680	20	13,888	9,142	4,746	6,987	1,973	5,014
50 " " 55	30,096	17,049	13,047	1,665	1,623	42	16,902	12,330	4,572	11,529	3,096	8,433
55 " " 60	10,048	5,745	4,303	525	516	9	5,487	4,049	1,438	4,036	1,180	2,856
60 and over	46,520	23,793	22,727	1,921	1,888	33	17,643	14,134	3,509	26,956	7,771	19,185
Total Sikhs	13,113	7,418	5,695	6,070	3,772	2,298	5,966	3,305	2,661	1,077	341	736
0 and under 1	515	258	257	515	258	257	...	...	...	...	...	...
1 " " 2	118	65	53	118	65	53	...	...	...	...	...	...
2 " " 3	346	184	162	346	184	162	...	...	...	...	...	...
3 " " 4	345	167	178	345	167	178	...	...	...	...	...	...
4 " " 5	373	196	177	373	196	177	...	...	...	...	...	...
Total 0 and under 5	1,697	870	827	1,697	870	827	...	...	...	...	...	...
II—Sikhs: 5 and under 10	1,789	999	790	1,759	991	768	27	8	19	3	...	3
10 " " 15	1,488	886	602	1,269	851	418	215	35	180	4	...	4
15 " " 20	1,131	670	461	581	521	60	531	145	386	19	4	15
20 " " 25	997	556	441	293	281	12	679	269	410	25	6	19
25 " " 30	1,017	511	506	183	177	6	786	319	467	48	15	33
30 " " 35	1,144	634	510	115	112	3	954	492	462	75	30	45
35 " " 40	765	454	311	44	42	2	652	393	259	69	19	50
40 " " 45	929	510	419	49	47	2	742	430	312	138	33	105
45 " " 50	452	280	172	17	17	...	361	240	121	74	23	51
50 " " 55	661	396	265	24	24	...	449	315	134	188	57	131
55 " " 60	190	129	61	5	5	...	132	101	31	53	23	30
60 and over	853	508	345	34	34	...	438	343	95	381	131	250

TABLE VII.

JAMMU AND KASHMIR STATE.

JAMMU PROVINCE.

AGE, SEX AND CIVIL CONDITION BY RELIGION—continued.

III—JAINS.

Age.	Population.			Unmarried.			Married.			Widowed.		
	Persons.	Males.	Females.	Persons.	Males.	Females.	Persons.	Males.	Females.	Persons.	Males.	Females.
1	2	3	4	5	6	7	8	9	10	11	12	13
Total Jains	439	252	187	190	124	66	194	102	92	55	26	29
0 and under 1	3	2	1	3	2	1	...	...	...	...	...	...
1 " " 2	6	3	3	6	3	3	...	...	...	...	...	...
2 " " 3	14	11	3	14	11	3	...	...	...	...	...	...
3 " " 4	9	4	5	9	4	5	...	...	...	...	...	...
4 " " 5	15	9	6	15	9	6	...	...	...	...	...	...
Total 0 and under 5	47	29	18	47	29	18	...	...	...	...	...	...
5 and under 10	45	22	23	43	21	22	2	1	1	...	...	...
10 " " 15	50	24	26	45	23	22	4	...	4	1	1	...
15 " " 20	41	26	15	13	11	2	27	14	13	1	1	...
20 " " 25	39	23	16	10	9	1	28	13	15	1	1	...
25 " " 30	41	33	8	10	10	...	27	19	8	4	4	...
30 " " 35	35	18	17	5	5	...	23	9	14	7	4	3
35 " " 40	23	12	11	3	3	...	17	8	9	3	1	2

IV—Buddhists.

40 " " 45 ...	30	10	20	2	2	...	20	15	14	8	2	6
45 " " 50 ...	20	13	7	3	3	...	14	8	6	3	2	1
50 " " 55 ...	25	16	9	4	4	...	14	8	6	7	4	3
55 " " 60 ...	8	5	3	1	1	...	3	2	1	4	2	2
60 " over ...	26	12	14	4	3	1	6	5	1	10	4	12
Total Budhists ...	4.831	2.431	2.400	2.445	1.305	1.140	2.016	1.015	1.001	370	111	259
0 and under 1 ...	45	22	24	46	22	24	...	...	...	...	...	...
1 " " 2 ...	68	31	37	68	31	37	...	...	...	...	...	...
2 " " 3 ...	70	31	39	70	31	39	...	...	...	...	...	...
3 " " 4 ...	77	29	48	77	29	48	...	...	...	...	...	...
4 " " 5 ...	100	55	54	100	55	54	...	...	...	...	...	...
Total 0 and under 5 ...	370	168	202	370	168	202	...	...	...	...	...	...
5 and under 10 ...	401	259	202	400	258	202	1	1	...	...	...	...
10 " " 15 ...	473	237	236	450	227	223	21	10	11	2	...	2
15 " " 20 ...	458	260	198	394	225	169	63	35	28	1	...	1
20 " " 25 ...	455	214	241	230	124	106	220	89	131	5	1	4
25 " " 30 ...	422	193	229	111	65	46	303	126	177	8	2	6
30 " " 35 ...	392	201	191	69	41	28	307	159	148	16	1	15
35 " " 40 ...	350	200	150	73	51	22	260	145	115	17	4	13
40 " " 45 ...	320	150	176	50	35	15	244	111	133	32	4	28
45 " " 50 ...	177	90	87	27	20	7	130	67	63	20	3	17
50 " " 55 ...	217	114	103	36	25	11	154	79	75	27	10	17
55 " " 60 ...	190	105	85	23	16	7	123	78	47	43	12	31
60 " over ...	540	240	300	153	51	102	188	115	73	199	74	125

TABLE VII.

JAMMU AND KASHMIR STATE.

JAMMU PROVINCE.

AGE, SEX AND CIVIL CONDITION BY RELIGION.—concluded.

Age.	Population.			Unmarried.			Married.			Widowed.		
	Persons.	Males.	Females.	Persons.	Males.	Females.	Persons.	Males.	Females.	Persons.	Males.	Females.
1	2	3	4	5	6	7	8	9	10	11	12	13
Total Musalmans	876.599	463.186	413.413	422.922	253.135	169.787	383.190	188.726	197.464	67.457	21.325	46.162
V.—Musalmans.												
0 and under 1	30,057	14,633	15,424	30,052	14,632	15,420	5	1	4	...	...	...
1 " " 2	13,538	7,409	6,039	13,525	7,406	6,029	13	3	10	...	...	...
2 " " 3	26,251	13,280	12,971	26,160	13,266	12,894	90	14	76	1	...	1
3 " " 4	27,303	13,946	13,357	27,135	13,905	13,230	163	39	123	6	2	4
4 " " 5	27,917	14,514	13,403	27,681	14,447	13,234	231	63	169	5	5	...
Total 0 and under 5	125.066	63.872	61.194	124.553	63.746	60.807	501	119	382	12	7	5
5 and under 10	129,101	66,850	62,251	124,275	65,836	58,430	4,691	978	3,713	135	36	99
10 " " 15	112,735	60,495	52,240	91,056	55,637	36,310	20,221	4,706	15,316	558	153	405
15 " " 20	77,587	40,783	36,804	40,840	30,614	10.226	35.123	9,459	25,664	1,624	710	914
20 " " 25	63,280	32,241	31,039	17,390	15,541	1,849	43,859	16,021	27.838	2,031	679	1,352
25 " " 30	66,239	33,331	32,608	10,233	9,421	812	52,808	22,685	30,123	3,188	1,225	1,963
30 " " 35	74,520	39,706	34,814	6,000	5,214	486	62,891	32,320	30,571	5,930	2,172	3,758
35 " " 40	45,643	25,105	20,538	2,271	2,088	183	39,027	21,461	17,566	4,345	1,566	2,789

VII—viA

	Age												
	40 and under 45 ...	57,490	30,965	26,523	2,486	2,217	260	45,876	20,111	19,765	9,128	2,640	6,483
	45 " " 50 ...	27,272	14,751	12,521	1,053	975	78	21,435	12,384	9,051	4,784	1,392	3,392
	50 " " 55 ...	37,903	21,249	15,054	965	861	104	25,931	17,478	8,353	10,407	2,910	7,497
	55 " " 60 ...	9,726	5,007	4,020	202	191	11	6,564	4,058	2,506	2,960	848	2,112
	60 " over ...	50,747	28,738	22,000	999	794	205	27,363	20,947	6,416	22,385	6,997	15,388
	Total Christians ...	**145**	**87**	**58**	**73**	**45**	**28**	**63**	**37**	**26**	**9**	**5**	**4**
VII.—Christians.	0 and under 1 ...	4	1	3	4	1	3	...	...	...	...	...	...
	1 " " 2 ...	4	2	2	4	2	2	...	...	...	...	...	...
	2 " " 3 ...	6	3	3	6	3	3	...	...	...	...	...	...
	3 " " 4 ...	8	7	1	8	7	1	...	...	...	...	...	...
	4 " " 5 ...	5	...	5	5	...	5	...	...	...	...	...	...
	Total 0 and under 5 ...	**27**	**13**	**14**	**27**	**13**	**14**	...	...	...	...	...	...
	5 and under 10 ...	20	9	11	19	9	10	1	...	1	...	...	...
	10 " " 15 ...	8	6	2	8	6	2	...	...	...	...	...	...
	15 " " 20 ...	10	6	4	5	4	1	5	2	3	...	...	...
	20 " " 25 ...	18	10	8	6	5	1	12	5	7	...	...	...
	25 " " 30 ...	15	11	4	3	3	...	9	6	3	3	2	1
	30 " " 35 ...	19	9	10	2	2	...	14	7	7	3	...	3
	35 " " 40 ...	11	10	1	2	2	...	8	7	1	1	1	...
	40 " " 45 ...	5	3	2	1	1	...	4	2	2	...	...	...
	45 " " 50 ...	3	2	1	...	...	...	3	2	1	...	...	...
	50 " " 55 ...	1	...	1	...	...	...	1	...	1	...	...	...
	60 and over ...	8	8	...	...	...	...	6	6	...	2	3	...
	Total Unspecified ...	**3**	...	**3**	**1**	...	**1**	**1**	...	**1**	**1**	...	**1**
VIII.—Unspecified.	5 and under 10 ...	1	...	1	1	...	1	...	...	...	...	...	...
	25 " " 30 ...	1	...	1	...	...	...	1	...	1	...	...	...
	60 and over ...	1	...	1	...	...	...	...	...	...	1	...	1

Note.—There were no figures under the age-periods which have been omitted from the table.

TABLE VII.

JAMMU AND KASHMIR STATE.

KASHMIR PROVINCE.

Age, Sex and Civil Condition by Religion.

TABLE VII.

JAMMU AND KASHMIR STATE.

KASHMIR PROVINCE.

AGE, SEX AND CIVIL CONDITION BY RELIGION.

Age.	Population.			Unmarried.			Married.			Widowed.		
	Persons.	Males.	Females.	Persons.	Males.	Females.	Persons.	Males.	Females.	Persons.	Males.	Females.
1	2	3	4	5	6	7	8	9	10	11	12	13
I—Hindus.												
Total Hindus	**60,682**	**34,281**	**26,421**	**28,718**	**19,420**	**9,238**	**24,974**	**12,830**	**12,144**	**6,990**	**2,011**	**4,979**
0 and under 1	2,119	1,053	1,036	2,113	1,081	1,035	3	2	1	...	...	...
1 " " 2	704	363	341	703	362	341	1	1	...	...	...	...
2 " " 3	1,539	764	775	1,535	764	771	2	...	2	2	...	2
3 " " 4	1,722	801	921	1,710	707	913	9	4	5	3	...	3
4 " " 5	1,433	741	692	1,428	738	690	4	2	2	1	1	...
Total 0 and under 5 ...	**7,517**	**3,752**	**3,765**	**7,432**	**3,742**	**3,750**	**19**	**9**	**10**	**6**	**1**	**5**
5 and under 10	7,690	3,919	3,771	7,387	3,880	3,698	89	24	64	15	6	9
10 " " 15	6,190	3,670	2,530	5,135	3,444	1,691	1,042	224	818	13	2	11
15 " " 20	5,168	3,045	3,121	2,524	2,429	95	2,565	600	1,965	77	16	61
20 " " 25	6,591	3,156	2,435	1,872	1,838	34	3,496	1,370	2,106	253	48	205
25 " " 30	5,677	3,354	2,323	1,255	1,247	8	4,025	2,016	2,009	207	91	306
30 " " 35	5,080	2,892	2,188	741	736	5	3,828	2,032	1,790	511	124	387
35 " " 40	3,612	2,231	1,381	459	458	1	2,646	1,635	1,011	507	138	369

	Age												
	40 and under 45 ...	4,095	2,237	1,838	540	542	7	2,456	1,394	1,062	1,090	321	769
	45 " " 50 ...	2,622	1,601	1,021	296	295	1	1,675	1,062	403	731	324	527
	50 " " 55 ...	2,852	1,713	1,139	300	307	2	1,592	1,170	412	961	236	725
	55 " " 60 ...	1,242	787	455	130	130	...	578	453	125	525	193	330
	60 and over ...	3,348	1,884	1,464	360	354	6	1,104	921	183	1,884	609	1,275
	Total Sikhs ...	**12,637**	**6,860**	**5,777**	**6,316**	**3,855**	**2,461**	**5,558**	**2,766**	**2,792**	**783**	**239**	**524**
II—Sikhs.	0 and under 1 ...	569	268	301	569	268	301	...	...	...	...	...	...
	1 " " 2 ...	212	111	101	212	111	101	...	...	...	...	...	...
	2 " " 3 ...	485	261	224	485	261	224	...	...	...	...	...	...
	3 " " 4 ...	439	239	200	435	237	198	3	1	2	1	1	...
	4 " " 5 ...	446	231	215	443	230	213	3	1	2	...	...	...
	Total 0 and under 5 ...	**2,151**	**1,110**	**1,041**	**2,144**	**1,107**	**1,037**	**6**	**2**	**4**	**1**	**1**	...
	5 and under 10 ...	2,027	1,095	932	1,993	1,088	905	32	6	26	2	1	1
	10 " " 15 ...	1,455	842	613	1,263	813	450	185	28	157	7	1	6
	15 " " 20 ...	1,150	596	554	186	445	41	656	150	506	8	1	7
	20 " " 25 ...	990	501	489	189	178	11	776	308	468	25	15	10
	25 " " 30 ...	1,053	596	457	129	123	6	889	461	428	35	12	23
	30 " " 35 ...	943	521	422	18	13	5	845	466	379	50	12	38
	35 " " 40 ...	594	331	263	10	10	...	528	300	228	56	21	35
	40 " " 45 ...	752	383	369	21	20	1	617	329	288	111	34	77
	45 " " 50 ...	270	170	91	13	12	1	219	158	61	38	9	29
	50 " " 55 ...	471	268	203	6	6		330	225	105	136	39	96
	55 " " 60 ...	102	58	44	1	1		75	48	27	26	9	17
	60 and over ...	670	380	289	11	10	1	400	285	115	268	85	183

TABLE VII.

JAMMU AND KASHMIR STATE.

KASHMIR PROVINCE.

AGE, SEX AND CIVIL CONDITION BY RELIGION.—continued.

	Age.	Population.			Unmarried.			Married.			Widowed.		
		Persons.	Males.	Females.	Persons.	Males.	Females.	Persons.	Males.	Females.	Persons.	Males.	Females.
	1	2	3	4	5	6	7	8	9	10	11	12	13
	Total Jains	2	1	1	1	1	...	1	...	1	...	...	...
III.—Jains.	40 and under 45	2	1	1	1	1	...	1	...	1	...	...	...
	Total Zoroastrians	11	8	3	3	3	...	8	5	3	...	...	...
IV.—Zoroastrians.	0 and under 1	2	2	...	2	2	...	...	...	...	...	...	...
	Total 0 and under 5	2	2	...	2	2	...	...	...	...	...	...	...
	5 and under 10	1	1	...	1	1	...	...	...	...	...	...	...
	20 " " 25	2	...	2	...	...	...	2	...	2	...		...
	25 " " 30	1	1	...	...	...	...	1	1	...	...	...	...
	30 " " 35	2	2	...	...	...	...	2	2	...	...	...	...
	40 " " 45	2	1	1	...	...	...	2	1	1	...	...	...
	45 " " 50	1	1	...	...	...	...	1	1	...	...	...	...

VII—A

VI.—MUSALMANS.

Total Musalmans	1,089,785	575,598	508,188	531,931	310,702	220,629	496,614	246,469	250,145	55,821	18,427	37,394
0 and under 1	51,392	26,053	25,339	51,360	26,089	25,321	31	14	17	1	...	1
1 " " 2	19,237	9,782	9,455	19,208	9,773	9,436	28	10	18	1	..	1
2 " " 3	38,998	19,275	19,723	38,885	19,239	19,646	113	36	77	...	...	...
3 " " 4	41,756	20,330	21,426	41,568	20,239	21,329	182	88	94	6	3	3
4 " " 5	37,776	19,359	18,417	37,596	19,288	18,308	167	66	101	13	5	8
Total 0 and under 5	189,159	94,799	94,360	188,617	94,577	94,040	521	214	307	21	8	13
5 and under 10	181,303	95,046	85,367	178,800	95,362	83,498	2,341	560	1,784	98	23	75
10 " " 15	129,848	72,717	57,131	104,586	67,200	37,386	24,916	5,429	19,486	347	88	259
15 " " 20	66,477	46,733	30,741	35,551	31,606	3,888	49,858	14,757	35,101	1,065	310	755
20 " " 25	79,053	36,754	42,299	13,186	12,478	707	64,273	23,576	40,697	1,505	700	805
25 " " 30	78,297	38,546	39,451	4,824	4,548	276	71,030	33,087	37,943	2,443	1,211	1,232
30 " " 35	90,222	48,679	41,543	2,009	2,302	307	83,294	44,501	38,702	4,320	1,876	2,444
35 " " 40	51,659	30,473	21,186	851	754	100	47,696	28,301	19,505	2,909	1,328	1,581
40 " " 45	62,663	32,780	29,883	898	739	166	54,663	29,742	24,921	7,102	2,306	4,796
45 " " 50	27,874	16,032	11,842	202	246	44	24,278	14,610	9,659	3,904	1,105	2,130
50 " " 55	45,020	25,727	19,293	388	300	88	31,548	22,677	11,071	10,094	2,850	7,234
55 " " 60	12,394	6,763	5,631	118	90	28	9,134	5,819	3,315	3,142	854	2,288
60 and over	40,798	20,350	20,448	546	445	101	29,861	23,197	6,664	19,391	5,708	13,683

TABLE VII.

JAMMU AND KASHMIR STATE.

KASHMIR PROVINCE.

AGE, SEX AND CIVIL CONDITION BY RELIGION.—concluded.

Age.	Population.			Unmarried.			Married.			Widowed.		
	Persons.	Males.	Females.	Persons.	Males.	Females.	Persons.	Males.	Females.	Persons.	Males.	Females.
1	2	3	4	5	6	7	8	9	10	11	12	13
Total Christians	**244**	**123**	**116**	**144**	**73**	**71**	**86**	**51**	**35**	**14**	**4**	**10**
0 and under 1	8	5	3	8	5	3	...	...	...	...	...	...
1 " " 2	3	2	1	3	2	1	...	...	...	...	...	...
2 " " 3	5	1	4	5	1	4	...	...	...	...	...	...
3 " " 4	7	4	3	7	4	3	...	...	...	...	...	...
4 " " 5	3	1	2	3	1	3	...	...	...	...	...	...
Total 0 and under 5	**26**	**13**	**13**	**26**	**13**	**13**	...	...	...	...	...	...
5 and under 10	23	11	12	23	11	12	...	...	...	...	...	...
10 " " 15	17	7	10	17	7	10	...	...	...	...	...	...
15 " " 20	14	6	8	14	6	8	...	...	...	...	...	...
20 " " 25	23	10	13	17	9	8	6	1	5	...	...	...
25 " " 30	37	19	18	25	13	12	12	6	6	...	...	...
30 " " 35	30	18	12	11	6	5	17	11	6	2	1	1
35 " " 40	20	11	9	4	1	3	14	9	5	2	1	1

Age-period												
40 „ „ 45	16	10	6	4	4	...	11	6	5	1	...	1
45 „ „ 50	7	4	3	2	2	...	3	1	2	2	1	1
50 „ „ 55	11	6	5	...	...	...	9	6	3	2	...	2
55 „ „ 60	6	2	4	...	...	...	5	2	3	1	...	1
60 „ over	14	11	3	1	1	...	9	9	...	4	1	3
Total Unspecified ...	**52**	**31**	**21**	**33**	**20**	**13**	**15**	**8**	**7**	**4**	**3**	**1**
VIII—Unspecified.												
0 and under 1	5	1	4	5	1	4	...	...	...	...	...	...
1 „ „ 2	2	1	1	2	1	1	...	...	...	...	...	...
2 „ „ 3	2	...	2	2	...	2	...	...	...	...	...	...
3 „ „ 4	3	2	1	3	2	1	...	...	...	...	...	...
Total 0 and under 5 ...	**12**	**4**	**8**	**12**	**4**	**8**	...	...	...	...	...	...
5 and under 10	7	3	4	7	3	4	...	...	...	...	...	...
10 „ „ 15	4	3	1	3	3	...	...	...	...	1	...	1
15 „ „ 20	2	1	1	2	1	1	...	...	...	...	...	...
20 „ „ 25	7	5	2	5	5	...	2	...	2	...	...	...
25 „ „ 30	4	4	...	3	3	...	1	1	...	...	...	...
30 „ „ 35	3	1	2	...	...	...	3	1	2	...	...	...
35 „ „ 40	2	1	1	...	...	...	2	1	1	...	...	...
40 „ „ 45	1	1	...	...	...	...	1	1	...	...	...	...
50 „ „ 55	2	3	...	...	...	...	1	1	...	1	1	...
55 „ „ 60	1	1	...	...	...	...	...	...	...	1	1	...
60 „ over	7	5	2	1	1	...	5	3	2	1	1	...

***Note.*—There were no figures under the age-periods which have been omitted from the table.**

TABLE VII.

JAMMU AND KASHMIR STATE.

FRONTIER DISTRICTS.

Age, Sex and Civil Condition by Religion.

TABLE VII.

JAMMU AND KASHMIR STATE.

FRONTIER DISTRICTS.

AGE, SEX AND CIVIL CONDITION BY RELIGION.

Age.	Population.			Unmarried.			Married.			Widowed.		
	Persons.	Males.	Females.	Persons.	Males.	Females.	Persons.	Males.	Females.	Persons.	Males.	Females.
1	2	3	4	5	6	7	8	9	10	11	12	13
I.—Hindus.												
Total Hindus	2,214	2,122	92	1,047	1,016	31	1,113	1,057	56	54	49	5
0 and under 1	4	...	4	4	...	4	...	...	...	...	...	...
1 " " 2	2	...	2	2	...	2	...	...	...	...	...	...
2 " " 3	9	5	4	9	5	4	...	...	...	...	...	...
3 " " 4	6	5	1	6	5	1	...	...	...	...	...	...
4 " " 5	10	3	7	10	3	7	...	...	...	...	...	...
Total 0 and under 5	31	13	18	31	13	18	...	...	...	...	...	...
5 and under 10	20	13	7	20	13	7	...	...	...	...	...	...
10 " " 15	14	9	5	13	9	4	1		1	...	...	...
15 " " 20	109	98	11	80	78	2	29	20	9	...	...	...
20 " " 25	476	462	14	311	311	...	160	146	14	5	5	...
25 " " 30	595	581	14	269	269	...	317	303	14	9	9	...
30 " " 35	494	483	11	217	217	...	269	258	11	8	8	...
35 " " 40	317	213	4	64	64	...	145	142	3	8	7	1

Age	1	2	3	4	5	6	7	8	9	10	11	12
40 „ „ 45	144	142	2	28	28	...	108	106	2	8	8	...
45 „ „ 50	57	54	3	6	6	...	45	44	1	6	4	2
50 „ „ 55	35	35	...	5	5	...	28	28	...	2	2	...
55 „ „ 60	9	8	1	...	...	...	7	7	...	2	1	1
60 and over	13	11	2	3	3	...	4	3	1	6	5	1
Total Sikhs	78	64	14	24	21	3	53	42	11	1	1	...
II.—Sikhs. 0 and under 1	1	...	1	1	...	1	...	...	...	...	...	...
3 „ „ 4	1	...	1	1	...	1	...	...	...	...	...	...
Total 0 and under 5 ...	2	...	2	2	...	2	...	...	...	...	...	...
5 and under 10	3	3	...	3	3	...	...	...	...	...	...	...
10 „ „ 15	2	2	...	2	2	...	...	...	...	...	...	...
15 „ „ 20	5	4	1	2	2	...	3	2	1	...	...	...
20 „ „ 25	14	12	2	6	6	...	8	6	2	...	...	...
25 „ „ 30	15	12	3	4	4	...	11	8	3	...	...	...
30 „ „ 35	14	11	3	3	3	...	11	8	3	...	...	...
35 „ „ 40	10	9	1	...	...	...	10	9	1	...	...	...
40 „ „ 45	8	7	1	2	1	1	6	6	...	...	...	...
45 „ „ 50	1	1	...	...	...	...	...	...	...	1	1	...
50 „ „ 55	2	1	1	...	...	...	2	1	1	...	...	...
60 and over	2	2	...	...	...	...	2	2	...	...	...	...
Total Jains	1	1	...	...	...	...	1	1	...	...	...	...
III.—Jains. 20 and under 25	1	1	...	...	...	...	1	1	...	...	...	...

TABLE VII.

JAMMU AND KASHMIR STATE.

FRONTIER DISTRICTS.

AGE, SEX AND CIVIL CONDITION BY RELIGION.—continued.

IV.—Budhists.

Age.	Population.			Unmarried.			Married.			Widowed.		
	Persons.	Males.	Females.	Persons.	Males.	Females.	Persons.	Males.	Females.	Persons.	Males.	Females.
1	2	3	4	5	6	7	8	9	10	11	12	13
Total Budhists ...	30,216	15,135	15,081	12,087	6,234	5,853	14,895	7,758	7,137	3,234	1,143	2,091
0 and under 1 ...	674	332	342	674	332	342	...	...	...	...	...	...
1 " " 2 ...	145	64	81	145	64	81	...	...	...	...	...	...
2 " " 3 ...	404	201	203	402	201	201	1	...	1	1	...	1
3 " " 4 ...	618	314	304	606	306	300	12	8	4	...	...	...
4 " " 5 ...	564	281	283	552	275	277	11	5	6	1	1	...
Total 0 and under 5 ...	2,405	1,192	1,213	2,379	1,178	1,201	24	13	11	2	1	1
5 and under 10 ...	3,363	1,692	1,071	3,203	1,613	1,590	158	78	80	2	1	1
10 " " 15 ...	2,740	1,395	1,345	2,295	1,113	1,182	425	270	146	20	3	17
15 " " 20 ...	2,503	1,271	1,232	1,538	752	786	924	490	428	41	23	18
20 " " 25 ...	2,077	1,020	1,057	708	330	378	1,249	612	637	120	78	42
25 " " 30 ...	2,387	1,274	1,113	439	257	182	1,679	801	878	269	216	53
30 " " 35 ...	2,324	1,328	996	270	188	82	1,835	932	903	219	208	11
35 " " 40 ...	2,174	1,161	1,013	308	149	59	1,712	877	835	254	135	119

40 " " 45	1,930	1,036	894	194	133	62	1,464	754	710	273	160	127
45 " " 50	1,744	896	848	136	82	42	1,344	711	633	276	103	173
50 " " 55	1,509	727	782	170	118	52	1,096	579	517	213	30	213
55 " " 60	867	421	446	71	61	20	669	358	311	127	12	115
60 " over	4,193	1,722	2,471	458	271	217	2,316	1,358	1,049	1,359	183	1,306
Total Musalmans	194,330	100,030	94,300	91,633	50,327	40,772	83,083	45,233	43,872	13,551	3,895	9,658
0 and under 1	6,324	3,197	3,127	6,348	3,180	3,108	30	17	19	...	...	...
1 " " 2	2,358	1,123	1,235	2,343	1,113	1,220	15	10	5	1	...	1
2 " " 3	4,821	2,446	2,375	4,780	2,427	2,353	30	10	20	2	...	2
3 " " 4	5,641	2,677	2,964	5,503	2,610	2,893	131	65	66	8	2	6
4 " " 5	5,014	2,438	2,576	4,911	2,398	2,513	97	39	58	6	1	5
Total 0 and under 5	24,158	11,881	12,277	23,423	11,723	12,035	318	150	168	17	3	14
5 and under 10	24,512	12,677	11,835	23,880	12,431	11,449	582	230	353	50	16	34
10 " " 15	17,953	9,633	8,320	16,527	8,926	6,601	2,307	685	1,083	60	23	37
15 " " 20	13,932	7,565	6,367	8,360	5,745	2,615	5,330	1,718	3,573	313	93	150
20 " " 25	18,469	9,004	9,465	4,699	3,316	1,383	13,049	5,393	7,646	721	205	436
25 " " 30	15,966	8,617	7,349	8,951	4,530	4,421	6,708	3,936	2,712	801	131	183
30 " " 35	12,708	6,691	6,017	2,451	1,203	1,251	9,583	5,148	4,137	670	341	329
35 " " 40	23,534	11,777	11,757	3,307	2,579	728	18,683	8,753	10,131	1,344	416	898
40 " " 45	15,104	7,926	7,178	339	252	87	13,900	7,012	6,894	1,869	632	1,227
45 " " 50	8,991	4,401	4,590	134	71	63	6,955	4,014	2,941	1,902	316	1,586
50 " " 55	3,536	1,996	1,540	44	35	9	2,685	1,800	885	807	161	646
55 " " 60	1,932	1,162	740	13	9	4	1,565	1,032	618	324	101	223
60 " over	13,565	6,700	6,865	157	94	63	8,157	5,358	2,899	5,251	1,348	3,903

VI.—Musalmans.

TABLE VII.

JAMMU AND KASHMIR STATE.

FRONTIER DISTRICTS.

AGE, SEX AND CIVIL CONDITION BY RELIGION.—concluded.

Age.	Population.			Unmarried.			Married.			Widowed.		
	Persons.	Males.	Females.	Persons.	Males.	Females.	Persons.	Males.	Females.	Persons.	Males.	Females.
1	2	3	4	5	6	7	8	9	10	11	12	13
Total Christians	33	21	12	19	13	6	13	7	6	1	1	...
VII.—Christians.												
0 and under 1	2	1	1	2	1	1	...	...	...	...	...	...
2 „ „ 3	1	1	...	1	1	...	...	...	...	...	...	...
3 „ „ 4	1	...	1	1	...	1	...	...	...	...	...	...
4 „ „ 5	1	...	1	1	...	1	...	...	...	...	...	...
Total 0 and under 5	5	2	3	5	2	3	...	...	...	...	...	...
20 and under 25	5	2	3	3	1	2	2	1	1	...	...	...
25 „ „ 30	5	2	3	2	2	...	3	...	3	...	...	...
30 „ „ 35	8	8	...	6	6	...	2	2	...	...	...	...
35 „ „ 40	4	2	2	1	1	...	3	1	2	...	...	...

VIII.—Unspecified.	1	2	3	4	5	6	7	8	9	10	11	12
40 " " 45	3	3	...	...	...	...	2	2	...	1	1	...
45 " " 50	1	1	...	...	...	...	1	1	...	...	...	...
50 " " 55	1	...	1	1	...	1	...	...	...	...	...	...
60 and over	1	1	...	1	1	...	...	...	...	...	...	...
Total Unspecified	5	5	...	3	3	...	2	2	...	...	...	...
15 and under 20	1	1	...	1	1	...	...	...	...	...	...	...
20 " " 52	4	4	...	2	2	...	2	2	...	...	...	...

Note—There were no figures under the age-periods which have been omitted from the table.

TABLE VII.

JAMMU AND KASHMIR STATE.

JAMMU CITY.

Age, Sex and Civil Condition by Religion.

TABLE VII.

JAMMU AND KASHMIR STATE.

JAMMU CITY.

AGE, SEX AND CIVIL CONDITION BY RELIGION.

Age.	Population.			Unmarried.			Married.			Widowed.		
	Persons.	Males.	Females.	Persons.	Males.	Females.	Persons.	Males.	Females.	Persons.	Males.	Females.
1	2	3	4	5	6	7	8	9	10	11	12	13
TOTAL JAMMU CITY ...	36,130	22,221	13,909	13,969	9,934	4,035	17,897	10,740	7,157	4,264	1,547	2,717
TOTAL ALL RELIGIONS:												
0 and under 1 ...	937	512	425	937	512	425	...	...	...	...	...	...
1 " " 2 ...	345	171	174	345	171	174	...	...	...	...	...	...
2 " " 3 ...	502	293	209	502	293	209	...	...	...	...	...	...
3 " " 4 ...	599	297	302	599	297	302	...	...	...	...	...	...
4 " " 5 ...	618	307	311	603	303	300	15	4	11	...	...	...
Total 0 and under 5 ...	3,061	1,580	1,481	3,046	1,576	1,470	15	4	11	...	...	...
5 and under 10 ...	3,242	1,731	1,511	3,142	1,704	1,438	100	27	73	...	...	...
10 " " 15 ...	3,481	2,103	1,378	2,775	1,907	868	684	180	406	22	10	12
15 " " 20 ...	3,502	2,195	1,307	1,659	1,502	157	1,758	594	1,163	87	39	48
20 " " 25 ...	3,970	2,543	1,427	1,264	1,228	36	2,521	1,342	1,179	185	73	112
25 " " 30 ...	4,445	2,987	1,458	953	931	22	3,173	1,901	1,272	319	155	164
30 " " 35 ...	4,073	2,634	1,439	526	513	13	3,062	1,917	1,145	485	304	181
35 " " 40 ...	2,300	1,517	783	179	175	4	1,748	1,201	547	372	141	231

40 and under 45	2,780	1,696	1,084	107	185	12	1,008	1,805	598	680	206	474
45 „ „ 50	1,310	850	460	70	68	2	885	668	317	361	120	241
50 „ „ 55	1,093	1,021	672	63	57	6	906	783	213	634	181	453
55 „ „ 60	512	364	148	18	18	...	311	204	47	183	82	101
60 „ over	1,750	1,054	702	77	70	7	743	648	95	936	336	600
TOTAL HINDUS	**21,112**	**12,881**	**8,231**	**7,752**	**5,712**	**2,040**	**10,613**	**6,228**	**4,385**	**2,747**	**941**	**1,806**
0 and under 1	541	296	245	541	296	245	...	...	...	...	...	...
1 „ „ 2	180	90	90	180	90	90	...	...	...	...	...	...
2 „ „ 3	306	152	154	306	152	154	...	...	...	...	...	...
3 „ „ 4	327	166	161	327	166	161	...	...	...	...	...	...
4 „ „ 5	321	154	167	308	152	156	13	2	11	...	...	...
Total 0 and under 5	1,675	858	817	1,662	856	806	13	2	11	...	...	...
5 and under 10	1,791	966	825	1,722	940	773	69	17	62	...	...	...
10 „ „ 15	1,865	1,120	748	1,372	992	380	481	124	457	15	4	11
15 „ „ 20	2,152	1,324	828	952	902	50	1,140	808	742	60	24	36
20 „ „ 25	2,390	1,525	865	744	735	9	1,532	745	787	114	45	69
25 „ „ 30	2,734	1,852	882	613	605	7	1,908	1,162	750	214	95	119
30 „ „ 35	2,321	1,445	876	303	299	4	1,702	1,048	650	310	103	213
35 „ „ 40	1,333	862	471	113	112	1	987	670	317	233	80	153
40 „ „ 45	1,657	967	690	136	181	5	1,060	700	354	401	130	231
45 „ „ 50	542	530	312	43	41	1	546	400	137	254	80	174
50 „ „ 55	1,013	586	427	36	34	2	575	444	131	402	108	294
55 „ „ 60	332	242	90	14	14	...	201	172	29	117	56	61
60 „ over	1,004	604	400	44	42	2	399	346	53	561	216	345

TABLE VII.

JAMMU AND KASHMIR STATE.

JAMMU CITY.

AGE, SEX AND CIVIL CONDITION BY RELIGION.—continued.

Age.	Population.			Unmarried.			Married.			Widowed.		
	Persons.	Males.	Females.	Persons.	Males.	Females.	Persons.	Males.	Females.	Persons.	Males.	Females.
1	2	3	4	5	6	7	8	9	10	11	12	13
Total Sikhs	885	548	337	315	222	93	494	291	203	76	35	41
III.—Sikhs. 0 and under 1	31	18	13	31	18	13	...	...	...	...	...	...
1 " " 2	8	6	2	8	6	2	...	...	...	...	...	...
2 " " 3	11	6	5	11	6	5	...	...	...	...	...	...
3 " " 4	12	6	6	12	6	6	...	...	...	...	...	...
4 " " 5	20	10	10	20	10	10	...	...	...	...	...	...
Total 0 and under 5 ...	82	46	36	82	46	36	...	...	...	...	...	...
5 and under 10	78	40	38	77	40	37	1	...	1	...	...	...
10 " " 15	70	43	27	60	41	19	10	2	8	...	...	...
15 " " 20	70	40	30	26	25	1	44	15	29	...	...	...
20 " " 25	89	57	32	21	21	...	66	36	30	2	...	2
25 " " 30	103	59	44	17	17	...	81	40	41	5	2	3
30 " " 35	115	76	39	18	18	...	86	53	34	11	6	6
35 " " 40	49	35	14	1	1	...	43	33	11	5	2	3

40 and under 45	67	36	31	...	...	...	57	33	24	10	8	7
45 " " 50	37	27	10	...	...	...	32	24	8	5	3	8
50 " " 55	45	30	15	1	1	...	34	26	5	10	3	7
55 " " 60	20	15	5	1	1	...	14	11	3	5	3	2
60 " over	51	35	16	2	2	...	26	20	6	23	13	10
Total Jains	**437**	**251**	**186**	**189**	**123**	**66**	**194**	**102**	**92**	**54**	**26**	**28**

IV.—Jains.

0 and under 1	3	2	1	3	2	1	...	...	...	...	...	...
1 " " 2	6	3	3	6	3	3	...	...	...	...	...	...
2 " " 3	14	11	3	14	11	3	...	...	...	...	...	...
3 " " 4	9	4	5	9	4	5	...	...	...	...	...	...
4 " " 5	15	9	6	15	9	6	...	...	...	...	...	...
Total 0 and under 5	47	29	18	47	29	18	...	...	...	...	...	...
5 and under 10	46	12	24	44	21	23	2	1	1	...	...	...
10 " " 15	50	21	26	45	23	22	1	...	4	1	1	...
15 " " 20	41	26	15	13	11	2	27	11	13	1	1	...
20 " " 25	40	25	15	11	11	...	28	13	15	1	1	...
25 " " 30	38	30	8	7	7	...	27	10	8	4	4	...
30 " " 35	35	18	17	5	5	...	23	9	14	7	4	3
35 " " 40	23	12	11	3	3	...	17	8	9	3	1	2
40 " " 45	30	10	20	2	2	...	20	15	14	8	2	6
45 " " 50	20	13	7	3	3	...	14	8	6	3	2	1
50 " " 55	25	16	9	4	4	...	14	8	6	7	4	3
55 " " 60	8	5	3	1	1	...	3	2	1	4	2	2
60 " over	25	12	13	4	3	1	6	5	1	15	4	11

TABLE VII.

JAMMU AND KASHMIR STATE.

JAMMU CITY.

AGE, SEX AND CIVIL CONDITION BY RELIGION.—concluded.

Age.	Population.			Unmarried.			Married.			Widowed.		
	Persons.	Males.	Females.	Persons.	Males.	Females.	Persons.	Males.	Females.	Persons.	Males.	Females.
1	2	3	4	5	6	7	8	9	10	11	12	13
Total Musalmans	**13,627**	**8,501**	**5,126**	**5,677**	**3,856**	**1,821**	**6,570**	**4,104**	**2,466**	**1,380**	**541**	**839**
V.—Musalmans. 0 and under 1	361	196	165	361	196	165	...	...	...	...	...	...
1 " " 2	149	71	78	149	71	78	...	...	...	...	...	...
2 " " 3	230	124	106	230	124	106	...	...	...	...	...	...
3 " " 4	246	117	129	246	117	129	...	...	...	...	...	...
4 " " 5	259	134	125	257	132	125	2	2	...	...	...	...
Total 0 and under 5	**1,245**	**642**	**603**	**1,243**	**640**	**603**	**2**	**2**	...	...	...	...
5 and under 10	1,308	690	618	1,280	681	599	28	9	19	...	...	...
10 " " 15	1,491	914	577	1,296	849	447	189	60	129	6	5	1
15 " " 20	1,234	742	492	665	562	103	543	166	377	26	14	12
20 " " 25	1,444	931	513	484	458	26	892	446	446	68	27	41
25 " " 30	1,561	1,041	520	317	302	15	1,151	687	464	93	52	41
30 " " 35	1,590	1,060	530	198	189	9	1,243	810	433	149	61	88
35 " " 40	887	601	286	60	57	3	697	487	210	130	57	73

Age		1	2	3	4	5	6	7	8	9	10	11	12
40 „ „ 45	... ...	1,018	673	343	65	51	7	757	651	906	201	71	190
45 „ „ 50	... ...	415	284	131	25	24	1	291	225	66	90	35	64
50 „ „ 55	... ...	600	380	220	22	18	1	372	305	67	215	66	140
55 „ „ 60	... ...	152	102	50	2	2		93	79	14	57	21	66
60 „ over	... ...	675	402	273	37	20	1	312	277	35	336	102	234
Total Christians	...	69	40	29	36	21	15	26	15	11	7	4	3

VI.—CHRISTIANS.

Age		1	2	3	4	5	6	7	8	9	10	11	12
0 and under 1	... ...	1	...	1	1	...	1	...	...	...	...	...	...
1 „ „ 2	... ...	2	1	1	2	1	1	...	...	...		...	...
2 „ „ 3	... ...	1		1	1	...	1	...	...	...	...	...	...
3 „ „ 4	... ...	6	4	1	5	1	1	...	...	...		...	...
4 „ „ 5	... ...	3		3	3		3	...	...	...	...		...
Total 0 and under 5	...	12	5	7	12	5	7		...	...	...	...	...
5 and under 10	... ...	10	4	6	10	4	6	...	...	...	...	...	...
10 „ „ 15	... ...	2	2	...	2	2	...	...	...	...	...	...	...
15 „ „ 20	... ...	5	3	2	3	2	1	2	1	1	...	...	...
20 „ „ 25	... ...	7	5	2	4	3	1	3	2	1	...	...	...
25 „ „ 30	... ...	9	5	4	...	...	...	6	3	3	3	2	1
30 „ „ 35	... ...	12	5	7	2	2	...	8	3	5	2	...	2
35 „ „ 40	... ...	7	7	...	2	2	...	4	4	...	1	1	...
40 „ „ 45	... ...	1	1	...	1	1	...	...	...	...	...	...	...
45 „ „ 50	... ...	2	2	...	...	...	...	2	2	...	...	...	...
50 „ „ 55	... ...	1	...	1	...	...	...	1	...	1	...	...	...
55 „ „ 60	... ...	...	...	...	...	...	...	...	...	...	...	...	...
60 „ over	... ...	1	1	...	...	...	...	...	...	...	1	1	...

TABLE VII.

JAMMU ADN KASHMIR STATE.

SRINAGAR CITY.

Age, Sex and Civil Condition by Religion.

TABLE VII.

JAMMU AND KASHMIR STATE.

SRINAGAR CITY.

AGE, SEX AND CIVIL CONDITION BY RELIGION.

Age.	Population.			Unmarried.			Married.			Widowed			Remarks.
	Persons.	Males.	Females.	Persons.	Males.	Females.	Persons.	Males.	Females.	Persons.	Males.	Females.	
1	2	3	4	5	6	7	8	9	10	11	12	13	14
TOTAL SRINAGAR CITY ...	122,618	65,542	57,076	55,333	34,274	21,059	56,347	28,013	28,334	10,938	3,255	7,683	
ALL RELIGIONS.													
0 and under 1	4,522	2,047	2,475	4,518	2,047	2,471	4	...	4	...	...	...	
1 " " 2	1,578	812	766	1,573	809	764	5	3	2	...	...	...	
2 " " 3	3,642	1,756	1,886	3,623	1,753	1,870	18	3	15	1	...	1	
3 " " 4	3,859	1,836	2,023	3,828	1,821	2,007	25	13	12	6	2	4	
4 " " 5	3,200	1,627	1,633	3,225	1,614	1,611	31	12	19	4	1	3	
Total 0 and under 5	16,861	8,078	8,783	16,787	8,044	8,723	53	31	52	11	3	8	
5 and under 10	17,066	8,934	8,132	16,870	8,870	8,000	172	58	114	24	6	18	
10 " " 15	13,994	8,250	5,744	11,639	7,807	3,832	2,311	430	1,881	44	13	31	
15 " " 20	10,619	5,687	4,932	4,683	4,382	301	5,755	1,266	4,489	181	39	142	
20 " " 25	11,341	5,849	5,492	2,456	2,375	81	8,485	3,329	5,156	400	145	255	
25 " " 30	10,103	5,124	4,979	1,088	1,054	34	8,405	3,874	4,531	610	196	414	
30 " " 35	11,384	6,009	5,375	648	618	30	9,375	5,067	4,308	1,361	324	1,037	
35 " " 40	6,110	3,408	2,702	288	277	11	5,134	2,910	2,224	688	221	467	

40 „ „ 45	8,201	4,375	3,826	383	368	20	6,278	3,489	2,787	1,542	533	1,019
45 „ „ 50	3,878	2,320	1,558	135	126	9	3,014	1,917	1,007	720	277	452
50 „ „ 55	5,790	3,687	2,163	156	150	6	4,069	3,010	1,079	1,554	479	1,076
55 „ „ 60	2,320	1,008	1,312	54	54	..	993	723	270	1,273	231	1,042
60 „ over	4,942	2,861	2,081	166	154	12	2,255	1,909	346	2,521	798	1,723
unspecified	...	...	...	...	...	...	...	...	...	...	...	...
TOTAL HINDUS ..	**27,873**	**15,260**	**12,613**	**12,065**	**8,076**	**3,989**	**12,258**	**6,135**	**6,123**	**3,550**	**1,049**	**2,501**
0 and under 1	859	424	435	859	424	435	...	...	...	...	...	...
1 „ „ 2 ...	297	150	147	297	150	147	...	...	...	...	...	...
2 „ „ 3	702	345	357	700	345	355	1	...	1	1	..	1
3 „ „ 4	780	368	412	772	366	400	6	2	4	2	...	2
4 „ „ 5	650	323	327	646	321	325	3	1	2	1	1	...
Total 0 and under 5 ...	**3,288**	**1,610**	**1,678**	**3,274**	**1,606**	**1,668**	**10**	**3**	**7**	**4**	**1**	**3**
5 and under 10	3,449	1,722	1,727	3,391	1,704	1,687	49	16	34	0	3	6
10 „ „ 15	2,695	1,640	1,055	2,058	1,456	662	630	182	448	7	2	5
15 „ „ 20	2,618	1,464	1,154	1,075	1,061	14	1,496	392	1,104	47	11	36
20 „ „ 25	2,812	1,583	1,229	771	765	6	1,884	779	1,105	157	39	118
25 „ „ 30	2,630	1,540	1,090	476	473	3	1,971	1,016	955	183	51	132
30 „ „ 35	2,399	1,280	1,119	280	278	2	1,820	925	895	290	77	222
35 „ „ 40	1,617	949	668	160	159	1	1,186	722	464	271	68	203
40 „ „ 45	2,048	1,075	973	267	262	5	1,140	586	554	641	227	414
45 „ „ 50	1,187	694	493	72	72	...	772	511	261	343	111	232
50 „ „ 55	1,345	699	646	102	101	1	699	511	188	544	87	457
55 „ „ 60	549	342	207	44	44	...	247	187	60	258	111	147
60 „ over	1,236	662	574	95	95	...	351	300	48	787	261	536
unspecified	..	..	..	...	...	...	...	...	...	...	...	...

I—HINDUS.

TABLE VII.

JAMMU AND KASHMIR STATE.

SRINAGAR CITY.

AGE, SEX AND CIVIL CONDITION BY RELIGION.—continued.

Age.	Population.			Unmarried.			Married.			Widowed.			Remarks.
	Persons.	Males.	Females.	Persons.	Males.	Females.	Persons.	Males.	Females.	Persons.	Males.	Females.	
1	2	3	4	5	6	7	8	9	10	11	12	13	14
II.—Sikhs.													
Total Sikhs ..	434	355	139	180	127	53	285	211	74	29	17	12	
0 and under 1	10	4	6	10	4	6	...	...	...	...	...	...	
1 „ „ 2	4	3	1	4	3	1	...	...	...	...	...	...	
2 „ „ 3	14	7	7	14	7	7	...	...	...	...	...	...	
3 „ „ 4	10	4	6	10	4	6	...	...	...	...	...	...	
4 „ „ 5	8	4	4	8	4	4	...	...	...	...	...	...	
Total 0 and under 5 ..	46	22	24	46	22	24	...	...	...	...	...	...	
5 and under 10	38	18	20	37	17	20	1	1	...	...	...	...	
10 „ „ 15	34	18	16	25	16	9	9	2	7	...	...	...	
15 „ „ 20	55	41	14	20	29	...	26	12	14	...	...	...	
20 „ „ 25	61	49	12	17	17	...	43	31	12	1	1	...	
25 „ „ 30	80	65	15	10	10	...	67	53	14	3	2	1	
30 „ „ 35	55	48	7	8	8	...	46	39	7	1	1	...	
35 „ „ 40	33	24	9	2	2	...	29	21	8	2	1	1	

40 and under 45	30	28	7	1	1	...	23	18	5	6	4	9
45 „ „ 50	18	15	3	3	3	...	11	10	1	5	3	3
50 „ „ 55	23	14	9	2	2	...	13	9	4	8	3	5
55 „ „ 60	2	2	...	1	1	...	1	1	...	...	...	...
60 „ „ over	10	16	3	...	...	...	16	14	2	3	2	1
unspecified	...	...	...	...	...	...	...	...	...	...	...	...
TOTAL JAINS	1	...	1	...	...	...	1	...	1	...	...	...
III.—JAINS.												
0 and under 1	...	...	...	...	...	...	...	...	...	...	...	...
1 „ „ 2	...	...	...	...	...	...	...	...	...	...	...	...
2 „ „ 3	...	...	...	...	...	...	...	...	...	...	...	...
3 „ „ 4	...	...	...	...	...	...	...	...	...	...	...	...
4 „ „ 5	...	...	...	...	...	...	...	...	...	...	...	...
Total 0 and under 5	...	...	...	...	...	...	...	...	...	...	...	...
5 and under 10	...	...	...	...	...	...	...	...	...	...	...	...
10 „ „ 15	...	...	...	...	...	...	...	...	...	...	...	...
15 „ „ 20	...	...	...	...	...	...	...	...	...	...	...	...
20 „ „ 25	...	...	...	...	...	...	...	...	...	...	...	...
25 „ „ 30	...	...	...	...	...	...	...	...	...	...	...	...
30 „ „ 35	...	...	...	...	...	...	...	...	...	...	...	...
35 „ „ 40	...	...	...	...	...	...	...	...	...	...	...	...
40 „ „ 45	1	...	1	...	...	...	1	...	1	...	...	...
45 „ „ 50	...	...	...	...	...	...	...	...	...	...	...	...
50 „ „ 55	...	...	...	...	...	...	...	...	...	...	...	...
55 „ „ 60	...	...	...	...	...	...	...	...	...	...	...	...
60 „ over	...	...	...	...	...	...	...	...	...	...	...	...
unspecified	...	...	...	...	...	...	...	...	...	...	...	...

TABLE VII.

JAMMU AND KASHMIR STATE.

SRINAGAR CITY.

AGE, SEX AND CIVIL CONDITION BY RELIGION.—continued.

Age.	Population.			Unmarried.			Married.			Widowed.			Remarks.
	Persons.	Males.	Females.	Persons.	Males.	Females.	Persons.	Males.	Females.	Persons.	Males.	Females.	
1	2	3	4	5	6	7	8	9	10	11	12	13	14
IV.—Zoroastrians.													
Total Zoroastrians ...	11	8	3	3	3	...	8	5	3	...	...	...	
0 and under 1 ...	2	2	...	2	2	...	...	...	...	...	...	...	
1 " " 2 ...	...	...	...	...	...	...	...	...	...	...	...	...	
2 " " 3 ...	...	...	...	...	...	...	...	...	...	...	...	...	
3 " " 4 ...	...	...	...	...	...	...	...	...	...	...	...	...	
4 " " 5 ...	...	...	...	...	...	...	...	...	...	...	...	...	
Total 0 and under 5 ...	2	2	...	2	2	...	...	...	...	...	...	...	
5 " " 10 ...	1	1	...	1	1	...	...	...	...	...	...	...	
10 " " 15 ...	...	...	...	...	...	...	...	...	...	...	...	...	
15 " " 20 ...	...	...	...	...	...	...	...	...	...	...	...	...	
20 " " 25 ...	2	...	2	...	...	...	2	...	2	...	...	...	
25 " " 30 ...	1	1	...	...	...	...	1	1	...	...	...	...	
30 " " 35 ...	2	2	...	...	...	...	2	2	...	...	...	...	
35 " " 40 ...		...	...	...	...	...	...	...	...	...	...	...	

VII—vii

V.—Musalmans.

Age												
40 ,, ,, 45	2	1	1	...	...	...	2	1	1	...	...	...
45 ,, ,, 50	1	1	...	...	...	...	1	1	...	...	...	...
50 ,, ,, 55	...	...	...	...	...	...	...	...	...	...	...	...
55 ,, ,, 60	...	...	...	...	...	...	...	...	...	...	...	...
60 ,, over	...	...	...	...	...	...	...	...	...	...	...	...
unspecified	...	...	...	...	...	...	...	...	...	...	...	...
Total Musalmans	**94,021**	**49,806**	**44,215**	**42,956**	**26,005**	**16,951**	**43,722**	**21,618**	**22,104**	**7,343**	**2,163**	**5,180**
0 and under 1	3,645	1,613	2,032	3,641	1,613	2,028	4	...	4	...	...	...
1 ,, ,, 2	1,273	657	616	1,268	654	614	5	3	2	...	...	...
2 ,, ,, 3	2,920	1,404	1,516	2,903	1,401	1,502	17	3	14	...	...	...
3 ,, ,, 4	3,061	1,458	1,603	3,038	1,445	1,593	10	11	8	4	2	2
4 ,, ,, 5	2,600	1,299	1,301	2,569	1,288	1,281	29	11	17	3	...	3
Total 0 and under 5	**13,499**	**6,431**	**7,068**	**13,419**	**6,401**	**7,018**	**73**	**28**	**45**	**7**	**2**	**5**
5 and under 10	13,561	7,186	6,375	13,424	7,141	6,283	122	42	80	13	3	12
10 ,, ,, 15	11,250	6,587	4,663	9,543	6,330	3,213	1,672	246	1,426	36	11	25
15 ,, ,, 20	7,934	4,176	3,758	3,567	3,286	281	4,233	862	3,371	134	28	106
20 ,, ,, 25	8,444	4,207	4,237	1,651	1,584	67	6,551	2,518	4,033	242	105	137
25 ,, ,, 30	7,360	3,501	3,859	581	559	22	6,355	2,799	3,556	424	143	281
30 ,, ,, 35	8,897	4,661	4,236	350	327	23	7,488	4,089	3,399	1,059	245	814
35 ,, ,, 40	4,444	2,426	2,018	123	116	7	3,906	2,150	1,749	413	151	262
40 ,, ,, 45	6,108	3,268	2,840	110	96	14	5,104	2,880	2,224	504	202	602
45 ,, ,, 50	2,668	1,608	1,060	60	51	9	2,228	1,395	833	380	162	218
50 ,, ,, 55	4,418	2,918	1,500	52	47	5	3,367	2,463	884	990	388	611
55 ,, ,, 60	1,764	662	1,102	9	9	...	742	534	208	1,013	119	894
60 ,, over	3,574	2,175	1,409	68	58	10	1,870	1,563	296	1,727	624	1,103
unspecified	...	...	...	...	...	...	...	...	...	...	...	...

TABLE VII.

JAMMU AND KASHMIR STATE.

SRINAGAR CITY.

AGE, SEX AND CIVIL CONDITION BY RELIGION.—concluded.

Age.	Population.			Unmarried.			Married.			Widowed.			Remarks.
	Persons.	Males.	Females.	Persons.	Males.	Females.	Persons.	Males.	Females.	Persons.	Males.	Females.	
1	2	3	4	5	6	7	8	9	10	11	12	13	14
Total Christians ...	184	92	92	107	50	57	65	39	26	12	3	9	
0 and under 1	4	3	1	4	3	1	...	...	...	...	...	...	
1 " " 2	2	1	1	2	1	1	...	...	...	...	...	...	
2 " " 3	4	...	4	4	...	4	...	...	...	...	...	...	
3 " " 4	5	4	1	5	4	1	...	...	...	...	...	...	
4 " " 5	2	1	1	2	1	1	...	...	...	...	...	...	
Total 0 and under 5 ...	17	9	8	17	9	8	...	...	...	...	...	...	
5 and under 10	13	6	7	13	6	7	...	...	...	...	...	...	
10 " " 15	12	3	9	12	3	9	...	...	...	...	...	...	
15 " " 20	10	5	5	10	5	5	...	...	...	...	...	...	
20 " " 25	20	8	12	15	7	8	5	1	4	...	...	...	
25 " " 30	30	15	15	19	10	9	11	5	6	...	...	...	
30 " " 35	28	17	11	10	5	5	16	11	5	2	1	1	
35 " " 40	14	8	6	3	...	3	9	7	2	2	1	1	

CAI—CHRISTIANS.

40 „ „ 45	11	7	4	5	4	1	5	8	9	1	...	1
45 „ „ 50	4	2	2	1	1	...	2	...	2	1	1	...
50 „ „ 55	11	6	5	...	...	...	9	6	3	2	...	2
55 „ „ 60	4	1	3	...	...	...	3	1	2	1	...	1
60 „ over	10	5	5	2	...	2	5	5	...	3	...	3
unspecified	...	...	...	...	...	...	...	...	...	...	...	–
Total Unspecified ...	**34**	**21**	**13**	**22**	**13**	**9**	**8**	**5**	**3**	**4**	**3**	**1**
0 and under 1	2	1	1	2	1	1	...	...	...	...	...	...
1 „ „ 2	2	1	1	2	1	1	...	...	...	...	...	...
2 „ „ 3	2	...	2	2	...	2	...	...	...	...	...	...
3 „ „ 4	3	2	1	3	2	1	...	...	...	...	...	...
4 „ „ 5	...	...	...	...	...	...	...	...	...	...	...	...
Total 0 and under 5 ...	**9**	**4**	**5**	**9**	**4**	**5**	...	...	...	...	...	...
5 and under 10	4	1	3	4	1	3	...	...	...	...	...	...
10 „ „ 15	3	2	1	3	2	...	...	...	...	1	...	1
15 „ „ 20	2	1	1	2	1	1	...	...	...	...	...	...
20 „ „ 25	2	2	...	2	2	...	...	...	...	...	...	...
25 „ „ 30	2	2	...	2	2	...	...	...	...	...	...	...
30 „ „ 35	3	1	2	...	...	...	3	1	2	...	...	...
35 „ „ 40	2	1	1	...	...	...	2	1	1	...	...	...
40 „ „ 45	1	1	...	...	...	...	1	1	...	...	...	...
45 „ „ 50	...	...	...	...	...	...	...	...	...	...	...	...
50 „ „ 55	2	2	...	...	...	...	1	1	...	1	1	...
55 „ „ 60	1	1	...	...	...	...	...	...	...	1	1	...
60 „ over	3	3	...	1	1	...	1	1	...	1	1	...
unspecified	...	...	...	...	...	...	...	...	...	...	...	...

VII.—Unspecified.

TABLE VIII.

EDUCATION.

JAMMU AND KASHMIR STATE.

TABLE

EDUCA

JAMMU AND

Age.		POPULATION.											
		Total.			Literate.			Illiterate.			Urdu or Hindustani.		
		Persons.	Males.	Females.	Persons.	Males.	Females.	Persons.	Males.	Females.	Persons.	Males.	Females.
1		2	3	4	5	6	7	8	9	10	11	12	13
	Total State ...	2.905.578	1.542.057	1.363.521	59.261	58.001	1.260	2.846.317	1.494.056	1.362.261	13.337	13.157	150
All Religions.	0 and under 10	852,244	437,036	415,208	956	867	89	851,288	436,169	415,119	326	319	7
	10 " " 15	341,555	189,531	152,024	4,263	4,128	135	337,292	185,103	151,889	1,577	1,558	19
	15 " " 20	239,676	128,389	111,287	5,885	5,721	164	233,791	122,668	111,123	2,084	2,062	22
	20 " over	1,472,103	787,101	685,002	48,157	47,285	872	1,423,946	739,816	684,130	9,356	9,248	102
	Total State ...	689,073	370.801	318.272	40.077	39.578	499	648.996	331.223	317.773	8.439	8.390	49
Hindus.	0 and under 10	164,333	83,515	80,818	583	563	20	163,750	82,952	80,798	219	216	3
	10 " " 15	74.752	43,284	31,498	2,830	2,794	45	71,949	40,490	31,453	1,137	1,132	5
	15 " " 20	56,365	30,467	25,898	3,897	3,837	60	52,468	26,630	25,838	1,466	1,458	8
	20 " over	393,593	213,535	180,058	32,758	32,384	374	360,835	181,151	179,684	5,617	5,581	33
	Total State ...	25,828	14.342	11.486	2.248	2.122	126	23.580	12.220	11.360	275	277	1
Sikhs.	0 and under 10	7,669	4,077	3,592	59	41	18	7,610	4,036	3,574	13	12	1
	10 " " 15	2,945	1,730	1,215	152	133	19	2,793	1,597	1,196	36	36	...
	15 " " 20	2,286	1,270	1,016	215	197	18	2.071	1,073	998	41	41	...
	20 " over	12.928	7,265	5,663	1,822	1,751	71	11.106	5,514	5.592	188	188	...
	Total State ...	442	254	188	153	153	...	289	101	188	6	6	...
Jains.	0 and under 10	92	51	41	6	6	...	86	45	41	1	1	...
	10 " " 15 — ...	50	24	26	12	12	...	38	12	26	1	1	...
	15 " " 20	41	26	15	18	18	...	23	8	15	2	2	...
	20 " over	259	153	106	117	117	...	142	36	106	2	2	...

VIII.

TION.

KASHMIR STATE.

LITERATE IN																							
PROVINCIAL VERNACULARS.																		OTHER LANGUAGES.			ENGLISH.		
Hindi or Bhasha.			*Gurmukhi.*			*Pashto.*			*Tibetan.*			*Dogri.*			*Lande or Mahajani.*								
Persons.	Males.	Females.	Persons.	Males.	Females.	Persons.	Males.	Females.	Persons.	Males.	Females.	Persons.	Males.	Females.	Persons.	Males.	Females.	Persons.	Males.	Females.	Persons.	Males.	Females.
14	15	16	17	18	19	20	21	22	23	24	25	26	27	28	29	30	31	32	33	34	35	36	37
8,987	**8,902**	**85**	**2,366**	**2,122**	**244**	**2**	**1**	**1**	**1**	**1**		**4,510**	**4,407**	**103**	**2,396**	**2,363**	**33**	**26,081**	**25,503**	**578**	**1,581**	**1,515**	**66**
63	59	4	61	38	23	...	...	...	...	...	...	22	21	1	7	6	1	449	402	47	28	22	6
269	265	4	155	116	39	...	...	...	...	...	...	119	114	5	44	41	3	1,947	1,882	65	152	152	...
496	483	13	238	209	29	1	...	1	...	...	...	247	240	7	85	82	3	2,438	2,354	84	296	291	5
8,159	8,095	64	1,912	1,759	153	1	1	...	1	1	...	4,122	4,032	90	2,260	2,234	26	21,247	20,865	382	1,105	1,050	55
8,284	**8,204**	**80**	**990**	**868**	**122**	...	...	...	...	...	...	**2,885**	**2,834**	**51**	**2,315**	**2,282**	**33**	**16,030**	**15,869**	**161**	**1,134**	**1,131**	**3**
55	52	3	18	11	7	...	...	...	...	...	...	13	13	...	7	6	1	257	251	6	14	14	...
240	236	4	61	41	20	...	...	...	...	...	...	82	81	1	43	40	3	1,140	1,134	12	131	131	...
455	442	13	102	90	12	...	...	...	...	...	...	177	172	5	84	81	3	1,356	1,341	15	254	253	1
7,534	7,474	60	810	726	84	...	...	...	...	...	...	2,613	2,568	45	2,182	2,156	26	13,268	13,143	125	736	733	3
351	**349**	**2**	**1,365**	**1,243**	**122**	**1**	...	**1**	...	...		**9**	**9**	...	**27**	**27**	...	**125**	**125**	...	**92**	**92**	...
2	1	1	43	27	16	...	...	...	...	...	...	...	...	...	...	...	...	1	1	...	...	...	...
11	11	...	92	73	19	...	...	...	...	...		1	1	...	...	...	...	10	10	...	2	2	...
21	21	...	136	119	17	1		1	...	...	...	...	...	...	...	...	...	10	10	...	6	6	...
317	316	1	1,094	1,024	70	...	...	...	...	...	...	8	8	...	27	27	...	104	101		84	84	...
144	**144**	...	...	...	...	...	...	...	...	...	...	...	...	...	...	...	...	...		...	**3**	**3**	...
5	6	...	...	...	...	...	...	...	...	...	...	...	...	...	...	...	...	...	...	...	...	...	...
11	11	...	...	...	...	...	...	...	...	...	...	...	...	...	...	...	...	...	...	...	...	...	...
16	16	...	...	...	...	...	...	...	...	...	...	...	...	...	...	...	...	...	...	...	...	...	...
112	112	...	...	...	...	...	...	...	...	...	...	...	...	...	...	...	...	...	...	...	3	3	...

TABLE

EDUCA

JAMMU AND

Religion	Age.	Population. Total. Persons.	Total. Males.	Total. Females.	Literate. Persons.	Literate. Males.	Literate. Females.	Illiterate. Persons.	Illiterate. Males.	Illiterate. Females.	*Urdu or Hindustani.* Persons.	*Urdu or Hindustani.* Males.	*Urdu or Hindustani.* Females.
	1	2	3	4	5	6	7	8	9	10	11	12	13
Zoroastrians.	**Total State** ...	**11**	**8**	**3**	**6**	**6**	...	**5**	**2**	**3**	...	...	...
	0 and under 10	3	3	...	1	1	...	2	2	...	...	...	...
	10 " " 15	...	...	...	...	...	...	...	...	...	...	...	...
	15 " " 20	...	...	...	...	...	...	...	...	...	...	...	...
	20 " over	8	5	3	5	5	...	3	...	3	...	...	...
Musalmans.	**Total State** ...	**2,154,635**	**1,138,814**	**1,015,881**	**14,942**	**14,466**	**476**	**2,139,753**	**1,124,349**	**1,015,405**	**4,588**	**4,492**	**96**
	0 and under 10	673,298	346,024	327,274	286	242	44	673,012	345,782	327,230	92	89	3
	10 " " 15	260,536	142,845	117,691	1,215	1,149	66	259,321	141,696	117,625	402	388	14
	15 " " 20	177,996	95,081	82,915	1,662	1,586	76	176,334	93,495	82,839	572	559	13
	20 " over	1,012,865	554,864	488,001	11,779	11,489	290	1,031,086	543,375	487,711	3,522	3,456	66
Christians.	**Total State** ...	**422**	**236**	**186**	**196**	**123**	**73**	**226**	**113**	**113**	**19**	**15**	**4**
	0 and under 10	100	48	52	12	6	6	88	42	46	1	1	...
	10 " " 15	25	13	12	7	7	...	18	6	12	1	1	...
	15 " " 20	24	12	12	10	4	6	14	8	6	2	1	1
	20 " over	273	163	110	167	106	61	106	57	49	15	12	3
Buddhists.	**Total State** ...	**35,047**	**17,586**	**17,461**	**1,637**	**1,551**	**86**	**33,410**	**16,015**	**17,395**	**6**	**6**	...
	0 and under 10	6,729	3,311	3,418	9	8	1	6,720	3,303	3,417	...	...	...
	10 " " 15	3,213	1,632	1,581	38	33	5	3,175	1,599	1,576	...	...	...
	15 " " 20	2,961	1,531	1,430	83	79	4	2,878	1,452	1,426	1	1	...
	20 " over	22,144	11,092	11,052	1,507	1,431	76	20,637	9,661	10,976	5	5	...
Unspecified.	**Total State** ...	**60**	**36**	**24**	**2**	**2**	...	**58**	**34**	**24**	**1**	**1**	...
	0 and under 10	20	7	13	...	—	...	20	7	13	...	...	...
	01 " " 15	4	3	1	...	...	...	4	3	1	...	...	...
	15 " " 20	3	2	1	...	...	...	3	2	1	...	...	...
	20 " over	33	24	9	2	2	...	31	22	9	1	1	...

KASHMIR STATE—concluded.

LITERATE IN																							
Provincial Vernaculars.																		Other Languages.			English.		
Hindi or Bhasha.			*Gurmukhi.*			*Pashto.*			*Tibetan.*			*Dogri.*			*Lande or Mahajani.*								
Persons.	Males.	Females.	Persons.	Males.	Females.	Persons.	Males.	Females.	Persons.	Males.	Females.	Persons.	Males.	Females.	Persons.	Males.	Females.	Persons.	Males.	Females.	Persons.	Males.	Females.
14	15	16	17	18	19	20	21	22	23	24	25	26	27	28	29	30	31	32	33	34	35	36	37
...	...	...	...	...	...	...	...	...	...	...	...	...	...	...	...	...	...	...	...	...	6	6	...
...	...	...	...	...	...	...	...	...	...	...	...	...	...	...	...	...	...	...	...	...	1	1	...
...	...	...	...	...	...	...	...	...	...	...	...	...	...	...	...	...	...	...	...	...	...	...	...
...	...	...	...	...	...	...	...	...	...	...	...	...	...	...	...	...	...	...	...	...	...	...	...
...	...	...	...	...	...	...	...	...	...	...	...	...	...	...	...	...	...	...	...	...	5	5	...
203	200	3	11	11	...	1	1	...	1	1	...	72	70	2	54	54	...	9,831	9,456	375	181	181	...
1	1	...	...	...	...	...	...	...	...	...	...	...	...	...	...	...	...	191	150	41	2	2	...
7	7	...	2	2	...	...	...	...	...	...	...	1	1	...	2	2	...	788	730	58	13	13	...
4	4	...	...	...	...	...	...	...	...	...	...	2	2	...	1	1	...	1,054	991	63	29	29	...
191	188	3	9	9	...	1	1	...	1	1	...	69	67	2	51	51	...	7,798	7,579	219	137	137	...
3	3	...	...	...	...	...	...	...	...	...	...	...	...	...	...	...	...	9	3	6	165	102	63
...	...	...	...	...	...	...	...	...	...	...	...	...	...	...	...	...	...	...	...	...	11	5	6
...	...	...	...	...	...	...	...	...	...	...	...	...	...	...	...	...	...	...	...	...	6	6	...
...	...	...	...	...	...	...	...	...	...	...	...	...	...	...	...	...	...	1	...	1	7	3	4
3	3	...	...	...	...	...	...	...	...	...	...	...	...	...	...	...	...	8	3	5	141	88	53
2	2	...	...	...	...	...	...	...	...	...	...	1,544	1,494	50	...	...	...	85	49	36	...	...	...
...	...	...	...	...	...	...	...	...	...	...	...	9	8	1	...	...	...	...	...	...	...	...	...
...	...	...	...	...	...	...	...	...	...	...	...	35	31	4	...	...	...	3	2	1	...	...	...
...	...	...	...	...	...	...	...	...	...	...	...	68	66	2	...	...	...	14	12	2	...	...	...
2	2	...	...	...	...	...	...	...	...	...	...	1,432	1,389	43	...	...	...	68	35	33	...	...	...
...	...	...	...	...	...	...	...	...	...	...	...	...	...	...	...	...	...	1	1	...	...	...	...
...	...	...	...	...	...	...	...	...	...	...	...	...	...	...	...	...	...	...	...	...	...	...	...
...	...	...	...	...	...	...	...	...	...	...	...	...	...	...	...	...	...	...	...	...	...	...	...
...	...	...	...	...	...	...	...	...	...	...	...	...	...	...	...	...	...	...	...	...	...	...	...
...	...	...	...	...	...	...	...	...	...	...	...	...	...	...	...	...	...	1	1	...	...	...	...

TABLE VIII.

EDUCATION.

JAMMU AND KASHMIR STATE.

Jammu Province.

TABLE

EDUCA

JAMMU AND

JAMMU

Age.		POPULATION. Total. Persons.	Total. Males.	Total. Females.	Literate. Persons.	Literate. Males.	Literate. Females.	Illiterate. Persons.	Illiterate. Males.	Illiterate. Females.	Urdu or Hindustani. Persons.	Urdu or Hindustani. Males.	Urdu or Hindustani. Females.
1		2	3	4	5	6	7	8	9	10	11	12	13
Total Province		**626 177**	**334 418**	**291 759**	**23·231**	**23 542**	**389**	**602 246**	**310 876**	**231 370**	**3 957**	**3 920**	**37**
Hindus	0 and under 10 ...	149,075	75,818	73,257	300	285	15	148,775	75,533	73,242	114	111	3
	10 " " 15 ...	68,578	39,605	28,073	1,377	1,342	35	67,201	38,263	28,038	547	543	4
	15 " " 20 ...	51,060	27,324	23,706	2,251	2,210	41	48,839	25,114	23,725	690	687	3
	20 " over ...	357,434	191,671	165,763	20,003	19,705	298	337,431	171,966	165,465	2,606	2,579	27
	Age not returned ...	...	...	...	...	...	...	...			...	...	...
Total Province		**13 113**	**7 418**	**5 695**	**1 318**	**1 230**	**88**	**11 795**	**6 188**	**5 607**	**149**	**148**	**1**
Sikhs	0 and under 10 ...	3,486	1,869	1,617	33	24	9	3,453	1,845	1,608	10	9	1
	10 " " 15 ...	1,488	886	602	91	81	10	1,397	805	592	22	22	...
	15 " " 20 ...	1,131	670	461	116	105	11	1,015	565	450	21	21	...
	20 " over ...	7,008	3,993	3,015	1,078	1,020	58	5,930	2,973	2,957	96	96	...
	Age not returned ...	...	...	...							...	...	...
Total Province		**439**	**252**	**187**	**153**	**153**	...	**286**	**99**	**187**	**8**	**8**	...
Jains	0 and under 10 ...	92	51	41	6	6	...	86	45	41	1	1	...
	10 " " 15 ...	50	24	26	12	12	...	38	12	26	1	1	...
	15 " " 20 ...	41	26	15	18	18	...	23	8	15	2	2	...
	20 " over ...	256	151	105	117	117	...	139	34	105	2	2	...
	Age not returned ...	...	...	...	...	...	...	...	...	...	...	...	...
Total Province		Nil											
Zoroastrians	0 and under 10 ...												
	10 " " 15 ...												
	15 " " 20 ...												
	20 " over ...												
	Age not returned ...												

VIII—ii

TION.

KASHMIR STATE.

PROVINCE.

LITERATE IN																							
PROVINCIAL VERNACULARS.																		Other Languages.			English.		
Hindi or Bhasha.			Gurmukhi			Dogri.			Tibetan.			Pashto.			Lande or Mahajani.								
Persons.	Males.	Females.	Persons.	Males.	Females.	Persons.	Males.	Females.	Persons.	Males.	Females.	Persons.	Males.	Females.	Persons.	Males.	Females.	Persons.	Males.	Females.	Persons.	Males.	Females.
14	15	16	17	18	19	20	21	22	23	24	25	26	27	28	29	30	31	32	33	34	35	36	37
7,847	**7,778**	**69**	**737**	**641**	**96**	**2,402**	**2,353**	**49**			...	...	...	...	**2,275**	**2,242**	**33**	**5,744**	**5,641**	**103**	**969**	**967**	**2**
54	52	2	14	7	7	11	11	...		...	...	...			7	6	1	86	84	2	14	14	...
240	236	4	41	26	15	52	52	...	...	...	...		...		42	39	3	353	344	9	102	102	...
423	412	11	78	71	7	167	162	5	...	...	...	...		...	84	81	3	583	572	11	226	225	1
7,130	7,078	52	604	537	67	2,172	2,128	44	...		...				2,142	2,116	26	4,722	4,641	81	627	626	1
...	...	...	...	...	...	...	...	...	...	...	...	...	...	...		...	...	...	...	...	...	...	...
328	**326**	**2**	**626**	**542**	**84**	**3**	**3**	...		...	...	**1**	...	**1**	**27**	**27**	...	**97**	**97**	...	**87**	**87**	...
2	1	1	20	13	7	...	...	...	...	...	...	...	...	...	...	...	...	1	1	...	...	...	...
10	10	...	47	37	10	1	1	...	...	...	...	...	...	...	...	...	...	10	10	...	1	1	...
18	18	...	66	56	10	...		...	...	...	...	1	...	1	...		...	5	5	...	5	5	...
298	297	1	493	436	57	2	2	...	...	...	...	...	...	...	27	27	...	81	81	...	81	81	...
...	...	...	...	...	...	...	...	...	...	...	...	...	...	...	...	...	...		...	...	...	...	...
144	**144**	...	...	...	...	...	...	...	...	...	...	...	...	...	...	...	...	...	...	...	**3**	**3**	...
5	5	...	...	...	...	...	...	...	...	...	...	...	...	...	...	...	...	...	...	...	...	...	...
11	11	...	...	...	...	...	...	...	...	...	...	...	...	...	...	...	...	...	...	...	...	...	...
16	16	...	...	...	...	...	...	...	...	...	...	...	...	...	...	...	...	...	...	...	...	...	...
112	112	...	...	...	...	...	...	...	...	...	...	...	...	...	...	...	...	...	...	...	3	3	...
...	...	...	...	...	...	...	...	...	...	...	...	...	...	...	...	...	...	...	...	...	...	...	...

Nil.

TABLE

EDUCA

JAMMU AND

JAMMU

	Age.	Population. Total. Persons.	Population. Total. Males.	Population. Total. Females.	Literate. Persons.	Literate. Males.	Literate. Females.	Illiterate. Persons.	Illiterate. Males.	Illiterate. Females.	Urdu or Hindustani. Persons.	Urdu or Hindustani. Males.	Urdu or Hindustani. Females.
	1	2	3	4	5	6	7	8	9	10	11	12	13
Muhammadans.	**Total Province**	**876,599**	**463,186**	**413,413**	**5,889**	**5,585**	**304**	**870,710**	**457,601**	**413,109**	**2,983**	**2,793**	**70**
	0 and under 10 ...	254,167	130,722	123,445	163	137	26	254,004	130,585	123,419	79	76	3
	10 " " 15 ...	112,735	60,495	52,240	492	450	42	112,243	60,045	52,198	269	259	10
	15 " " 20 ...	77,587	40,783	36,804	672	625	47	76,915	40,158	36,757	353	347	6
	20 " over ...	432,110	231,186	200,924	4,562	4,373	189	427,548	226,813	200,735	2,162	2,111	51
	Age not returned.	...	...	...	...	...	...	...	...	...	...	...	...
Christians.	**Total Province**	**145**	**87**	**58**	**41**	**30**	**11**	**104**	**57**	**47**	**14**	**11**	**3**
	0 and under 10 ...	46	22	24	2	1	1	44	21	23	1	1	...
	10 " " 15 ...	8	6	2	3	3	...	5	3	2	1	1	...
	15 " " 20 ...	10	6	4	4	2	2	6	4	2	2	1	1
	20 " over ...	81	53	28	32	24	8	49	29	20	10	8	2
	Age not returned ...	...	...	...	...	...	...	...	...	...	...	...	...
Buddhists.	**Total Province**	**4,531**	**2,431**	**2,400**	**527**	**459**	**68**	**4,304**	**1,972**	**2,332**	**1**	**1**	...
	0 and under 10 ...	925	427	498	5	4	1	920	423	497	...	...	...
	10 " " 15 ...	473	237	236	9	4	5	464	233	231	...	...	...
	15 " " 20 ...	458	260	198	30	26	4	428	234	194	...	...	...
	20 " over ...	2,975	1,507	1,468	483	425	58	2,492	1,082	1,410	1	1	...
	Age not returned ...	...	...	...	...	...	...	...	...	...	...	...	...
Unclassified.	**Total Province** ...	**3**	...	**3**	...	...	...	**3**	...	3	...	...	...
	0 and under 10 ...	1	...	1	...	...	...	1	...	1	...	...	...
	10 " " 15 ...	...	...	...	...	...	...	...	...	...	...	...	...
	15 " " 20 ...	...	...	...	...	...	...	...	...	...	...	...	...
	20 " over ...	2	...	2	...	...	...	3	...	2	...	...	...
	Age not returned ...	...	...	...	...	...	...	...	...	...	...	...	...

TION.

KASHMIR STATE.

PROVINCE—concluded.

LITERATE IN																							
PROVINCIAL VERNACULARS.																		OTHER LANGUAGES.			ENGLISH.		
Hindi or Bhasha.			*[illegible].*			*[illegible].*			*Tibetan.*			*Takri.*			*Lande or Mahajani.*								
Persons.	Males.	Females.	Persons.	Males.	Females.	Persons.	Males.	Females.	Persons.	Males.	Females.	Persons.	Males.	Females.	Persons.	Males.	Females.	Persons.	Males.	Females.	Persons.	Males.	Females.
14	15	16	17	18	19	20	21	22	23	24	25	26	27	28	29	30	31	32	33	34	35	36	37
187	186	1	7	7	...	23	23	...	...	...	...	...	...	...	53	53	...	2,605	2,372	233	151	151	...
1	1	...	...	...	...	...	...	...	...	...	...	...	...	...	...	...	...	[illegible]	58	23	2	2	...
7	7	...	1	1	...	...	...	...	...	...	...	...	...	...	2	2	...	201	169	32	12	12	...
4	4	...	...	...	...	1	1	...	...	...	...	...	...	...	...	...	...	287	246	41	27	27	...
175	174	1	6	6	...	22	22	...	...	...	...	...	...	...	51	51	...	2,036	1,899	137	110	110	...
...	...	...	...	...	...	...	...	...	...	...	...	...	...	...	...	...	...	...	...	...	...	...	...
1	1	...	...	...	...	...	...	...	...	...	...	...	...	...	...	...	...	...	...	...	26	18	8
...	...	...	...	...	...	...	...	...	...	...	...	...	...	...	...	...	...	...	...	...	1	...	1
...	...	...	...	...	...	...	...	...	...	...	...	...	...	...	...	...	...	...	...	...	2	2	...
...	...	...	...	...	...	...	...	...	...	...	...	...	...	...	...	...	...	...	...	...	2	1	1
1	1	...	...	...	...	...	...	...	...	...	...	...	...	...	...	...	...	...	...	...	21	15	6
...	...	...	...	...	...	...	...	...	...	...	...	...	...	...	...	...	...	...	...	...	...	...	...
...	...	...	...	...	...	443	411	32	...	...	...	...	...	...	...	...	...	[illegible]	47	36	...	...	...
...	...	...	...	...	...	5	4	1	...	...	...	...	...	...	...	...	...	...	...	...	...	...	...
...	...	...	...	...	...	6	[illegible]	[illegible]	...	...	...	...	...	...	...	...	...	[illegible]	2	1	...	...	...
...	...	...	...	...	...	16	1	...	...	...	...	...	...	...	...	...	...	14	12	2	...	...	...
...	...	...	...	...	...	[illegible]	[illegible]	[illegible]	...	...	...	...	...	...	...	...	...	[illegible]	[illegible]	[illegible]	...	...	...
...	...	...	...	...	...	...	...	...	...	...	...	...	...	...	...	...	...	...	...	...	...	...	...
...	...	...	...	...	...	...	...	...	...	...	...	...	...	...	...	...	...	...	...	...	...	...	...
...	...	...	...	...	...	...	...	...	...	...	...	...	...	...	...	...	...	...	...	...	...	...	...
...	...	...	...	...	...	...	...	...	...	...	...	...	...	...	...	...	...	...	...	...	...	...	...
...	...	...	...	...	...	...	...	...	...	...	...	...	...	...	...	...	...	...	...	...	...	...	...
...	...	...	...	...	...	...	...	...	...	...	...	...	...	...	...	...	...	...	...	...	...	...	...
...	...	...	...	...	...	...	...	...	...	...	...	...	...	...	...	...	...	...	...	...	...	...	...

TABLE

JAMMU AND

EDUCA

JAMMU

Age.	POPULATION.											
	Total.			Literate.			Illiterate.			*Urdu or Hindustani.*		
	Persons.	Males.	Females.	Persons.	Males.	Females.	Persons.	Males.	Females.	Persons.	Males.	Females.
1	2	3	4	5	6	7	8	9	10	11	12	13
Total Province ...	1,521,307	[illegible]07,732	713,515	31,85[illegible]	33,[illegible]93	83[illegible]	1,429,448	776,7[illegible]3	712,655	6,390	6,879	111
All Religions. 0 and under 10 ...	407,792	208,900	198,88[illegible]	509	457	53	407,283	208,452	198,831	205	198	7
All Religions. 10 " " 15 ...	183,332	101,253	82,079	1,984	1,893	92	181,348	99,361	81,087	840	826	14
All Religions. 15 " " 20 ...	130,317	69,069	61,248	3,091	2,986	105	127,226	66,083	61,143	1,068	1,055	10
All Religions. 20 " over ...	799,866	428,561	371,305	26,275	25,664	611	773,591	402,897	370,694	4,877	4,797	80

KASHMIR STATE.

TION.

PROVINCE.

LITERATE IN																							
PROVINCIAL VERNACULARS.																		OTHER LANGUAGES.			ENGLISH.		
Hindi or Bhasha.			*Gurmukhi.*			*Dogri.*			*Tibetan.*			*Pashtu.*			*Lande or Mahajani.*								
Persons.	Males.	Females.	Persons.	Males.	Females.	Persons.	Males.	Females.	Persons.	Males.	Females.	Persons.	Males.	Females.	Persons.	Males.	Females.	Persons.	Males.	Females.	Persons.	Males.	Females.
14	15	16	17	18	19	20	21	22	23	24	25	26	27	28	29	30	31	32	33	34	35	36	37
8,507	8,435	72	1,370	1,190	180	2,871	2,730	51	...	..	..	1	...	1	2,355	2,322	33	8,529	8,157	372	1,236	1,226	10
62	59	3	34	20	14	16	15	1	...	...	...	...	...		7	6	1	168	143	25	17	16	1
268	265	4	89	64	25	59	55	4	...	..	...	...	...	...	44	41	3	567	525	42	117	117	...
461	450	11	144	127	17	184	177	7	...	...	...	1	...	1	84	81	3	889	835	54	260	258	2
7,716	7,662	54	1,103	979	124	2,612	2,5[illegible]	60	...	...	...	..	...	...	2,22[illegible]	2,194	26	6,905	6,654	251	842	835	7

TABLE VIII.

JAMMU AND KASHMIR STATE.

EDUCATION.

KASHMIR PROVINCE.

TABLE

JAMMU AND

EDUCA

KASHMIR

Age.	POPULATION. Total. Persons.	Males.	Females.	Literate. Persons.	Males.	Females.	Illiterate. Persons.	Males.	Females.	*Urdu or Hindustani.* Persons.	Males.	Females.
1	2	3	4	5	6	7	8	9	10	11	12	13
TOTAL PROVINCE ...	**60,682**	**34,261**	**26,421**	**15,240**	**15,137**	**103**	**45,442**	**19,124**	**26,318**	**4,296**	**4,285**	**11**
HINDUS. 0 and under 10	15,207	7,671	7,536	282	278	4	14,925	7,393	7,532	105	105	...
HINDUS. 10 " " 15	6,190	3,670	2,520	1,461	1,451	10	4,729	2,210	2,510	590	589	1
HINDUS. 15 " " 20	5,166	3,045	2,121	1,606	1,591	15	3,560	1,454	2,106	762	758	4
HINDUS. 20 " over	34,119	19,875	14,244	11,891	11,817	74	22,228	8,058	14,170	2,839	2,833	6
TOTAL PROVINCE ..	**12,637**	**6,860**	**5,777**	**886**	**849**	**37**	**11,751**	**6,011**	**5,740**	**106**	**105**	...
SIKHS. 0 and under 10	4,178	2,205	1,973	26	17	9	4,152	2,188	1,964	3	3	...
SIKHS. 10 " " 15	1,455	842	613	60	51	9	1,395	791	604	13	18	...
SIKHS. 15 " " 20	1,150	596	554	95	89	6	1,055	507	548	19	19	...
SIKHS. 20 " over	5,854	3,217	2,637	705	692	13	5,149	2,525	2,624	73	73	...
TOTAL PROVINCE ...	**2**	**1**	**1**	...	...	...	**2**	**1**	**1**			...
JAINS. 20 and over	2	1	1	...	...	...	2	1	1	...	...	...
TOTAL PROVINCE ...	**11**	**8**	**3**	**6**	**6**	...	**5**	**2**	**3**	...	...	...
ZOROASTRIANS. 0 and under 10	3	3	...	1	1	...	2	2	...	...	...	...
ZOROASTRIANS. 20 " over	8	5	3	5	5	...	3	...	3	...	...	...

VIII—ii

KASHMIR STATE.

TION.

PROVINCE.

LITERATE IN

Provincial Vernaculars.																		Other Languages.			English.		
Hindi or Bhasha.			*Gurmukhi.*			*Dogri.*			*Tibetan.*			*Pashto.*			*Landi or Mahajani.*								
Persons.	Males.	Females.	Persons.	Males.	Females.	Persons.	Males.	Females.	Persons.	Males.	Females.	Persons.	Males.	Females.	Persons.	Males.	Females.	Persons.	Males.	Females.	Persons.	Males.	Females.
14	15	16	17	18	19	20	21	22	23	24	25	26	27	28	29	30	31	32	33	34	35	36	37
215	228	7	234	210	24	137	135	2	...	...	...	...	...	...	3	37		10,338	10,00[illegible]	52	163	162	1
...	...	...	4	4		2	2	...	...	...			...					171	167	4	...		...
...	...	...	20	15	5	30	29	1		...	...	...	...	...				792	789	3	29	29	...
19	19	...	23	19	4	4	4	...	...				...		...		...	770	763	7	28	28	...
228	221	7	187	172	15	161	160	1	...		...	...			37	37		8,[illegible]	8,29[illegible]	41	106	105	1
21	21	...	722	685	37	4	4	...	...			...						23	2		3	3	...
...	...	...	23	14	9	...	...	...	...	...	...	...	...	...	...					...	...	...	...
1	1	...	45	36	9	...	...	...	...	...	...	...	...	...	...	...		...	...	...	1	1	...
3	3	...	67	61	6	...		...	...			...						5	5	...	1	1	...
17	17		587	574	13	4	4		...			...	...			...	...	23	23		1	1	...
...	...	...	...	...	...	...	...		...		...	...		...	...	...		...		...	...	...	...
...	...		...		...	...	...		...	...	...	...						...		...	...	...	...
...	...	...	...	...	...	...	...	...				...	...	...		...				...	6	6	...
...	...		...	...			...				...									...	1	1	...
...	...	...	...	...	...			...	...	...		...		...					...		5	5	...

TABLE

JAMMU AND

EDUCA

KASHMIR

Age.	POPULATION.											
	Total.			Literate.			Illiterate.			Urdu or Hindustani.		
	Persons.	Males.	Females.	Persons.	Males.	Females.	Persons.	Males.	Females.	Persons.	Males	Females.
1	2	3	4	5	6	7	8	9	10	11	12	13
Total Province ...	**1,083,766**	**575,598**	**508,168**	**8,367**	**8,228**	**159**	**1,075,379**	**567,370**	**508,009**	**1,376**	**1,356**	**20**
Musalmans. 0 and under 10	370,461	190,744	179,717	119	101	18	370,342	190,643	179,699	10	10	...
Musalmans. 10 " " 15	129,848	72,717	57,131	710	686	24	129,138	72,031	57,107	126	122	4
Musalmans. 15 " " 20	86,477	46,733	39,744	919	931	28	85,528	45,812	39,716	189	183	6
Musalmans. 20 " over	496,980	265,401	231,576	6,609	6,520	89	490,371	258,884	231,487	1,051	1,041	10
Total Province ...	**244**	**128**	**116**	**131**	**76**	**55**	**113**	**52**	**61**	**4**	**3**	**1**
Christians. 0 and under 10	49	24	25	10	5	5	39	19	20	...	...	...
Christians. 10 " " 15	17	7	10	4	4	...	13	3	10	...	...	...
Christians. 15 " " 20	14	6	8	6	2	4	8	4	4	...	...	...
Christians. 20 " over	164	91	73	111	65	46	53	26	27	4	3	1
Total Province ...	**52**	**31**	**21**	**2**	**2**	...	**50**	**29**	**21**	**1**	**1**	...
Unspecified. 0 and under 10	19	7	12	...	...	...	19	7	12	...	...	...
Unspecified. 10 " " 15	4	3	1	...	...	...	4	3	1	...	...	...
Unspecified. 15 " " 20	2	1	1	...	...	...	2	1	1	...	...	...
Unspecified. 20 " over	27	20	7	2	2	...	25	18	7	1	1	...

KASHMIR STATE.

TION.

PROVINCE.—concluded.

LITERATE IN

Provincial Vernaculars: *Hindi or Bhasha.* Persons.	Males.	Females.	*Gurmukhi.* Persons.	Males.	Females.	*Dogri.* Persons.	Males.	Females.	*Tibetan.* Persons.	Males.	Females.	*Pashto.* Persons.	Males.	Females.	*Landi or Mahajani.* Persons.	Males.	Females.	Other Languages. Persons.	Males.	Females.	English. Persons.	Males.	Females.
14	15	16	17	18	19	20	21	22	23	24	25	26	27	28	29	30	31	32	33	34	35	36	37
14	13	1	3	3	...	16	16		1	1	..	1	1	..	1	1	..	6,945	6,807	138	30	30	...
...	...	..	..	...	...	..	...	...	..	..	..				..	..	..	109	91	18	...	...	...
...	...	..	...	...	...	1	1	..	..	...	..	..	..	...	...	...	...	582	562	20	1	1	...
...	...	..	...	...	...	...	..	..	..					...	1	1	...	757	735	22	2	2	...
14	13	1	3	3	...	15	15	...	1	1	...	1	1	..	...	..	..	5,497	5,419	78	27	27	...
2	2	.	.	...	...	...	...	..	..	...	..	..	..	...	..	..		9	3	6	116	68	48
...	...	...	...	...	...	...	...		...	...	..	..	..	...	...		..	..	..	..	10	5	5
...	...	...	...	...	...	...	..	...	..	..	..	..		...	..	..	..	..		..	4	4	...
...	...	..	..	..	..	...	..	...	...	...	..	..	..	..	...	...	...	1	...	1	5	2	3
2	2	...	...	..	...	...		...	...	...	..		...	..	..	..	..	8	3	5	97	57	40
...	...	...	..	..	...	...	...	...		..	..	..	..	..	...	..	..	1	1	...	..	...	...
...	...	...	...	...	...	..	...	...	..	...	..	...	...	...	...	...	...	...	...	...	..	..	...
...	...	...	...	...	...	...	...	...	...	...	...	...	...	...	...	...	...	...	...	...	...	..	...
...	...	...	...	...	...	...	...	...	..	..	..	..	..	...	...	...	...	...	...	...	...	...	...
...	...	...	...	...	...	...	...	...	...	...	...	...	...	...	...	...	...	1	1	...	...	...	...

TABLE

JAMMU AND

EDUCA

KASHMIR

Age.	POPULATION.											
	Total.			Literate.			Illiterate.			*Urdu or Hindustani.*		
	Persons.	Males.	Females.	Persons.	Males.	Females.	Persons.	Males.	Females.	Persons.	Males.	Females.
1	2	3	4	5	6	7	8	9	10	11	12	13
Total Province ...	1.157.394	616.887	540.507	24.652	24.298	354	1.132.742	592.589	540.153	5.785	5.753	32
All Religions. 0 and under 10	389,917	200,654	189,263	438	402	36	389.479	200,252	189.227	118	118	...
10 " " 15	137,514	77,239	60,275	2,235	2,192	43	135,279	75,047	60.232	729	724	5
15 " " 20	92,809	50,381	42,428	2,656	2,603	53	90,153	47,778	42,375	970	960	10
20 " over	537.154	288,613	248,541	19,323	19.101	222	517,831	269.512	248.319	3.968	3,951	17

VIII.

KASHMIR STATE.

TION.

PROVINCE.

LITERATE IN																							
Provincial Vernaculars.																		Other Languages.			English.		
Hindi or Bhasha.			*Gurmukhi.*			*Dogri.*			*Tibetan.*			*Pashtu.*			*Lande or Mahajani.*								
Persons.	Males.	Females.	Persons.	Males.	Females.	Persons.	Males.	Females.	Persons.	Males.	Females.	Persons.	Males.	Females.	Persons.	Males.	Females.	Persons.	Males.	Females.	Persons.	Males.	Females.
14	15	16	17	18	19	20	21	22	23	24	25	26	27	28	29	30	31	32	33	34	35	36	37
284	276	8	959	898	61	217	215	2	1	1	...	1	1	...	38	38	...	17,049	16,847	202	318	269	49
...	...	...	27	18	9	2	2	...	...	...	...	...	...	...	...	...	...	280	258	22	11	6	5
1	1	...	65	51	14	31	30	1	...	...	...	...		...	...	...	...	1,374	1,351	23	35	35	...
22	22	...	90	80	10	4	4	...	...	...	...	...	...	...	1	1	...	1,533	1,503	30	36	33	3
261	253	8	777	749	28	180	179	1	1	1	...	1	1	...	37	37	...	13,862	13,735	127	236	195	41

TABLE VIII.

JAMMU AND KASHMIR STATE.

EDUCATION.

Frontier Districts.

JAMMU AND
EDUCA
FRONTIER

Religion	Age	Population: Total: Persons	Total: Males	Total: Females	Literate: Persons	Literate: Males	Literate: Females	Illiterate: Persons	Illiterate: Males	Illiterate: Females
	1	2	3	4	5	6	7	8	9	10
Hindus.	Total ...	2,214	2,122	92	906	899	7	1,308	1,223	25
	0 and under 10 ...	51	26	25	1	...	1	50	26	24
	10 " " 15 ...	14	9	5	1	1	...	13	8	5
	15 " " 20 ...	109	98	11	40	36	4	69	62	7
	20 " over ...	2,040	1,989	51	864	862	2	1,176	1,127	49
Sikhs.	Total ...	78	64	14	44	43	1	34	21	13
	0 and under 10 ...	5	3	2	...	...	...	5	3	2
	10 " " 15 ...	2	2	...	1	1	...	1	1	...
	15 " " 20 ...	5	4	1	4	3	1	1	1	...
	20 " over ...	66	55	11	39	39	...	27	16	11
Jains.	Total ...	1	1	...	...	...	...	1	1	...
	0 and under 10 ...	...	...	...	...	...	...	...	...	...
	10 " " 15 ...	...	...	...	...	...	...	...	...	...
	15 " " 20 ...	...	...	...	...	...	...	...	...	...
	20 " over ...	1	1	...	...	...	...	1	1	...
Musalmans.	Total ...	1,94,330	1,00,030	94,300	666	653	13	1,93,684	99,377	94,287
	0 and under 10 ...	48,670	24,558	24,112	4	4	...	48,666	24,554	24,112
	10 " " 15 ...	17,953	9,633	8,320	13	13	...	17,940	9,620	8,320
	15 " " 20 ...	13,932	7,565	6,367	41	40	1	13,891	7,525	6,366
	20 " over ...	1,13,775	58,274	55,501	608	596	12	1,13,167	57,678	55,489

VIII.

KASHMIR STATE.

TION.

DISTRICTS.

LITERATE IN																				
PROVINCIAL VERNACULARS.															OTHER LANGUAGES.			ENGLISH.		
Urdu or Hindustani			*Hindi or Bhasha.*			*Gurmukhi.*			*Dogri.*			*Lande or Mahajani*								
Persons.	Males.	Females.	Persons.	Males.	Females.	Persons.	Males.	Females.	Persons.	Males.	Females.	Persons.	Males.	Females.	Persons.	Males.	Females.	Persons.	Males.	Females.
11	12	13	14	15	16	17	18	19	20	21	22	23	24	25	26	27	28	29	30	31
186	**185**	**1**	**190**	**186**	**4**	**19**	**17**	**2**	**286**	**285**	.	**3**	**3**		**220**	**220**	...	**2**	**2**	.
...	...	.	1	...	1	...	.	.	...	.	.			..	..	...	...	...	...	...
...	...	..	..		...	..		.		..			...	..	1	1	...		..	...
14	13	1	3	11	2	1	...	1	6	6	..		...	...	6	6	..			..
172	172	...	176	175	1	18	17	1	280	280	..	3	3	...	213	213	...	2	2	...
21	**21**	..	**2**	**2**	...	**17**	**16**	**1**	**2**	**2**				..	..	...	...	**2**	**2**	...
...	...	..	...	...	...	...	..	...	..	.	.				...		.	...	...	...
1	1	..	.	...	...	...	...	.	...	...	.	..	..			.	.	.	..	...
1	1	..	...	..	...	3	2	1	...	...	.	..			..	..	...	.	..	...
10	10	...	2	2	..	14	14	.	2	2	..		.			..	...	2	2	...
...	...	...	...	..	...	...	..	...	...	...		.			.	.	..	...	...	...
...	...	...	...		..	...			.	.		...	..		...		..	...	..	...
...	...	..	...	...	...					..	.			.	..	..	...	...	...	...
...	...	..	...				..	..	...		.			..		..	...	...	...	...
...	...	..	.	..	...	...		..		..				...		..		...	...	...
349	**343**	**6**	**2**	**1**	**1**	**1**	**1**	..	**33**	**31**	**2**		.		**281**	**277**	**4**		...	..
3	3	...	..	.		...		...	.	.	..	..	...		1	1		.	...	...
7	7	.	...	...	..	1	1	.	...	...	..	..		.	5	5			.	...
30	29	1	.		...	..			1	1	...	...	...		10	10	...		...	...
309	304	5	2	1	1	..	...	...	32	30	2			.	265	261	4		...	...

TABLE

JAMMU AND

EDUCA

FRONTIER

Age.		POPULATION.								
		Total.			Literate.			Illiterate.		
		Persons.	Males.	Females.	Persons.	Males.	Females.	Persons.	Males.	Females.
1		2	3	4	5	6	7	8	9	10
Christians.	Total ...	23	21	12	24	17	7	9	4	5
	0 and under 10 ...	3	2				...	3	2	3
	10 " " 15 ...	..					...	...	...	...
	15 " " 20 ...	...					...	...	..	.
	20 " over ...	[illegible]	19	[illegible]	21	17	7	4	2	2
Buddhists.	Total ...	30,2[illegible]	15,1[illegible]	15,071	1,110	1,092	18	29,106	14,043	15,063
	0 and under 10 ...	5,904	2,884	2,020	4	4	.	5,[illegible]	2,880	2,020
	10 " " 15 ...	2,740	1,395	1,345	29	20	...	2,711	1,366	1,345
	15 " " 20 ...	2,503	1,271	1,232	53	53	...	2,450	1,218	1,232
	20 " over ...	19,169	9,585	9,584	1,024	1,006	18	18,145	8,579	9,568
Unspecified.	Total ...	5	5	...	...	...	...	5	5	...
	0 and under 10 ...	...	...	...	...	...	...	...	...	...
	10 " " 15 ...	...	...	...	...	...	...	...	...	...
	15 " " 20 ...	1	1	...	...	...	...	1	1	...
	20 " over ...	4	4	...	...	...	...	4	4	...

KASHMIR STATE.
TION.
DISTRICTS.—concluded.

LITERATE IN																				
Provincial Vernaculars.															Other Languages.			English.		
Urdu or Hindustani.			*Hindi or Bhasha.*			*Gurmukhi.*			*Dogri.*			*Lande or Mahajani*								
Persons.	Males.	Females.	Persons.	Males.	Females.	Persons.	Males.	Females.	Persons.	Males.	Females.	Persons.	Males.	Females.	Persons.	Males.	Females.	Persons.	Males.	Females.
11	12	13	14	15	16	17	18	19	20	21	22	23	24	25	26	27	28	29	30	31
1	1	...	...	...	...	...	...	...	...	...	...	...	...	...	...	...	...	23	16	7
...	...	...	...	...	...	...	...	...	...	...	...	...	...	...	...	...	...	...	...	...
...	...	...	...	...	...	...	...	...	...	...	...	...	...	...	...	...	...	...	...	...
...	...	...	...	...	...	...	...	...	...	...	...	...	...	...	...	...	...	...	...	...
1	1	...	...	...	...	...	...	...	...	...	...	...	...	...	...	...	...	23	16	7
5	5	...	2	2	...	...	...	...	1,101	1,083	18	...	...	...	2	2	...	...	...	...
...	...	...	...	...	...	...	...	...	4	4	...	...	...	...	...	...	...	...	...	...
...	...	...	...	...	...	...	...	...	29	29	...	...	...	...	...	...	...	...	...	...
1	1	...	...	...	...	...	...	...	52	52	...	...	...	...	...	...	...	...	...	...
4	4	...	2	2	...	...	...	...	1,016	998	18	...	...	...	2	2	...	...	...	...
...	...	...	...	...	...	...	...	...	...	...	...	...	...	...	...	...	...	...	...	...
...	...	...	...	...	...	...	...	...	...	...	...	...	...	...	...	...	...	...	...	...
...	...	...	...	...	...	...	...	...	...	...	...	...	...	...	...	...	...	...	...	...
...	...	...	...	...	...	...	...	...	...	...	...	...	...	...	...	...	...	...	...	...
...	...	...	...	...	...	...	...	...	...	...	...	...	...	...	...	...	...	...	...	...

TABLE
JAMMU AND
EDUCA
FRONTIER

AGE.		POPULATION.								
		TOTAL.			LITERATE.			ILLITERATE		
		Persons.	Males.	Females.	Persons	Males.	Females.	Persons	Males	Females
1		2	3	4	5	6	7	8	9	10
	TOTAL ...	226.877	117.378	109 499	2.750	2.704	46	224.127	114.674	109.453
ALL RELIGIONS.	0 and under 10	54.535	27.473	27.062	9	8	1	54.526	27.465	27.061
	10 " " 15	20.709	11.039	9,670	14	14	..	20,665	10,995	9.670
	15 " " 20	16.550	8.939	7.611	138	132	6	16.412	8.807	7.605
	20 " over	135,083	69.927	65.156	2.559	2.520	39	132.524	67.407	65,117

KASHMIR STATE.

TION.

DISTRICTS.

LITERATE IN																				
PROVINCIAL VERNACULARS.															OTHER LANGUAGES.			ENGLISH.		
Urdu or Hindustani.			*Hindi or Bhasha.*			*Gurmukhi.*			*Dogri.*			*Lande or Mahajani.*								
Persons.	Males.	Females.	Persons.	Males.	Females.	Persons.	Males.	Females.	Persons.	Males.	Females.	Persons.	Males.	Females.	Persons.	Males.	Females.	Persons.	Males.	Females.
11	12	13	14	15	16	17	18	19	20	21	22	23	24	25	26	27	28	29	30	31
582	**555**	**7**	**196**	**191**	**5**	**37**	**34**	**3**	**1,422**	**1,402**	**20**	**3**	**3**		**503**	**499**	**4**	**27**	**20**	**7**
3	3	..	1	..	1	..			4	4			..	...	1	1	...	...	.	...
8	8	...		..	..	1	1		20	20		..		...	6	6	...	...	...	...
46	44	2	13	11	2	4	2	2	59	59		...	..	...	16	16	...	..	...	...
505	500	5	182	180	2	32	31	1	1,330	1,310	20	3	3	...	480	476	4	27	20	7

TABLE VIII.

JAMMU AND KASHMIR STATE.

Jammu City.

Age	POPULATION											
	Total.			Literate.			Illiterate.			*Urdu or Hindustani.*		
	Persons.	Males.	Females.	Persons.	Males.	Females.	Persons.	Males.	Females.	Persons.	Males.	Females.
1	2	3	4	5	6	7	8	9	10	11	12	13
Total City ...	**36,130**	**22,221**	**13,909**	**6,320**	**6,022**	**298**	**29,810**	**16,199**	**13,611**	**2,224**	**2,173**	**51**
All Religions. 0 and under 10	6,303	3,311	2,992	135	120	15	6,168	3,191	2,977	73	70	3
10 " " 15 ...	3,481	2,103	1,378	471	439	32	3,010	1,664	1,346	228	220	8
15 " " 20 ...	3,502	2,135	1,367	719	688	31	2,783	1,447	1,336	262	258	4
20 " over	22,844	14,672	8,172	4,995	4,775	220	17,849	9,897	7,952	1,661	1,625	36
Age not returned ...	...	...	...	...		...	...		...		...	...
Total City ...	**21,112**	**12,881**	**8,231**	**4,899**	**4,706**	**193**	**16,213**	**8,175**	**8,036**	**1,471**	**1,450**	**21**
Hindus. 0 and under 10	3,466	1,824	1,642	88	78	10	3,378	1,746	1,632	41	38	3
10 " " 15	1,868	1,120	748	327	314	13	1,541	806	735	139	138	1
15 " " 20	2,152	1,324	828	558	536	22	1,594	788	806	173	172	1
20 " over	13,626	8,613	5,013	3,926	3,778	148	9,700	4,835	4,865	1,118	1,102	16
Age not returned	...	...	...	...	...	...	...	...	...		...	...
Total City ...	**885**	**548**	**337**	**305**	**268**	**37**	**580**	**280**	**300**	**19**	**19**	...
Sikhs. 0 and under 10	169	95	74	6	6	...	163	89	74	3	3	...
10 " " 15	70	43	27	26	20	6	44	23	21	6	6	...
15 " " 20	70	40	30	27	22	5	43	18	25	3	3	...
20 " over	576	370	206	246	220	26	330	150	180	7	7	...
Age not returned	...	...	...	...	...	...	...	...	...	...	...	...
Total City ...	**437**	**251**	**186**	**152**	**152**	...	**285**	**99**	**186**	**5**	**5**	...
Jains. 0 and under 10	93	51	42	6	6	...	87	45	42	1	1	...
10 " " 15	50	24	26	12	12	...	38	12	26	1	1	...
15 " " 20	41	26	15	18	18	...	23	8	15	2	2	...
20 " over	253	150	103	116	116	...	137	34	103	1	1	...
Age not returned	...	...	...	...	...	...	...	...	...	...	...	...

VIII.

KASHMIR STATE.

CITY.

LITERATE IN.																							
PROVINCIAL VERNACULARS.																		OTHER LANGUAGES.			ENGLISH.		
Hindi or Bhasha.			*Gurmukhi.*			*Dogri.*			*Tibetan.*			*Tankri.*			*Lande or Mahajani.*								
Persons.	Males.	Females.	Persons.	Males.	Females.	Persons.	Males.	Females.	Persons.	Males.	Females.	Persons.	Males.	Females.	Persons.	Males.	Females.	Persons.	Males.	Females.	Persons.	Males.	Females.
14	15	16	17	18	19	20	21	22	23	24	25	26	27	28	29	30	31	32	33	34	35	36	37
533	515	18	356	258	98	1,325	1,281	44	...	...	...	...	...	...	30	30	...	984	904	80	868	861	7
13	12	1	9	5	4	4	4	...	...	...	...	...	...	...	...	...	...	22	16	6	14	13	1
30	20	...	25	12	13	39	38	1	...	...	...	...	...	...	1	1	...	64	54	10	94	94	...
34	29	5	28	18	10	113	108	5	...	...	...	...	...	...	...	...	...	122	116	6	160	159	1
466	454	12	294	223	71	1,169	1,131	38	...	...	...	...	...	...	29	29	...	776	718	58	600	595	5
...	...	...	...	...	...	...	...	...	...	...	...	...	...	...	...	...	...	...	...	...	...	...	...
322	304	18	192	131	61	1,325	1,281	44	...	...	...	...	...	...	29	29	...	901	854	47	659	657	2
7	6	1	6	2	4	4	4	...	...	...	...	...	...	...	...	...	...	17	15	2	13	13	...
7	7	...	10	3	7	39	38	1	...	...	...	...	...	...	1	1	...	50	46	4	81	81	...
18	13	5	9	4	5	113	108	5	...	...	...	...	...	...	...	...	...	110	105	5	135	134	1
290	278	12	167	122	45	1,169	1,131	38	...	...	...	...	...	...	28	28	...	724	688	36	430	429	1
...	...	...	...	...	...	...	...	...	...	...	...	...	...	...	...	...	...	...	...	...	...	...	...
38	38	...	163	126	37	...	...	...	...	...	...	...	...	...	...	...	...	9	9	...	78	78	...
...	...	...	3	3	...	...	...	...	...	...	...	...	...	...	...	...	...	...	...	...	...	...	...
1	1	...	14	8	6	...	...	...	...	...	...	...	...	...	...	...	...	4	4	...	1	1	...
...	...	...	19	14	5	...	...	...	...	...	...	...	...	...	...	...	...	1	1	...	4	4	...
37	37	...	127	101	26	...	...	...	...	...	...	...	...	...	...	...	...	4	4	...	71	71	...
...	...	...	...	...	...	...	...	...	...	...	...	...	...	...	...	...	...	...	...	...	...	...	...
144	144	...	...	...	...	...	...	...	...	...	...	...	...	...	...	...	...	...	...	...	3	...	3
5	5	...	...	...	...	...	...	...	...	...	...	...	...	...	...	...	...	...	...	...	...	...	...
11	11	...	...	...	...	...	...	...	...	...	...	...	...	...	...	...	...	...	...	...	...	...	...
16	16	...	...	...	...	...	...	...	...	...	...	...	...	...	...	...	...	...	...	...	...	...	...
112	112	...	...	...	...	...	...	...	...	...	...	...	...	...	...	...	...	...	...	...	3	3	...
...	...	...	...	...	...	...	...	...	...	...	...	...	...	...	...	...	...	...	...	...	...	...	...

Age.	Population. Total. Persons.	Total. Males.	Total. Females.	Literate. Persons.	Literate. Males.	Literate. Females.	Illiterate. Persons.	Illiterate. Males.	Illiterate. Females.	*Urdu or Hindustani.* Persons.	*Urdu or Hindustani.* Males.	*Urdu or Hindustani.* Females.
1	2	3	4	5	6	7	8	9	10	11	12	13
ZOROASTRIANS. Total City.												
0 and under 10	Nil											
10 " " 15												
15 " " 20												
20 " over												
Age not returned												
MUHAMMADANS. Total City ...	**13,627**	**8,501**	**5,126**	**935**	**875**	**60**	**12,692**	**7,626**	**5,066**	**718**	**691**	**27**
0 and under 10	2,553	1,332	1,221	33	20	4	2,520	1,303	1,217	27	27	...
10 " " 15	1,491	914	577	104	91	13	1,387	823	564	81	74	7
15 " " 20	1,234	742	492	113	110	3	1,121	632	489	82	80	2
20 " over	8,349	5,513	2,836	685	645	40	7,664	4,868	2,796	528	510	18
Age not returned	...	...	...	...	...	...	...	...	...	...	...	...
CHRISTIANS. Total City ...	**69**	**40**	**29**	**29**	**21**	**8**	**40**	**19**	**21**	**11**	**8**	**3**
0 and under 10	22	9	13	2	1	1	20	8	12	1	1	...
10 " " 15	2	2	...	2	2	...	...	...	...	1	1	...
15 " " 20	5	3	2	2	2	1	2	1	1	2	1	1
20 " over	40	26	14	22	16	6	18	10	8	7	5	2
Age not returned	...	...	...	...	...	...	...	...	...	...	...	...
UNSPECIFIED. Total City ...												
0 and under 10	Nil											
10 " " 15												
15 " " 20												
20 " over												
Age not returned												

KASHMIR STATE.

***CITY*—concluded.**

LITERATE IN																							
PROVINCIAL VERNACULARS.																		OTHER LANGUAGES.			ENGLISH.		
Hindi or Bhasha.			*Gurmukhi.*			*Dogri.*			*Tibetan.*			*Takri.*			*Lande or Mahajani.*								
Persons.	Males.	Females.	Persons.	Males.	Females.	Persons.	Males.	Females.	Persons.	Males.	Females.	Persons.	Males.	Females.	Persons.	Males.	Females.	Persons.	Males.	Females.	Persons.	Males.	Females.
14	15	16	17	18	19	20	21	22	23	24	25	26	27	28	29	30	31	32	33	34	35	36	37
									Nil														
29	29	...	1	1	...	...		...	...	...	...	...	...	...	1	1	...	74	41	33	112	112	...
1	1	...	...	...	...	...	...	...	...	...	...	...	...	...	...	...	...	[illegible]	1	4	...	...	...
1	1	...	1	1	...	...	...	...	...	...	...	...	...	...	...	...	...	10	4	6	11	11	...
...	...	...	...	...	...	...	...	...	...	...	...	...	...	...	...	...	...	11	10	1	20	20	...
27	27	...	...	...	...	...	...	...	...	...	...	...	...	...	1	1	...	48	26	22	81	81	...
...	...		...	...	...	...		...	...	...	...	...	...	...	...	...	...	...	...	...	...	...	...
...	...	...	...	...	...	...	...	...	...	...	...	...	...	...	...	...	...			...	18	13	5
...	...	...	...	...	...	...	...	...	...	...	...	...	...	...	...				...	...	1	...	1
...	...	...	...	...	...	...	...	...	...	...	...	...	...	...	...	...	...	...	...	...	1	1	...
...		...	...	...	...	...	...	...	...	...	...	...	...	...	...	...	...	...	...	...	1	1	...
...	...	...	...	...	...	...	...	...	...	...	...	...	...	...	...	...	...	...	...		15	11	4
...		...		...	...	...	...															...	...
									Nil														

TABLE VIII.

EDUCATION.

JAMMU AND KASHMIR STATE.

Srinagar City.

EDUCA

JAMMU AND

SRINAGAR

Age.		Population. Total. Persons.	Total. Males.	Total. Females.	Literate. Persons.	Literate. Males.	Literate. Females.	Illiterate. Persons.	Illiterate. Males.	Illiterate. Females.
1		2	3	4	5	6	7	8	9	10
	Total City	**122.618**	**65.542**	**57.076**	**10.301**	**10.161**	**140**	**112.317**	**55.381**	**56.936**
All Religions.	0 and under 10	33,927	17,012	16,915	265	251	14	33,662	16,761	16,901
	10 " " 15	13,994	8,250	5,744	1.207	1.194	13	12,787	7,056	5,731
	15 " " 20	10,619	5,687	4,932	1.215	1,194	21	9.404	4,493	4,911
	20 " over	64,078	34,593	29,485	7,614	7,522	92	56,464	27,071	29,393
	Age not returned	...	...	...	...	...	...	...	...	...
	Total City	**27.873**	**15.260**	**12.613**	**8.326**	**8.276**	**50**	**19.547**	**6.684**	**12.563**
Hindus.	0 and under 10	6,737	3,332	3,405	195	192	3	6,542	3,140	3,402
	10 " " 15	2,695	1,640	1,055	955	953	2	1,740	687	1,053
	15 " " 20	2,618	1,464	1,154	959	947	12	1,659	517	1,142
	20 " over	15,823	8,524	6,999	6,217	6.184	33	9.606	2.040	6,966
	Age not returned	...	...	...	...	...	...	...	...	...
	Total City	**494**	**355**	**139**	**179**	**176**	**3**	**315**	**179**	**136**
Sikhs.	0 and under 10	84	40	44	2	2	...	82	38	44
	10 " " 15	34	18	16	10	10	...	24	8	16
	15 " " 20	55	41	14	23	21	2	32	20	12
	20 " over	321	256	65	144	143	1	177	113	64
	Age not returned	...	...	...	...	...	...	...	...	...
	Total City ...	**1**	...	**1**	...	...	...	**1**	...	**1**
Jains.	0 and under 10	...	...	...	...	...	...	...	...	...
	10 " " 15	...	...	...	...	...	...	...	...	...
	15 " " 20	...	...	...	...	...	...	...	...	...
	20 " over	1	...	1	...	...	...	1	...	1
	Age not returned	...	...	...	...	...	...	...	...	...

TION.

KASHMIR STATE.

CITY.

LITERATE IN																							
PROVINCIAL VERNACULARS.																		OTHER LANGUAGES.			ENGLISH.		
Urdu or Hindustani.			*Hindi or Bhasha.*			*Gurmukhi.*			*Tibetan.*			*Dogri.*			*Landi or Mahajani.*								
Persons.	Males.	Females.	Persons.	Males.	Females.	Persons.	Males.	Females.	Persons.	Males.	Females.	Persons.	Males.	Females.	Persons.	Males.	Females.	Persons.	Males.	Females.	Persons.	Males.	Females.
11	12	13	14	15	16	17	18	19	20	21	22	23	24	25	26	27	28	29	30	31	32	33	34
3,794	**3,722**	**12**	**52**	**51**	**1**	**146**	**134**	**12**	...	...	...	**24**	**24**	...	**37**	**37**	...	**6,218**	**6,138**	**80**	**90**	**55**	**35**
77	77	...	...	...	...	...	...	...	...	...	...	...	...	...	...	...	...	186	172	14	2	2	...
564	563	1	5	5	...	7	6	1	...	...	...	...	...	...	...	...	...	629	618	11	2	2	...
734	731	3	5	5	...	19	13	6	...	...	...	...	...	...	...	...	...	453	442	11	4	3	1
2,359	2,351	8	42	41	1	[illegible]	115	5	...	...	...	24	24	...	37	37	...	4,950	4,906	44	82	48	34
...	...	...	...	...	...	...	...	...	...	...	...	...	...	...	...	...	...	...	...	...	...	...	...
3,159	**3,152**	**7**	**42**	**42**	...	**26**	**17**	**9**	...	...	...	**22**	**22**	...	**37**	**37**	...	**5,033**	**5,000**	**33**	**7**	**6**	**1**
68	68	...	...	...	...	...	...	...	...	...	...	...	...	...	...	...	...	127	124	3	...	...	...
486	486	...	5	5	...	1	...	1	...	...	...	...	...	...	...	...	...	462	461	1	1	1	...
634	632	2	5	5	...	5	1	4	...	...	...	...	...	...	...	...	...	314	308	6	1	1	...
1,971	1,966	5	32	32	...	20	16	4	...	...	...	22	22		37	37	...	4,130	4,107	23	5	4	1
...	...	...	...	...	...	...	...		...	...	...	...	...	...	...	...	...	...	...	...	...	...	...
57	**57**	...	**2**	**2**	...	**119**	**116**	**3**	...	...	...	...	...		...	...	...	**1**	**1**	...	...	...	...
2	2	...	...	...	...	...				...	...	...			...	...	...	...	...	...	...	...	...
4	4	...	...	...	...	6	6		...	...	...	...		...	...	...	...	...	...	...	...	...	...
9	9	...	...	...	...	14	12	2	...	...	...	...			...	...	...	...	...	...	...	...	...
42	42	...	2	2	...	99	98	1	...	...	...	...	...	...	...	...	...	1	1			...	...
...	...	...	...	...	...	...		...	...	...	...	...	...	...	...	...	...	...	...	...	...	...	...
...	...	...	...	...	...	...	...		...	...	...	...	...	...	...	...	...	...	...	...	...	...	...
...	...	...	...	...	...	...	...		...	...	...	...	...	...	...	...	...	...	...	...	...	...	...
...		...	...	...	...	...			...	...	...	...	...	...	...	...	...	...	...	...	...	...	...
...	...	...	...	...	...	...	...		...	...	...	...	...	...	...	...	...	...	...	...	...	...	...
...	...	...	...	...	...	...	...	...	...	...	...	...	...	...	...	...	...	...	...	...	...	...	...
...	...	...	...	...	...	...	...	...	...	...	...	...	...	...	...	...	...	...	...	...	...	...	...

TABLE

EDUCA

JAMMU AND

SRINAGAR

Age.		Population. Total. Persons.	Total. Males.	Total. Females.	Literate. Persons.	Literate. Males.	Literate. Females.	Illiterate. Persons.	Illiterate. Males.	Illiterate. Females.
1		2	3	4	5	6	7	8	9	10
	TOTAL CITY ...	11	8	3	6	6	...	5	2	3
Zoroastrians.	0 and under 10	3	3	...	1	1	...	2	2	...
	10 " " 15	...	...	...	...	...	...	...	...	...
	15 " " 20	[illegible]	...	...	...	...	...	...	...	...
	20 " over	8	5	3	5	5		3	...	3
	Age not returned	...	...	...	...	...	...	...	...	...
	TOTAL CITY ...	94,021	49,806	44,215	1,703	1,654	49	92,318	48,152	44,166
Mohammedans.	0 and under 10	27,060	13,617	13,443	66	55	11	26,994	[illegible]	13,432
	10 " " 15	11,250	6,587	4,663	241	[illegible]	11	11,009	6,[illegible]37	4,652
	15 " " 20	7,934	4,176	3,758	230	224	6	7,701	3,952	3,762
	20 " over	47,777	25,426	22,351	1,166	1,145	21	46,611	21,281	22,330
	Age not returned	...	...	...	...	...		...	...	...
	TOTAL CITY ...	184	92	92	85	47	38	99	45	54
Christians.	0 and under 10	30	15	15	1	1	...	29	14	15
	10 " " 15	12	3	9	1	1	...	11	2	9
	15 " " 20	10	5	5	3	2	1	7	3	4
	20 " over	132	69	63	80	43	37	53	26	26
	Age not returned	...	...		...	...	...	...	...	...
	TOTAL CITY ...	34	21	13	2	2	...	32	19	13
Unspecified.	0 and under 10	13	5	8	...	...	...	13	5	8
	10 " " 15	3	2	1	...	...	...	3	2	1
	15 " " 20	2	1	1	...	...	...	2	1	1
	20 " over	16	13	3	2	2	...	14	11	3
	Age not returned	...	...	...	...	...	...	...	...	...

KASHMIR STATE.

CITY.—concluded.

LITERATE IN																							
PROVINCIAL VERNACULARS.																		OTHER LANGUAGES.			ENGLISH.		
Urdu or Hindustani			*Hindi or Bhasha*			*Gurmukhi.*			*Tibetan.*			*Dogri.*			*Landi or Mahajani*								
Persons.	Males.	Females.	Persons.	Males.	Females.	Persons.	Males.	Females.	Persons.	Males.	Females.	Persons.	Males.	Females.	Persons.	Males.	Females.	Persons.	Males.	Females.	Persons.	Males.	Females.
11	12	13	14	15	16	17	18	19	20	21	22	23	24	25	26	27	28	29	30	31	32	33	34
...	...	...	...	...	...	...	...	...	...	...	...	...	...	...	...	...	...	...	...	...	6	6	...
...	...	...	...	...	...	...	...	...	...	...	...	...	...	...	...	...	...	...	...	...	1	1	...
...	...	...	...	...	...	...	...	...	...	...	...	...	...	...	...	...	...	...	...	...	...	...	...
...	...	...	...	...	...	...	...	...	...	...	...	...	...	...	...	...	...	...	...	...	...	...	...
...	...	...	...	...	...	...	...	...	...	...	...	...	...	...	...	...	...	...	...	...	5	5	...
...	...	...	...	...	...	...	...	...	...	...	...	...	...	...	...	...	...	...	...	...	...	...	...
515	**511**	**4**	**6**	**5**	**1**	**1**	**1**	...	...	...	...	**2**	**2**	...	...	...	...	**1,179**	**1,135**	**44**	...	...	...
7	7	...	...	...	...	...	...	...	...	...	...	...	...	...	...	...	...	59	48	11	...	...	...
74	73	1	...	...	...	...	...	...	...	...	...	...	...	...	...	...	...	167	157	10	...	...	...
91	90	1	...	...	...	...	...	...	...	...	...	...	...	...	...	...	...	139	134	5	...	...	...
343	341	2	6	5	1	1	1	...	...	...	...	2	2	...	...	...	...	814	796	18	...	...	...
...	...	...	...	...	...	...	...	...	...	...	...	...	...	...	...	...	...	...	...	...	...	...	...
2	**1**	**1**	**2**	**2**	...	...	...	...	...	...	...	...	...	...	...	...	...	**4**	**1**	**3**	**77**	**43**	**34**
...	...	...	...	...	...	...	...	...	...	...	...	...	...	...	...	...	...	...	...	...	1	1	...
...	...	...	...	...	...	...	...	...	...	...	...	...	...	...	...	...	...	...	...	...	1	1	...
...	...	...	...	...	...	...	...	...	...	...	...	...	...	...	...	...	...	...	...	...	3	2	1
2	1	1	2	2	...	...	...	...	...	...	...	...	...	...	...	...	...	4	1	3	72	39	33
...	...	...	...	...	...	...	...	...	...	...	...	...	...	...	...	...	...	...	...	...	...	...	...
1	**1**	...	...	...	...	...	...	...	...	...	...	...	...	...	...	...	...	**1**	**1**	...	...	...	...
...	...	...	...	...	...	...	...	...	...	...	...	...	...	...	...	...	...	...	...	...	...	...	...
...	...	...	...	...	...	...	...	...	...	...	...	...	...	...	...	...	...	...	...	...	...	...	...
...	...	...	...	...	...	...	...	...	...	...	...	...	...	...	...	...	...	...	...	...	...	...	...
1	1	...	...	...	...	...	...	...	...	...	...	...	...	...	...	...	...	1	1	...	...	...	...
...	...	...	...	...	...	...	...	...	...	...	...	...	...	...	...	...	...	...	...	...	...	...	...

TABLE X.

JAMMU AND KASHMIR STATE.

LANGUAGE.

Part I—Classified Totals.

TABLE X.

JAMMU AND KASHMIR STATE.

LANGUAGE.

PART I.—CLASSIFIED TOTALS.

Family.	Branch.	Language or Dialect	Total.			Remarks.
			Persons.	Males.	Females.	
1	2	3	4	5	6	7
INDO-EUROPEAN FAMILY. ARYAN SUB-FAMILY.	I—IRANIAN.	**POPULATION**	**2.905.578**	**1.542.057**	**1.366.521**	
		I. **Western Group**	**552**	**433**	**119**	
		1. Persian	552	433	119	
		II. **Eastern Group**	**1.954**	**1.395**	**559**	
		3. Balochi	1	...	1	
		13. Pashtoo	1,253	958	295	
		13. Kaboli	1	1	...	
		1?. Afghani	273	221	25	
		Tagati	116	46	70	
		Yaghistani	13	4	9	
		Kaghani	297	165	132	
	II—INDIAN.	III. **Shina—Khowar Group**...	**54.364**	**29.107**	**25.257**	
		31. Khowar, Arniya and Chitrari ...	228	115	110	
		32. Shina	46,813	25,282	21,531	
		34. Chilasi	8	2	6	
		35. Brokpa	7,315	3,705	3,610	
		IV. **North-Western Group**...	**998.193**	**533.999**	**464.194**	
		38. Kashmiri	981,628	525,197	456,431	
		Dardah	3,807	2,087	1,720	
		40. Kishtwari	12.078	6.347	5,731	
		Bambaghi	320	172	148	
		41. Rambani	359	195	164	
		48. Multani	1	1	...	

TABLE X.

JAMMU AND KASHMIR STATE

LANGUAGE.

PART I.—CLASSIFIED TOTALS.

Family.	Branch.	Language or Dialect.	Total. Persons.	Total. Males.	Total. Females.	Remarks.
1	2	3	4	5	6	7
INDO-EUROPEAN FAMILY. ARYAN SUB-FAMILY.	II—Indian—continued.	**Dialects North of the Salt Range ... ..**	**193**	**157**	**36**	
		50. Chhibhali	86	61	25	
		56. Pothwari	107	96	11	
		Dialects South of the Salt Range	**25**	**11**	**14**	
		65. Sindhi	25	11	14	
		V. South-Western Group ... — ...	**31**	**30**	**1**	
		95. Kulwadi	28	28	...	
		105. Marheti	3	2	1	
		VI. Western Group	**1.429-218**	**761-831**	**667.367**	
		125. Gujrati	56	13	43	
		131. Kachchhi	18	18	...	
		149. Punjabi	863,539	455,934	404,605	
		149. Gurmukhi	654	588	66	
		150. Dogri	436,211	233,142	203,069	
		Andhri	1	...	1	
		152. Powadi	5	3	2	
		157. Bikaneri	13	7	6	
		159. Dakhni	10	9	1	
		161. Vanis	33	...	33	
		161. Marwari	266	141	125	
		166. Gujari	136,849	67,784	59,065	
		167. Rathi	1	...	1	
		170. Nagasi	3	3	..	
		172. Mathuri	2	2	...	

TABLE X.

JAMMU AND KASHMIR STATE

LANGUAGE.

PALT I.—CLASSIFIED TOTALS.

Family.	Branch.	Language or Dialect.	Total. Persons.	Total. Males.	Total. Females.	Remarks.
1	2	3	4	5	6	7
INDO-EUROPEAN FAMILY. ARYAN SUB-FAMILY.	II.—Indian—concluded.	179. Hindustani	1,150	890	260	
		182. Hindi	23	13	10	
		Sanskrit	9	9	...	
		Negri	2	...	2	
		186. Urdu	369	273	96	
		190. Bangrahi	4	2	2	
		VII. Northern Group	156,141	80,774	75,367	
		192 Pahari	103,686	53,991	49,695	
		193. Bhadarwahi	21,298	10,438	10,800	
		195. Chambiali	5	4	1	
		196. Gadi	4,620	2,151	2,469	
		201. Padri	4,540	2,362	2,178	
		201. Dogri	6,351	3,266	3,085	
		202. Kangri	10	10	...	
		204. Mandiali	32	32	...	
		223 Siraji	14,743	7,806	6,987	
		251. Naipali	62	44	18	
		Gorkhali	794	670	124	
		IX. Eastern Group	111	90	21	
		270. Bengali	62	43	19	
		279. Parbi	49	47	2	
		Gipsy Dialects	2,920	1,459	1,461	
		323. Labhani	2,528	1,253	1,275	
DRAVIDIAN FAMILY. }		Dravid	392	206	186	

TABLE X.

JAMMU AND KASHMIR STATE.

LANGUAGE.

PART I.—CLASSIFIED TOTALS.

Family.	Branch.	Language or Dialect.	Total: Persons.	Total: Males.	Total: Females.	Remarks.
1	2	3	4	5	6	7
		I. Himalayan Group	**168,216**	**84,876**	**83,340**	
		448. Bhotia (Balti)	130,678	65,844	64,834	
		Bhutti	6,104	3,167	2,937	
		454. Tibetan...	1,445	834	611	
		Badhi	29,718	14,888	14,830	
		482. Malheeti	7	7		
		488. Kanashi	264	136	128	
	INDO-EUROPEAN.	Romance ... { French	6	2	4	
		Romance ... { Portuguese ...	7	7	...	
			13	**9**	**4**	
		Balto-Slavonic ... b. Slavonic ... } Russian	1	1	...	
		Teutonic ... { English	177	111	66	
		Teutonic ... { Dutch	1	1	...	
			179	**113**	**66**	
SEMITIC.	SOUTHERN BRANCH.	{ Bagdadi ... ... —	1	1	...	
		{ Arabic —	19	18	1	
			20	**19**	**1**	
MANGOLIAN.	URAL ALTAIC.	} Turkish	33	26	7	
			33	**26**	**7**	
		Unspecified ...	93,415	47,728	45,687	

TABLE X.

JAMMU AND KASHMIR STATE.

LANGUAGE.

Part II—Distribution by Districts in the Jammu and Kashmir State.

TABLE

JAMMU AND

LANGU

PART II.—DISTRIBUTION BY DISTRICTS

District or State.	Population.			A.—(1) Provincial					
				Dogri.			*Pahari.*		
	Persons.	Males.	Females.	Persons.	Males.	Females.	Persons.	Males.	Females.
1	2	3	4	5	6	7	8	9	10
Jammu	3,44,018	1,85,722	1,58,296	2,04,745	1,08,986	95,759	137	133	4
Udhampur	2,84,048	1,51,425	1,32,623	1,28,724	60,098	50,626	16,795	9,059	7,736
Bhimbar	4,00,229	2,10,075	1,90,154	4,751	2,556	2,195	118	86	33
Jasrota	1,54,213	82,591	71,632	93,056	48,959	44,097	9,061	4,[illegible]7	4,554
Poonch	3,04,488	1,60,679	1,43,809	595	415	180	...	...	...
Bhadarwah	34,311	17,500	16,811	2,194	1,336	858	...	...	...
Srinagar	9,89,196	5,26,158	4,63,038	892	554	338	22,274	11,543	10,731
Muzaffarabad	1,68,198	90,739	77,469	10	8	2	55,281	28,643	26,638
Ladakh	1,65,992	83,600	82,392	6	6	...	...	...	...
Gilgit	60,885	33,778	27,107	1,238	1,224	14	...	...	...

X.

KASHMIR STATE.

AGE.

IN THE JAMMU AND KASHMIR STATE.

VERNACULARS.

Gojari.			*Bhadarwahi.*			*Kishtwari.*			*Paddri.*		
Persons.	Males.	Females.	Persons.	Males.	Females.	Persons.	Males.	Females.	Persons.	Males.	Females.
11	12	13	14	15	16	17	18	19	20	21	22
24,844	13,755	11,089	167	153	14	17	16	1	...	...	...
25,749	13,691	12,058	128	122	6	11,975	6,268	6,707	4,540	2,362	2,178
1,646	993	653	...	...	...	...	...	...	...	...	...
2,085	1,053	1,032	7	7	...	...	...	...	...	...	...
59,920	31,688	28,232	...	...	...	...	...	...	...	...	...
1,099	472	627	20,977	10,145	10,832	63	45	18	...	...	...
3,957	2,051	1,906	3	2	1	19	15	4	...	...	...
7,360	3,976	3,384	...	...	...	...	...	...	...	...	...
...	...	...	16	9	7	4	3	1	...	...	...
159	75	84	...	...	...	...	...	...	...	...	...

TABLE

JAMMU AND

LANGU

PART II.—DISTRIBUTION BY DISTRICTS

A.—(1) Provincial

District or State.	*Rambani.*			*Balti.*			*Chilasi.*		
	Persons.	Males.	Females.	Persons.	Males.	Females.	Persons.	Males.	Females.
1	23	24	25	26	27	28	29	30	31
Jammu	...	...	...	8	8	...	...	...	...
Udhampur	359	195	164	...	...	...	...	...	...
Bhimbar	...	...	...	...	...	...	...	...	...
Jasrota	...	...	...	...	...	...	...	...	...
Poonch	...	...	...	...	...	...	...	...	...
Bhadarwah	...	...	...	...	...	...	8	2	6
Srinagar	...	...	...	181	65	116	...	...	...
Muzaffarabad	...	...	...	...	...	...	...	...	...
Ladakh	...	...	...	1,21,302	60,950	60,352	...	...	...
Gilgit	...	...	...	9,187	4,821	4,366	...	...	...

X.

KASHMIR STATE

AGE.

IN THE JAMMU AND KASHMIR STATE.—continued.

VERNACULARS—*continued.*

Bhuti.			*Kashmiri.*			*Shina.*			*Budhi.*		
Persons.	Males.	Females.	Persons.	Males.	Females.	Persons.	Males.	Females.	Persons.	Males.	Females.
32	33	34	35	36	37	38	39	40	41	42	43
...	...	...	857	634	223	...	...	...	...	...	...
5,349	2,795	2,554	50,114	26,136	23,978		...	...	...	...	...
...	...	...	2,605	1,127	1,478	...	...		...	...	...
...	...	...	1,237	603	634	...	...	...	...	...	...
...	...	...	14,802	9,323	5,479	...	...	...	...	...	...
...			8,682	4,684	3,998	...	...	...	...	...	...
39	29	10	8,88,108	4,73,250	4,14,858		...	...	...	...	...
...	...		13,966	8,660	5,306	...	...	...	...	...	...
716	343	373	1,105	638	467	1	...	1	29,716	14,886	14,830
...	...	...	152	142	10	46,813	25,282	21,531	2	2	...

TABLE

JAMMU AND

LANGU

PART II.—DISTRIBUTION BY DISTRICTS

A.—(1) PROVINCIAL

DISTRICT OR STATE.	Brokpa.			Pogli.			Bambhogy		
	Persons.	Males.	Females.	Persons.	Males.	Females.	Persons.	Males.	Females.
1	44	45	46	47	48	49	50	51	52
Jammu	...	...	...	...	...	..		...	...
Udhampur ...	..	...	...	6,351	3,266	3,085	320	172	148
Bhimbar	...	...	...	...		..	...	..	...
Jasrota .. .	...	...	...	...	...	..	...	...	
Poonch		...	..	...	...	...	...	...	...
Bhadarwah	...	..	.	...	...	..	..	.	.
Srinagar	...	...	...	..	..	...	..	...	..
Muzaffarabad	...	...	...	...	..	..	...	...	..
Ladakh . ..	7,315	3,705	3,610	...	..	...	...	...	...
Gilgit	...	...	...	...		...	...	...	...

X.

KASHMIR STATE

AGE.

***IN THE JAMMU AND KASHMIR STATE.*—continued.**

Vernaculars —concluded.									A.(2) Other Indian Vernaculars.		
Awdhi.			*Punchi.*			*Gadi.*			*Panjabi.*		
Persons.	Males.	Females.	Persons.	Males.	Females.	Persons.	Males.	Females.	Persons.	Males.	Females.
53	54	55	56	57	58	59	60	61	62	63	64
...	...			...	...	6	6	...	1,00,459	54,904	45,555
...	...	...		...	...	4,370	2,000	2,370	5,939	3,878	2,061
...	...	...	...	...	...	2	2	...	3,81,905	2,00,665	1,81,240
1	...	1		...	...	180	107	73	45,379	24,993	20,386
	...	...	...	...	...	...	...		2,20,069	1,14,042	1,06,027
...	...	...	...	...	...	62	36	26	255	213	42
...		...	3,807	2,087	1,720		...	...	24,533	13,973	10,560
		...	...	...	...	...	...	...	84,134	45,509	38,625
...	...	...	...	...	...	...	...	...	267	248	19
...	...	...	...	...	...	...	...	...	699	609	90

TABLE

JAMMU AND
LANGU

PART II.—DISTRIBUTION BY DISTRICTS

A.—(3) OTHER INDIAN

District or State.	Pothwari.			Kulwadi.			Yaghistani		
	Persons.	Males.	Females.	Persons.	Males.	Females.	Persons.	Males.	Females.
1	65	66	67	68	69	70	71	72	73
Jammu ...	50	47	3	...	...	...	...	...	...
Udhampur ...	17	17	...	...	...	...	...	...	...
Bhimber ...	22	15	7	...	...	...	...	...	...
Jasrota ...	1	1	...	...	...	...	...	...	...
Poonch ...	...	...	...	...	...	...	...	...	...
Bhadarwah ...	2	2	...	28	28	...	...	...	...
Srinagar ...	6	6	...	...	...	...	13	4	9
Muzaffarabad ...	9	8	1	...	...	...	...	...	...
Ladakh ...	...	...	...	...	...	...	...	...	...
Gilgit ...	...	...	...	...	...	...	...	...	...

X.

KASHMIR STATE.

AGE.

IN THE JAMMU AND KASHMIR STATE.—continued.

VERNACULARS.—*continued.*

Gurmukhi.			*Multani.*			*Sindhi.*			*Kangri.*		
Persons.	Males.	Females.	Persons.	Males.	Females.	Persons.	Males.	Females.	Persons.	Males.	Females.
74	75	76	77	78	79	80	81	82	83	84	85
596	532	64	...	...	...	7	7	...	4	4	...
58	56	2	...	...	...	16	3	13	6	6	...
...	...	...	...	...	...	1	...	1	...	...	...
...	...	...	...	...	...	1	1	...	...	...	...
...	...	...	...	...	...	...	...	...	...	...	...
...	...	...	...	...	...	...	...	...	...	...	...
...	...	...	1	1	...	...	...	...	...	...	...
...	...	...	...	...	...	...	...	...	...	...	...
...	...	...	...	...	...	...	...	...	...	...	...
...	...	...	...	...	...	...	...	...	...	...	...

PART II.—DISTRIBUTION BY DISTRICTS

District or State	A.—(2) Other Indian								
	Koghani.			*Lubhani.*			*Siraji*		
	Persons.	Males.	Females.	Persons.	Males.	Females.	Persons.	Males.	Females.
1	86	87	88	89	90	91	92	93	94
Jammu	158	79	79	2,371	1,131	1,240	...	...	...
Udhampur	...	...	...	...	...	...	14,743	7,806	6,937
Bhimbar	139	86	53	68	68	...	...	...	...
Jasrota	...	...	...	46	28	18	...	...	...
Poonch	...	...	...	...	...	...	...	...	...
Bhadarwah	...	...	...	43	26	17	...	...	...
Srinagar	...	...	...	...	...	...	...	...	...
Muzaffarabad	...	...	...	...	...	...	...	...	...
Ladakh	...	...	...	...	...	...	...	...	...
Gilgit	...	...	...	...	...	...	...	...	...

AGE.

IN THE JAMMU AND KASHMIR STATE.—continued.

Vernacular languages.—continued.

Bangri or Bangrehi.			*Mandiali.*			*Vani.*			*Chambiali.*		
Persons.	Males.	Females.	Persons.	Males.	Females.	Persons.	Males.	Females.	Persons.	Males.	Females.
95	96	97	98	99	100	101	102	103	104	105	106
...	...	...	...	...	...	...	...	...	...	...	...
4	2	2	16	16	...	...	...	...	1	1	...
...	...	...	...	...	...	...	...	...	...	...	...
...	...	...	...	...	...	...	...	...	4	3	1
...	...	...	...	...	...	...	...	...	...	...	...
...	...	...	16	16	...	33	...	33	...	...	...
...	...	...	...	...	...	...	...	...	...	...	...
...	...	...	...	...	...	...	...	...	...	...	...
...	...	...	...	...	...	...	...	...	...	...	...
...	...	...	...	...	...	...	...	...	...	...	...

TABLE

JAMMU AND

LANGU

PART II.—DISTRIBUTION BY DISTRICTS

A.—(2) Other Indian

District or State.	Chhibhali.			Hindi.			Bikaneri.		
	Persons.	Males.	Females.	Persons.	Males.	Females.	Persons.	Males.	Females.
1	107	108	109	110	111	112	113	114	115
Jammu	...	...	...	4	4	...	8	4	4
Udhampur	...	...	...	...	...	...	1	...	1
Bhimbar	...	...	...	...	...	...	...	...	...
Jasrota	...	...	...	...	...	...	4	3	1
Poonch	...	...	...	3	3	..	...	...	...
Bhadarwah	86	61	25	...	...	...	...	...	...
Srinagar	...	...	...	...	...	...	...	...	...
Muzaffarabad	...	...	...	16	6	10	...	...	...
Ladakh	...	...	...	...	...	...	...	...	...
Gilgit	...	...	...	...	...	...	...	...	...

KASHMIR STATE.

AGE.

IN THE JAMMU AND KASHMIR STATE.—continued.

VERNACULARS—*continued.*

Hindustani.			*Urdu.*			*Dakhni or Maharashtri.*			*Marwari.*		
Persons.	Males.	Females.	Persons.	Males.	Females.	Persons.	Males.	Females.	Persons.	Males.	Females.
116	117	118	119	120	121	122	123	124	125	126	127
702	511	191	75	70	5	9	8	1	236	127	109
140	125	15	5	5	...	...	...	...	7	3	4
55	47	8	1	1	...	...	...	...	20	10	10
93	72	21	2	2	...	...	...	...	...	...	...
30	28	2	...	...	...	...	...	...	3	1	2
24	23	1	...	...	...	...	...	...	...	...	...
...			277	191	86	1	1	...	...	...	...
67	52	15	...	...	...	...	...	...	...	...	...
5	2	3	2	1	1	...	...	...	...	...	...
34	30	4	7	3	4	...	...	...	...	...	...

TABLE

JAMMU AND

LANGU

PART II.—DISTRIBUTION BY DISTRICTS

A.—(2) OTHER INDIAN

District or State.	Sanskrit.			Purbi.			Marhoti.		
	Persons.	Males.	Females.	Persons.	Males.	Females.	Persons.	Males.	Females.
1	128	129	130	131	132	133	134	135	136
Jammu	3	3	...	15	14	1	3	2	1
Udhampur	...	...	...	21	21	...	...	...	...
Bhimbar	...	...	...	2	2	...	...	...	...
Jasrota	...	...	...	7	6	1	...	...	...
Poonch	...	...	...	...	...	...	...	...	...
Bhadarwah	...	...	...	...	...	...	...	...	...
Srinagar	4	4		4	4	...	...	...	...
Muzaffarabad	...	...	...	...	...	...	...	...	...
Ladakh	...		...	...	...	...	...	...	...
Gilgit	2	2	...	...	...	...	...	...	...

X.

KASHMIR STATE

AGE.

IN THE JAMMU AND KASHMIR STATE.— continued.

VERNACULARS — *continued.*

Bengali.			*Gujrati.*			*Pawadi.*			*Rathi.*		
Persons.	Males.	Females.	Persons.	Males.	Females.	Persons.	Males.	Females.	Persons	Males.	Females.
137	138	139	140	141	142	143	144	145	146	147	148
6	5	1	8	5	3	5	3	2	..	...	...
1	1	...	1	1	...	...	...	...	..	...	...
...	...	...	..	...	...	...	...	...	...	...	...
2	...	2	..	..	..	...	...	...	...	...	...
24	20	4	...	...	...	...	...	...	1	...	1
...	...	...	...	..	...	...	...	...	..	...	...
28	16	12	47	7	40	...	...	...	...	...	...
...	...	...	...	...	...	...	.	...	...	...	...
...	...	...	...	...	..	...	.	...	...	...	...
1	1	...	..	...	...	...	...	...	...	...	...

TABLE

JAMMU AND

LANGU

PART II.—DISTRIBUTION BY DISTRICTS

A.—(2) Other Indian

District or State	*Naipali.*			*Darawari.*			*Gorkhali.*		
	Persons.	Males.	Females.	Persons.	Males.	Females.	Persons.	Males.	Females.
1	149	150	151	152	153	154	155	156	157
Jammu	...	...	...	...	...	...	...	...	...
Udhampur	26	17	9	...	...	...	...	...	...
Bhimbar	...	...	...	...	...	...	3	3	...
Jasrota	4	4	...	...	...	...	9	8	1
Poonch	2	...	3	...	...	...	43	37	6
Bhadarwah	4	4	...	...	...	...	...	...	...
Srinagar	26	19	7	...	...	...	282	178	104
Muzaffarabad	...	...	...	392	206	186	...	...	...
Ladakh	...	...	...	..	...	...	9	8	1
Gilgit	...	...	...	...	...	...	448	436	12

KASHMIR STATE.

AGE.

***IN THE JAMMU AND KASHMIR STATE.*—continued.**

VERNACULARS—*continued.*

Nagri.			*Melkesti.*			*Mathuri.*			*Nagasi.*		
Persons.	Males.	Females.	Persons.	Males.	Females.	Persons.	Males.	Females.	Persons.	Males.	Females.
158	159	160	161	162	163	164	165	166	167	168	169
2	...	2	7	7	...	...	...	...	...	...	...
...	...	...			...	2	2	...	3	3	...
...	...	...	...	...	...	...	...	...	...	...	...
...	...	...	...	...	...	...	...	...	...	...	...
...	...	...	...		...	...	...	...	...	...	...
...	...	...	...	...	...		...	...	...	...	...
...	...	...	...	...	...	...	...	...	...	...	...
...	...	...	...	...	...	...	...	...	...	...	...
...	...	...	...	...	...	...	...	...	...	...	...
...	...	...	...	...	...	...	...	...	...	...	...

TABLE

JAMMU AND

LANGU

PART II.—DISTRIBUTION BY DISTRICTS.

A.—(2) Other Indian

District or State.	*Kanashi.*			*Kachhi.*			*Pushtoo.*		
	Persons.	Males.	Females.	Persons.	Males.	Females.	Persons.	Males.	Females.
1	170	171	172	173	174	175	176	177	178
Jammu ...	...	...	...	...	...	...	320	299	21
Udhampur	264	136	128	...	...	...	128	117	11
Bhimbar	...	...	...	...	...	...	214	127	87
Jasrota	...	...	...	...		...	10	10	...
Poonch	...	...	...	...	...	...	34	15	19
Bhadarwah	...	...	...	18	18		...		...
Srinagar	...	...	...	...			345	240	105
Muzaffarabad ...	...	...	...				110	62	48
Ladakh	...	...	...	...			9	9	...
Gilgit ...	...	...	...				83	79	4

X.

KASHMIR STATE

AGE.

IN THE JAMMU AND KASHMIR STATE.—continued.

VERNACULARS—*continued.*

Afghani.			*Chitrari.*			*Kabuli.*			*Balochi.*		
Persons.	Males.	Females.	Persons.	Males.	Females.	Persons.	Males.	Females.	Persons.	Males.	Females.
179	180	181	182	183	184	185	186	187	188	189	190
17	17	...	...	...						...	...
141	140	1		...							...
1	1	...	...	...			...		...	...	...
...	...	...	...	...	...	1	1	...	...		...
...	...	...	...	...	...		...	...	...	...	...
...	...		...	...	...	...	...	...		...	...
114	63	51	...	...	...	...	...	...	1	...	1
...	...		...	...	...	...	...	...	...	...	...
...	...		...	...		...	...	...	...	...	...
...	...	...	228	118	110	...	...	...	...	...	...

TABLE

JAMMU AND

LANGU

PART II.—DISTRIBUTION BY DISTRICTS

District or State	A.—(2) Other Indian Vernaculars.—*concluded.*			B.—Vernaculars of Asiatic					
	Tagalo.			*Persian.*			*Tibetan.*		
	Persons.	Males.	Females.	Persons.	Males.	Females.	Persons.	Males.	Females.
1	191	192	193	194	195	196	197	198	199
Jammu	...	...	...	126	123	3	81	79	2
Udhampur	116	46	70	124	124	...	127	122	5
Bhimber	...	...	...	2	2	...	...	...	...
Jasrota	...	...	...	1	1	...	...	...	...
Poonch	...	...	...	...	...	...	...	...	...
Bhadarwah	...	...	...	...	...	...	...	...	...
Srinagar ...	...	...	...	224	118	106	20	12	8
Muzaffarabad	...	...	...	15	12	3	...	...	...
Ladakh	...	...	...	12	11	1	20	9	11
Gilgit	...	...	...	48	42	6	1,157	612	655

X.

KASHMIR STATE.

AGE.

IN THE JAMMU AND KASHMIR STATE.—continued.

Countries beyond India.						C.—European Languages.								
Bagdadi.			*Arabic.*			*English.*			*Russian*			*Turkish.*		
Persons.	Males.	Females.	Persons.	Males.	Females.	Persons.	Males.	Females.	Persons.	Males.	Females.	Persons.	Males.	Females.
200	201	202	203	204	205	206	207	208	209	210	211	212	213	214
1	1	...	4	4	...	11	6	5	1	1		1	1	...
...	...	..	9	8	1	...	...	...				...	...	...
...	...	...	1	1	.	1	1	...	...	..	...	...	...	...
...	...	...	...	...	..	...		...	.		.	..	...	...
...	...	...	1	1	...	4	1	3	..	...	..	3	..	3
...	...	...	...	..	..	1	1	...	...	..		...	..	...
...	...	...	1	1	...	127	[illegible]	15	...		...	19	17	2
...	..	...	1	1	...	2	2	...		..	..	...	...	...
...	...	...	2	2	..	5	1	4	...	...		8	8	...
...	...	...	...	...	...	26	17	9	...	.		2	...	2

TABLE X.

JAMMU AND KASHMIR STATE.

LANGUAGE.

PART II.—DISTRIBUTION BY DISTRICTS IN THE JAMMU AND KASHMIR STATE.—concluded.

District or State.	C.—European Languages—*concluded.*									Unspecified.		
	French.			*Dutch.*			*Portuguese.*					
	Persons.	Males.	Females.	Persons.	Males.	Females.	Persons.	Males.	Females.	Persons.	Males.	Females.
1	215	216	217	218	219	220	221	222	223	224	225	226
Jammu	...	...	...	...	...	...	...	...	...	7,947	4,033	3,914
Udhampur	...	...	...	...	...	...	...	...	...	7,358	3,605	3,753
Bhimbar	...	...	...	...	...	...	...	...	...	8,772	4,382	4,390
Jasrota	...	...	...	...	...	...	...	...	...	3,002	2,003	1,000
Poonch ...	...	...	...	...	...	...	...	...	...	8,954	5,105	3,849
Bhadarwah	...	...	...	...	...	...	...	...	...	716	388	328
Srinagar	6	2	[illegible]	[illegible]	1	[illegible]	2	2	...	43,799	21,585	22,214
Muzaffarabad	...	...	...	...	...	...	...	...	...	6,835	3,584	3,251
Ladakh	...	...	...	...	...	...	...	...	...	5,359	2,714	2,645
Gilgit ...	...	...	...	...	...	...	...	...	...	673	330	343

TABLE XI.

JAMMU AND KASHMIR STATE.

BIRTH-PLACE.

TABLE XI.

JAMMU AND KASHMIR STATE.

BIRTH-PLACE.

District, State, Province or Country where born.	Population of Jammu and Kashmir State			Province, District or State where enumerated. Jammu.			Udhampur.			Bhimbar.			Jasrota.		
	Persons.	Males.	Females.	Persons.	Males.	Females.	Persons.	Males.	Females.	Persons.	Males.	Females.	Persons.	Males.	Females.
1	2	3	4	5	6	7	8	9	10	11	12	13	14	15	16
TOTAL STATE ...	2.905.578	1.542.057	1.363.521	344.018	185.722	158.296	284.048	151.425	132.623	400.229	210.075	190.154	154.213	82.391	71.822
A.—District within the State ...	2.819.981	1.499.401	1.320.580	308.305	170.548	137.757	281.563	149.588	131.975	387.728	204.043	183.685	139.535	77.015	62.520
a.—Jammu Province ...	1.460.231	783.439	676.792	306.823	169.741	137.088	280.094	148.528	131.566	385.961	203.175	182.786	139.502	76.996	62.506
Jammu	314,017	176,492	137,525	204,271	104,041	130,230	5,215	3,039	2,170	1,350	753	603	3,785	1,621	2,164
Udhampur	283,828	148,654	134,674	4,124	1,718	2,406	272,316	144,051	128,265	707	537	260	3,836	838	2,998
Bhimber	389,564	205,501	184,003	5,031	2,894	3,727	1,371	822	549	380,657	200,424	180,238	45	32	13
Jasrota	135,537	76,469	59,068	2,421	816	1,605	943	455	488	424	418	6	130,859	74,085	56,774
Punch Jagir	303,959	159,255	144,704	205	104	101	194	120	74	2,736	1,043	1,083	16	10	6
Bhadarwah Jagir	33,796	16,978	16,818	184	168	16	55	41	14	1	...	1	961	410	551
b.—Kashmir Province ...	1.136.118	601.651	534.467	1.357	701	656	1.325	939	386	1.766	868	898	32	18	14
Khas	976,313	518,445	457,868	1,240	627	613	954	691	263	988	334	654	33	18	14
Muzaffarabad	159,805	83,206	76,599	117	74	43	371	248	123	778	534	244	...	...	...
c.—Frontier Districts ...	223.632	114.311	109.321	119	106	13	144	121	23	1	...	1	1	1	...
Ladakh	165,422	83,169	82,253	8	8	...	128	113	15	...	...	...	1	1	...
Gilgit	58,210	31,142	27,068	111	98	13	16	8	8	1	...	1	...	...	...

B.—PROVINCES OR STATES IN INDIA BEYOND THE STATE.	82.607	40.383	42.224	34.836	14.411	20.465	2.352	1.739	643	12.378	5.946	6.432	14.861	5.362	9.299
a.—CONTIGUOUS DISTRICTS OR STATES IN PUNJAB.	72.533	33.158	39.435	31.369	12.146	19.223	1.648	1.157	491	11.680	5.372	6.308	13.911	4.938	8.973
1.—DISTRICTS	71.533	32.813	39.025	31.367	12.146	19.221	1.604	1.130	474	11.678	5.370	6.303	13.336	4.701	8.635
Chitral	30	5	15	...	...	...	1	1	...	...	...	...	...	...	...
Kangra	2,605	915	1,780	817	250	567	180	112	68	38	34	4	1,367	279	1,088
Gurdaspur	14,289	5,112	9,177	2,598	684	1,914	190	125	65	151	59	92	10,969	3,948	7,021
Sialkote	26,767	10,446	16,321	22,652	8,093	14,559	648	446	202	1,346	497	849	891	403	488
Gujrat	10,322	4,827	5,495	3,123	1,736	1,387	195	140	55	6,378	2,484	3,894	37	24	13
Gujranwala	1,844	1,173	671	1,218	745	473	154	113	41	195	121	74	34	20	14
Jhelum	3,315	2,129	1,186	438	257	181	93	87	6	1,521	836	685	22	16	6
Rawalpindi	3,509	2,542	967	325	232	93	77	68	9	1,108	708	400	16	11	5
Hazara (including Swat) ...	9,077	5,664	3,413	196	149	47	63	38	25	878	661	217	...	...	...
2.—NATIVE STATES ...	755	345	410	2		2	44	27	17	2	2	...	575	237	338
Chamba	755	345	410	2	...	2	44	27	17	2	2	...	575	237	338
b.—REMOTE DISTRICTS OR STATES IN PUNJAB	8.565	6.123	2.442	2.933	1.841	1.152	487	387	100	611	506	105	638	346	292
1.—DISTRICTS	8.223	5.848	2.375	2.882	1.754	1.128	431	335	96	596	493	103	559	309	250
Hissar	30	22	8	20	17	3	...	...	...	2	2	...	4	1	3
Rohtak	5	5	...	...	...	...	...	...	...	...	...	...	3	3	...
Gurgaon	16	10	6	15	9	6	...	...	...	1	1	...	...	...	...
Delhi	166	124	42	81	61	20	13	12	1	2	2	...	6	6	...
Karnal	17	17	...	6	6	...	5	5	...	2	2	...	1	1	...
Umballa	113	84	29	44	36	8	9	9	...	5	4	1	9	4	5
Simla	44	30	14	20	12	8	5	4	1	1	1	...	5	2	3
Hoshiarpur	1,224	893	331	388	249	139	32	28	4	41	35	6	288	145	143
Jullundhar...	639	431	208	356	218	138	53	37	16	33	25	8	40	30	10
Ludhiana	183	95	88	53	35	18	9	5	4	8	6	2	11	5	6

TABLE XI.

JAMMU AND KASHMIR STATE.

BIRTH-PLACE—continued.

District, State, Province or Country where born.	Punch Jagir. Persons.	Punch Jagir. Males.	Punch Jagir. Females.	Bhadarwah Jagir. Persons.	Bhadarwah Jagir. Males.	Bhadarwah Jagir. Females.	Srinagar. Persons.	Srinagar. Males.	Srinagar. Females.	Muzaffarabad. Persons.	Muzaffarabad. Males.	Muzaffarabad. Females.	Ladakh. Persons.	Ladakh. Males.	Ladakh. Females.	Gilgit. Persons.	Gilgit. Males.	Gilgit. Females.
	Province, District or State where enumerated.																	
1	17	18	19	20	21	22	23	24	25	26	27	28	29	30	31	32	33	34
TOTAL STATE ...	**304.468**	**160.679**	**143.609**	**34.311**	**17.500**	**16.811**	**989.196**	**526.158**	**463.038**	**168.198**	**90.729**	**77.469**	**165.992**	**83.600**	**82.392**	**60.885**	**33.778**	**27.107**
A.—District within the State ...	**301.480**	**158.621**	**142.859**	**33.871**	**17.177**	**16.694**	**980.756**	**521.290**	**459.466**	**161.317**	**84.974**	**76.343**	**165.799**	**83.427**	**82.372**	**59.627**	**32.718**	**26.909**
a.—Jammu Province ...	**301.121**	**158.422**	**142.699**	**33.732**	**17.084**	**16.648**	**6.843**	**4.149**	**2.694**	**4.357**	**3.631**	**726**	**132**	**93**	**39**	**1.660**	**1.620**	**40**
Jammu ...	4.106	2.749	1.447	301	196	105	2.186	1,498	688	1,534	1,469	65	37	21	16	1 136	1 105	31
Udhampur ...	701	437	264	717	445	272	574	396	178	58	40	18	46	34	12	159	158	1
Bhimber ...	266	169	97	23	10	13	752	428	324	560	521	39	10	9	1	259	252	7
Jasrota ...	6	6	...	93	63	30	43	38	5	659	499	160	12	12	...	77	77	...
Punch Jagir ...	295.951	155.061	140,890	29	25	4	3.285	1.789	1.100	1,516	1.102	144	5	3	2	29	28	1
Bhadarwah Jagir ...	1	...	1	32,569	16,345	16,224	3		3	–		...	22	14	8	...	...	...
b.—Kashmir Province ...	**359**	**199**	**160**	**139**	**93**	**46**	**973.854**	**516.997**	**456.657**	**156.936**	**81.338**	**75.598**	**338**	**301**	**37**	**212**	**197**	**15**
Khas ...	...	...	...	137	92	45	972.369	516.226	456,143	244	126	118	215	202	13	134	129	5
Muzaffarabad ...	359	199	160	2	1	1	1 285	771	514	156,692	81,212	75,480	123	99	24	78	68	10
c.—Frontier Districts ...	...	...	...	...	...	...	**259**	**144**	**115**	**24**	**5**	**19**	**165.329**	**83.033**	**82.296**	**57.755**	**30.901**	**26.854**
Ladakh ...	...	...	...	...	...	...	20	7	13	10	...	10	165.098	83.015	82 183	167	125	232
Gilgit ...	...	...	...	...	...	...	239	137	102	14	5	9	231	118	113	57,696	30,776	[illegible]

B.—Provinces or States in India beyond the State.	2,888	1,992	896	418	301	117	7,450	4,303	3,147	6,826	5,710	1,116	126	113	13	582	506	76
a.—Contiguous Districts or States in Punjab.	2,399	1,608	791	304	205	99	5,474	3,012	2,462	5,430	4,395	1,035	42	39	3	336	286	50
1.—Districts	2,337	1,606	791	175	129	46	5,473	3,011	2,462	5,430	4,395	1,035	42	39	3	336	286	50
Chitral	...	...	...	...	...	...	2	1	1	2	2	...	...	...	...	15	1	14
Kangra	91	66	25	78	55	23	33	28	5	34	34	...	...	...	...	57	57	...
Gurdaspur	59	39	20	56	44	12	62	33	29	172	151	21	1	1	...	31	28	3
Sialkote	165	127	38	17	10	7	314	200	114	623	577	46	9	8	1	102	85	17
Gujrat	199	158	41	9	8	1	262	189	73	73	47	26	1	1	...	45	40	5
Gujranwalla	46	35	11	5	3	2	133	90	43	41	28	13	18	18	...	...	...	...
Jhelum	716	468	248	3	3	...	109	66	43	386	376	10	1	1	...	23	19	4
Rawalpindi	440	304	136	7	6	1	444	321	123	994	862	132	12	10	2	26	20	6
Hazara (including Swat) ...	681	409	272	...	...	...	4,114	2,083	2,031	3,105	2,318	787	...	...	...	37	36	1
2.—Native States	2	2	...	129	76	53	1	1	...	...	...	...	...	...	...	...	...	...
Chamba	2	2	...	129	76	53	1	1	...	...	...	...	...	...	...	...	...	...
b.—Remote Districts or States in Punjab.	409	313	96	105	87	18	1,676	1,096	580	1,368	1,295	73	77	68	9	201	184	17
1.—Districts	378	289	89	59	53	6	1,644	1,069	575	1,366	1,294	72	77	68	9	201	184	17
Hissar	...	...	...	...	...	...	4	2	2	...	...	...	...	...	...	...	...	...
Rohtak	...	...	...	...	...	...	...	...	...	...	...	...	...	...	...	2	2	...
Gurgaon	...	...	...	...	...	...	...	...	...	...	...	...	...	...	...	...	...	...
Delhi	2	2	...	7	4	3	35	21	14	15	11	4	...	...	...	5	5	...
Karnal	...	...	...	...	...	...	2	2	...	1	1	...	...	...	...	...	...	...
Umballa	12	9	3	2	...	2	13	9	4	3	2	1	1	1	...	15	10	5
Simla	...	...	...	5	5	...	8	6	2	...	...	...	...	...	...	...	...	...
Hoshiarpur	65	58	7	9	9	...	69	54	15	276	265	11	22	16	6	34	34	...
Jullundhar...	25	24	1	3	3	...	103	82	21	8	4	4	...	...	...	9	8	1
Ludhiana	2	3	...	2	2	...	38	31	7	5	5	...	...	...	...	5	4	1

TABLE XI.

JAMMU AND KASHMIR STATE.

BIRTH-PLACE—continued.

District, State, Province or Country where born.	Population of Jammu and Kashmir State.			Jammu.			Udhampur.			Bhimbar.			Jasrota.		
	Persons.	Males.	Females.	Persons.	Males.	Females.	Persons.	Males.	Females.	Persons.	Males.	Females.	Persons.	Males.	Females.
1	2	3	4	5	6	7	8	9	10	11	12	13	14	15	16
Ferozepur	59	43	16	10	12	7	7	1	6	...	...	...	8	5	3
Multan	96	57	39	20	12	8	2	2		17	16	1	6	3	3
Jhang	56	36	20	37	23	14	3	3	...	4	2	2	1	1	...
Montgomery	22	16	6	16	11	5	1	1	...	1	...	1	...	...	...
Lahore	2,146	1,474	672	581	330	251	108	87	19	234	212	22	30	15	15
Amritsar	1,199	718	481	617	359	258	100	60	40	29	23	6	130	67	72
Shahpur	455	302	153	253	154	99	13	13	...	72	43	29	20	13	7
Peshawar	1,686	1,446	240	330	190	140	59	55	4	135	114	21	5	5	...
Kohat	31	9	22	8	4	4	2	2	...	...	...	...	...	...	...
Bannu	44	6	38	3	1	2	...	...	...	4	4	...	...	...	...
Dera Ismail Khan ...	28	19	9	4	4	...	2	1	1	2	...	2	2	2	...
Dera Ghazi Khan ...	3	3	...	1	1	...	1	1	...	1	1	...	...	...	...
Muzaffar Garh	6	6	...	...	...	...	...	...	...	...	...	...	...	...	...
Chenab Valley	5	2	3	1	1	...	...	...	...	2	...	2	2	1	1
2.—Native States in Punjab	342	275	67	111	87	24	56	52	4	15	13	2	49	37	12
Patiala	78	64	14	41	32	9	8	7	1	6	6	...	6	4	2
Nabha	5	5	...	5	5	...	...	...	...	...	...	...	...	...	...

Kapurthala	...	100	73	27	54	42	12	11	9	2	...	...	...	18	7	9
Bahawalpur	...	4	2	2	...	...	...	2	1	1	1	...	1	...	...	...
Maler Kotla	...	3	3	...	3	3	...	...	...	...	...	...	...	...	...	...
Mandi	...	51	33	18	...	...	...	...	...	...	...	...	...	...	...	...
Suket	...	59	58	1	1	...	1	33	33	...	...	...	...	25	25	...
Faridkota	...	7	6	1	3	2	1	2	2	...	...	...	...	...	...	...
Simla's State Balaspur	...	36	32	4	5	4	1	...	...	...	8	7	1	3	1	1
C.—Other Provinces or States in India.																
a.—Bengal	...	198	146	52	16	13	3	29	27	2	7	6	1	...	...	...
1.—Districts	...	194	145	49	16	13	3	29	27	2	7	6	1	...	...	...
Patna	...	1	1	...	...	...	...	...	...	...	...	...	...	...	...	...
Gaya	...	2	2	...	...	...	...	...	...	...	...	...	...	...	...	...
Dinajpur	...	2	1	1	...	...	...	...	...	...	...	...	...	...	...	...
Bardwan	...	8	7	1	3	3	...	...	...	...	...	...	...	...	...	...
Calcutta	...	178	132	46	12	9	3	29	27	2	7	6	1	...	...	...
Chaubis Pargana	...	3	2	1	1	1	...	...	...	...	...	...	...	...	...	...
2.—Bengal States	...	4	1	3	...	...	...	...	...	...	...	...	...	...	...	...
Orissa	...	2	1	1	...	...	...	...	...	...	...	...	...	...	...	...
Chotta Nagpur	...	2	...	2	...	...	...	...	...	...	...	...	...	...	...	...
D.—North-Western Provinces and Oudh.		751	609	142	338	326	72	45	42	3	38	33	5	38	35	3
a.—North-Western Provinces		582	476	116	296	241	55	35	32	3	33	28	5	33	31	2
Muradabad	...	11	10	1	4	4	...	...	...	...	1	1	...	...	...	...
Bijnour	...	14	9	5	4	2	2	1	1	...	1	1	...	...	...	...
Saharanpur	...	45	33	12	30	10	11	...	...	...	...	...	...	6	6	...
Agra	...	68	57	11	15	15	...	7	7	...	4	4	...	1	1	...
Cawnpur	...	60	51	9	36	30	6	1	1	...	10	9	1	...	...	...
Meerut	...	58	43	15	31	23	9	7	7	...	2	2	...	2	1	1

TABLE XI.

JAMMU AND KASHMIR STATE.

BIRTH-PLACE—continued.

District, State, Province or Country where born.	Punnch Jagir.			Bhadarwah Jagir.			Srinagar.			Muzaffarabad.			Ladakh.			Gilgit.		
	Persons.	Males.	Females.	Persons.	Males.	Females.	Persons.	Males.	Females.	Persons.	Males.	Females.	Persons.	Males.	Females.	Persons.	Males.	Females.
1	17	18	19	20	21	23	23	24	25	26	27	28	29	30	31	32	33	34
Ferozepur	1	1	...	...	...	...	14	14	...	10	10	...	...	...	...	...	...	...
Multan	2	2	...	...	...	...	40	22	27	...	...	...	...	...	...	...	...	...
Jhang	...	...	...	2	2	...	9	5	4	...	...	...	...	...	...	...	...	...
Montgomery	1	1	...	1	1	...	...	...	...	2	2	...	...	...	...	...	...	...
Lahore	156	114	42	12	12	...	814	525	289	75	46	29	46	44	2	92	89	3
Amritsar	36	23	13	15	15	...	223	141	82	16	9	7	3	3	1	12	10	2
Shahpur	8	7		...	...	...	61	47	14	15	15	...	...	...	...	13	10	3
Peshawar	55	36	19	1	...	1	142	97	45	932	924	8	4	4	...	14	12	2
Kohat	...	...	...	...	...	...	20	2	18	...	...	...	1	1	...	...	...	...
Bannu	1	...	1	...	...	...	28	1	27	8	...	8	...	...	...	...	...	...
Dera Ismail Khan ...	6	4	2	...	...	...	12	8	4	...	...	...	...	...	...	...	...	...
Dera Ghazi Khan ...	...	...	...	...	...	...	...	...	...	...	...	...	...	...	...	..	...	...
Muzaffar Garh	6	6	...	...	...	...	...	...	...	...	...	...	...	...	...	...	...	...
Chenab Valley	...	...	...	...	...	...	...	...	...	...	...	...	...	...	...	...	...	...
2.—Native States in Punjab	31	24	7	46	34	12	32	27	5	2	1	1	...	...	...	...	...	...
Patiala	2	2	...	1	1	...	13	11	2	1	1	...	...	...	...	...	...	...
Nabha	...	...	...	...	...	...	...	...	...	...	...	...	...	...	...	...	...	...

Kapurthala	...	...	2	2	...	...	...	...	16	13	3		...	1	...	...	...	...	...	...
Bahawalpur	...	...	...	...	...	...	...	...	1	1	...	...	...	...	...	...	...	...	...	...
Maler Kotla	...	...	...	...	...	...	...	...	...	...	...	...	...		...	...	...	...	...	...
Manji	...	...	6	...	6	45	33	12	...	...	...	...	...	...	...	...	...	...	...	...
Suket	...	...	...	...	...	...	...	...	...	...	...	...	...	...	...	...	...	...	...	...
Faridkote	...	...	...	...	...	...	...	...	2	2	...	...	...	...	...	...	...	...	...	...
Simla's State Balaspur	...	21	20	1	...	...	...	...	...	...	...	...	...	...	...	...	...	...	...	...
C.—OTHER PROVINCES OR STATES IN INDIA.																				
a.—BENGAL	...	...	37	34	3	...	...	...	96	54	42	...	...	...	5	5	...	8	7	1
1.—DISTRICT	...	...	37	34	3	...	...	...	92	53	39	...	...	...	5	5	...	8	7	1
Patna	...	...	...	...	...	...	...	...	1	1		...	...	...	...	...	...	...	...	...
Gaya	...	...	...	...	...	...	...	...	2	2	...	...	...	...	...	...	...	...	...	...
Dinajpur	...	...	...	...	...	...	...	...	2	1	1	...	...	...	...	...	...	...	...	...
Bardwan	...	...	...	...	...	...	...	...	5	4	1	...	...	...	...	...	...	...	...	...
Calcutta	...	...	37	34	3	...	...	...	80	44	36	...	...	...	5	5	...	8	7	1
Chaubis Pargana	...	...	...	...	...	...	...	...	2	1	1	...	...	...	...	...	...	...	...	...
2.—BENGAL STATES	...	...	...	...	...	...	...	...	4	1	3	...	...	...	...	...	...	...	...	...
Orissa	...	...	...	...	...	...	...	...	2	1	1	...	...	...	...	...	...	...	...	...
Chota Nagpur	...	...	...	...	...	...	...	...	2	...	2	...	...	...	...	...	...	...	...	...
D.—NORTH-WESTERN PROVINCES AND OUDH.		32	30	2	9	9	...	138	96	42	18	12	6	2	1	1	33	25	8
a.—NORTH-WESTERN PROVINCES		29	27	2	5	5	...	118	82	36	11	7	4	2	1	1	30	22	8
Muradabad	...	...	...	...	...	...	...	...	4	4	...	...	...	...	2	1	1	...	...	...
Bijnour	...	...	...	...	...	...	...	...	5	2	3	...	...	...	...	...	...	...	...	...
Saharanpur	...	...	...	...	...	1	1	...	7	6	1	1	1	...	...	...	...	...	...	...
Agra	...	...	13	11	2	...	...	...	27	19	8	1	...	1	...	...	...	...	...	...
Cawnpur	...	...	2	2	...	...	...	...	7	5	2	...	...	...	...	...	...	4	4	...
Meerut	...	...	...	...	...	...	...	...	7	3	4	...	...	...	...	...	...	9	8	1

TABLE XI.

JAMMU AND KASHMIR STATE.

BIRTH-PLACE—continued.

District, State, Province or Country where born.	Population of Jammu and Kashmir State.			Province, District or State where enumerated. Jammu.			Udhampur.			Bhimber.			Jasrota.		
	Persons.	Males.	Females.	Persons.	Males.	Females.	Persons.	Males.	Females.	Persons.	Males.	Females.	Persons.	Males.	Females.
1	2	3	4	5	6	7	8	9	10	11	12	13	14	15	16
Bareilly	17	17	...	...	...	...	4	4	...	...	.	...	..	...	...
Aligarh	13	10	3	11	8	3	...	...	...	.	...	...	...	..	...
Dera Dun	14	5	9	...	...	...	1	...	1	..	...	...	...	...	...
Mathra	51	43	8	20	21	5	4	3	1	4	2	2	11	11	...
Garhwal	3	3	...	...	...	...	...		...	...	.	...	...	..	...
Farrakhabad	25	21	4	21	17	4	—	.	...	2	2	..	...	...	...
Muzaffarnagar	37	27	10	10	8	2	3	3	...	.	.	..	.	...	...
Allahabad	48	37	11	17	16	1	4	3	1	4	3	1	..	...	...
Ghazipur	11	10	1	...	...	...	...	...	...	...		.	10	9	1
Benares	72	62	10	55	47	8	2	2	.	3	2	1	3	3	...
Bulandshahr	24	22	2	21	19	2		...	...	1	1	...	...	...	...
Etawah	9	9	.	9	9	...	...	...	..	...	.	..	..	...	...
Azimgarh	1	1	...	1	1		...	...	...	.	..	...	..	...	...
Mirzapur	1	1	...	...	...	..	...	...	..	1	1	..	.	...	...
Hamirpur	2	1	1	2	1	1	...	...	...	...	...	...	..	...	...
Shahjahanpur	8	4	4	3	2	1	1	1	..	..	...	..	...	...	...
6.—Oudh	159	133	26	102	85	17	10	10	...	5	5	...	5	4	1

Lucknow	80	62	18	47	33	12	4	4	...	1	1	...	3	2	1
Sultanpur	12	6	4	10	7	3	...	...	..	..	...	..	...	...	...
Faizabad	41	38	8	23	22	1	6	6	...	4	4	..	2	2	...
Gonda	16	15	1	16	15	1	...	...	...		...	...	...	...	...
Bara Banki	6	6	...	6	6	...	..	.		...	...	...	..	...	...
Oudh (Unspecified) ..	4	4	...	...	...	...	...	...	..	...	...	...	..	...	...
E.—Central India Agency ..	23	24	5	8	6	2	5	3	2	8	8	..	1	1	...
Gowaliar	23	20	3	5	6	2	1	1	...	6	6	...	1	1	...
Indore	6	4	2	...	..	..	4	2	2	2	2	.	...	...	...
F.—Rajputana Agency	199	172	77	74	47	27	22	15	7	25	14	11	62	36	26
Jaipur	21	21	3	18	16	2	1	1		...	...	...	1	1	...
Marwar	23	18	5	3	3	...	3	3	...	1	1	..	15	10	5
Bhartpur	12	4	8	4	1	3	5	3	2	...	...	...	3	..	3
Bikanir	105	60	45	17	10	7	13	8	5	24	13	11	43	23	18
Alwar	3	1	2	1	..	1	...	...	...		...	...	...	...	...
Partabgarh	1	1	..	...	.	...	...	...	...	...	..	...	...	...	...
Rajputana (Unspecified) ...	31	17	11	31	17	14	...	.	...	..	...	...	...	...	...
G.—Central Provinces ...	8	8	...	6	6	...	...		..	...	...	...	...	...	...
Jabalpur	1	1	...	1	1	...	..	...	...	...	..	...	...	...	...
Sagar	7	7	...	5	5	...	...	...	..	...	...	...	...	...	...
H.—Bombay Presidency Districts and States.	218	160	58	24	21	3	141	103	38	5	3	2	4	2	2
a.—Districts	142	93	49	17	15	2	76	46	30	3	1	2	4	2	2
Shikarpur	70	47	32	2	2	...	72	42	30	3	1	2	1	1	...
Karrachi	4	1	3	...	...	...	...	...	...	...	...	...	1	...	1
Bombay	38	72	11	12	10	2	3	3	...	...	...	...	2	1	1
Belgam	1	...	1	...	...	...	...	...	...	...	...	...	...	...	...

TABLE XI.

JAMMU AND KASHMIR STATE.

BIRTH-PLACE—continued.

District, State, Province or Country where born.	PROVINCE, DISTRICT OR STATE WHERE ENUMERATED.																	
	Poonch Jagir.			Bhadarwah Jagir.			Srinagar.			Muzaffarabad.			Ladakh.			Gilgit.		
	Persons.	Males.	Females.	Persons.	Males.	Females.	Persons.	Males.	Females.	Persons.	Males.	Females.	Persons.	Males.	Females.	Persons.	Males.	Females.
1	17	18	19	20	21	22	23	24	25	26	27	28	29	30	31	32	33	34
Bareilly	4	4	...	...	...	...	3	3	...	1	1	...	...	...	...	5	5	...
Aligarh	...	...	...	...	...	...	2	2	...	...	...	...	...	...	...	...	...	...
Dera Dun	...	...	...	...	...	...	3	2	1	...	...	...	...	...	...	10	3	7
Mathra	2	2	...	2	2	...	1	1	...	1	1	...	...	...	...	...	...	...
Garhwal	...	...	...	2	2	...	1	1	...	...	...	...	...	...	...	...	...	...
Farrukhabad	...	...	...	...	...	...	2	2	...	...	...	...	...	...	...	...	...	...
Muzaffarnagar	6	6	...	...	...	...	18	10	8	...	...	...	...	...	...	...	...	...
Allahabad	2	2	...	...	...	...	19	11	8	...	...	...	...	...	...	2	2	...
Ghazipur	...	...	...	...	...	...	1	1	...	...	...	...	...	...	...	...	...	...
Benares	...	...	...	...	...	...	6	5	1	3	3	...	...	...	...	...	...	...
Bulandshahr	...	...	...	...	...	...	2	2	...	...	...	...	...	...	...	...	...	...
Etawah	...	...	...	...	...	...	...	...	...	...	...	...	...	...	...	...	...	...
Azimgarh	...	...	...	...	...	...	...	...	...	...	...	...	...	...	...	...	...	...
Mirzapur	...	...	...	...	...	...	...	...	...	...	...	...	...	...	...	...	...	...
Hamirpur	...	...	...	...	...	...	...	...	...	...	...	...	...	...	...	...	...	...
Shahjahanpur	...	...	...	...	...	...	...	...	...	4	1	3	...	...	...	...	...	...
b.—Oudh	3	3	...	4	4	...	20	14	6	7	5	2	...	...	...	3	3	...

Lucknow	3	3	.	4	4	...	11	8	3	7	6	2	...	...	...	...	...	...
Sultanpur	...	...	...	...	...	..	2	1	1	...	.	...	...	.	...	...	...	...
Faizabad	...	...	..	...	...	...	3	1	2	...	..	...	...	...	...	3	3	..
Gonda	...	...	.	...	...	...	...	...	...	..	..	.	...	...	...	...	...	...
Bara Banki	...	...	.	...	...	...	...	...	...	...	...		...	..	.	..	...	.
Oudh (Unspecified)	.	...	...	...	...	...	4	4	..	...	...	..	...	..	...	...	..	...
E.—Central India Agency	2	2	...	...	...	...		1	1	3	3	.	...	.	..	.	...	.
Gowaliar	2	2	...	..	...	...	2	1	1	3	3	...	...	...	..	...	.	...
Indore	...	...	...	...	...	...	...	...	..	..	...	...	...	-	...	...	..	...
F.—Rajputana Agency	8	4	4	...	...	...	7	5	2	1	1	...	...	...	...	...	...	..
Jaipur	..	.	...	...	.	..	4	3	1	...	...	...	...	...	...	...	...	...
Marwar	...	..	...	..	..	...	...	...	..	1	1	...	...	...	...		...	...
Bhartpur	...	..	...	...	...	...	...	...	...	...	..	..	...	...	...	...	...	..
Bakanir	7	3	4		...	...	1	1	...	...	.	...	..	.	...	...	...	...
Alwar	.	.	..	...	...	...	2	1	1	..		...	...	..	...	...	.	
Partabgarh	1	1	...	...	...	..	...	..	.	.	...	.	...	...	..	...	..	..
Rajputana (Unspecified)	...	...	...	..	...	...	...	.	...	...	...	...	...	...	..	...	...	...
G.—Central Provinces	...	...	...	...	...	...	2	2	..	...	...	...	...	...	..	...	...	.
Jabalpur	...	...	...	...	...	...	...	...	..	..		..	...	...	...	...	...	..
Sagar	..	...		...	...	...	2	2	...	..	..	...	...	...	.	...	...	...
H.—Bombay Presidency Districts and States	..	...	...	..	...	...	34	23	11	6	4	2		...	...	4	4	.
a.—Districts	...	...	.	...	..	...	32	21	11	6	4	2	..	..	...	4	4	...
Shikarpur	...	...	...	...	..	..	1	1	...	..	...	...	...	...	...	...	...	..
Karrachi	..	..	..	...	...	...	3	1	2	...	...	...	...	...	...	...	...	...
Bombay	...	...	...	..	...	...	17	9	8	...	...	...	...	...	...	4	4	...
Belgam	...	...	...	...	...	...	1	...	1	..	...	..	...	...	...	...	...	...

TABLE XI.

JAMMU AND KASHMIR STATE.

BIRTH-PLACE—continued.

District, State, Province or Country where born.	Population of Jammu and Kashmir State.			Province, District or State where enumerated.											
				Jammu.			Udhampur.			Bhimbar			Jasrota.		
	Persons.	Males.	Females.	Persons.	Males.	Females.	Persons.	Males.	Females.	Persons.	Males.	Females.	Persons.	Males.	Females.
1	2	3	4	5	6	7	8	9	10	11	12	13	14	15	16
French and Portuguese Settlements	10	10	...	...	...	...	...	...	...	...	...	...	...	...	...
Hyderabad (Sindh) ...	10	8	2	3	3	...	1	1	...	...	...	...	...	...	...
(b).—States	76	67	9	7	6	1	65	57	8	2	2	...	...	...	...
Baroda	6	5	1	4	3	1	...	...	...	2	2	...	...	...	...
Kutchh	70	62	8	3	3	...	65	57	8	...	...	...	...	...	...
I.—Madras Presidency ...	9	7	2	1	1	...	2	2	...	1	1	...	...	...	...
Madras (Unspecified) ...	9	7	2	1	1	...	2	2	...	1	1	...	...	...	...
J.—Ajmere Merwara ...	10	7	3	3	2	1	1	1	...	...	...	...	...	...	...
Ajmere Merwara ...	10	7	3	3	2	1	1	1	...	...	...	...	...	...	...
K.—Hyderabad Nizam ...	18	15	3	3	2	1	2	2	...	2	2	...	4	4	...
Hyderabad Nizam ...	18	15	3	3	2	1	2	2	...	2	2	...	4	4	...
L.—Assam	2	1	1	...	...	...	...	...	...	...	...	...	...	...	...
Sylhet	2	1	1	...	...	...	...	...	...	...	...	...	...	...	...
M.—Andaman and Nicobars	1	...	1	1	...	1	...	...	...	...	...	...	...	...	...

Andaman	1	...	1	1	...	1	...	...	...	...	...	...	...	...	...
N.—BURMA	3	3	...	...	...	...	...	...	...	1	1	...	...	...	...
Burma	3	3	...	...	...	...	...	...	...	1	1	...	...	...	...
O.—BIRTH PLACE NOT RETURNED	3	...	3	...	...	...	...	...	...	...	...	...	3	...	3
P.—BORN IN COUNTRIES ADJACENT TO INDIA.	2,840	2,186	654	808	756	52	98	95	3	121	64	57	17	14	3
(a). AFGHANISTAN ...	1,038	687	351	199	194	5	97	94	3	43	23	20	6	6	...
Kabul	947	601	346	150	146	4	67	64	3	42	23	19	4	4	...
Kandhar	34	32	2	2	1	1	29	29	...	1	...	1	...	...	...
Ghazni	46	46	...	44	44	...	...	...	...	...	...	...	2	2	...
Jalalabad	6	6	...	3	3	...	1	1	...	...	...	...	...	...	...
Herat	5	2	3	...	...	...	...	...	...	...	...	...	...	...	...
(b) YAGHISTAN	309	178	131	8	8	...	...	...	...	57	43	14	...	...	...
Yaghistan	309	178	131	8	8	...	...	...	...	57	43	14	...	...	...
(c) BALUCHISTAN ...	16	15	1	13	13	...	...	...	...	1	1	...	...	...	...
Baluchistan	16	15	1	13	13	...	...	...	...	1	1	...	...	...	...
(d) TURKISTAN	33	28	5	3	3	...	...	...	...	...	...	...	...	...	...
Badakhshan	3	1	2	...	...	...	...	...	...	...	...	...	...	...	...
Samarkand	4	4	...	3	3	...	...	...	...	...	...	...	...	...	...
Yarkand	26	23	3	...	...	...	...	...	...	...	...	...	...	...	...
(e). TIBET	60	35	25	...	...	...	1	1	...	5	5	...	...	...	...
Tibet	60	35	25	...	...	...	1	1	...	5	5	...	...	...	...
(f). NEPAL	1,384	1,243	141	585	538	47	...	...	...	15	12	3	11	8	3
Nepal	1,384	1,243	141	585	538	47	...	...	...	15	12	3	11	8	3

TABLE XI.

JAMMU AND KASHMIR STATE.

***BIRTH-PLACE*—continued.**

District, State, Province or Country where born.	PROVINCE, DISTRICT OR STATE WHERE ENUMERATED.																	
	Punch Jagir.			Bhadarwah Jagir.			Srinagar.			Muzaffarabad.			Ladakh.			Gilgit.		
	Persons.	Males.	Females.	Persons.	Males.	Females.	Persons.	Males.	Females.	Persons.	Males.	Females.	Persons.	Males.	Females.	Persons.	Males.	Females.
1	17	18	19	20	21	22	23	24	25	26	27	28	29	30	31	32	33	34
French and Portuguese Settlements	...	...	...	...	...	...	10	10	...	...	...	...	...	...	...	...	...	...
Hyderabad (Sind) ...	...	...	...	...	...	...	...	...	...	6	4	2	...	...	...	...	...	...
(b) States	...	...	...	...	...	...	2	2	...	...	...	...	...	...	...	...	...	...
Baroda ...	...	...	...	...	...	...	...	...	...	...	...	...	...	...	...	...	...	...
Kutchh	...	...	...	...	...	...	2	2	...	...	...	...	...	...	...	...	...	...
I.—Madras Presidency ...	...	...	...	...	...	...	5	3	2	...	...	...	...	...	...	...	...	...
Madras (Unspecified) ...	...	...	...	...	...	...	5	3	2	...	...	...	...	...	...	...	...	...
J.—Ajmere Merwara ...	...	...	...	...	...	...	6	4	2	...	...	...	...	...	...	...	...	...
Ajmere Merwara ...	...	...	...	...	...	...	6	4	2	...	...	...	...	...	...	...	...	...
K.—Hyderabad Nizam ...	1	1	...	...	...	...	6	4	2	...	...	...	...	...	...	...	...	...
Hyderabad Nizam ...	1	1	...	...	...	...	6	4	2	...	...	...	...	...	...	...	...	...
L.—Assam	...	...	...	...	...	...	2	1	1	...	...	...	...	...	...	...	...	...
Sylhet	...	...	...	...	...	...	2	1	1	...	...	...	...	...	...	...	...	...
M.—Andaman and Nicobars ...	...	...	...	...	...	...	...	...	...	...	...	...	...	...	...	...	...	...

Andaman	...	...	...	...	...	...	...	...	...	...	...	...	...	...	...	...	...	...
N.—BURMA	...	...	...	...	...	...	2	2	...	...	...	...	...	...	...	...	...	...
Burma	...	...	...	...	...	...	2	2	...	...	...	...	...	...	...	...	...	...
O.—BIRTH PLACE NOT RETURNED	...	...	...	...	...	...	...	...	...	...	...	...	...	...	...	...	...	...
P.—BORN IN COUNTRIES ADJACENT TO INDIA.	117	65	52	21	21	...	895	514	381	54	44	10	49	48	1	660	545	115
(a) AFGHANISTAN ...	87	41	46	3	3	...	361	199	162	...	...	...	12	12	...	230	115	115
Kabul	87	41	46	3	3	...	352	193	160	...	...	...	12	12	...	230	115	115
Kandhar	...	...	...	...	...	...	2	2	...	...	...	...	...	...	...	...	...	...
Ghazni	...	...	...	...	...	...	...	...	...	...	...	...	...	...	...	...	...	...
Jalalabad	...	...	...	...	...	...	2	2	...	...	...	...	...	...	...	...	...	...
Herat	...	...	...	...	...	...	5	2	3	...	...	...	...	...	...	...	...	...
(b) YAGHISTAN	1	...	1	3	3	...	211	105	106	29	19	10	...		...	...	...	...
Yaghistan	1	...	1	3	3	...	211	105	106	29	19	10	...	...	...	...	...	...
(c) BALUCHISTAN	...	...	...	...	...	...	2	1	1	...	...	...	...	...	...	...	...	...
Baluchistan	...	...	...	...	...	...	2	1	1	...	...	...	...	...	...	...	...	...
(d) TURKISTAN	...	...	...	...	...	...	23	18	5	7	7	...	...	...	...	...	...	...
Badakhshan	...	...	...	...	...	...	3	1	2	...	...	...	...	...	...	...	...	...
Samarkand	...	...	...	...	...	...	1	1	...	...	...	...	...	...	...	...	...	...
Yarkand	...	...	...	...	...	...	19	16	3	7	...	...	...	...	...	...	...	...
(e) TIBET	...	...	...	...	...	...	37	12	25	17	17	...	...	...	...	...	...	...
Tibet	...	...	...	...	...	...	37	12	25	17	17	...	...	...	...	...	...	...
(f) NEPAL	29	34	5	15	15	...	261	179	82	1	1	...	37	36	1	430	430	...
Nepal	29	34	5	15	15	...	261	179	82	1	1	...	37	36	1	430	430	...

TABLE XI.

JAMMU AND KASHMIR STATE.

BIRTH-PLACE—continued.

District, State, Province or Country where born.	Province, District or State where enumerated.														
	Population of Jammu and Kashmir State.			Jammu.			Udhampur.			Bhimbar.			Jasrota.		
	Persons.	Males.	Females.	Persons.	Males.	Females.	Persons.	Males.	Persons.	Persons.	Males.	Females.	Persons.	Males.	Females.
1	2	3	4	5	6	7	8	9	10	11	12	13	14	15	16
Q.—Born in other Asiatic Countries.	28	25	3	4	4	...	5	3	2	2	2	...	...	...	...
China	15	12	3	...	...	...	4	2	2	...	...	...	...	...	...
Tartary China	1	1	...	1	1	...	...	...	...	...	...	...	...	...	...
Arabia	4	4	...	1	1	...	1	1		...	...	...	...	...	...
Baghdad	8	8	...	2	2	...	...	...		2	2	...	...	...	...
R.—Born in other Continents	122	82	60	5	3	2	...	...	...	...	...	...	...	...	...
(a) Born in Countries in Europe.	110	58	52	5	3	2	...	...	...	...	...	...	...	...	...
United Kingdom ...	92	45	47	5	3	2	...	...	...	...	...	...	...	...	...
England	74	34	40	2	1	1	...	...	...	...	...	...	...	...	...
Wales	2	1	1	...	...	...	...	...	...	...	...	...	...	...	...
Scotland	8	4	4	2	1	1	...	...	...	...	...	...	...	...	...

Ireland	8	6	2	1	1	...	...	...	...	...	...	...	...	...	...
Malta	2	...	2	...	...	...	...	...	...	...	...	...	...	...	...
France	6	3	3	...	...	...	...	...	...	...	...	...	...	...	...
Belgium	1	1	...	...	...	...	...	...	...	...	...	...	...	...	...
Holland	1	1	...	...	...	...	...	...	...	...	...	...	...	...	...
Portugal	7	7	...	...	...	...	...	...	...	...	...	...	...	...	...
Switzerland	1	1	...	...	...	...	...	...	...	...	...	...	...	...	...
S.—BORN IN AFRICA	8	2	6	...	...	...	...	...	...	...	...	...	...	...	...
Cape Colony	3	1	2	...	...	...	...	...	...	...	...	...	...	...	...
Egypt	2	1	1	...	...	...	...	...	...	...	...	...	...	...	...
Africa (Unspecified)	3	...	3	...	...	...	...	...	...	...	...	...	...	...	...
T.—BORN IN AMERICA	2	1	1	...	...	...	...	...	...	...	...	...	...	...	...
America (Unspecified)	2	1	1	...	...	...	...	...	...	...	...	...	...	...	...
U.—BORN IN AUSTRALIA	2	1	1	...	...	...	...	...	...	...	...	...	...	...	...
Australia	2	1	1	...	...	...	...	...	...	...	...	...	...	...	...

TABLE XI.

JAMMU AND KASHMIR STATE.

BIRTH-PLACE—concluded.

District, State, Province or Country where born.	Punch Jagir.			Bhadarwah Jagir.			Srinagar.			Muzaffarabad.			Ladakh.			Gilgit.		
	Persons.	Males.	Females.	Persons.	Males.	Females.	Persons.	Males.	Females.	Persons.	Males.	Females.	Persons.	Males.	Females.	Persons.	Males.	Females.
1	17	18	19	20	21	22	23	24	25	20	27	28	29	30	31	32	33	34
Q.—Born in other Asiatic Countries.	1	1	...	...	...	...	3	3	...	...	...	...	11	10	1	2	2	...
China	...	...	...	...	...	...	...	...	...	...	...	...	11	10	1	...	...	...
Tartary China	...	...	...	...	...	...	...	...	...	...	...	...	...	...	...	...	...	...
Arabia	1	1	...	...	...	...	1	1	...	...	...	...	...	...	...	...	...	...
Baghdad	...	...	...	...	...	...	2	2	...	...	...	...	...	...	...	2	2	...
R.—Born in other Continents ...	2	...	2	1	1	...	92	48	44	1	1	...	7	2	5	14	7	7
(a). Born in Countries in Europe.	2	...	2	1	1	...	83	45	38	1	1	...	4	1	3	14	7	7
United Kingdom	2	...	2	1	1	...	65	32	33	1	1	...	4	1	3	14	7	7
England	...	...	...	1	1	...	62	33	29	1	1	...	4	1	3	14	7	7
Wales	...	...	...	...	...	...	2	1	1	...	...	...	...	...	...	...	...	...
Scotland	2	...	2	...	...	...	4	3	1	...	...	...	...	...	...	...	...	...

Ireland ...	...	...	...	...	...	...	...	7	5	2	...	...	...	...	...	...	...	...	...
Malta ...	...	...	...	...	...	...	...	2	...	2	...	...	...	...	...	...	...	...	...
France ...	...	...	...	...	...			6	3	3	...		...		...	...	...	...	...
Belgium ...	...	...	...	...	...	...	...	1	1	...	...	...	...	...	...	...	...	...	...
Holland ...	...	...	...	...	...	...	...	1	1	...	...		...			...	...	...	...
Portugal ...	...	...	...	...	...	...	...	7	7		...		...	...	...	...	...	...	...
Switzerland ...	...	...	...	...	...	...	...	1	1	...	...	...	...	...	...	...	...	...	...
S.—Born in Africa	...	...		...	...	...	...	5	1	1	...	...		3	1	2	...	...	...
Cape Colony ...	...	...		...	...	...	...				...	...		3	1	2	...	...	...
Egypt ...	...	...	...	...	...	...	...	2	1	1					...		...	...	...
Africa (Unspecified)	...	...	...	...	...	...	...	3	...	3	...			...	...	...	...	...	...
T.—Born in America	...	...	...	...	...	...	...	2	1	1			...		...	...	...	...	...
America (Unspecified)	...	...	...	...	...	...		2	1	1	...		...			...	...	...	...
V.—Born in Australia	...	...	...	...				2	1	1			...		...	...	...	...	...
Australia ...		...	...	...	...	...		2	1	1		...	...		...		...	...	...

TABLE XI.

JAMMU AND KASHMIR STATE.

BIRTH-PLACE.

Part II—Detailed distribution of population by birth-place.

TABLE XI.

JAMMU AND KASHMIR STATE.

BIRTH-PLACE.

Part II.—Detailed distribution of population by birth-place.

			BIRTH-PLACE.	Population. Persons.	Males.	Females.
			TOTAL ENUMERATED POPULATION	2.905.578	1.542.057	1.363.521
			BORN IN INDIA	2.902.588	1.539.784	1.362.804
A.			DISTRICTS WITHIN THE STATE	2.819.981	1.499.401	1.320.580
	(a).		JAMMU PROVINCE	1.460.231	763.439	676.792
			Jammu	314,017	176,492	137,525
			Udhampur	283,328	148,654	134,674
			Bhimber	389,564	205,561	184,003
			Jasrota	135,537	76,469	59,068
			Punch Jagir	303,989	159,285	144,704
			Bhadarwah Jagir	33,796	16,978	16,818
	(b).		KASHMIR PROVINCE	1.136.118	601.651	534.467
			Khas	976,313	518,445	457,868
			Muzaffarabad	159,805	83,206	76,599
	(c).		FRONTIER DISTRICTS	223.632	114.311	109.321
			Ladakh	165.422	83.169	82,253
			Gilgit	58.210	31,142	27,068
B.			PROVINCES OR STATES IN INDIA BEYOND THE STATE ...	82.607	40.353	42.234
	(a).		CONTIGUOUS DISTRICTS OR STATES IN PUNJAB	72.593	33.158	39.435
		1	DISTRICTS	71.838	32.813	39.025
		2	NATIVE STATES	755	345	410

TABLE XI.

JAMMU AND KASHMIR STATE.

BIRTH-PLACE.

Part II.—Detailed distribution of population by birth-place.—continued.

			BIRTH-PLACE.	POPULATION. Persons.	Males.	Females.
	(b).		REMOTE DISTRICTS OR STATES IN PUNJAB	8,565	6,123	2,442
		1	Districts	8,223	5,848	2,375
		2	Native States in Punjab	342	275	67
C.			OTHER PROVINCES OR STATES IN INDIA.			
	(a).		BENGAL	198	146	52
		1	Districts	194	145	49
		2	Bengal States	4	1	3
D.			NORTH-WESTERN PROVINCES AND OUDH	751	609	142
	(a)		North-Western Provinces	592	476	116
	(b).		Oudh	159	133	26
E.			CENTRAL INDIA AGENCY	29	24	5
F.			RAJPUTANA AGENCY	199	122	77
G.			CENTRAL PROVINCES	8	8	...
H.			BOMBAY PRESIDENCY DISTRICTS AND STATES...	218	160	58
	(a).		Districts	142	93	49
	(b).		States	76	67	9
I.			MADRAS PRESIDENCY	9	7	2
J.			AJMERE-MERWARA	10	7	3
K. / L.			HYDERABAD NIZAM	18	15	3
M.			ASSAM	2	1	1

TABLE XI.

JAMMU AND KASHMIR STATE.

BIRTH-PLACE.

Part II.—Detailed distribution of population by birth-place.—continued.

BIRTH-PLACE.			Population. Persons.	Males.	Females.
N.		Andaman and Nicobars	1	...	1
O.		Burma	3	3	...
P.		Birth-place not returned	3	...	3
Q.		Countries adjacent to India	2,840	2,186	654
	a.	Afghanistan	1,038	687	351
	b	Yaghistan	309	178	131
	c.	Baluchistan	16	15	1
	d.	Turkistan	33	28	5
	e.	Tibbet	60	35	25
	f.	Nepal	1,384	1,243	141
R.		Other Asiatic Countries	28	25	3
		China	15	12	3
		Tartary China	1	1	...
		Arabia	4	4	...
		Baghdad	8	8	...
S.		Other Continents	122	62	60
	a.	Countries in Europe	110	58	52
		United Kingdom	92	45	47
		England	74	34	40
		Wales	2	1	1

TABLE XI.

JAMMU AND KASHMIR STATE.

BIRTH-PLACE.

Part II.—Detailed distribution of population by birth-place.—concluded.

	BIRTH-PLACE.	Population. Persons.	Males.	Females.
	Scotland	8	4	4
	Ireland	8	6	2
	Malta	2	...	2
	France	6	3	3
	Belgium	1	1	...
	Holland	1	1	...
	Portugal	7	7	...
	Switzerland	1	1	...
T.	AFRICA	8	2	6
	Cape Colony	3	1	2
	Egypt	2	1	1
	Africa (Unspecified)	3	...	3
U.	AMERICA	2	1	1
	America (Unspecified)	2	1	1
V.	AUSTRALIA	2	1	1
	Australia	2	1	1

TABLE XI.

JAMMU AND KASHMIR STATE.

BIRTH-PLACE.

Part III.—Internal Migration.

TABLE

JAMMU AND

BIRTH-

Part III.—

PROVINCE, STATE OR AGENCY.	Immigrants born in India.	Emigrants born in Province or State.	Excess of Immigrants (+) or emigrants (—).	NET		
				Jammu.	Udhampur.	Bhimbar.
1	2	3	4	5	6	7
INDIA.						
Within the State.						
1. Jammu	49,747	21,651	+28,006	...	— 1,001	+ 4,365
2. Udhampur	11,732	11,012	+720	+1,091	...	+574
3. Bhimber	19,672	8,907	+10,665	— 4,265	— 574	...
4. Jasrota	23,354	4,678	+18,676	+1,384	+2,893	— 379
5. Poonch	8,537	10,034	— 1,497	+3,988	+507	— 2,460
6 Bhadarwah	1,742	1,227	+515	+117	+662	+22
7. Khas Kashmir	16,827	84,796	— 67,969	+946	— 380	— 236
8. Muzaffarabad	11,506	3,113	+8,393	+1,417	— 313	— 218
9. Gilgit	3,287	612	+2,675	+1,025	+143	+258
10. Ladakh	894	382	+512	+20	— 82	+10
OTHER PARTS OF INDIA.						
Provinces.						
11. Ajmere-Merwara	...	.	..	— 3	— 1	...
12. Andamans and Nicobars	...	...	...	— 1	.	..
13. Assam	..		..	...	...	...
14. Baluchistan British and administered districts	...	...	...	— 13	...	— 1
15. Bengal	...	..	...	+21	— 29	— 7
16. Berar	...	..		...	...	...
17. Bombay	...	...	...	— 29	— 141	— 8
18. Burma	...	...	..	...	...	— 1
19. Central Provinces	...	.	...	— 6	...	...
20. Madras	..	...	...	— 1	— 2	— 1
21. North-West Provinces and Oudh	...	...	...	— 318	— 45	— 38
22. Punjab and North-West Frontier Province...	..	...	...	— 32,404	— 2,135	12,291
States and Agencies.						
23. Baroda State	...		..	— 4	...	— 2
24. Central India Agency...	.	...	...	— 8	— 5	— 8
25. Hyderabad State	.	...	...	— 3	— 2	— 2
26. Mysore State	.	...	...	...	...	...
27. Rajputana State	...	...	...	— 74	— 22	— 25
28. Birth-place not returned	3	.	...	...	..	...

KASHMIR STATE.

PLACE.

Internal Migration.

INTERCHANGE OF POPULATION BETWEEN STATE DISTRICTS AND OTHER PROVINCES AND STATES.

Jasrota.	Poonch.	Bhadarwah.	Khas Kashmir.	Muzaffarabad.	Gilgit.	Ladakh.	Ajmere-Merwara.	Andamans and Nicobars.	Assam.
8	9	10	11	12	13	14	15	16	17
— 1,364	— 3,988	— 117	— 946	— 1,417	— 1,025	— 29	+ 3	+ 1	...
— 2,893	— 507	— 662	+ 380	+ 313	— 143	+ 82	+ 1	...	...
+ 379	+ 2,460	— 22	+ 236	+ 218	— 258	— 10	...	...	...
...	+ 10	+ 868	— 11	— 659	— 77	— 11	...	...	...
— 10	...	— 28	— 3,285	— 1,187	— 29	— 5	...	...	...
— 868	+ 28	...	+ 134	+ 2	...	— 22	...	...	...
+ 11	+ 3,285	— 134	...	+ 1,041	+ 105	— 195	+ 6	...	+ 2
+ 659	+ 1,187	— 2	— 1,041	...	— 64	— 113	...	...	...
+ 77	+ 29	...	— 105	+ 64	...	— 74	...	...	...
+ 11	+ 5	+ 22	+ 195	+ 113	+ 74	...	...	...	...
...	...	...	— 6	...	...	...	...	...	...
...	...	...	...	...	...	...	...	...	...
...	...	...	— 2	...	...	...	...	...	...
...	...	...	+ 447	...	...	...	...	...	...
...	— 37	...	+ 193	...	— 8	— 5	...	...	...
...	...	...	+ 2	...	...	...	...	...	...
— 4	...	...	+ 613	— 6	— 4		...	...	...
...	...	...	— 2	...			...	...	...
...	...	...	2	...			...	...	...
...	...	...	+ 27	...		...		...	...
— 38	— 32	— 9	— 138	— 18	— 33	— 2		...	...
— 14,549	— 812	— 409	+ 72,170	— 6,708	— 337	— 61		...	...
...	...	...	+ 15	...	...		...	...	...
— 1	— 2	...	— 2	— 3	...			...	...
— 4	— 1	...	— 6	...		...	...	...	...
...	...	...	+ 11	...		...	...	...	...
— 62	— 8	...	+ 82	— 1		...		...	...
+ 3	...	...	...	...	...	...	...	...	...

TABLE

JAMMU AND

BIRTH-

Part III.—

PROVINCE, STATE OR AGENCY.	Baluchistan British and administered districts.	Bengal.	Berar.	Bombay.	Burma.
1	18	19	20	21	22
INDIA.					
Within the State.					
1. Jammu	+ 13	— 21	...	+ 20	.
2. Udhampur	...	+ 29	.	+ 141	...
3. Bhimber	+ 1	+ 7	...	+ 3	+ 1
4. Jasrota	...	...	..	+ 4	...
5. Poonch	...	+ 37	..	.	..
6. Bhadarwar	...	..	...	..	.
7. Khas Kashmir	— 447	— 193	— 2	— 613	+ 2
8. Muzaffarabad	...	...	..	+ 6	.
9. Gilgit	...	+ 8	...	+ 4	...
10. Ladakh	...	+ 5	...	.	..
OTHER PARTS OF INDIA.					
Provinces.					
11. Ajmere-Merwara	...	...	...	.	...
12. Andamans and Nicobars	...		.		..
13. Assam	...	..	.		...
14. Baluchistan British and administered districts		...	...	.	.
15. Bengal		...	..	.	.
16. Berar	...	...		.	...
17. Bombay	..	...	.	..	.
18. Burma	.	.	.	..	...
19. Central Provinces	...	...	.	.	...
20. Madras	...	.	..	.	...
21. North-West Provinces and Oudh	...	...	...	.	...
22. Punjab and North-West Frontier Province	...	...	.	.	...
States and Agencies.					
23. Baroda State	...	...	..	.	...
24. Central India Agency	...	...	.	...	...
25. Hyderabad State	...	...	...	...	...
26. Mysore State	...	.	...	.	...
27. Rajputana State	...	...	...	..	...
28. Birth-place not returned	...	...	...	.	...

XI.

KASHMIR STATE.

PLACE.

Internal Migration.—concluded.

INTERCHANGE OF POPULATION BETWEEN STATE, DISTRICTS AND OTHER PROVINCES AND STATES.

Central Provinces.	Madras.	North-West Provinces and Oudh.	Punjab and North-West Frontier Province.	Baroda State.	Central India Agency.	Hyderabad State.	Mysore State.	Rajputana State.	Birth-place not returned.
23	24	25	26	27	28	29	30	31	32
+6	+1	+398	+32,494	+4	+8	+3	...	+74	...
...	+2	+45	+2,135	...	+5	+2	...	+22	...
...	+1	+38	+12,291	+2	+8	+2		+25	...
...	...	+38	+14,540	...	+1	+4		+62	−3
...	...	+32	+812	...	+2	+1	...	+8	...
...	...	+9	+409	.	...	..		...	...
+2	−27	+138	−72,170	−15	+2	+6	−11	−82	...
..	...	+18	+6,798		+3		.	+1	...
...	...	+33	+537	...	..		...	.	...
...	...	+2	+81	...	..	...	..	...	...
...	...	...	...	...	..	.	..	...	...
...	...	...	...	.	...	...		..	...
...	...	...	...	...			..		...
..	...	..	...	..	..	...		...	...
...	...	...	.	..	..	...	..	...	...
...	...	...	..	.	...	..	...	.	...
...	...	...	..	...	..	...	...	...	...
...	...	...	..	...	...	..		..	...
...	...	...	...		..			...	...
...	...	...	...	..		...	...	...	...
..	...	...	.	.	..	..	...		...
...	...	...	...	..		...		...	...
...	...	...	...	...	.	...	...	..	...
.	...	...		..		...		..	...
...	...			...		...			...
...	...	...	...	.		...		.	...
...	...	...	.	...	...	...	...	.	...
...	...	..	...	...	.				...

TABLE XI.

JAMMU AND KASHMIR STATE.

JAMMU CITY.

(BIRTH-PLACE.)

Part II—Detailed distribution of population by birth-place.

TABLE XI.

JAMMU AND KASHMIR STATE.

JAMMU CITY.

(BIRTH-PLACE.)

Part II.—Detailed distribution of population by birth-place.

BIRTH-PLACE	POPULATION		
	Persons.	Males.	Females.
TOTAL JAMMU CITY	36130	22221	13909
A.—DISTRICTS WITHIN THE STATE	26713	16049	10664
(a).—JAMMU PROVINCE	26150	15616	10534
Jammu	23,415	13,527	9,888
Udhampur	1,132	706	426
Bhimber	1,144	1,037	1[illegible]7
Jasrota	364	279	85
Punch Jagir	70	50	20
Bhadarwah Jagir	25	17	8
(b).—KASHMIR PROVINCE	540	417	123
Srinagar	522	402	120
Muzaffarabad	18	15	
(c).—FRONTIER DISTRICTS	23	16	7
Laddakh	8	8	..
Gilgit	15	8	7
B.—PROVINCES OR STATES IN INDIA BEYOND THE STATE	8660	5473	3157
(a).—CONTIGUOUS DISTRICTS OR STATES IN THE PUNJAB	6335	3947	2388
Kangra	242	199	43
Gurdaspur	501	320	181
Sialkote	3,545	2,115	1,432
Gujrat	718	465	253
Gujranwala	847	515	332

TABLE XI.

JAMMU AND KASHMIR STATE.

JAMMU CITY—continued.

(BIRTH-PLACE.)

Part II.—Detailed distribution of population by birth-place.

BIRTH-PLACE.	POPULATION.		
	Persons.	Males.	Females.
Jhelum	211	149	62
Rawalpindi	236	158	78
Hazara	32	26	6
(b).—REMOTE DISTRICTS OR STATES IN PUNJAB	1.925	1.223	702
(1) DISTRICTS	1.250	1.165	685
Hissar	9	3	6
Gurgaon	15	9	6
Delhi	36	21	15
Karnal	3	3	...
Umballa	27	23	4
Simla	13	11	2
Hoshiarpur	273	180	93
Jallundhar	262	168	94
Ludhiana	42	25	17
Ferozepur	16	9	7
Multan	11	6	5
Jhang	30	19	11
Montgomery	5	6	2
Lahore	306	210	156
Amritsar	452	260	192
Shahpur	159	109	50
Malakand	1	1	...
Peshawar	113	94	19
Kohat	7	4	3

TABLE XI.

JAMMU AND KASHMIR STATE.

JAMMU CITY—continued.

(BIRTH-PLACE.)

Part II.—Detailed distribution of population by birth-place.

BIRTH-PLACE.	POPULATION.		
	Persons.	Males.	Females.
Bannoo	2	1	1
Dera Ismail Khan	2	2	...
Dera Ghazi Khan	2	1	1
Sakhar	1	...	1
(2). NATIVE STATES	75	58	17
Patiala	29	20	9
Nabha	5	5	
Kapurthala	33	27	6
Bilaspur	5	4	1
Malerkotla	2	2	
Faridkot	1	...	1
(c).—OTHER PROVINCES OR STATES IN INDIA	400	303	97
(1). CALCUTTA	7	5	2
Calcutta	7	5	2
(3). NORTH-WESTERN PROVINCES AND OUDH	303	241	62
(a).—NORTH-WESTERN PROVINCES	231	184	47
Bajnour	3	2	1
Saharanpur	18	11	7
Muradabad	4	4	...
Cawnpur	28	23	5
Agra	28	18	10
Aligarh	9	6	3
Meerut	22	17	5

TABLE XI.

JAMMU AND KASHMIR STATE.

JAMMU CITY—continued.

(BIRTH-PLACE.)

Part II.—Detailed distribution of population by birth-place.

BIRTH-PLACE.	POPULATION.		
	Persons.	Males.	Females.
Mathra	18	14	4
Farakhabad	14	10	4
Muzafar Nagar	3	2	1
Allahabad	12	11	1
Benares	41	37	4
Bulandshahar	16	16	..
Attawa	9	9	...
Azimgarh	1	1	...
Shahjahanpur	3	2	1
Hamirpur	2	1	1
(b).—OUDH	72	57	15
Lucknow	37	26	11
Faizabad	10	9	1
Barabanki	6	6	...
Gonda	11	11	...
Sultanpur	8	5	3
(3) CENTRAL INDIA AGENCY	4	2	2
Gawaliar	4	2	2
(4) RAJPUTANA AGENCY	65	39	26
Marwar	3	2	
Rajputana	31	17	14
Bharatpur	4	1	3
Bikanir	17	10	7

TABLE XI.

JAMMU AND KASHMIR STATE.

JAMMU CITY.—continued.

(BIRTH-PLACE.)

Part II.—Detailed distribution of population by birth-place

BIRTH-PLACE.	POPULATION.		
	Persons.	Males.	Females.
Alwar	1	..	1
Jaipur	10	9	1
(5). CENTRAL PROVINCES	1	1	..
Jabalpur	1	1	..
(6). BOMBAY PRESIDENCY	11	9	2
Bombay	10	8	..
Haidrabad (Sindh)	1	1	.
(7). BOMBAY PRESIDENCY STATES	1		1
Baroda	1	...	1
(8). BENGAL PRESIDENCY	2	2	..
Bardwan	2	2	..
(9). MADRAS PRESIDENCY	6	4	2
Madras (Unspecified)	2	1	1
Ajmere (Merwara)	4	3	1
C.—BORN IN COUNTRIES ADJACENT TO INDIA	750	694	56
(a).—AFGHANISTAN	171	161	10
Kabul	95	92	3
Kandhar	2	1	1
Jallalabad	2	2	...
Afghanistan (Unspecified)	72	66	6
(b).—YAGISTAN	7	7	...
Yagistan	7	7	...

TABLE XI.

JAMMU AND KASHMIR STATE.

JAMMU CITY.—concluded.

(BIRTH-PLACE.)

Part II.—Detailed distribution of population by birth-place.

BIRTH-PLACE.	POPULATION.		
	Persons.	Males.	Females.
(c)—BALOCHISTAN	2	2	...
Balochistan	2	2	...
(d)—TURKISTAN	3	3	...
Turkistan	3	3	...
( )—NEPAL	567	521	46
Nepal	567	521	46
D.—BORN IN OTHER ASIATIC COUNTRIES	2	2	...
Tartary China	1	1	...
Baghdad	1	1	...
E.—BORN IN COUNTRIES IN EUROPE	5	3	2
England	2	2	...
Scotland	2	1	1
Ireland	1	...	1

TABLE XI.

BIRTH-PLACE.

JAMMU AND KASHMIR STATE.

SRINAGAR CITY.

Part II.—Detailed distribution of population by birth-place.

TABLE XI.

JAMMU AND KASHMIR STATE.

SRINAGAR CITY.

(BIRTH-PLACE.)

Part II.—Detailed distribution of population by birth-place.

			BIRTH-PLACE.	POPULATION. Persons.	Males.	Females.
			TOTAL CITY	**122.618**	**65.542**	**57.376**
A.			DISTRICTS WITHIN THE STATE	**120.279**	**63.922**	**56.357**
	(a).		JAMMU PROVINCE	**1.233**	**966**	**267**
			Jammu	919	731	188
			Udhampur	65	43	22
			Bhimber	131	100	31
			Jasrota	4	1	3
			Punch Jagir	82	64	18
			Bhadarwah Jagir	32	27	5
	(b).		KASHMIR PROVINCE	**118.925**	**62.886**	**56.039**
			Khas	118,863	62,838	56,025
			Muzaffarabad	62	48	14
	(c).		FRONTIER DISTRICTS	**121**	**70**	**51**
			Gilgit	121	70	51
B.			PROVINCES OR STATES IN INDIA BEYOND THE STATE	**1.842**	**1.325**	**517**
	(a).		CONTIGUOUS DISTRICTS OR STATES IN PUNJAB ..	**768**	**570**	**198**
		1	DISTRICTS	**766**	**568**	**198**
			Chitral	2	1	1
			Kangra	21	20	1
			Gurdaspur	33	29	4
			Sialkote	196	131	65

TABLE XI.

JAMMU AND KASHMIR STATE.

SRINAGAR CITY—continued.

(BIRTH-PLACE.)

Part II.—Detailed distribution of population by birth-place.—continued.

		BIRTH-PLACE.	POPULATION.		
			Persons.	Males.	Females.
		Gujrat	143	131	12
		Gujranwala	102	69	33
		Jhelum	41	32	9
		Rawalpindi	228	155	73
	2	STATES	2	2	...
		Chamba	2	2	...
(b)		REMOTE DISTRICTS OR STATES IN PUNJAB	827	583	244
	1	DISTRICTS	787	549	238
		Delhi	25	15	10
		Karnal	2	2	...
		Umballa	12	8	4
		Simla	8	6	2
		Hoshiarpur	61	48	13
		Jullundur	47	34	13
		Ludhiana	34	27	7
		Ferozepur	3	3	...
		Multan	1	1	...
		Jhang	7	3	4
		Lahore	302	196	106
		Amritsar	149	103	46
		Shahpur	57	43	14
		Peshawar	63	50	13
		Kohat			...

TABLE XI.

JAMMU AND KASHMIR STATE.

SRINAGAR CITY.—continued.

(BIRTH-PLACE.)

***Part II.—Detailed distribution of population by birth-place.*—continued.**

			BIRTH PLACE	Population. Persons.	Males.	Females.
			Bannu	4	2	
			Dera Ismail Khan	12	8	
			Dera Ghazi Khan			
		2	NATIVE STATES IN PUNJAB ...	40	34	
			Patiala	12	10	
			Bahawalpur	4	4	
			Kapurthala	16	13	
			Faridkote	2	2	
			Simla State—Bilaspur	6	5	
			OTHER PROVINCES OR STATES IN INDIA	247	172	
	a.		BENGAL	79	44	
		1	DISTRICTS	75	43	
			Gaya	6	6	
			Dinajpur	2	1	
			Bardawan	1		
			Calcutta	64	35	
			Choubis Pargana	2	1	
		2	BENGAL STATES	4	1	
	a.		Orissa	2	1	
			Chetta Nagpur	2		
B.			NORTH-WESTERN PROVINCES AND OUDH	126	100	
	a.		NORTH-WESTERN PROVINCES	108	88	
			Muradabad	3	3	...

TABLE XI.

JAMMU AND KASHMIR STATE.

SRINAGAR CITY.—**continued.**

(BIRTH-PLACE).

Part II — Detailed distribution of population by birth-place.—continued.

			BIRTH-PLACE.	Persons.	Males.	Females.
			Bijnour	19	18	1
			Saharanpur	8	6	2
			Agra	22	15	7
			Cawnpur	6	4	2
			Meerut	8	4	4
			Bareilly	3	3	...
			Aligarh	2	2	...
			Dera Dun	3	2	1
			Mathura	2	2	...
			Garhwal	2	2	...
			Farrakhabad	2	2	...
			Muzaffar Nagar	11	10	1
			Allahabad	9	9	...
			Ghazipur	2	1	1
			Banares	4	3	1
			Bulandshaher	2	2	...
	b.		OUDH	18	12	6
			Oudh	4	4	...
			Lucknow	9	6	3
			Sultanpur	2	1	1
			Faizabad	3	1	2
E.			CENTRAL INDIA AGENCY	2	1	1
			Gawaliar	2	1	1

TABLE XI.

JAMMU AND KASHMIR STATE.

SRINAGAR CITY—continued.

BIRTH-PLACE.)

Part II.—Detailed distribution of population by birth-place.—continued.

		BIRTH PLACE	Population. Persons.	Males.	Females.
F.		RAJPUTANA AGENCY	9	8	1
		Bikanir	7	7	...
		Alwar	2	1	1
G.		CENTRAL PROVINCES	2	2	...
		Sagar	2	2	...
H.		BOMBAY PRESIDENCY DISTRICTS AND STATES	18	10	8
	a.	DISTRICTS	18	10	8
		Shikarpur	4	4	...
		Karrachi	3	1	2
		Bombay	9	4	5
		Balgam	2	1	1
	b.	STATES	...	...	...
I.		MADRAS PRESIDENCY	5	4	1
		Madras	5	4	1
J.		AJMERE-MERWARA	4	2	2
		Ajmere-Merwara	4	2	2
K.		ASSAM	2	1	1
		Salhat	2	1	1
L.		BORN IN COUNTRIES ADJACENT TO INDIA ...	417	256	161
	a.	AFGHANISTAN	170	88	82
		Kabul	155	77	78
		Herat	9	6	3
		Kandhar	6	5	1

TABLE XI.

JAMMU AND KASHMIR STATE.

SRINAGAR CITY.—concluded.

(BIRTH-PLACE.)

Part II.—Detailed distribution of population by birth-place.—concluded.

		BIRTH-PLACE.	Population. Persons.	Population. Males.	Population. Females.
	b.	YAGISTAN	**17**	**15**	**2**
		Yagistan	17	15	2
	c.	TURKISTAN	**21**	**17**	**4**
		Badakhshan	2	1	1
		Yarkand	19	16	3
	d.	NEPAL	**209**	**136**	**73**
		Nepal	209	136	73
M.		BORN IN COUNTRIES IN EUROPE	**71**	**36**	**35**
		UNITED KINGDOM	**53**	**25**	**22**
		England	42	17	
		Wales	2	1	1
		Scotland	4	3	1
		Ireland	5	4	1
		France	7	2	5
		Belgium	2	1	1
		Portugal	7	7	...
		Switzerland	2	1	1
N.		BORN IN AFRICA	**5**	**1**	**4**
		Egypt	2	1	1
		Africa (Unspecified)	3	...	3
O.		BORN IN AMERICA	**2**	**1**	**1**
		America (Unspecified)	2	1	1
P.		BORN IN AUSTRALIA	**2**	**1**	**1**
		Australia (Unspecified)	2	1	1

TABLE XII.—INFIRMITIES.

PART I.—DISTRIBUTION BY AGES.

PART II.—DISTRIBUTION BY DISTRICTS.

TABLE XII.—Infirmities.

PART I.—Distribution by Ages.

Age	Population afflicted. Persons.	Males.	Females.	Insane. Persons.	Males.	Females.	Deaf-mutes. Persons.	Males.	Females.	Blind. Persons.	Males.	Females.	Lepers. Persons.	Males.	Females.	Remarks.
1	2	3	4	5	6	7	8	9	10	11	12	13	14	15	16	17
Total State ...	**9,449**	**5,896**	**3,553**	**1,419**	**919**	**500**	**3,349**	**2,101**	**1,248**	**3,084**	**1,769**	**1,315**	**1,597**	**1,107**	**490**	
0 and under 1 ...	17	8	9	2	1	1	2	1	1	11	5	6	2	1	1	
1 " " 2 ...	20	14	6	4	2	2	9	5	4	6	6	...	1	1	...	
2 " " 3 ...	68	36	32	7	3	4	38	20	18	20	12	8	3	1	2	
3 " " 4 ...	130	76	54	20	14	6	75	37	38	27	22	5	8	3	5	
4 " " 5 ...	156	96	60	25	17	8	83	53	30	37	18	19	11	8	3	
Total 0 and under 5 ...	391	230	161	58	37	21	207	116	91	101	63	38	25	14	11	
5 and under 10 ...	961	589	372	196	118	78	407	294	203	195	126	69	73	51	22	
10 " " 15 ...	1,001	628	373	195	122	73	484	316	168	235	134	101	87	56	31	
15 " " 20 ...	846	509	337	154	107	47	364	211	153	227	127	100	101	64	37	
20 " " 25 ...	748	466	282	148	92	56	296	190	106	207	119	88	97	65	32	
25 " " 30 ...	812	530	282	134	100	34	324	213	111	225	131	94	129	86	43	
30 " " 35 ...	785	496	289	141	95	46	264	164	100	221	127	94	159	110	49	
35 " " 40 ...	520	342	178	79	54	25	161	110	51	139	78	61	141	100	41	
40 " " 45 ...	679	434	245	75	45	30	188	119	69	224	118	106	192	152	40	
45 " " 50 ...	338	243	95	31	25	6	88	63	25	121	79	42	98	76	22	
50 " " 55 ...	609	370	230	65	37	28	154	91	63	238	126	112	152	116	36	
55 " " 60 ...	209	125	84	21	10	11	37	21	16	106	63	43	45	31	14	
60 " over ...	1,550	934	616	122	77	45	285	193	92	845	478	367	298	186	112	
Unspecified ...	...	...	...	...	...	...	...	...	...	...	...	...	...	...	...	
Total Jammu Province ...	**4,253**	**2,716**	**1,537**	**534**	**365**	**169**	**1,833**	**1,161**	**672**	**1,214**	**709**	**505**	**672**	**481**	**191**	
0 and under 1 ...	3	1	2	1	...	1	1	...	1	1	1	...	...	...	...	
1 " " 2 ...	4	2	2	...	...	...	4	2	2	...	...	...	...	...	...	
2 " " 3 ...	22	9	13	...	...	...	17	8	9	5	1	4	...	...	...	
3 " " 4 ...	37	20	17	7	5	2	25	11	14	5	4	1	...	...	...	
4 " " 5 ...	55	33	22	8	5	3	39	24	15	5	2	3	3	2	1	
Total 0 and under 5 ...	121	65	56	16	10	6	86	45	41	16	8	8	3	2	1	
5 and under 10 ...	325	195	130	51	30	21	223	130	93	43	30	13	8	5	3	
10 " " 15 ...	367	236	131	47	34	13	231	151	80	73	40	33	16	11	5	
15 " " 20 ...	322	206	116	52	39	13	180	111	69	61	38	23	29	18	11	
20 " " 25 ...	304	198	106	49	35	14	168	107	61	58	36	22	29	20	9	
25 " " 30 ...	397	273	124	75	58	17	198	136	62	75	48	27	49	31	18	
30 " " 35 ...	392	253	139	62	42	20	187	113	74	76	48	28	67	50	17	
35 " " 40 ...	243	160	83	39	25	14	83	56	27	56	35	21	65	44	21	
40 " " 45 ...	372	251	121	40	23	17	131	83	48	98	60	38	103	85	18	
45 " " 50 ...	175	128	47	12	9	3	58	40	18	48	34	14	57	45	12	
50 " " 55 ...	297	185	112	28	17	11	94	54	40	96	54	42	79	60	19	
55 " " 60 ...	125	76	40	12	7	5	26	14	12	58	32	25	29	22	7	
60 " over ...	813	490	323	51	36	15	168	121	47	456	245	211	138	88	50	
Unspecified ...	...	...	...	...	...	...	...	...	...	...	...	...	...	...	...	

Total Kashmir Province	**4,518**	**2,845**	**1,673**	**845**	**536**	**309**	**1,183**	**760**	**423**	**1,653**	**968**	**685**	**837**	**581**	**256**
0 and under 1	11	5	6	1	1	...	...	...	...	8	3	5	2	1	1
1 " " 2	13	11	2	4	2	2	2	2	...	6	6	...	1	1	...
2 " " 3	29	17	12	7	3	4	8	4	4	11	9	2	3	1	2
3 " " 4	62	41	21	11	8	3	27	14	13	19	16	3	5	3	2
4 " " 5	75	48	27	17	12	5	25	17	8	25	13	12	8	6	2
Total 0 and under 5	190	122	68	40	26	14	62	37	25	69	47	22	19	12	7
5 and under 10	544	349	195	140	86	54	203	134	69	142	89	53	59	40	19
10 " " 15	562	346	216	143	86	57	198	126	72	155	92	63	66	42	24
15 " " 20	472	283	189	96	67	29	152	89	63	154	81	73	70	46	24
20 " " 25	405	249	156	91	54	37	112	75	37	137	77	60	65	43	22
25 " " 30	388	241	147	57	41	16	111	67	44	144	80	64	76	53	23
30 " " 35	361	222	139	77	53	24	62	40	22	138	74	64	84	55	29
35 " " 40	226	159	67	36	26	10	55	41	14	67	39	28	68	53	15
40 " " 45	285	173	112	34	21	13	48	31	17	118	55	63	85	66	19
45 " " 50	119	90	29	16	14	2	23	17	6	48	32	16	32	27	5
50 " " 55	281	170	111	36	19	17	50	31	19	131	69	62	64	51	13
55 " " 60	71	44	27	8	2	6	8	5	3	43	29	14	12	8	4
60 " over	614	397	217	71	41	30	99	67	32	307	204	103	137	85	52
Unspecified	...	...	...	...	...	...	...	...	...	...	...	...	...	...	...
Total Frontier Districts	**678**	**335**	**343**	**40**	**18**	**22**	**333**	**180**	**153**	**217**	**92**	**125**	**88**	**45**	**43**
0 and under 1	3	2	1	...	...	...	1	1	...	2	1	1	...	...	
1 " " 2	3	1	2	...	...	...	3	1	2	...	...		...	...	...
2 " " 3	17	10	7	...	...	...	13	8	5	4	2	2	...	...	...
3 " " 4	31	15	16	2	1	1	23	12	11	3	2	1	3	...	3
4 " " 5	26	15	11	...	...	...	19	12	7	7	3	4	...	...	...
Total 0 and under 5	80	43	37	2	1	1	59	34	25	16	8	8	3	...	3
5 and under 10	92	45	47	5	2	3	71	30	41	10	7	3	6	6	...
10 " " 15	72	46	26	5	2	3	55	39	16	7	2	5	5	3	2
15 " " 20	52	20	32	6	1	5	32	11	21	12	8	4	2	...	2
20 " " 25	39	19	20	8	3	5	16	8	8	12	6	6	3	2	1
25 " " 30	27	16	11	2	1	1	15	10	5	6	3	3	4	2	2
30 " " 35	32	21	11	2	...	2	15	11	4	7	5	2	8	5	3
35 " " 40	51	23	28	4	3	1	23	13	10	16	4	12	8	3	5
40 " " 45	22	10	12	1	1	...	9	5	4	8	3	5	4	1	3
45 " " 50	44	25	19	3	2	1	7	6	1	25	13	12	9	4	5
50 " " 55	31	15	16	1	1	...	10	6	4	11	3	8	9	5	4
55 " " 60	13	5	8	1	1	...	3	2	1	5	1	4	4	1	3
60 " over	123	47	76	...	...	...	18	5	13	82	29	53	23	13	10
Unspecified	...	...	...	...	...	...	...	...	...	...	...	...	...	...	...

TABLE XII.—Infirmities.

PART II.—Distribution by Districts.

District	Afflicted.			Insane.			Deaf-mutes.			Blind.			Lepers.			Remarks.
	Persons.	Males.	Females.	Persons.	Males.	Females.	Persons.	Males.	Females.	Persons.	Males.	Females.	Persons.	Males.	Females.	
1	2	3	4	5	6	7	8	9	10	11	12	13	14	15	16	17
Total State	9,449	5,896	3,553	1,419	919	500	3,349	2,101	1,248	3,084	1,769	1,315	1,597	1,107	490	
Total Jammu Province	4,253	2,716	1,537	534	365	169	1,533	1,161	672	1,214	709	505	672	481	191	
Jammu	923	571	352	85	57	28	391	248	143	407	228	179	40	38	2	
Udhampur	1,146	733	413	167	114	53	515	334	181	251	141	110	213	144	69	
Bhimber	1,106	714	392	150	107	43	484	301	183	278	172	106	194	134	60	
Jasrota	683	457	226	87	56	31	293	191	102	207	129	78	96	81	15	
Punch Jagir	236	153	83	32	22	10	82	50	32	38	21	17	84	60	24	
Bhadarwah Jagir	159	88	71	13	9	4	68	37	31	33	18	15	45	24	21	
Total Kashmir Province	4,518	2,845	1,673	845	536	309	1,183	760	423	1,653	968	685	837	581	256	
Khas	3,956	2,496	1,460	779	501	278	980	637	343	1,503	887	616	694	471	223	
Musaffarabad	562	349	213	66	35	31	203	123	80	150	81	69	143	110	33	
Total Frontier Districts	678	335	343	40	18	22	333	180	153	217	92	125	88	45	43	

TABLE XIII.

CASTE, TRIBE, RACE OR NATIONALITY.

TABLE XIII.

Caste, Tribe, Race or Nationality.

Caste, Tribe, Race or Nationality.	Total Population.			Provinces with Districts. — Jammu Province.																				
				Jammu District.			Udhampur District.			Bhimber District.			Jasrota District			Punch Jágir.			Bhadarwah Jágir.			Total Jammu Province.		
	Persons.	Males.	Females.	Persons.	Males.	Females.	Persons.	Males.	Females.	Persons.	Males.	Females.	Persons.	Males.	Females.	Persons.	Males.	Females.	Persons.	Males.	Females.	Persons	Males.	Females.
1	2	3	4	5	6	7	8	9	10	11	12	13	14	15	16	17	18	19	20	21	22	23	24	25
Grand Total ...	2,905,578	1,542,057	1,363,521	344,018	185,722	158,296	284,048	151,425	132,623	400,229	210,075	190,154	154,213	82,391	71,822	304,488	160,679	143,809	34,311	17,500	16,811	1,521,307	807,792	713,515
Total Hindus (including Aryans) ...	689,073	370,801	318,272	207,412	111,757	95,655	171,470	91,050	80,420	83,051	44,459	38,592	121,779	64,674	57,105	20,519	11,482	9,037	21,946	10,996	10,950	626,177	334,418	291,759
Attarda Samko ...	21	1	20	...	...	...	...	...	...	...	...	...	...	...	...	...	...	...	...	...	...	...	...	...
Arora ...	5,164	4,297	867	28	17	11	1,049	962	87	318	107	211	137	5	132	1,827	1,792	35	34	11	23	3,393	2,894	499
Acharaj ...	219	116	103	15	14	1	77	8	69	9	6	3	65	55	10	7	5	2	1	1	...	174	89	85
Antrade matter ...	3	3	...	3	3	...	...	...	...	...	...	...	...	...	...	...	...	...	...	...	...	3	3	...
Aisar ...	2	2	...	2	2	...	...	...	...	...	...	...	...	...	...	...	...	...	...	...	...	2	2	...
Anand ...	113	63	50	...	...	...	...	...	...	...	...	...	...	...	...	...	...	...	...	...	...	...	...	...
Abadpa ...	52	32	20	...	...	...	...	...	...	...	...	...	...	...	...	...	...	...	...	...	...	...	...	...
Abotra ...	1	1	...	...	...	...	...	...	...	...	...	...	...	...	...	...	...	...	...	...	...	...	...	...
Athcari ...	5	5	...	...	...	...	...	...	...	...	...	...	...	...	...	...	...	...	...	...	...	...	...	...
Achhar ...	1	1	...	...	...	...	...	...	...	...	...	...	...	...	...	...	...	...	...	...	...	...	...	...
Arotra ...	3	3	...	...	...	...	...	...	...	...	...	...	...	...	...	...	...	...	...	...	...	...	...	...
Bania ...	80	56	24	80	56	24	...	...	...	...	...	...	...	...	...	...	...	...	...	...	...	80	56	24
Banjo ...	1	1	...	1	1	...	...	...	...	...	...	...	...	...	...	...	...	...	...	...	...	1	1	...
Bhatti ...	4	4	...	1	1	...	...	...	...	...	...	...	...	...	...	...	...	...	...	...	...	1	1	...
Badhan ...	16	...	16	...	...	...	...	...	...	16	...	16	...	...	...	...	...	...	...	...	...	16	...	16
Bhat ...	53	27	26	30	23	7	21	3	18	2	1	1	...	...	...	...	...	...	...	...	...	53	27	26
Baloch ...	10	10	...	10	10	...	...	...	...	...	...	...	...	...	...	...	...	...	...	...	...	10	10	...
Bhatra ...	26	16	10	...	...	...	...	...	...	...	...	...	...	...	...	...	...	...	...	...	...	...	...	...
Bazigar ...	35	14	21	...	...	...	...	...	...	31	13	18	...	...	...	...	...	...	...	...	...	31	13	18
Bhut ...	4	3	1	...	...	...	4	3	1	...	...	...	...	...	...	...	...	...	...	...	...	4	3	1
Bharni ...	1	...	1	...	...	...	1	...	1	...	...	...	...	...	...	...	...	...	...	...	...	1	...	1
Bharot ...	1	...	1	...	...	...	1	...	1	...	...	...	...	...	...	...	...	...	...	...	...	1	...	1
Badu ...	26	13	13	...	...	...	26	13	13	...	...	...	...	...	...	...	...	...	...	...	...	26	13	13
Barwala ...	1,184	622	562	...	...	...	315	171	144	560	295	265	104	35	69	...	...	...	196	115	81	1,175	616	559
Brahmin ...	185,869	98,159	87,710	45,960	21,960	24,000	42,357	22,653	19,704	23,332	12,748	10,584	37,419	20,107	17,312	3,140	2,343	797	9,430	4,604	4,826	161,638	84,415	77,223
Do. Pandit ...	579	335	244	30	14	16	...	...	...	...	...	...	7	3	4	...	...	...	1	1	...	38	18	20
Batwal ...	3,234	1,785	1,449	2,886	1,696	1,190	97	65	32	34	10	24	216	13	203	...	...	...	...	...	...	3,233	1,784	1,449
Baisht ...	8,159	3,997	4,162	...	...	...	...	...	...	6,159	2,997	3,162	2,000	1,000	1,000	...	...	...	...	...	...	8,159	3,997	4,162
Banial ...	1	...	1	...	...	...	...	...	...	1	...	1	...	...	...	...	...	...	...	...	...	1	...	1
Bathoria ...	9	9	...	...	...	...	...	...	...	...	...	...	9	9	...	...	...	...	...	...	...	9	9	...
Baotra ...	15	8	7	...	...	...	...	...	...	...	...	...	15	8	7	...	...	...	...	...	...	15	8	7
Bakal ...	578	478	100	...	...	...	...	...	...	...	...	...	...	...	...	...	...	...	...	...	...	...	...	...
Beragi ...	12	10	2	...	...	...	...	...	...	...	...	...	...	...	...	...	...	...	...	...	...	...	...	...
Bakla ...	1	1	...	...	...	...	...	...	...	...	...	...	...	...	...	...	...	...	...	...	...	...	...	...
Bajal ...	2	2	...	...	...	...	...	...	...	...	...	...	...	...	...	...	...	...	...	...	...	...	...	...
Bagial ...	2	2	...	...	...	...	...	...	...	...	...	...	...	...	...	...	...	...	...	...	...	...	...	...
Badiarattar ...	5	3	2	...	...	...	...	...	...	...	...	...	...	...	...	...	...	...	...	...	...	...	...	...

PROVINCES WITH DISTRICTS.

Caste, Tribe, Race or Nationality.	Kashmir Province. Khás District. Persons.	Males.	Females.	Muzaffarabad District. Persons.	Males.	Females.	Total Kashmir Province. Persons.	Males.	Females.	Frontier Districts. Ladakh District. Persons.	Males.	Females.	Gilgit District. Persons.	Males.	Females.	Total Frontier Districts. Persons.	Males.	Females.
	26	27	28	29	30	31	32	33	34	35	36	37	38	39	40	41	42	43
Grand Total ...	989,196	526,158	463,038	168,198	90,729	77,469	1,157,394	616,887	540,507	165,992	83,600	82,392	60,885	33,768	27,107	226,877	117,378	109,499
Total Hindus (including Aryans) ...	56,517	31,718	24,799	4,165	2,543	1,622	60,682	34,261	26,421	213	189	24	2,001	1,933	68	2,214	2,122	92
Attarda Bamko ...	21	1	20	...	...	...	21	1	20	...	...	...	...	...	...	...	...	...
Arora ...	1,023	991	32	445	110	335	1,468	1,101	367	63	62	1	240	240	...	303	302	1
Aoharaj ...	40	26	14	5	1	4	45	27	18	...	...	...	...	...	...	...	...	...
Antrade mattor ...	...	...	...	...	...	...	...	...	...	...	...	...	...	...	...	...	...	...
Aisar ...	...	...	...	...	...	...	...	...	...	...	...	...	...	...	...	...	...	...
Anand ...	113	63	50	...	...	...	113	63	50	...	...	...	...	...	...	...	...	...
Abadpa ...	52	32	20	...	...	...	52	32	20	...	...	...	...	...	...	...	...	...
Abotra ...	...	...	...	...	...	...	...	...	...	...	...	...	1	1	...	1	1	...
Athsari ...	...	...	...	...	...	...	...	...	...	...	...	...	5	5	...	5	5	...
Achhar ...	...	...	...	...	...	...	...	...	...	...	...	...	1	1	...	1	1	...
Arotra ...	...	...	...	...	...	...	...	...	...	...	...	...	3	3	...	3	3	...
Bania ...	...	...	...	...	...	...	...	...	...	...	...	...	...	...	...	...	...	...
Banjo ...	...	...	...	...	...	...	...	...	...	...	...	...	...	...	...	...	...	...
Bhatti ...	...	...	...	3	3	...	3	3	...	...	...	...	...	...	...	...	...	...
Badhau ...	...	...	...	...	...	...	...	...	...	...	...	...	...	...	...	...	...	...
Bhat ...	...	...	...	...	...	...	...	...	...	...	...	...	...	...	...	...	...	...
Baloch ...	...	...	...	...	...	...	...	...	...	...	...	...	...	...	...	...	...	...
Bhatre ...	...	...	...	26	16	10	26	16	10	...	...	...	...	...	...	...	...	...
Bazigar ...	...	...	...	...	...	...	...	...	...	4	1	3	...	...	...	4	1	3
Bhut ...	...	...	...	...	...	...	...	...	...	...	...	...	...	...	...	...	...	...
Bharai ...	...	...	...	...	...	...	...	...	...	...	...	...	...	...	...	...	...	...
Bharot ...	...	...	...	...	...	...	...	...	...	...	...	...	...	...	...	...	...	...
Badu ...	...	...	...	...	...	...	...	...	...	...	...	...	...	...	...	...	...	...
Barwala ...	...	...	...	6	3	3	6	3	3	...	...	...	3	3	...	3	3	...
Brahmin ...	23,526	13,291	10,235	705	453	252	24,231	13,744	10,487	...	...	...	...	...	...	...	...	...
Do. Pandit ...	539	316	223	2	1	1	541	316	224	...	...	...	...	...	...	...	...	...
Batwal ...	...	...	...	1	1	...	1	1	...	...	...	...	...	...	...	...	...	...
Basisht ...	...	...	...	...	...	...	...	...	...	...	...	...	...	...	...	...	...	...
Banial ...	...	...	...	...	...	...	...	...	...	...	...	...	...	...	...	...	...	...
Batheria ...	...	...	...	...	...	...	...	...	...	...	...	...	...	...	...	...	...	...
Baotra ...	...	...	...	...	...	...	...	...	...	...	...	...	...	...	...	...	...	...
Bakal ...	205	135	70	373	334	39	578	469	109	...	...	...	...	...	...	...	...	...
Beragi ...	12	10	2	...	...	...	12	10	2	...	...	...	...	...	...	...	...	...
Bakla ...	...	...	...	1	1	...	1	1	...	...	...	...	...	...	...	...	...	...
Bajal ...	...	...	...	...	...	...	...	...	...	2	2	...	...	...	...	2	2	...
Bagial ...	...	...	...	...	...	...	...	...	...	2	2	...	...	...	...	2	2	...
Badiaratar ...	...	...	...	...	...	...	...	...	...	5	3	2	...	...	...	5	3	2

TABLE XIII.

Caste, Tribe, Race or Nationality.

Caste, Tribe, Race or Nationality.	Total Population.			Provinces with Districts. — Jammu Province. — Jammu District.			Udhampur District.			Bhimber District.			Jasrota District.			Punch Jagir.			Bhadarwah Jagir.			Total Jammu Province.		
	Persons.	Males.	Females.	Persons.	Males.	Females.	Persons.	Males.	Females.	Persons.	Males.	Females.	Persons.	Males.	Females.	Persons.	Males.	Females.	Persons.	Males.	Females.	Persons.	Males.	Females.
1	2	3	4	5	6	7	8	9	10	11	12	13	14	15	16	17	18	19	20	21	22	23	24	25
Balla	1	1	...	...	...	...	...	...	...	...	...	...	...	...	...	...	...	...	...	...	...	...	...	...
Bandear	1	1	...	...	...	...	...	...	...	...	...	...	...	...	...	...	...	...	...	...	...	...	...	...
Bachge	20	20	...	...	...	...	...	...	...	...	...	...	...	...	...	...	...	...	...	...	...	...	...	...
China	154	94	60	48	42	6	...	...	...	...	...	...	...	...	...	...	...	...	8	8	...	56	50	6
Chharmara	14	9	5	...	...	...	...	...	...	...	...	...	...	...	...	...	...	...	...	...	...	...	...	...
Chmar	35,123	18,251	16,872	12,320	6,555	5,765	7,434	3,887	3,547	7,791	3,868	3,923	6,625	3,499	3,126	314	139	175	405	208	257	34,940	18,156	16,798
Chohra	39	18	21	3	1	2	1	1	...	...	...	...	...	...	...	33	16	17	...	...	...	37	18	19
Challa	54	33	21	...	...	...	9	9	...	...	...	...	...	...	...	...	...	...	...	...	...	9	9	...
Darojirahmatri	3	2	1	...	...	...	...	...	...	...	...	...	...	...	...	...	...	...	...	...	...	...	...	...
Darzi	139	60	79	...	...	...	...	...	...	...	...	...	...	...	...	...	...	...	...	...	...	...	...	...
Dosali	3	3	...	...	...	...	...	...	...	...	...	...	...	...	...	...	...	...	...	...	...	...	...	...
Darda	4	4	...	...	...	...	...	...	...	...	...	...	...	...	...	...	...	...	...	...	...	...	...	...
Dhobi	227	123	104	...	...	...	...	...	...	225	121	104	...	...	...	...	...	...	...	...	...	225	121	104
Diwan	159	95	64	...	...	...	...	...	...	...	...	...	...	...	...	...	...	...	...	...	...	...	...	...
Dand	470	188	282	...	...	...	...	...	...	...	...	...	...	...	...	...	...	...	...	...	...	...	...	...
Darbari	223	148	75	...	...	...	...	...	...	...	...	...	...	...	...	...	...	...	...	...	...	...	...	...
Degu	62	30	32	...	...	...	...	...	...	...	...	...	...	...	...	...	...	...	...	...	...	...	...	...
Danafanja	107	56	51	...	...	...	...	...	...	...	...	...	...	...	...	...	...	...	...	...	...	...	...	...
Darwas	47	16	31	...	...	...	...	...	...	...	...	...	...	...	...	...	...	...	...	...	...	...	...	...
Deskoshki	31	31	...	...	...	...	...	...	...	...	...	...	...	...	...	...	...	...	...	...	...	...	...	...
Donial	13,912	6,825	7,087	480	260	220	590	300	290	336	161	175	80	45	35	...	...	...	...	...	...	1,486	766	720
Dhaigari	1	1	...	...	...	...	...	...	...	...	...	...	...	...	...	...	...	...	...	...	...	...	...	...
Fakir	18,070	9,319	8,751	1,605	960	735	1,674	885	789	4,903	3,337	2,566	2,781	1,371	1,410	1,748	1,051	697	547	321	226	13,348	6,925	6,423
Inderpal	25	...	25	...	...	...	...	...	...	...	...	...	...	...	...	...	...	...	...	...	...	...	...	...
Jat	24,837	12,872	11,965	8,302	4,696	3,606	366	156	210	13,281	6,898	6,383	2,737	1,006	1,731	93	61	32	...	...	...	24,779	12,817	11,962
Jhiwar	12,748	6,743	6,005	7,739	4,154	3,585	814	521	293	1,036	563	473	2,837	1,323	1,514	182	104	78	17	10	7	12,625	6,675	5,950
Jhwar	84	59	25	4	4	...	...	...	...	4	4	...	76	51	25	...	...	...	...	...	...	84	59	25
Janny	145	84	61	...	...	...	...	...	...	...	...	...	...	...	...	...	...	...	...	...	...	...	...	...
Khattri	47,887	27,929	19,958	16,173	9,757	6,416	11,522	5,951	5,571	5,086	2,925	2,161	5,431	3,941	1,490	2,700	1,434	1,356	1,213	617	596	40,215	22,625	17,590
" Kapur	126	61	65	...	...	...	...	...	...	115	56	59	...	...	...	...	...	...	...	...	...	115	56	59
" Malhottray ..	150	79	71	...	...	...	...	...	...	141	71	70	...	...	...	...	...	...	...	...	...	141	71	70
" Khanna	254	103	151	...	...	...	...	...	...	23	12	11	...	...	...	231	91	140	...	...	...	254	103	151
" Bedi	9	7	2	...	...	...	...	...	...	9	7	2	...	...	...	...	...	...	...	...	...	9	7	2
" Sodhi	11	6	5	...	...	...	...	...	...	11	6	5	...	...	...	...	...	...	...	...	...	11	6	5
" Kambilla	5	3	2	...	...	...	...	...	...	...	...	...	...	...	...	...	...	...	...	...	...	...	...	...
Labana	5,769	3,096	2,673	3,555	1,712	1,843	146	96	50	684	409	275	700	326	374	575	452	123	...	...	...	5,660	2,995	2,665
Lakhi	11	11	...	...	...	...	...	...	...	...	...	...	...	...	...	...	...	...	...	...	...	...	...	...
Langrea	222	206	16	...	...	...	...	...	...	...	...	...	...	...	...	...	...	...	...	...	...	...	...	...
Ladari	153	72	81	...	...	...	...	...	...	...	...	...	...	...	...	...	...	...	...	...	...	...	...	...
Lohar	1,345	660	685	54	35	19	...	...	...	931	488	443	...	...	...	282	96	186	3	3	...	1,270	622	648
Mahájan	27,459	13,771	13,688	9,815	5,560	4,255	3,432	1,877	1,555	3,062	2,130	1,832	3,534	1,844	1,690	6,234	2,102	4,132	230	98	132	27,207	13,611	13,596
Megh	4,713	3,642	671	32	19	13	838	786	52	275	82	193	153	6	147	2,001	1,981	20	23	6	17	3,332	2,880	442

PROVINCES WITH DISTRICTS.

KASHMIR PROVINCE.

Caste, Tribe, Race or Nationality.	Khas District. Persons.	Khas District. Males.	Khas District. Females.	Muzaffarabad District. Persons.	Muzaffarabad District. Males.	Muzaffarabad District. Females.	Total Kashmir Province. Persons.	Total Kashmir Province. Males.	Total Kashmir Province. Females.
	26	27	28	29	30	31	32	33	34
Balla	...	...	...	...	...	...	...	...	...
Bandear	...	...	...	...	...	...	...	...	...
Bachgo	...	...	...	...	...	...	...	...	...
China	98	44	54	...	...	...	98	44	54
Chhharmara	...	...	...	...	...	...	...	...	...
Chmar	146	74	72	9	6	3	155	80	75
Chohra	...	...	...	2	...	2	2	...	2
Challa	45	24	21	...	...	...	45	24	21
Darojirahmatri	...	...	...	...	28	...	...	...	...
Darzi	139	60	79	...	...	...	139	60	79
Doaali	...	...	...	...	...	...	...	...	...
Darda	...	...	...	...	...	...	...	...	...
Dhobi	...	...	...	2	2	...	2	2	...
Diwan	150	95	64	...	...	...	150	95	64
Dand	470	188	282	...	...	...	470	188	282
Darbari	223	148	75	...	...	...	223	148	75
Degu	62	30	32	...	...	...	62	30	32
Danafanja	107	56	51	...	...	...	107	56	51
Darwas	47	16	31	...	...	...	47	16	31
Deskoshki	31	31	...	...	...	...	31	31	...
Donial	12,426	6,059	6,367	...	...	...	12,426	6,059	6,367
Dhaigari	1	1	...	...	...	...	1	1	...
Fakir	4,366	2,200	2,166	55	40	15	4,421	2,240	2,181
Inderpal	...	...	...	25	...	25	25	...	25
Jat	...	...	...	10	7	3	10	7	3
Jhiwar	115	63	52	8	5	3	123	68	55
Jhwar	...	...	...	...	...	...	...	...	...
Janny	145	84	61	...	...	...	145	84	61
Khattri	4,947	2,674	2,273	616	538	78	5,563	3,212	2,351
" Kapur ...	4	1	3	5	4	1	9	5	4
" Malhottray ...	1	1	...	8	7	1	9	8	1
" Khanna ...	...	...	...	...	...	...	...	...	...
" Bedi ...	...	...	...	...	...	...	...	...	...
" Sodhi	...	...	...	...	...	...	...	...	...
" Kambilla ...	...	...	...	...	...	...	...	...	...
Labana	19	12	7	68	68	...	87	80	7
Lakhi	...	...	...	11	11	...	11	11	...
Langria	...	...	...	222	206	16	222	206	16
Ladari	153	72	81	...	...	...	153	72	81
Lohar	...	...	...	159	122	37	159	122	37
Mahajan	133	66	67	65	40	25	198	106	93
Megh	758	721	37	233	41	192	991	762	229

FRONTIER DISTRICTS.

Caste, Tribe, Race or Nationality.	Ladakh District. Persons.	Ladakh District. Males.	Ladakh District. Females.	Gilgit District. Persons.	Gilgit District. Males.	Gilgit District. Females.	Total Frontier Districts. Persons.	Total Frontier Districts. Males.	Total Frontier Districts. Females.
	35	36	37	38	39	40	41	42	43
Balla	1	1	...	...	...	...	1	1	...
Bandear	1	1	...	...	...	...	1	1	...
Bachgo	...	...	...	20	20	...	20	20	...
China	...	...	...	...	...	...	...	...	...
Chhharmara	14	9	5	...	...	...	14	9	5
Chmar	...	...	...	19	15	4	19	15	4
Chohra	...	...	...	...	...	...	...	...	...
Challa	...	...	...	...	...	...	...	...	...
Darojirahmatri	3	2	1	...	...	...	3	2	1
Darzi	...	...	...	...	...	...	...	...	...
Doaali	...	...	...	3	3	...	3	3	...
Darda	...	...	...	4	4	...	4	4	...
Dhobi	...	...	...	...	...	...	...	...	...
Diwan	...	...	...	...	...	...	...	...	...
Dand	...	...	...	...	...	...	...	...	...
Darbari	...	...	...	...	...	...	...	...	...
Degu	...	...	...	...	...	...	...	...	...
Danafanja	...	...	...	...	...	...	...	...	...
Darwas	...	...	...	...	...	...	...	...	...
Deskoshki	...	...	...	...	...	...	...	...	...
Donial	...	...	...	...	...	...	...	...	...
Dhaigari	...	...	...	...	...	...	...	...	...
Fakir	132	56	76	169	98	71	301	154	147
Inderpal	...	...	...	...	...	...	...	...	...
Jat	1	1	...	47	47	...	48	48	...
Jhiwar	...	...	...	...	...	...	...	...	...
Jhwar	...	...	...	...	...	...	...	...	...
Janny	...	...	...	...	...	...	...	...	...
Khattri	2	1	1	107	91	16	109	92	17
" Kapur ...	...	...	...	2	...	2	2	...	2
" Malhottray ...	...	...	...	...	...	...	...	...	...
" Khanna ...	...	...	...	...	...	...	...	...	...
" Bedi ...	...	...	...	...	...	...	...	...	...
" Sodhi	...	...	...	...	...	...	...	...	...
" Kambilla ...	...	...	...	5	3	2	5	3	2
Labana	4	4	...	18	17	1	22	21	1
Lakhi	...	...	...	...	...	...	...	...	...
Langria	...	...	...	...	...	...	...	...	...
Ladari	...	...	...	...	...	...	...	...	...
Lohar	...	...	...	...	...	...	...	...	...
Mahajan	54	54	...	...	...	...	54	54	...
Megh	...	...	...	...	...	...	...	...	...

TABLE XIII.

Caste, Tribe, Race or Nationality

Caste, Tribe, Race or Nationality.	Total Population.			Provinces with Districts. Jammu Province. Jammu District.			Udhampur District.			Bhimber District.			Jasrota District.			Punch Jagir.			Bhadarwah Jagir.			Total Jammu Province.		
	Persons.	Males.	Females.	Persons.	Males.	Females.	Persons.	Males.	Females.	Persons.	Males.	Females.	Persons.	Males.	Females.	Persons.	Males.	Females.	Persons.	Males.	Females.	Persons.	Males.	Females.
1	2	3	4	5	6	7	8	9	10	11	12	13	14	15	16	17	18	19	20	21	22	23	24	25
Total Mohial ...	**4,833**	**2,617**	**2,216**	**1,032**	**469**	**563**	**304**	**176**	**128**	**1,001**	**546**	**455**	**276**	**136**	**140**	**397**	**268**	**129**	**70**	**37**	**33**	**3,060**	**1,632**	**1,448**
Mohial Bali	1,693	914	770	100	62	128	92	64	28	295	151	144	38	18	20	147	118	29	8	4	4	770	417	353
" Bamwal	417	208	209	232	115	117	40	27	13	68	30	38	11	5	6	...	...	...	12	5	7	363	182	181
" Chibbar	525	250	275	194	69	125	13	8	5	196	103	93	17	9	8	36	26	10	...	...	...	456	215	241
" Datt	975	578	397	123	93	30	58	29	29	65	34	31	197	98	99	96	52	44	50	28	22	580	384	255
" Lau	523	307	216	29	21	8	23	12	11	158	92	66	13	6	7	82	52	30	...	...	...	305	183	122
" Mohan	342	172	170	123	56	67	50	24	26	133	72	61	...	...	...	36	20	16	...	...	...	342	172	170
" Wald	358	188	170	141	53	88	28	12	16	86	64	22	...	...	...	...	...	...	...	...	...	255	129	126
Marhatta	4	...	4	...	...	...	...	...	...	...	...	...	...	...	...	...	...	...	...	...	...	...	...	...
Malhial	177	5	172	...	...	...	...	...	...	...	...	...	...	...	...	...	...	...	...	...	...	...	...	...
Nai	4,312	3,310	1,002	37	16	21	832	708	124	405	110	295	181	7	174	581	541	40	62	9	53	2,098	1,391	707
Nakib	423	227	196	...	...	...	...	...	...	...	...	...	...	...	...	...	...	...	...	...	...	...	...	...
Nath	761	369	392	...	...	...	...	...	...	...	...	...	...	...	...	...	...	...	...	...	...	...	...	...
Nohla	124	66	58	...	...	...	...	...	...	...	...	...	...	...	...	...	...	...	...	...	...	...	...	...
Phalasar	2	2	...	...	...	...	...	...	...	...	...	...	...	...	...	...	...	...	...	...	...	...	...	...
Pandolo	1	1	...	...	...	...	...	...	...	...	...	...	...	...	...	...	...	...	...	...	...	...	...	...
Palial	1	1	...	...	...	...	...	...	...	...	...	...	...	...	...	...	...	...	...	...	...	...	...	...
Palolara	2	2	...	...	...	...	...	...	...	...	...	...	...	...	...	...	...	...	...	...	...	...	...	...
Pachla	1	1	...	...	...	...	...	...	...	...	...	...	...	...	...	...	...	...	...	...	...	...	...	...
Padias	45	17	28	...	...	...	45	17	28	...	...	...	...	...	...	...	...	...	...	...	...	45	17	28
Purboa	26	11	15	22	7	15	...	...	...	...	...	...	...	...	...	...	...	...	...	...	...	22	7	15
Total Rajputs ...	**166,547**	**85,892**	**80,655**	**69,873**	**35,212**	**34,661**	**40,905**	**20,959**	**19,946**	**28,390**	**14,123**	**12,267**	**24,545**	**12,719**	**11,826**	**1,794**	**798**	**996**	**452**	**249**	**203**	**163,959**	**84,060**	**79,899**
Rajput Augdia Raiwal ...	3	3	...	3	3	...	...	...	...	...	...	...	...	...	...	...	...	...	...	...	...	3	3	...
" Agotir	1	1	...	1	1	...	...	...	...	...	...	...	...	...	...	...	...	...	...	...	...	1	1	...
" Athal	275	175	100	21	20	1	254	155	99	...	...	...	...	...	...	...	...	...	...	...	...	275	175	100
" Alar	32	19	13	...	...	...	32	19	13	...	...	...	...	...	...	...	...	...	...	...	...	32	19	13
" Andhotara ...	573	344	220	...	...	...	...	...	...	...	...	...	573	344	229	...	...	...	...	...	...	543	344	229
" Agni	147	98	49	...	...	...	...	...	...	...	...	...	147	98	49	...	...	...	...	...	...	147	98	49
" Bandwal	42	27	15	42	27	15	...	...	...	...	...	...	...	...	...	...	...	...	...	...	...	42	27	15
" Bindral	1,492	937	555	280	71	209	1,043	744	299	...	...	...	153	106	47	...	...	...	...	...	...	1,476	921	555
" Bhalwal	457	212	245	163	89	74	82	58	24	...	...	...	212	65	147	...	...	...	...	...	...	457	212	245
" Bhardwaj ...	74	53	21	60	46	14	7	3	4	...	...	...	3	3	...	...	...	...	4	1	3	74	53	21
" Balori	784	437	347	238	59	179	2	2	...	...	...	...	542	374	168	...	...	...	...	...	...	782	435	347
" Bijoo	225	19	206	223	18	205	...	...	...	2	1	1	...	...	...	...	...	...	...	...	...	225	19	206
" Bambal	137	112	25	94	93	1	43	19	24	...	...	...	...	...	...	...	...	...	...	...	...	137	112	25
" Barkat	4	1	3	1	...	1	3	1	2	...	...	...	...	...	...	...	...	...	...	...	...	4	1	3
" Basne	5	1	4	4	...	4	1	1	...	...	...	...	...	...	...	...	...	...	...	...	...	5	1	4
" Bajial	8	7	1	8	7	1	...	...	...	...	...	...	...	...	...	...	...	...	...	...	...	8	7	1
" Baseth	1	1	...	1	1	...	...	...	...	...	...	...	...	...	...	...	...	...	...	...	...	1	1	...

Caste, Tribe, Race or Nationality.	Kashmir Province. Khas District. Persons.	Males.	Females.	Muzaffarabad District. Persons.	Males.	Females.	Total Kashmir Province. Persons.	Males.	Females.	Frontier Districts. Ladakh District. Persons.	Males.	Females.	Gilgit District. Persons.	Males.	Females.	Total Frontier Districts. Persons.	Males.	Females.
	26	27	28	29	30	31	32	33	34	35	36	37	38	39	40	41	42	43
Total Mohial ...	**1,288**	**703**	**585**	**465**	**282**	**183**	**1,753**	**985**	**768**	...	...	...	...	...	...	...	...	...
Mohial Bali	878	459	419	45	38	7	923	497	426	...	...	...	...	...	...	...	...	...
" Bamwal	...	...	...	54	26	28	54	26	28	...	...	...	...	...	...	...	...	...
" Chibbar	...	...	...	69	35	34	69	35	34	...	...	...	...	...	...	...	...	...
" Datt	277	169	108	109	75	34	386	244	142	...	...	...	...	...	...	...	...	...
" Lau	133	75	58	85	49	36	218	124	94	...	...	...	...	...	...	...	...	...
" Mohan	...	...	...	...	...	...	...	...	...	...	...	...	...	...	...	...	...	...
" Waid	...	...	...	103	59	44	103	59	44	...	...	...	...	...	...	...	...	...
Marhatta	...	...	...	4	...	4	4	...	4	...	...	...	...	...	...	...	...	...
Malhial	...	...	...	177	5	172	177	5	172	...	...	...	...	...	...	...	...	...
Nai	1,650	1,595	55	344	104	240	1,994	1,699	295	120	120	...	100	100	...	220	220	...
Nakib	423	227	196	...	...	...	423	227	196	...	...	...	...	...	...	...	...	...
Nath	761	369	392	...	...	...	761	369	392	...	...	...	...	...	...	...	...	...
Nehla	124	66	58	...	...	...	124	66	58	...	...	...	...	...	...	...	...	...
Phalasar	...	...	...	...	...	...	...	...	...	2	2	...	...	...	...	2	2	...
Pundolo	...	...	...	...	...	...	...	...	...	...	...	...	1	1	...	1	1	...
Palial	...	...	...	...	...	...	...	...	...	...	...	...	1	1	...	1	1	...
Palolara	...	...	...	...	...	...	...	...	...	...	...	...	2	2	...	2	2	...
Pachla	...	...	...	...	...	...	...	...	...	...	...	...	1	1	...	1	1	...
Padias	...	...	...	...	...	...	...	...	...	...	...	...	...	...	...	...	...	...
Purbos	4	4	...	...	...	...	4	4	...	...	...	...	...	...	...	...	...	...
Total Rajputs ...	**1,602**	**884**	**718**	**127**	**96**	**31**	**1,729**	**980**	**749**	**25**	**20**	**5**	**834**	**832**	**2**	**859**	**852**	**7**
Rajput Angdia Raiwal ...	...	...	...	...	...	...	...	...	...	...	...	...	...	...	...	...	...	...
" Agotir	...	...	...	...	...	...	...	...	...	...	...	...	...	...	...	...	...	...
" Athal	...	...	...	...	...	...	...	...	...	...	...	...	...	...	...	...	...	...
" Alar	...	...	...	...	...	...	...	...	...	...	...	...	...	...	...	...	...	...
" Andhotara ...	...	...	...	...	...	...	...	...	...	...	...	...	...	...	...	...	...	...
" Agni	...	...	...	...	...	...	...	...	...	...	...	...	...	...	...	...	...	...
" Bandwal	...	...	...	...	...	...	...	...	...	...	...	...	...	...	...	...	...	...
" Bindral	...	...	...	1	1	...	1	1	...	...	...	...	15	15	...	15	15	...
" Bhalwal	...	...	...	...	...	...	...	...	...	...	...	...	...	...	...	...	...	...
" Bhardwaj	...	...	...	...	...	...	...	...	...	...	...	...	...	...	...	...	...	...
" Balori	...	...	...	...	...	...	...	...	...	...	...	...	2	2	...	2	2	...
" Bijoo	...	...	...	...	...	...	...	...	...	...	...	...	...	...	...	...	...	...
" Bambal	...	...	...	...	...	...	...	...	...	...	...	...	...	...	...	...	...	...
" Barkat	...	...	...	...	...	...	...	...	...	...	...	...	...	...	...	...	...	...
" Bazno	...	...	...	...	...	...	...	...	...	...	...	...	...	...	...	...	...	...
" Bájial	...	...	...	...	...	...	...	...	...	...	...	...	...	...	...	...	...	...
" Baseth	...	...	...	...	...	...	...	...	...	...	...	...	...	...	...	...	...	...

TABLE XIII.

CASTE, TRIBE, RACE OR NATIONALITY.

Caste, Tribe, Race or Nationality.	Total Population.			Provinces with Districts. Jammu Province. Jammu Districts.			Udhampur District.			Bhimber District.			Jasrota District.			Punch Jágir.			Bhadarwah Jágir.			Total Jammu Province.		
	Persons.	Males.	Females.	Persons.	Males.	Females.	Persons.	Males.	Females.	Persons.	Males.	Females.	Persons.	Males.	Females.	Persons.	Males.	Females.	Persons.	Males.	Females.	Persons.	Males.	Females.
1	2	3	4	5	6	7	8	9	10	11	12	13	14	15	16	17	18	19	20	21	22	23	24	25
Rajput Bahlolna ...	1	...	1	1	...	1	...	...	...	...	...	...	...	...	...	...	...	...	...	...	...	1	...	1
" Batwalia ...	6	6	...	6	6	...	...	...	...	...	...	...	...	...	...	...	...	...	...	...	...	6	6	...
" Bharondh ...	2	2	...	2	2	...	...	...	...	...	...	...	...	...	...	...	...	...	...	...	...	2	2	...
" Bangal ...	92	84	8	92	84	8	...	...	...	...	...	...	...	...	...	...	...	...	...	...	...	92	84	8
" Bandwali ...	3	3	...	3	3	...	...	...	...	...	...	...	...	...	...	...	...	...	...	...	...	3	3	...
" Bangwati ...	49	33	16	5	5	...	44	28	16	...	...	...	...	...	...	...	...	...	...	...	...	49	33	16
" Banglah ...	20	15	5	1	...	1	19	15	4	...	...	...	...	...	...	...	...	...	...	...	...	20	15	5
" Batti ...	7	3	4	...	...	...	2	2	...	...	...	...	...	...	...	...	...	...	5	1	4	7	3	4
" Balana ...	10	10	...	...	...	...	10	10	...	...	...	...	...	...	...	...	...	...	...	...	...	10	10	...
" Banawal ...	1	1	...	...	...	...	1	1	...	...	...	...	...	...	...	...	...	...	...	...	...	1	1	...
" Baila ...	62	41	21	...	...	...	46	25	21	...	...	...	16	16	...	...	...	...	...	...	...	62	41	21
" Bharatpuria ...	62	53	9	...	...	...	62	53	9	...	...	...	...	...	...	...	...	...	...	...	...	62	53	9
" Bansalgos ...	28	28	...	...	...	...	...	...	...	...	...	...	28	28	...	...	...	...	...	...	...	28	28	...
" Chohan ...	162	54	108	25	16	9	...	...	...	65	8	57	28	19	9	...	...	...	44	11	33	162	54	108
" Chandhal ...	30	7	23	...	...	...	30	7	23	...	...	...	...	...	...	...	...	...	...	...	...	30	7	23
" Chanial ...	157	103	54	3	2	1	154	101	53	...	...	...	...	...	...	...	...	...	...	...	...	157	103	54
" Chandarbansi ...	2	2	...	1	1	...	1	1	...	...	...	...	...	...	...	...	...	...	...	...	...	2	2	...
" Chanalia ...	1	1	...	...	...	...	1	1	...	...	...	...	...	...	...	...	...	...	...	...	...	1	1	...
" Dalpatia ...	153	113	40	153	113	40	...	...	...	...	...	...	...	...	...	...	...	...	...	...	...	153	113	40
" Dialia ...	9	8	1	7	6	1	2	2	...	...	...	...	...	...	...	...	...	...	...	...	...	9	8	1
" Dadwal ...	89	65	24	17	12	5	...	...	...	3	3	...	68	49	19	...	...	...	...	...	...	88	64	24
" Danikal ...	1	1	...	1	1	...	...	...	...	...	...	...	...	...	...	...	...	...	...	...	...	1	1	...
" Danlia ...	10	7	3	...	...	...	10	7	3	...	...	...	...	...	...	...	...	...	...	...	...	10	7	3
" Dantal ...	40	26	14	...	...	...	9	7	2	...	...	...	...	...	...	31	19	12	...	...	...	40	26	14
" Dandus ...	1	1	...	...	...	...	1	1	...	...	...	...	...	...	...	...	...	...	...	...	...	1	1	...
" Dhati ...	5	2	3	...	...	...	4	2	2	1	...	1	...	...	...	...	...	...	...	...	...	5	2	3
" Dakoria ...	1	...	1	...	...	...	1	...	1	...	...	...	...	...	...	...	...	...	...	...	...	1	...	1
" Digria ...	5	5	...	...	...	...	...	...	...	5	5	...	...	...	...	...	...	...	...	...	...	5	5	...
" Goria ...	2,437	1,228	1,209	52	36	16	2,385	1,192	1,193	...	...	...	...	...	...	...	...	...	...	...	...	2,437	1,228	1,209
" Gobal ...	5,721	3,138	2,583	517	229	288	527	290	237	1,733	1,116	617	2,942	1,500	1,442	...	...	...	...	...	...	5,719	3,136	2,583
" Indarmati ...	364	209	155	364	209	155	...	...	...	...	...	...	...	...	...	...	...	...	...	...	...	364	209	155
" Jaswal ...	40,183	25,175	15,008	20,183	11,175	9,008	10,000	7,000	3,000	...	...	...	10,000	6,000	4,000	...	...	...	...	...	...	40,183	25,175	15,008
" Jasrotia ...	582	421	161	119	95	24	39	21	18	...	...	...	408	289	119	...	...	...	...	...	...	566	405	161
" Jamwal ...	4,053	2,512	1,541	2,756	1,717	1,039	820	484	336	229	116	113	113	95	18	77	57	20	26	13	13	4,021	2,482	1,539
" Jakaria ...	1	1	...	...	...	...	...	...	...	1	1	...	...	...	...	...	...	...	...	...	...	1	1	...
" Janjua ...	6	4	2	3	3	...	2	...	2	...	...	...	...	...	...	1	1	...	...	...	...	6	4	2
" Jajabi ...	30	15	15	30	15	15	...	...	...	...	...	...	...	...	...	...	...	...	...	...	...	30	15	15
" Janti ...	1	1	...	1	1	...	...	...	...	...	...	...	...	...	...	...	...	...	...	...	...	1	1	...
" Jandial ...	8	7	1	4	3	1	4	4	...	...	...	...	...	...	...	...	...	...	...	...	...	8	7	1
" Jandarwalia ...	11	11	...	...	...	...	...	...	...	...	...	...	11	11	...	...	...	...	...	...	...	11	11	...
" Janial ...	30	24	6	...	...	...	7	7	...	...	...	...	23	17	6	...	...	...	...	...	...	30	24	6

PROVINCES WITH DISTRICTS.

Caste, Tribe, Race or Nationality.	Kashmir Province. Khas District. Persons.	Males.	Females.	Muzaffarabad District. Persons.	Males.	Females.	Total Kashmir Province. Persons.	Males.	Females.	Frontier Districts. Ladakh District. Persons.	Males.	Females.	Gilgit District. Persons.	Males.	Females.	Total Frontier Districts. Persons.	Males.	Females.
	26	27	28	29	30	31	32	33	34	35	36	37	38	39	40	41	42	43
Rajput Bahloina ...	...	...	...	...	...	...	...	...	...	...	...	...	...	...	...	...	...	...
" Batwalia ...	...	...	...	...	...	...	...	...	...	...	...	...	...	...	...	...	...	...
" Bharondh ...	...	...	...	...	...	...	...	...	...	...	...	...	...	...	...	...	...	...
" Bangal ...	...	...	...	...	...	...	...	...	...	...	...	...	...	...	...	...	...	...
" Bandwali ...	...	...	...	...	...	...	...	...	...	...	...	...	...	...	...	...	...	...
" Bangwati ...	...	...	...	...	...	...	...	...	...	...	...	...	...	...	...	...	...	...
" Banglah ...	...	...	...	...	...	...	...	...	...	...	...	...	...	...	...	...	...	...
" Batti ...	...	...	...	...	...	...	...	...	...	...	...	...	...	...	...	...	...	...
" Balans ...	...	...	...	...	...	...	...	...	...	...	...	...	...	...	...	...	...	...
" Banawal ...	...	...	...	...	...	...	...	...	...	...	...	...	...	...	...	...	...	...
" Baila ...	...	...	...	...	...	...	...	...	...	...	...	...	...	...	...	...	...	...
" Bharat puria ...	...	...	...	...	...	...	...	...	...	...	...	...	...	...	...	...	...	...
" Banalgos ...	...	...	...	...	...	...	...	...	...	...	...	...	...	...	...	...	...	...
" Chohan ...	...	...	...	...	...	...	...	...	...	...	...	...	...	...	...	...	...	...
" Chandhal ...	...	...	...	...	...	...	...	...	...	...	...	...	...	...	...	...	...	...
" Chanial ...	...	...	...	...	...	...	...	...	...	...	...	...	...	...	...	...	...	...
" Chandar bansi ...	...	...	...	...	...	...	...	...	...	...	...	...	...	...	...	...	...	...
" Chanalia ...	...	...	...	...	...	...	...	...	...	...	...	...	...	...	...	...	...	...
" Dalpatia ...	...	...	...	...	...	...	...	...	...	...	...	...	...	...	...	...	...	...
" Dinlia ...	...	...	...	...	...	...	...	...	...	...	...	...	...	...	...	...	...	...
" Dadwal ...	...	...	...	1	1	...	1	1	...	...	...	...	...	...	...	...	...	...
" Danikal ...	...	...	...	...	...	...	...	...	...	...	...	...	...	...	...	...	...	...
" Dáolia ...	...	...	...	...	...	...	...	...	...	...	...	...	...	...	...	...	...	...
" Dántál ...	...	...	...	...	...	...	...	...	...	...	...	...	...	...	...	...	...	...
" Dandas ...	...	...	...	...	...	...	...	...	...	...	...	...	...	...	...	...	...	...
" Dhati ...	...	...	...	...	...	...	...	...	...	...	...	...	...	...	...	...	...	...
" Dakoria ...	...	...	...	...	...	...	...	...	...	...	...	...	...	...	...	...	...	...
" Digria ...	...	...	...	...	...	...	...	...	...	...	...	...	...	...	...	...	...	...
" Goria ...	...	...	...	...	...	...	...	...	...	...	...	...	...	...	...	...	...	...
" Gobal ...	...	...	...	...	...	...	...	...	...	...	...	...	2	2	...	2	2	...
" Indarsati ...	...	...	...	...	...	...	...	...	...	...	...	...	...	...	...	...	...	...
" Jaswal ...	...	...	...	...	...	...	...	...	...	...	...	...	...	...	...	...	...	...
" Jasrotia ...	...	...	...	...	...	...	...	...	...	...	...	...	16	16	...	16	16	...
" Jamwal ...	6	4	2	5	5	...	11	9	2	...	...	...	21	21	...	21	21	...
" Jakaria ...	...	...	...	...	...	...	...	...	...	...	...	...	...	...	...	...	...	...
" Janjua ...	...	...	...	...	...	...	...	...	...	...	...	...	...	...	...	...	...	...
" Jajabi ...	...	...	...	...	...	...	...	...	...	...	...	...	...	...	...	...	...	...
" Janti ...	...	...	...	...	...	...	...	...	...	...	...	...	...	...	...	...	...	...
" Jandial ...	...	...	...	...	...	...	...	...	...	...	...	...	...	...	...	...	...	...
" Jandarwalia ...	...	...	...	...	...	...	...	...	...	...	...	...	...	...	...	...	...	...
" Jainal ...	...	...	...	...	...	...	...	...	...	...	...	...	...	...	...	...	...	...

TABLE XIII.

Caste, Tribe, Race or Nationality.

Caste, Tribe, Race or Nationality.	Total Population.			Provinces with Districts. Jammu Province. Jammu District.			Udhampur District.			Bhimber District.			Jasrota District.			Punch Jágir.			Bhaderwah Jágir.			Total Jammu Province.		
	Persons.	Males.	Females.	Persons.	Males.	Females.	Persons.	Males.	Females.	Persons.	Males.	Females.	Persons.	Males.	Females.	Persons.	Males.	Females.	Persons.	Males.	Females.	Persons.	Males.	Females.
1	2	3	4	5	6	7	8	9	10	11	12	13	14	15	16	17	18	19	20	21	22	23	24	25
Rajput Jidia	5	2	3	5	2	3	...	...	...	...	...	...	...	...	...	...	...	...	...	...	...	5	2	3
" Kapura	29	22	7	29	22	7	...	...	...	...	...	...	...	...	...	...	...	...	...	...	...	29	22	7
" Katal	284	199	85	104	42	62	...	...	...	...	...	...	180	157	23	...	...	...	...	...	...	284	190	85
" Kotoch	270	166	104	37	15	22	118	66	52	29	25	4	30	24	6	...	...	...	56	36	20	270	166	104
" Kandel	2	2	...	...	...	...	2	2	...	...	...	...	...	...	...	...	...	...	...	...	...	2	2	...
" Katuria	40	24	16	7	4	3	29	18	11	...	...	...	4	2	2	...	...	...	...	...	...	40	24	16
" Kalial	249	119	130	3	2	1	...	...	...	235	106	129	11	11	...	...	...	...	...	...	...	249	119	130
" Kalotara	916	648	268	1	1	...	...	...	...	915	647	268	...	...	...	...	...	...	...	...	...	916	648	268
" Kabluria	12	10	2	12	10	2	...	...	...	...	...	...	...	...	...	...	...	...	...	...	...	12	10	2
" Kamial	25	25	...	25	25	...	...	...	...	...	...	...	...	...	...	...	...	...	...	...	...	25	25	...
" Kour	917	475	442	...	...	...	16	8	8	...	...	...	901	467	434	...	...	...	...	...	...	917	475	442
" Logario	6	1	5	6	1	5	...	...	...	...	...	...	...	...	...	...	...	...	...	...	...	6	1	5
" Lagnas	26	25	1	1	...	1	...	...	...	...	...	...	...	...	...	...	...	...	...	...	...	1	...	1
" Langoti	23	18	5	23	18	5	...	...	...	...	...	...	...	...	...	...	...	...	...	...	...	23	18	5
" Manhas	5,504	3,121	2,473	4,834	2,551	2,283	...	...	...	254	123	131	154	154	...	65	44	21	80	44	36	5,387	2,916	2,471
" Malotro	3	...	3	3	...	3	...	...	...	...	...	...	...	...	...	...	...	...	...	...	...	3	...	3
" Madkalia	1	...	1	1	...	1	...	...	...	...	...	...	...	...	...	...	...	...	...	...	...	1	...	1
" Mandi	28	9	19	28	9	19	...	...	...	...	...	...	...	...	...	...	...	...	...	...	...	28	9	19
" Mangral	110	95	15	5	5	...	...	...	...	90	81	9	...	...	...	...	...	...	15	9	6	110	95	15
" Mian	6	6	...	6	6	...	...	...	...	...	...	...	...	...	...	...	...	...	...	...	...	6	6	...
" Mahila	290	74	216	...	...	...	...	...	...	281	65	216	...	...	...	9	9	...	...	...	...	290	74	216
" Manglah	4	4	...	4	4	...	...	...	...	...	...	...	...	...	...	...	...	...	...	...	...	4	4	...
" Mardoal	462	193	269	...	...	...	...	...	...	...	...	...	462	193	269	...	...	...	...	...	...	462	193	269
" Nagial	4	4	...	4	4	...	...	...	...	...	...	...	...	...	...	...	...	...	...	...	...	4	4	...
" Narania	19	10	9	19	10	9	...	...	...	...	...	...	...	...	...	...	...	...	...	...	...	19	10	9
" Pathania ...	386	325	61	71	57	14	105	105	...	1	1	...	209	162	47	...	...	...	...	...	...	386	325	61
" Palin	5	5	...	...	...	...	5	5	...	...	...	...	...	...	...	...	...	...	...	...	...	5	5	...
" Parbal	19	16	3	1	1	...	18	15	3	...	...	...	...	...	...	...	...	...	...	...	...	19	16	3
" Pagiár	318	27	291	318	27	291	...	...	...	...	...	...	...	...	...	...	...	...	...	...	...	318	27	291
" Pawair	37	16	21	...	...	...	37	16	21	...	...	...	...	...	...	...	...	...	...	...	...	37	16	21
" Poni	81	61	20	...	...	...	...	...	...	...	...	...	81	61	20	...	...	...	...	...	...	81	61	20
" Patial	180	178	2	...	...	...	180	178	2	...	...	...	...	...	...	...	...	...	...	...	...	180	178	2
" Rajput	269	269	...	...	...	...	...	...	...	—	...	...	...	...	...	...	...	...	...	...	...	...	...	...
" Rangaria ...	28	15	13	19	14	5	9	1	8	...	...	...	...	...	...	...	...	...	...	...	...	28	15	13
" Rana	214	118	96	...	...	...	214	118	96	...	...	...	...	...	...	...	...	...	...	...	...	214	118	96
" Raghubansi ...	142	142	...	142	142	...	...	...	...	...	...	...	...	...	...	...	...	...	...	...	...	142	142	...
" Rathaur	6	3	3	6	3	3	...	...	...	...	...	...	...	...	...	...	...	...	...	...	...	6	3	3
" Ratial	4,887	2,923	1,964	277	149	128	768	515	253	562	508	54	2,188	1,020	1,168	202	140	62	121	101	20	4,118	2,433	1,685
" Rajial	19	1	18	3	1	2	...	...	...	16	...	16	...	...	...	...	...	...	...	...	...	19	1	18
" Rasial	26	4	22	...	...	...	26	4	22	...	...	...	...	...	...	...	...	...	...	...	...	26	4	22
" Rupial	17	3	14	...	...	...	...	...	...	17	3	14	...	...	...	...	...	...	...	...	...	17	3	14

Caste, Tribe, Race or Nationality.	Kashmir Province. Khas District. Persons.	Males.	Females.	Muzaffarabad District. Persons.	Males.	Females.	Total Kashmir Province. Persons.	Males.	Females.	Frontier Districts. Ladakh District. Persons.	Males.	Females.	Gilgit District. Persons.	Males.	Females.	Total Frontier Districts. Persons.	Males.	Females.
	26	27	28	29	30	31	32	33	34	35	36	37	38	39	40	41	42	43
Rajput Jidia	...	...	...	...	...	...	...	...	...	...	...	...	...	...	...	...	...	...
„ Kapura	...	...	...	...	...	...	...	...	...	...	...	...	...	...	...	...	...	...
„ Katal ...	...	...	...	...	...	...	...	...	...	...	...	...	...	...	...	...	...	...
„ Kotoch	...	...	...	...	...	...	...	...	...	...	...	...	...	...	...	...	...	...
„ Kandel	...	...	...	...	...	...	...	...	...	...	...	...	...	...	...	...	...	...
„ Katuria ...	...	...	...	...	...	...	...	...	...	...	...	...	...	...	...	...	...	...
„ Kalial	...	...	...	...	...	...	...	...	...	...	...	...	...	...	...	...	...	...
„ Kalotara... ...	...	...	...	...	...	...	...	...	...	...	...	...	...	...	...	...	...	...
„ Kabluria... ...	...	...	...	...	...	...	...	...	...	...	...	...	...	...	...	...	...	...
„ Kamial ...	...	...	...	...	...	...	...	...	...	...	...	...	...	...	...	...	...	...
„ Kour ...	...	...	...	...	...	...	...	...	...	...	...	...	...	...	...	...	...	...
„ Logarea	...	...	...	...	...	...	...	...	...	...	...	...	...	...	...	...	...	...
„ Lognas	...	...	...	...	...	...	...	...	...	...	...	...	25	25	...	25	25	...
„ Longoti	...	...	...	...	...	...	...	...	...	...	...	...	...	...	...	...	...	...
„ Manhas	4	3	1	2	1	1	6	4	2	...	...	...	201	201	...	201	201	...
„ Malotro	...	...	...	...	...	...	...	...	...	...	...	...	...	...	...	...	...	...
„ Madkalia... ...	...	...	...	...	...	...	...	...	...	...	...	...	...	...	...	...	...	...
„ Mandi	...	...	...	...	...	...	...	...	...	...	...	...	...	...	...	...	...	...
„ Mangral ...	...	...	...	...	...	...	...	...	...	...	...	...	...	...	...	...	...	...
„ Miau	...	...	...	...	...	...	...	...	...	...	...	...	...	...	...	...	...	...
„ Mahola	...	...	...	...	...	...	...	...	...	...	...	...	...	...	...	...	...	...
„ Manglah ...	...	...	...	...	...	...	...	...	...	...	...	...	...	...	...	...	...	...
„ Mardeal	...	...	...	...	...	...	...	...	...	...	...	...	...	...	...	...	...	...
„ Nageal	...	...	...	...	...	...	...	...	...	...	...	...	...	...	...	...	...	...
„ Narania	...	...	...	...	...	...	...	...	...	...	...	...	...	...	...	...	...	...
„ Pathania ...	...	...	...	...	...	...	...	...	...	...	...	...	...	...	...	...	...	...
„ Palian	...	...	...	...	...	...	...	...	...	...	...	...	...	...	...	...	...	...
„ Parbal	...	...	...	...	...	...	...	...	...	...	...	...	...	...	...	...	...	...
„ Pagiar	...	...	...	...	...	...	...	...	...	...	...	...	...	...	...	...	...	...
„ Pawair	...	...	...	...	...	...	...	...	...	...	...	...	...	...	...	...	...	...
„ Pani	...	...	...	...	...	...	...	...	...	...	...	...	...	...	...	...	...	...
„ Patial	...	...	...	...	...	...	...	...	...	...	...	...	...	...	...	...	...	...
„ Rajput	...	...	...	...	...	...	...	...	...	...	...	...	269	269	...	269	269	...
„ Rangaria ...	...	...	...	...	...	...	...	...	...	...	...	...	...	...	...	...	...	...
„ Rana	...	...	...	...	...	...	...	...	...	...	...	...	...	...	...	...	...	...
„ Raghubansi ...	...	...	...	...	...	...	...	...	...	...	...	...	...	...	...	...	...	...
„ Rathaur	...	...	...	...	...	...	...	...	...	...	...	...	...	...	...	...	...	...
„ Ratial	656	399	257	91	74	17	747	473	274	22	17	5	...	...	...	22	17	5
„ Rajial	...	...	...	...	...	...	...	...	...	...	...	...	...	...	...	...	...	...
„ Rasial	...	...	...	...	...	...	...	...	...	...	...	...	...	...	...	...	...	...
„ Rupial	...	...	...	...	...	...	...	...	...	...	...	...	...	...	...	...	...	...

TABLE XIII.

CASTE, TRIBE, RACE OR NATIONALITY.

Caste, Tribe, Race or Nationality.	TOTAL POPULATION.			PROVINCES WITH DISTRICTS. — JAMMU PROVINCE. — Jammu District.			Udhampur District.			Bhimber District.			Jasrota District.			Punch Jágir.			Bhadarwah Jágir.			Total Jammu Province.		
	Persons.	Males.	Females.	Persons.	Males.	Females.	Persons.	Males.	Females.	Persons.	Males.	Females.	Persons.	Males.	Females.	Persons.	Males.	Females.	Persons.	Males.	Females.	Persons.	Males.	Females.
1	2	3	4	5	6	7	8	9	10	11	12	13	14	15	16	17	18	19	20	21	22	23	24	25
Rajput Saniai	790	554	236	689	497	192	101	57	44	...	...	...	...	...	...	...	...	...	...	...	...	790	554	236
" Sultani	1	1	...	1	1	...	...	...	...	...	...	...	...	...	...	...	...	...	...	...	...	1	1	...
" Saroj	266	159	107	266	159	107	...	...	...	...	...	...	...	...	...	...	...	...	...	...	...	266	159	107
" Salattira	537	446	91	537	446	91	...	...	...	...	...	...	...	...	...	...	...	...	...	...	...	537	446	91
" Sinl	69	15	54	69	15	54	...	...	...	...	...	...	...	...	...	...	...	...	...	...	...	69	15	54
" Sonkhla	244	...	244	244	...	244	...	...	...	...	...	...	...	...	...	...	...	...	...	...	...	244	...	244
" Sial	126	97	29	2	...	2	...	...	...	2	2	...	104	77	27	...	...	...	...	...	...	108	79	29
" Sanne	195	22	173	195	22	173	...	...	...	...	...	...	...	...	...	...	...	...	...	...	...	195	22	173
" Sotwar	16	16	...	16	16	...	...	...	...	...	...	...	...	...	...	...	...	...	...	...	...	16	16	...
" Saratea	9	4	5	6	5	1	3	3	...	...	...	...	...	...	...	...	...	...	...	...	...	9	4	5
" Sogial	42	32	10	2	2	...	40	30	10	...	...	...	...	...	...	...	...	...	...	...	...	42	32	10
" Saryana	759	382	377	758	381	377	...	...	...	1	1	...	...	...	...	...	...	...	...	...	...	759	382	377
" Saknia	61	49	12	4	...	4	16	8	8	41	41	...	...	...	...	...	...	...	...	...	...	61	49	12
" Surajbansi	48,583	19,638	28,945	20,117	9,001	11,116	21,197	9,103	12,094	...	...	...	6,154	1,879	4,275	...	...	...	...	...	...	47,468	18,983	28,485
" Sotra	177	88	89	3	...	3	174	88	86	...	...	...	...	...	...	...	...	...	...	...	...	177	88	89
" Samaria	238	166	72	...	...	...	53	23	30	...	...	...	136	136	...	...	...	...	49	7	42	238	166	72
" San Chondhri	2,512	1,308	1,204	2,135	1,083	1,052	168	111	57	65	32	33	69	25	44	35	23	13	12	7	5	2,484	1,280	1,204
" San Mohta Rakwal	806	393	413	622	291	331	147	86	61	4	2	2	31	12	19	...	...	...	...	...	...	804	391	413
" San Khan Chib	5,111	2,955	2,156	2,840	1,432	1,408	202	104	98	1,978	1,344	634	64	53	11	16	11	5	11	11	...	5,111	2,955	2,156
" San Khan Charak	8,275	3,826	4,449	6,500	3,254	3,246	17	15	2	1,187	424	763	13	2	11	525	111	414	...	...	...	8,242	3,806	4,436
" San Kutwal	2,140	979	1,161	1,834	810	1,024	142	97	45	112	48	64	39	13	26	13	11	2	...	...	...	2,140	979	1,161
" San Mian	3,080	1,550	1,529	2,821	1,443	1,378	73	32	41	127	57	70	13	5	8	33	1	32	3	3	...	3,070	1,541	1,529
" San Dhan	1,190	717	473	123	59	64	3	1	2	1,050	651	399	10	2	8	4	4	...	...	...	...	1,190	717	473
" San Bhagal	445	319	126	354	233	121	11	11	...	...	...	...	80	75	5	...	...	...	...	...	...	445	319	126
" San Jaral	1,030	414	616	485	17	468	368	258	110	77	59	18	40	29	11	43	36	7	17	15	2	1,030	414	616
" San Chowdri Salarna	8,548	4,303	4,245	185	138	47	6,758	3,364	3,394	1,080	555	525	...	...	...	503	233	270	9	...	9	8,535	4,290	4,245
" San Bajial	4,808	1,393	3,415	4,201	1,125	3,076	92	46	46	208	90	118	73	36	37	232	94	138	...	...	...	4,806	1,391	3,415
" San Mian Andorana	1,074	495	579	702	293	409	123	86	37	17	6	11	227	105	122	5	5	...	...	...	...	1,074	495	579
" San Mian Rahal	741	326	415	683	282	401	33	19	14	2	2	...	5	5	...	...	...	...	...	...	...	723	308	415
" Thákar	1	1	...	...	...	...	...	...	...	...	...	...	...	...	...	...	...	...	...	...	...	...	...	...
Thakkur	93,364	51,042	42,322	5,966	3,607	2,359	50,351	26,771	23,580	1,450	1,081	369	25,768	14,364	11,404	278	200	78	9,187	4,692	4,495	93,000	50,715	42,285
Bania	219	117	102	...	...	...	...	...	...	...	...	...	...	...	...	...	...	...	...	...	...	...	...	...
Haann	12	12	...	...	...	...	...	...	...	...	...	...	...	...	...	...	...	...	...	...	...	...	...	...
Rawal	7	7	...	7	7	...	...	...	...	...	...	...	...	...	...	...	...	...	...	...	...	7	7	...
Ratal	553	149	404	288	41	247	143	51	92	...	...	...	122	57	65	...	...	...	...	...	...	553	149	404
Saryarn	984	295	689	...	...	...	676	193	483	53	26	27	244	55	189	...	...	...	...	...	...	973	274	699
Soohi	232	106	126	31	1	30	154	105	49	...	...	...	47	...	47	...	...	...	...	...	...	232	106	126
Tarkhan	10,080	5,332	4,748	4,693	2,673	2,020	1,211	687	524	477	258	219	3,067	1,087	1,980	12	8	4	7	6	1	10,067	5,319	4,748
Thapa	294	231	63	66	61	5	2	2	...	...	...	...	...	...	...	...	...	...	...	...	...	68	63	5
Tihar	137	62	65	...	...	...	...	...	...	...	...	...	...	...	...	...	...	...	...	...	...	...	...	...

Caste, Tribe, Race or Nationality.	PROVINCES WITH DISTRICTS.																	
	KASHMIR PROVINCE.									FRONTIER DISTRICTS.								
	Khas District.			Muzaffarabad District.			Total Kashmir Province.			Ladakh District.			Gilgit District.			Total Frontier Districts.		
	Persons.	Males.	Females.	Persons.	Males.	Females.	Persons.	Males.	Females.	Persons.	Males.	Females.	Persons.	Males.	Females.	Persons.	Males.	Females.
	26	27	28	29	30	31	32	33	34	35	36	37	38	39	40	41	42	43
Rajput Samal	...	...	...	...	...	...	...	...	...	...	...	...	...	...	...	...	...	...
" Sultani	...	...	...	...	...	...	...	...	...	...	...	...	...	...	...	...	...	...
" Saraj	...	...	...	...	...	...	...	...	...	...	...	...	...	...	...	...	...	...
" Sallattira	...	...	...	...	...	...	...	...	...	...	...	...	...	...	...	...	...	...
" Sini	...	...	...	...	...	...	...	...	...	...	...	...	...	...	...	...	...	...
" Sonkhla	...	...	...	...	...	...	...	...	...	...	...	...	...	...	...	...	...	...
" Sial	...	...	...	...	...	...	...	...	...	...	...	...	18	18	...	18	18	...
" Sanan	...	...	...	...	...	...	...	...	...	...	...	...	...	...	...	...	...	...
" Sotwar	...	...	...	...	...	...	...	...	...	...	...	...	...	...	...	...	...	...
" Sarates	...	...	...	...	...	...	...	...	...	...	...	...	...	...	...	...	...	...
" Sagial	...	...	...	...	...	...	...	...	...	...	...	...	...	...	...	...	...	...
" Saryana	...	...	...	...	...	...	...	...	...	...	...	...	...	...	...	...	...	...
" Saknia	...	...	...	...	...	...	...	...	...	...	...	...	...	...	...	...	...	...
" Sarajhansi	936	478	458	...	...	...	936	478	458	...	...	...	169	167	2	169	167	2
" Sotre	...	...	...	...	...	...	...	...	...	...	...	...	...	...	...	...	...	...
" Samaria	...	...	...	...	...	...	...	...	...	...	...	...	...	...	...	...	...	...
" Sau Choudhri	...	...	...	...	...	...	...	...	...	...	...	...	28	28	...	28	28	...
" Sau Mahta Rakwal	...	...	...	...	...	...	...	...	...	2	2	...	...	...	...	2	2	...
" Sau Khan Chib	...	...	...	...	...	...	...	...	...	...	...	...	...	...	...	...	...	...
" Sau Khan Charak	...	...	...	14	1	13	14	1	13	...	...	...	19	19	...	19	19	...
" Sau Kutwal	...	...	...	...	...	...	...	...	...	...	...	...	...	...	...	...	...	...
" Sau Mian	...	...	...	...	...	...	...	...	...	...	...	...	19	19	...	19	19	...
" Sau Bhan	...	...	...	...	...	...	...	...	...	...	...	...	...	...	...	...	...	...
" Sau Bhagal	...	...	...	...	...	...	...	...	...	...	...	...	...	...	...	...	...	...
" Sau Jarral	...	...	...	...	...	...	...	...	...	...	...	...	...	...	...	...	...	...
" Sau Chowdri Salaria	...	...	...	13	13	...	13	13	...	...	...	...	...	...	...	...	...	...
" Sau Bajial	...	...	...	...	...	...	...	...	...	...	...	...	2	2	...	2	2	...
" Sau Mian andorann	...	...	...	...	...	...	...	...	...	...	...	...	...	...	...	...	...	...
" Sau Mian Bahal	...	...	...	...	...	...	...	...	...	...	...	...	18	18	...	18	18	...
" Thakar	...	...	...	...	...	...	...	...	...	1	1	...	...	...	...	1	1	...
Thakkar	61	32	29	1	...	1	62	32	30	15	8	7	287	287	...	302	295	7
Bania	197	95	102	...	...	...	197	95	102	...	...	...	22	22	...	22	22	...
Basan	12	12	...	...	...	...	12	12	...	...	...	...	...	...	...	...	...	...
Rawal	...	...	...	...	...	...	...	...	...	...	...	...	...	...	...	...	...	...
Batal	...	...	...	...	...	...	...	...	...	...	...	...	...	...	...	...	...	...
Saryara	...	...	...	...	...	...	...	...	...	...	...	...	11	11	...	11	11	...
Sochi	...	...	...	...	...	...	...	...	...	...	...	...	...	...	...	...	...	...
Tarkhan	...	...	...	...	...	...	...	...	...	...	...	...	13	13	...	13	13	...
Thaga	143	85	58	...	...	...	143	85	58	1	1	...	82	82	...	83	82	...
Tihar	119	54	65	...	...	...	119	54	65	...	...	...	8	8	...	8	8	...

TABLE XIII.

Caste, Tribe, Race or Nationality.

Caste, Tribe, Race or Nationality.	Total Population: Persons.	Total Population: Males.	Total Population: Females.	Jammu District: Persons.	Jammu District: Males.	Jammu District: Females.	Udhampur District: Persons.	Udhampur District: Males.	Udhampur District: Females.	Bhimber District: Persons.	Bhimber District: Males.	Bhimber District: Females.	Jasrota District: Persons.	Jasrota District: Males.	Jasrota District: Females.	Punch Jágir: Persons.	Punch Jágir: Males.	Punch Jágir: Females.	Bhadarwah Jágir: Persons.	Bhadarwah Jágir: Males.	Bhadarwah Jágir: Females.	Total Jammu Province: Persons.	Total Jammu Province: Males.	Total Jammu Province: Females.
1	2	3	4	5	6	7	8	9	10	11	12	13	14	15	16	17	18	19	20	21	22	23	24	25
Thathiar ...	114	54	60	38	18	20	73	34	39	...	...	...	3	2	1	...	...	...	...	...	...	114	54	60
Total Sikhs ...	25,828	14,342	11,486	2,257	1,333	924	155	102	53	2,638	1,537	1,101	179	123	56	7,868	4,312	3,556	16	11	5	13,113	7,418	5,695
Arora ...	70	34	36	10	5	5	...	...	...	60	29	31	...	...	...	...	...	...	...	...	...	70	34	36
Ahluwalia ...	78	43	35	30	14	16	...	...	...	...	...	...	7	3	4	...	...	...	1	1	...	38	18	20
Akali ...	445	216	229	...	...	...	...	...	...	...	...	...	...	...	...	...	...	...	...	...	...	...	...	...
Agangat ...	120	54	75	...	...	...	...	...	...	...	...	...	...	...	...	...	...	...	...	...	...	...	...	...
Bania ...	12	5	7	...	...	...	12	5	7	...	...	...	...	...	...	...	...	...	...	...	...	12	5	7
Bhatti ...	15	8	7	...	...	...	2	1	1	...	...	...	...	...	...	...	...	...	...	...	...	2	1	1
Barmane ...	5	3	2	5	3	2	...	...	...	...	...	...	...	...	...	...	...	...	...	...	...	5	3	2
Bangial ...	24	5	19	...	...	...	...	...	...	...	...	...	...	...	...	24	5	19	...	...	...	24	5	19
Bhat ...	47	31	16	...	...	...	...	...	...	21	16	5	...	...	...	19	10	9	...	...	...	40	26	14
Barwala ...	1	1	...	...	...	...	...	...	...	...	...	...	1	1	...	...	...	...	...	...	...	1	1	...
Brahmin ...	16,844	8,563	7,281	1,680	980	700	25	13	12	104	57	47	4	2	2	5,718	3,076	2,642	...	...	...	7,531	4,128	3,403
Bhanjra ...	26	16	10	...	...	...	...	...	...	...	...	...	26	16	10	...	...	...	...	...	...	26	16	10
Balas ...	18	10	8	...	...	...	...	...	...	...	...	...	...	...	...	...	...	...	...	...	...	...	...	...
Banjala ...	154	51	103	...	...	...	...	...	...	...	...	...	...	...	...	...	...	...	...	...	...	...	...	...
Dhobi ...	22	11	11	...	...	...	...	...	...	22	11	11	...	...	...	...	...	...	...	...	...	22	11	11
Jat ...	755	406	254	352	220	132	8	5	3	120	74	46	58	46	12	32	24	8	1	1	...	571	370	201
Jatoor ...	18	12	6	16	10	6	1	1	...	...	...	...	1	1	...	...	...	...	...	...	...	18	12	6
Jinsi ...	2,888	1,697	1,191	...	...	...	...	...	...	...	...	...	...	...	...	...	...	...	...	...	...	...	...	...
Manhas ...	66	37	29	...	...	...	...	...	...	...	...	...	...	...	...	66	37	29	...	...	...	66	37	29
Mazbi ...	4,680	2,746	1,934	162	100	62	109	78	31	2,311	1,350	961	75	49	26	2,009	1,160	849	14	9	5	4,680	2,746	1,934
Rania ...	190	130	69	...	...	...	...	...	...	...	...	...	...	...	...	...	...	...	...	...	...	...	...	...
Ramdasi ...	7	5	2	...	...	...	...	...	...	...	...	...	7	5	2	...	...	...	...	...	...	7	5	2
Ramdeo ...	136	68	68	...	...	...	...	...	...	...	...	...	...	...	...	...	...	...	...	...	...	...	...	...
Tarkhan ...	189	95	94	...	...	...	...	...	...	...	...	...	...	...	...	...	...	...	...	...	...	...	...	...
Thapa ...	5	5	...	...	...	...	...	...	...	...	...	...	...	...	...	...	...	...	...	...	...	...	...	...
Jain ...	442	254	188	437	251	186	2	1	1	...	...	...	...	...	...	...	...	...	...	...	...	439	252	187
Buddhist ...	35,047	17,566	17,481	...	...	...	4,831	2,431	2,400	...	...	...	...	...	...	...	...	...	...	...	...	4,831	2,431	2,400
Zoroastrian ...	11	8	3	...	...	...	...	...	...	...	...	...	...	...	...	...	...	...	...	...	...	...	...	...
Total Muhammadans ...	2,154,695	1,138,814	1,015,881	133,775	72,301	61,474	107,588	57,839	49,749	314,539	164,078	150,461	32,255	17,594	14,661	276,094	144,882	131,212	12,348	6,492	5,856	876,599	463,186	413,413
Ali ...	167	83	84	...	...	...	...	...	...	...	...	...	...	...	...	...	...	...	...	...	...	...	...	...
Alam ...	9	6	3	...	...	...	...	...	...	...	...	...	...	...	...	...	...	...	...	...	...	...	...	...
Asi ...	26	13	13	...	...	...	...	...	...	...	...	...	...	...	...	...	...	...	...	...	...	...	...	...
Attar ...	60	29	31	...	...	...	...	...	...	...	...	...	...	...	...	...	...	...	...	...	...	...	...	...
Akik ...	83	35	48	...	...	...	...	...	...	...	...	...	...	...	...	...	...	...	...	...	...	...	...	...

Caste, Tribe, Race or Nationality.	PROVINCES WITH DISTRICTS.																	
	KASHMIR PROVINCE									FRONTIER DISTRICTS.								
	Khas District.			Muzaffarabad District.			Total Kashmir Province.			Ladakh District.			Gilgit District.			Total Frontier Districts.		
	Persons.	Males.	Females.	Persons.	Males.	Females.	Persons.	Males.	Females.	Persons.	Males.	Females.	Persons.	Males.	Females.	Persons.	Males.	Females.
	26	27	28	29	30	31	32	33	34	35	36	37	38	39	40	41	42	43
Thathiar	...	...	...	...	...	...	...	...	...	...	...	...	...	...	...	...	...	...
Total Sikhs ...	6,027	3,253	2,744	6,610	3,577	3,033	12,637	6,860	5,777	4	3	1	74	61	13	78	64	14
Arora	...	...	...	...	...	...	...	...	...	...	...	...	...	...	...	...	...	...
Ahluwalia ...	38	24	14	2	1	1	10	35	15	...	...	...	...	...	...	...	...	...
Akali	5	3	2	140	213	227	145	216	229	...	...	...	...	...	...	...	...	...
Agangal	129	54	75	...	...	...	129	54	75	...	...	...	...	...	...	...	...	...
Bania	...	...	...	...	...	...	...	...	...	...	...	...	...	...	...	...	...	...
Bhatti	...	...	...	13	7	6	13	7	6	...	...	...	...	...	...	...	...	...
Barmano	...	...	...	...	...	...	...	...	...	...	...	...	...	...	...	...	...	...
Bangial	...	...	...	...	...	...	...	...	...	...	...	...	...	...	...	...	...	...
Bhat	...	...	...	...	...	...	...	...	...	...	...	...	7	5	2	7	5	2
Barwala	...	...	...	...	...	...	...	...	...	...	...	...	...	...	...	...	...	...
Brahmin	3,161	1,662	1,499	5,152	2,773	2,379	8,313	4,435	3,878	...	...	...	...	...	...	...	...	...
Bhanjra	...	...	...	...	...	...	...	...	...	...	...	...	...	...	...	...	...	...
Balas	18	10	8	...	...	...	18	10	8	...	...	...	...	...	...	...	...	...
Baujaic	154	51	103	...	...	...	154	51	103	...	...	...	...	...	...	...	...	...
Dhobi	...	...	...	...	...	...	...	...	...	...	...	...	...	...	...	...	...	...
Jat	116	89	27	60	35	25	176	124	52	...	...	...	3	2	1	3	2	1
Jatoor	...	...	...	...	...	...	...	...	...	...	...	...	...	...	...	...	...	...
Jinsi	2,013	1,160	853	807	480	327	2,820	1,640	1,180	4	3	1	64	54	10	68	57	11
Manhas	...	...	...	...	...	...	...	...	...	...	...	...	...	...	...	...	...	...
Mazbi	...	...	...	...	...	...	...	...	...	...	...	...	...	...	...	...	...	...
Rania	199	130	169	...	...	...	199	130	169	...	...	...	...	...	...	...	...	...
Ramdasi	...	...	...	...	...	...	...	...	...	...	...	...	...	...	...	...	...	...
Ramdeo	...	...	...	136	68	68	136	68	68	...	...	...	...	...	...	...	...	...
Tarkhan	189	95	94	...	...	...	189	95	94	...	...	...	...	...	...	...	...	...
Thapa	5	5	...	...	...	...	5	5	...	...	...	...	...	...	...	...	...	...
Jain	2	1	1	...	...	...	2	1	1	...	...	...	1	1	...	1	1	...
Buddhist	...	...	...	...	...	...	...	...	...	30,216	15,135	15,081	...	...	...	30,216	15,135	15,081
Zoroastrian ...	11	8	3	...	...	...	11	8	3	...	...	...	...	...	...	...	...	...
Total Muhammadans ...	926,360	491,000	435,360	157,406	84,598	72,808	1,083,766	575,598	508,168	135,551	68,268	67,283	58,779	31,762	27,017	194,330	1,00,030	94,300
Ali	167	83	84	...	...	...	167	83	84	...	...	...	...	...	...	...	...	...
Alam	9	6	3	...	...	...	9	6	3	...	...	...	...	...	...	...	...	...
Asi	26	13	13	...	...	...	26	13	13	...	...	...	...	...	...	...	...	...
Attar	60	29	31	...	...	...	60	29	31	...	...	...	...	...	...	...	...	...
Akik	83	35	48	...	...	...	83	35	48	...	...	...	...	...	...	...	...	...

TABLE XIII.

Caste, Tribe, Race or Nationality.

Caste, Tribe, Race or Nationality	Total Population.			Provinces with Districts. Jammu Province. Jammu District.			Udhampur District.			Bhimber District.			Jasrota District.			Punch Jagir.			Bhadarwah Jagir.			Total Jammu Province.		
	Persons.	Males.	Females.	Persons.	Males.	Females.	Persons.	Males.	Females.	Persons.	Males.	Females.	Persons.	Males.	Females.	Persons.	Males.	Females.	Persons.	Males.	Females.	Persons.	Males.	Females.
1	2	3	4	5	6	7	8	9	10	11	12	13	14	15	16	17	18	19	20	21	22	23	24	25
Alipa	48	20	28	...	...	...	...	...	...	...	...	...	...	...	...	...	...	...	...	...	...	...	...	...
Abdulpa	65	43	22	...	...	...	...	...	...	...	...	...	...	...	...	...	...	...	...	...	...	...	...	...
Azispa	49	30	19	...	...	...	...	...	...	...	...	...	...	...	...	...	...	...	...	...	...	...	...	...
Asurpa	78	51	27	...	...	...	...	...	...	...	...	...	...	...	...	...	...	...	...	...	...	...	...	...
Audangpa	46	35	11	...	...	...	...	...	...	...	...	...	...	...	...	...	...	...	...	...	...	...	...	...
Alpa	42	34	8	...	...	...	...	...	...	...	...	...	...	...	...	...	...	...	...	...	...	...	...	...
Algripa	53	49	4	...	...	...	...	...	...	...	...	...	...	...	...	...	...	...	...	...	...	...	...	...
Abadpa	10	7	3	...	...	...	...	...	...	...	...	...	...	...	...	...	...	...	...	...	...	...	...	...
Amnapa	11	7	4	...	...	...	...	...	...	...	...	...	...	...	...	...	...	...	...	...	...	...	...	...
Abdullapa	9	3	6	...	...	...	...	...	...	...	...	...	...	...	...	...	...	...	...	...	...	...	...	...
Alamkhan	36	16	20	...	...	...	...	...	...	...	...	...	...	...	...	...	...	...	...	...	...	...	...	...
Arsulpa	10	10	...	...	...	...	...	...	...	...	...	...	...	...	...	...	...	...	...	...	...	...	...	...
Aloo	4	4	...	...	...	...	...	...	...	...	...	...	...	...	...	...	...	...	...	...	...	...	...	...
Alampa	581	440	141	...	...	...	...	...	...	...	...	...	...	...	...	...	...	...	...	...	...	...	...	...
Amropa	8	4	4	...	...	...	...	...	...	...	...	...	...	...	...	...	...	...	...	...	...	...	...	...
Askaupa	1	1	...	...	...	...	...	...	...	...	...	...	...	...	...	...	...	...	...	...	...	...	...	...
Ayun	4	2	2	...	...	...	...	...	...	...	...	...	...	...	...	...	...	...	...	...	...	...	...	...
Ajmi	4	1	3	...	...	...	...	...	...	...	...	...	...	...	...	...	...	...	...	...	...	...	...	...
Arab	11,954	6,335	5,619	...	...	...	...	...	...	...	...	...	...	...	...	...	...	...	...	...	...	...	...	...
Akla	5	...	5	...	...	...	...	...	...	...	...	...	...	...	...	...	...	...	...	...	...	...	...	...
Aursab	36	11	25	...	...	...	...	...	...	...	...	...	...	...	...	...	...	...	...	...	...	...	...	...
Total Awan	22,610	12,301	10,309	2,474	1,327	1,147	193	124	69	5,354	2,947	2,407	145	99	46	5,847	3,282	2,565	...	...	...	14,013	7,779	6,234
Awana	7,669	4,235	3,434	244	133	111	71	64	7	672	305	367	23	4	10	2,710	1,782	928	...	...	...	3,720	2,288	1,432
" Aman	2	2	...	2	2	...	...	...	...	...	...	...	...	...	...	...	...	...	...	...	...	2	2	...
" Badar	322	158	164	...	...	...	...	...	...	130	94	46	...	...	...	...	...	...	...	...	...	130	94	45
" Bhalwal	55	44	11	...	...	...	...	...	...	55	44	11	...	...	...	...	...	...	...	...	...	55	44	11
" Bhatti	281	222	59	...	...	...	...	...	...	281	223	59	...	...	...	...	...	...	...	...	...	281	223	59
" Bhagwal	70	34	36	10	5	5	...	...	...	60	29	31	...	...	...	...	...	...	...	...	...	70	34	36
" Bajra	371	200	171	361	196	165	...	...	...	10	4	6	...	...	...	...	...	...	...	...	...	371	200	171
" Bahuise	73	37	36	25	19	6	...	...	...	48	18	30	...	...	...	...	...	...	...	...	...	73	37	36
" Badan	231	116	115	...	...	...	...	...	...	86	46	40	...	...	...	...	...	...	...	...	...	86	46	40
" Bodi	20	18	2	...	...	...	...	...	...	20	18	2	...	...	...	...	...	...	...	...	...	20	18	2
" Barnal	10	6	4	...	...	...	...	...	...	10	6	4	...	...	...	...	...	...	...	...	...	10	6	4
" Chowhan	518	188	330	49	17	32	1	1	...	416	146	270	...	...	...	...	...	...	...	...	...	466	164	302
" Chhan	29	3	26	29	3	26	...	...	...	...	...	...	...	...	...	...	...	...	...	...	...	29	3	26
" Charasi	485	338	147	...	...	...	...	...	...	485	338	147	...	...	...	...	...	...	...	...	...	485	338	147
" Dadhal	65	22	43	65	22	43	...	...	...	...	...	...	...	...	...	...	...	...	...	...	...	65	22	43
" Golra	1,962	1,126	836	1,304	789	605	...	...	...	357	164	193	...	...	...	127	118	9	...	...	...	1,878	1,071	807
" Jangua	499	304	195	...	...	...	...	...	...	...	...	...	...	...	...	379	246	183	...	...	...	379	246	133

Caste, Tribe, Race or Nationality.	PROVINCES WITH DISTRICTS.																	
	KASHMIR PROVINCE.									FRONTIER DISTRICTS.								
	Khas District.			Muzaffarabad District.			Total Kashmir Province			Ladakh District.			Gilgit District.			Total Frontier Districts.		
	Persons.	Males.	Females.	Persons.	Males.	Females.	Persons.	Males.	Females.	Persons.	Males.	Females.	Persons.	Males.	Females.	Persons.	Males.	Females.
	26	27	28	29	30	31	32	33	34	35	36	37	38	39	40	41	42	43
Alipa	...	...	...	...	...	...	...	...	...	48	20	28	...	...	...	48	20	28
Abdulpa	...	...	...	...	...	...	...	...	...	65	43	22	...	...	...	65	43	22
Asixpa	...	...	...	...	...	...	...	...	...	49	30	19	...	...	...	49	30	19
Asurpa	...	...	...	...	...	...	...	...	...	78	51	27	...	...	...	78	51	27
Audangpa	...	...	...	...	...	...	...	...	...	46	35	11	...	...	...	46	35	11
Alpa	...	...	...	...	...	...	...	...	...	42	34	8	...	...	...	42	34	8
Algripa	...	...	...	...	...	...	...	...	...	53	49	4	...	...	...	53	49	4
Abadpa	...	...	...	...	...	...	...	...	...	10	7	3	...	...	...	10	7	3
Amaspa	...	...	...	...	...	...	...	...	...	11	7	4	...	...	...	11	7	4
Abadlopa	...	...	...	...	...	...	...	...	...	9	3	6	...	...	...	9	3	6
Alamkhan	...	...	...	...	...	...	...	...	...	36	16	20	...	...	...	36	16	20
Arsulpa	...	...	...	...	...	...	...	...	...	10	10	...	...	...	...	10	10	...
Alla	...	...	...	...	...	...	...	...	...	4	4	...	...	...	...	4	4	...
Alampa	...	...	...	...	...	...	...	...	...	581	440	141	...	...	...	581	440	141
Amropa	...	...	...	...	...	...	...	...	...	8	4	4	...	...	...	8	4	4
Askanpa	...	...	...	...	...	...	...	...	...	1	1	...	...	...	...	1	1	...
Ayun	...	...	...	...	...	...	...	...	...	4	2	2	...	...	...	4	2	2
Ajmi	...	...	...	...	...	...	...	...	...	...	...	...	4	1	3	4	1	3
Arab	...	...	...	...	...	...	...	...	...	...	...	...	11,954	6,335	5,619	11,954	6,335	5,619
Akla	...	...	...	5	...	5	5	...	5	...	...	...	...	...	...	...	...	...
Aursah	...	...	...	36	11	25	36	11	25	...	...	...	...	...	...	...	...	...
Total Awan ...	1,039	577	462	7,558	3,945	3,613	8,597	4,522	4,075	...	...	...	...	...	...	...	...	...
Awan	838	473	365	3,111	1,474	1,637	3,949	1,947	2,002	...	...	...	...	...	...	...	...	...
" Aman	...	...	...	...	...	...	...	...	...	...	...	...	...	...	...	...	...	...
" Badar	...	...	...	183	64	119	183	64	119	...	...	...	...	...	...	...	...	...
" Bhalwal	...	...	...	...	...	...	...	...	...	...	...	...	...	...	...	...	...	...
" Bhatti	...	...	...	...	...	...	...	...	...	...	...	...	...	...	...	...	...	...
" Bhagwal	...	...	...	...	...	...	...	...	...	...	...	...	...	...	...	...	...	...
" Bajra	...	...	...	...	...	...	...	...	...	...	...	...	...	...	...	...	...	...
" Bahulac	...	...	...	...	...	...	...	...	...	...	...	...	...	...	...	...	...	...
" Badan	...	...	...	145	70	75	145	70	75	...	...	...	...	...	...	...	...	...
" Bodi	...	...	...	...	...	...	...	...	...	...	...	...	...	...	...	...	...	...
" Barnal	...	...	...	...	...	...	...	...	...	...	...	...	...	...	...	...	...	...
" Chowhan	...	...	...	52	24	28	52	34	28	...	...	...	...	...	...	...	...	...
" Chhan	...	...	...	...	...	...	...	...	...	...	...	...	...	...	...	...	...	...
" Charasi	...	...	...	...	...	...	...	...	...	...	...	...	...	...	...	...	...	...
" Dadhal	...	...	...	...	...	...	...	...	...	...	...	...	...	...	...	...	...	...
" Golra	...	...	...	84	55	29	84	55	29	...	...	...	...	...	...	...	...	...
" Jangua	...	...	...	120	58	62	120	58	62	...	...	...	...	...	...	...	...	...

TABLE XIII.

Caste, Tribe, Race or Nationality.

Caste, Tribe, Race or Nationality.	Total Population.			Provinces with Districts. Jammu Province. Jammu District.			Udhampur District.			Bhimber District.			Jasrota District.			Punch Jágir.			Bhadarwah Jágir.			Total Jammu Province.		
	Persons.	Males.	Females.	Persons.	Males.	Females.	Persons.	Males.	Females.	Persons.	Males.	Females.	Persons.	Males.	Females.	Persons.	Males.	Females.	Persons.	Males.	Females.	Persons.	Males.	Females.
1	2	3	4	5	6	7	8	9	10	11	12	13	14	15	16	17	18	19	20	21	22	23	24	25
Awan Jat	116	65	51	...	...	...	...	...	...	...	...	...	...	...	...	...	...	...	...	...	...	...	...	...
" Jathlo	4	1	3	...	...	...	...	...	...	4	1	3	...	...	...	...	...	...	...	...	...	4	1	3
" Jagran	272	149	123	...	...	...	...	...	...	...	...	...	...	...	...	...	...	...	...	...	...	...	...	...
" Jhanwal	169	92	77	...	...	...	...	...	...	...	...	...	...	...	...	...	...	...	...	...	...	...	...	...
" Kuchhbi	439	184	255	...	...	...	...	...	...	...	...	...	...	...	...	...	...	...	...	...	...	...	...	...
" Kalpan	1,450	865	585	1	1	...	...	...	...	506	272	234	...	...	...	...	...	...	...	...	...	507	273	234
" Karial	4	3	1	4	3	1	...	...	...	...	...	...	...	...	...	...	...	...	...	...	...	4	3	1
" Khokhar	2,511	1,372	1,139	171	80	91	52	17	35	232	110	122	122	95	27	1,011	541	470	...	...	...	1,588	843	745
" Kutab Shai	2,738	1,220	1,518	32	22	10	...	...	...	123	67	56	...	...	...	1,407	479	988	...	...	...	1,622	608	1,054
" Karwal	14	13	1	...	...	...	...	...	...	14	13	1	...	...	...	...	...	...	...	...	...	14	13	1
" Khurana	927	601	326	29	4	25	...	...	...	898	597	301	...	...	...	...	...	...	...	...	...	927	601	326
" Katwal	249	175	74	...	...	...	...	...	...	156	82	74	...	...	...	93	93	...	...	...	...	249	175	74
" Karol	32	12	20	...	...	...	...	...	...	1	...	1	...	...	...	...	...	...	...	...	...	1	...	1
" Khal	8	...	8	...	...	...	...	...	...	8	...	8	...	...	...	...	...	...	...	...	...	8	...	8
" Kausia	31	19	12	...	...	...	...	...	...	31	19	12	...	...	...	...	...	...	...	...	...	31	19	12
" Lattia	14	14	...	...	...	...	...	...	...	14	14	...	...	...	...	...	...	...	...	...	...	14	14	...
" Manghal	93	43	50	33	20	13	...	...	...	...	...	...	...	...	...	60	23	37	...	...	...	93	43	50
" Molwage	6	...	6	...	...	...	...	...	...	6	...	6	...	...	...	...	...	...	...	...	...	6	...	6
" Manjal	6	2	4	...	...	...	...	...	...	6	2	4	...	...	...	...	...	...	...	...	...	6	2	4
" Mandial	168	87	81	...	...	...	...	...	...	113	58	55	...	...	...	...	...	...	...	...	...	113	58	55
" Maliak	382	184	198	9	7	2	...	...	...	373	177	196	...	...	...	...	...	...	...	...	...	382	184	198
" Mir Sultani	43	22	21	...	...	...	43	22	21	...	...	...	...	...	...	...	...	...	...	...	...	43	22	21
" Ranga	26	20	6	...	...	...	26	20	6	...	...	...	...	...	...	...	...	...	...	...	...	26	20	6
" Sindhia	230	101	129	...	...	...	...	...	...	230	101	129	...	...	...	...	...	...	...	...	...	230	101	129
" Sarhal	6	1	5	6	1	5	...	...	...	...	...	...	...	...	...	...	...	...	...	...	...	6	1	5
" Sibbi	4	1	3	4	1	3	...	...	...	...	...	...	...	...	...	...	...	...	...	...	...	4	1	3
" Sogi	4	1	3	4	1	3	...	...	...	...	...	...	...	...	...	...	...	...	...	...	...	4	1	3
" Suruba	2	1	1	2	1	1	...	...	...	...	...	...	...	...	...	...	...	...	...	...	...	2	1	1
Ahmedpa	752	486	266	...	...	...	...	...	...	...	...	...	...	...	...	...	...	...	...	...	...	...	...	...
Asadpa	149	44	105	...	...	...	...	...	...	...	...	...	...	...	...	...	...	...	...	...	...	...	...	...
Abapa	166	34	132	...	...	...	...	...	...	...	...	...	...	...	...	...	...	...	...	...	...	...	...	...
Alirpa	15	9	6	...	...	...	...	...	...	...	...	...	...	...	...	...	...	...	...	...	...	...	...	...
Attarpa	11	8	3	...	...	...	...	...	...	...	...	...	...	...	...	...	...	...	...	...	...	...	...	...
Akhunpa	5,404	2,994	2,410	...	...	...	...	...	...	...	...	...	...	...	...	...	...	...	...	...	...	...	...	...
Arghunpa	408	193	215	...	...	...	...	...	...	...	...	...	...	...	...	...	...	...	...	...	...	...	...	...
Alupa	78	45	33	...	...	...	...	...	...	...	...	...	...	...	...	...	...	...	...	...	...	...	...	...
Alpoh	7	4	3	...	...	...	...	...	...	...	...	...	...	...	...	...	...	...	...	...	...	...	...	...
Alchakpa	190	63	127	...	...	...	...	...	...	...	...	...	...	...	...	...	...	...	...	...	...	...	...	...
Aripa	30	28	2	...	...	...	...	...	...	...	...	...	...	...	...	...	...	...	...	...	...	...	...	...
Anakakpa	105	20	85	...	...	...	...	...	...	...	...	...	...	...	...	...	...	...	...	...	...	...	...	...
Alukpa	145	27	118	...	...	...	...	...	...	...	...	...	...	...	...	...	...	...	...	...	...	...	...	...

PROVINCES WITH DISTRICTS.

Caste, Tribe, Race or Nationality.	Kashmir Province. Khas District. Persons.	Males.	Females.	Muzaffarabad District. Persons.	Males.	Females.	Total Kashmir Province. Persons.	Males.	Females.	Frontier Districts. Ladakh District. Persons.	Males.	Females.	Gilgit District. Persons.	Males.	Females.	Total Frontier Districts. Persons.	Males.	Females.
	26	27	28	29	30	31	32	33	34	35	36	37	38	39	40	41	42	43
Awan Jat	116	65	51	...	...	...	110	65	51	...	...	...	...	...	...	...	...	...
" Juthlo	...	...	...	...	...	...	...	...	...	...	...	...	...	...	...	...	...	...
" Juggan	...	...	...	272	149	123	272	149	123	...	...	...	...	...	...	...	...	...
" Jhatwal	...	...	...	169	92	77	169	92	77	...	...	...	...	...	...	...	...	...
" Kuchhal	...	...	...	439	184	255	439	184	255	...	...	...	...	...	...	...	...	...
" Kalgan	64	27	27	889	565	324	943	592	351	...	...	...	...	...	...	...	...	...
" Karial	...	...	...	...	...	...	...	...	...	...	...	...	...	...	...	...	...	...
" Khokhar	...	...	...	923	529	394	923	529	394	...	...	...	...	...	...	...	...	...
" Kutab Shai	...	...	...	1,116	652	464	1,116	652	464	...	...	...	...	...	...	...	...	...
" Karwal	...	...	...	...	...	...	...	...	...	...	...	...	...	...	...	...	...	...
" Khurana	...	...	...	...	...	...	...	...	...	...	...	...	...	...	...	...	...	...
" Awans Katwal	...	...	...	...	...	...	...	...	...	...	...	...	...	...	...	...	...	...
" Karol	31	12	19	...	...	...	31	12	19	...	...	...	...	...	...	...	...	...
" Khal	...	...	...	...	...	...	...	...	...	...	...	...	...	...	...	...	...	...
" Kansia	...	...	...	...	...	...	...	...	...	...	...	...	...	...	...	...	...	...
" Luttia	...	...	...	...	...	...	...	...	...	...	...	...	...	...	...	...	...	...
" Maughal	...	...	...	...	...	...	...	...	...	...	...	...	...	...	...	...	...	...
" Malwago	...	...	...	...	...	...	...	...	...	...	...	...	...	...	...	...	...	...
" Manjal	...	...	...	...	...	...	...	...	...	...	...	...	...	...	...	...	...	...
" Mandial	...	...	...	55	29	26	55	29	26	...	...	...	...	...	...	...	...	...
" Mallak	...	...	...	...	...	...	...	...	...	...	...	...	...	...	...	...	...	...
" Mir Sultani	...	...	...	...	...	...	...	...	...	...	...	...	...	...	...	...	...	...
" Ranga	...	...	...	...	...	...	...	...	...	...	...	...	...	...	...	...	...	...
" Sindhia	...	...	...	...	...	...	...	...	...	...	...	...	...	...	...	...	...	...
" Sarhal	...	...	...	...	...	...	...	...	...	...	...	...	...	...	...	...	...	...
" Sibbi	...	...	...	...	...	...	...	...	...	...	...	...	...	...	...	...	...	...
" Sogi	...	...	...	...	...	...	...	...	...	...	...	...	...	...	...	...	...	...
" Suruba	...	...	...	...	...	...	...	...	...	...	...	...	...	...	...	...	...	...
Ahmodpa	...	...	...	...	...	...	...	...	...	752	486	266	...	...	...	752	486	266
Asadpa	...	...	...	...	...	...	...	...	...	149	44	105	...	...	...	149	44	105
Abapa	...	...	...	...	...	...	...	...	...	166	34	132	...	...	...	166	34	132
Alirpa	...	...	...	...	...	...	...	...	...	15	9	6	...	...	...	15	9	6
Attarpa	...	...	...	...	...	...	...	...	...	11	8	3	...	...	...	11	8	3
Akhunpa	4,607	2,599	2,008	22	10	12	4,629	2,609	2,020	742	366	376	33	19	14	775	385	390
Arghunpa	...	...	...	...	...	...	...	...	...	405	190	215	3	3	...	408	193	215
Alupa	...	...	...	...	...	...	...	...	...	78	45	33	...	...	...	78	45	33
Alpoh	...	...	...	...	...	...	...	...	...	7	4	3	...	...	...	7	4	3
Alchakpa	...	...	...	...	...	...	...	...	...	190	63	127	...	...	...	190	63	127
Aripa	...	...	...	...	...	...	...	...	...	30	28	2	...	...	...	30	28	2
Anachakpa	...	...	...	...	...	...	...	...	...	105	20	85	...	...	...	105	20	85
Alukpa	...	...	...	...	...	...	...	...	...	145	27	118	...	...	...	145	27	118

TABLE XIII.

Caste, Tribe, Race or Nationality.

PROVINCES WITH DISTRICTS.

JAMMU PROVINCE.

Caste, Tribe, Race or Nationality.	Total Population.			Jammu District.			Udhampur District.			Bhimber District.			Jasrota District.			Punch Jágír.			Bhadarwah Jágír.			Total Jammu Province.		
	Persons.	Males.	Females.	Persons.	Males.	Females.	Persons.	Males.	Females.	Persons.	Males.	Females.	Persons.	Males.	Females.	Persons.	Males.	Females.	Persons.	Males.	Females.	Persons.	Males.	Females.
1	2	3	4	5	6	7	8	9	10	11	12	13	14	15	16	17	18	19	20	21	22	23	24	25
Abbupa	112	36	76	...	...	...	...	...	...	...	...	...	...	...	...	...	...	...	...	...	...	...	...	...
Aahpa	106	55	51	...	...	...	...	...	...	...	...	...	...	...	...	...	...	...	...	...	...	...	...	...
Amus	128	53	75	...	...	...	...	...	...	...	...	...	...	...	...	...	...	...	...	...	...	...	...	...
Arak	68	33	35	...	...	...	...	...	...	...	...	...	...	...	...	...	...	...	...	...	...	...	...	...
Aonkpa	216	98	118	...	...	...	...	...	...	...	...	...	...	...	...	...	...	...	...	...	...	...	...	...
Akbarpa	124	47	77	...	...	...	...	...	...	...	...	...	...	...	...	...	...	...	...	...	...	...	...	...
Akwarpa	60	6	54	...	...	...	...	...	...	...	...	...	...	...	...	...	...	...	...	...	...	...	...	...
Amarchakpa	52	40	12	...	...	...	...	...	...	...	...	...	...	...	...	...	...	...	...	...	...	...	...	...
Ajurpa	22	10	12	...	...	...	...	...	...	...	...	...	...	...	...	...	...	...	...	...	...	...	...	...
Amriakapa	19	5	14	...	...	...	...	...	...	...	...	...	...	...	...	...	...	...	...	...	...	...	...	...
Auladopa	17	8	9	...	...	...	...	...	...	...	...	...	...	...	...	...	...	...	...	...	...	...	...	...
Amsha	38	24	14	...	...	...	...	...	...	...	...	...	...	...	...	...	...	...	...	...	...	...	...	...
Aoonkpa	20	10	10	...	...	...	...	...	...	...	...	...	...	...	...	...	...	...	...	...	...	...	...	...
Armanpa	99	44	55	...	...	...	...	...	...	...	...	...	...	...	...	...	...	...	...	...	...	...	...	...
Alumahorpa	47	26	21	...	...	...	...	...	...	...	...	...	...	...	...	...	...	...	...	...	...	...	...	...
Apadi	75	16	59	...	...	...	...	...	...	...	...	...	...	...	...	...	...	...	...	...	...	...	...	...
Ambo	48	27	21	...	...	...	...	...	...	...	...	...	...	...	...	...	...	...	...	...	...	...	...	...
Aguntar	5,461	2,920	2,541	...	...	...	...	...	...	...	...	...	...	...	...	...	...	...	...	...	...	...	...	...
Anjarni	39	23	16	...	...	...	...	...	...	...	...	...	...	...	...	...	...	...	...	...	...	...	...	...
Arwal	451	259	192	451	259	192	...	...	...	...	...	...	...	...	...	...	...	...	...	...	...	451	259	192
Aghalt	14	10	4	...	...	...	...	...	...	...	...	...	...	...	...	...	...	...	...	...	...	...	...	...
Ashraf	62	29	33	...	...	...	...	...	...	...	...	...	...	...	...	...	...	...	...	...	...	...	...	...
Alu	7,948	4,292	3,656	...	...	...	...	...	...	...	...	...	...	...	...	...	...	...	...	...	...	...	...	...
Adand	25	10	15	...	...	...	...	...	...	...	...	...	...	...	...	...	...	...	...	...	...	...	...	...
Alu	43	16	27	...	...	...	...	...	...	...	...	...	...	...	...	...	...	...	...	...	...	...	...	...
Arna	519	349	170	...	...	...	...	...	...	...	...	...	...	...	...	...	...	...	...	...	...	...	...	...
Agarman	28	7	21	...	...	...	...	...	...	...	...	...	...	...	...	...	...	...	...	...	...	...	...	...
Aucku	41	12	29	...	...	...	...	...	...	...	...	...	...	...	...	...	...	...	...	...	...	...	...	...
Amri	7	1	6	...	...	...	...	...	...	...	...	...	...	...	...	...	...	...	...	...	...	...	...	...
Ammu	9	4	5	...	...	...	...	...	...	...	...	...	...	...	...	...	...	...	...	...	...	...	...	...
Aham	12	7	5	...	...	...	...	...	...	...	...	...	...	...	...	...	...	...	...	...	...	...	...	...
Atanto	38	23	15	...	...	...	...	...	...	...	...	...	...	...	...	...	...	...	...	...	...	...	...	...
Adasi	21	17	4	...	...	...	...	...	...	...	...	...	...	...	...	...	...	...	...	...	...	...	...	...
Adrung	4	3	1	...	...	...	...	...	...	...	...	...	...	...	...	...	...	...	...	...	...	...	...	...
Arkhand	12	4	8	...	...	...	...	...	...	...	...	...	...	...	...	...	...	...	...	...	...	...	...	...
Achat	1	1	...	...	...	...	...	...	...	...	...	...	...	...	...	...	...	...	...	...	...	...	...	...
Aohul	8	4	4	...	...	...	...	...	...	...	...	...	...	...	...	...	...	...	...	...	...	...	...	...
Abichair	1	1	...	...	...	...	...	...	...	...	...	...	...	...	...	...	...	...	...	...	...	...	...	...
Akz	5	2	3	...	...	...	...	...	...	...	...	...	...	...	...	...	...	...	...	...	...	...	...	...
Akhar	1	1	...	...	...	...	...	...	...	...	...	...	...	...	...	...	...	...	...	...	...	...	...	...
Aosha	7	3	4	...	...	...	...	...	...	...	...	...	...	...	...	...	...	...	...	...	...	...	...	...

PROVINCES WITH DISTRICTS.

Caste, Tribe, Race or Nationality.	Kashmir Province. Khas District. Persons.	Males.	Females.	Muzaffarabad District. Persons.	Males.	Females.	Total Kashmir Province. Persons.	Males.	Females.	Frontier Districts. Ladakh District. Persons.	Males.	Females.	Gilgit District. Persons.	Males.	Females.	Total Frontier Districts. Persons.	Males.	Females.
	26	27	28	29	30	31	32	33	34	35	36	37	38	39	40	41	42	43
Abbupa	...	...	...	...	...	...	...	...	...	112	36	76	...	...	...	112	36	76
Ashpa	...	...	...	...	...	...	...	...	...	106	55	51	...	...	...	106	55	51
Amna	...	...	...	...	...	...	...	...	...	128	53	75	...	...	...	128	53	75
Arak	...	...	...	...	...	...	...	...	...	68	33	35	...	...	...	68	33	35
Asakpa	...	...	...	...	...	...	...	...	...	216	98	118	...	...	...	216	98	118
Akbarpa	...	...	...	...	...	...	...	...	...	124	47	77	...	...	...	124	47	77
Akwarpa	...	...	...	...	...	...	...	...	...	60	6	54	...	...	...	60	6	54
Amarchakpa	...	...	...	...	...	...	...	...	...	52	40	12	...	...	...	52	40	12
Ajarpa	...	...	...	...	...	...	...	...	...	22	10	12	...	...	...	22	10	12
Amrinkapa	...	...	...	...	...	...	...	...	...	19	5	14	...	...	...	19	5	14
Auladepa	...	...	...	...	...	...	...	...	...	17	8	9	...	...	...	17	8	9
Amshu	...	...	...	...	...	...	...	...	...	38	24	14	...	...	...	38	24	14
Asonkpa	...	...	...	...	...	...	...	...	...	20	10	10	...	...	...	20	10	10
Armanpa	...	...	...	...	...	...	...	...	...	99	44	55	...	...	...	99	44	55
Alamshorpa	...	...	...	...	...	...	...	...	...	47	26	21	...	...	...	47	26	21
Apadi	73	14	59	...	...	...	73	14	59	2	2	...	...	...	...	2	2	...
Ambo	...	...	...	...	...	...	...	...	...	34	20	14	14	7	7	48	27	21
Agantor	5,461	2,920	2,541	...	...	...	5,461	2,920	2,541	...	...	...	...	...	...	...	...	...
Anjarni	39	23	16	...	...	...	39	23	16	...	...	...	...	...	...	...	...	...
Awal	...	...	...	...	...	...	...	...	...	...	...	...	...	...	...	...	...	...
Aghait	14	10	4	...	...	...	14	10	4	...	...	...	...	...	...	...	...	...
Ashraf	62	29	33	...	...	...	62	29	33	...	...	...	...	...	...	...	...	...
Aitu	7,048	4,202	3,656	...	...	...	7,048	4,202	3,656	...	...	...	...	...	...	...	...	...
Adand	25	10	15	...	...	...	25	10	15	...	...	...	...	...	...	...	...	...
Atu	43	16	27	...	...	...	43	16	27	...	...	...	...	...	...	...	...	...
Arum	519	349	170	...	...	...	519	340	170	...	...	...	...	...	...	...	...	...
Agarman	28	7	21	...	...	...	28	7	21	...	...	...	...	...	...	...	...	...
Andku	41	12	29	...	...	...	41	12	29	...	...	...	...	...	...	...	...	...
Amri	7	1	6	...	...	...	7	1	6	...	...	...	...	...	...	...	...	...
Aman	9	4	5	...	...	...	9	4	5	...	...	...	...	...	...	...	...	...
Aham	12	7	5	...	...	...	12	7	5	...	...	...	...	...	...	...	...	...
Atanto	38	23	15	...	...	...	38	23	15	...	...	...	...	...	...	...	...	...
Adasi	21	17	4	...	...	...	21	17	4	...	...	...	...	...	...	...	...	...
Adrong	4	3	1	...	...	...	4	3	1	...	...	...	...	...	...	...	...	...
Achhaad	12	4	8	...	...	...	12	4	8	...	...	...	...	...	...	...	...	...
Achat	1	1	...	...	...	...	1	1	...	...	...	...	...	...	...	...	...	...
Aohni	8	4	4	...	...	...	8	4	4	...	...	...	...	...	...	...	...	...
Abkhair	1	1	...	...	...	...	1	1	...	...	...	...	...	...	...	...	...	...
Akk	5	2	3	...	...	...	5	2	3	...	...	...	...	...	...	...	...	...
Akhar	1	1	...	...	...	...	1	1	...	...	...	...	...	...	...	...	...	...
Aosha	7	3	4	...	...	...	7	3	4	...	...	...	...	...	...	...	...	...

TABLE XIII.

Caste, Tribe, Race or Nationality.

Caste, Tribe, Race or Nationality.	Total Population. Persons.	Total Population. Males.	Total Population. Females.	Provinces with Districts. Jammu Province. Jammu District. Persons.	Jammu District. Males.	Jammu District. Females.	Chhampur District. Persons.	Chhampur District. Males.	Chhampur District. Females.	Bhimber District. Persons.	Bhimber District. Males.	Bhimber District. Females.	Jasrota District. Persons.	Jasrota District. Males.	Jasrota District. Females.	Punch Jágir. Persons.	Punch Jágir. Males.	Punch Jágir. Females.	Bhadarwah Jágir. Persons.	Bhadarwah Jágir. Males.	Bhadarwah Jágir. Females.	Total Jammu Province. Persons.	Total Jammu Province. Males.	Total Jammu Province. Females.
1	2	3	4	5	6	7	8	9	10	11	12	13	14	15	16	17	18	19	20	21	22	23	24	25
Ambor	44	24	20	...	...	...	...	...	...	...	...	...	...	...	...	...	...	...	...	...	...	...	...	...
Aranga	8	...	8	...	...	...	...	...	...	...	...	...	...	...	...	...	...	...	...	...	...	...	...	...
Abju	11	8	3	...	...	...	...	...	...	...	...	...	...	...	...	...	...	...	...	...	...	...	...	...
Aunt	44	22	22	...	...	...	...	...	...	...	...	...	...	...	...	...	...	...	...	...	...	...	...	...
Aopi	20	13	7	...	...	...	...	...	...	...	...	...	...	...	...	...	...	...	...	...	...	...	...	...
Arda	72	63	9	...	...	...	...	...	...	...	...	...	...	...	...	...	...	...	...	...	...	...	...	...
Afa	9	6	3	...	...	...	...	...	...	...	...	...	...	...	...	...	...	...	...	...	...	...	...	...
Ansari	66	59	7	...	...	...	...	...	...	...	...	...	...	...	...	...	...	...	...	...	...	...	...	...
Achami	53	28	25	...	...	...	...	...	...	...	...	...	...	...	...	...	...	...	...	...	...	...	...	...
Abahwadi	32	12	20	...	...	...	...	...	...	...	...	...	...	...	...	...	...	...	...	...	...	...	...	...
Asbar	10	4	6	...	...	...	...	...	...	...	...	...	...	...	...	...	...	...	...	...	...	...	...	...
Ababho	82	46	36	...	...	...	...	...	...	...	...	...	...	...	...	...	...	...	...	...	...	...	...	...
Afghan	343	296	47	...	...	...	...	...	...	...	...	...	...	...	...	...	...	...	...	...	...	...	...	...
Afridi	19	19	...	...	...	...	...	...	...	...	...	...	...	...	...	...	...	...	...	...	...	...	...	...
Adrash	21	21	...	...	...	...	...	...	...	...	...	...	...	...	...	...	...	...	...	...	...	...	...	...
Achal	9	9	...	...	...	...	...	...	...	...	...	...	...	...	...	...	...	...	...	...	...	...	...	...
Asia	10	10	...	...	...	...	...	...	...	...	...	...	...	...	...	...	...	...	...	...	...	...	...	...
Aghauri	17	17	...	...	...	...	...	...	...	...	...	...	...	...	...	...	...	...	...	...	...	...	...	...
Alasy	592	332	260	...	...	...	...	...	...	...	...	...	...	...	...	...	...	...	...	...	...	...	...	...
Arash	5	5	...	...	...	...	...	...	...	...	...	...	...	...	...	...	...	...	...	...	...	...	...	...
Antmehtor	8	4	4	8	4	4	...	...	...	...	...	...	...	...	...	...	...	...	...	...	...	8	4	4
Agga	96	52	44	...	...	...	...	...	...	...	...	...	...	...	...	...	...	...	...	...	...	...	...	...
Arosy	4	2	2	...	...	...	...	...	...	...	...	...	...	...	...	...	...	...	...	...	...	...	...	...
Andh	3	1	2	...	...	...	...	...	...	...	...	...	...	...	...	...	...	...	...	...	...	...	...	...
Armun	3	1	2	...	...	...	...	...	...	...	...	...	...	...	...	...	...	...	...	...	...	...	...	...
Arkouh	3	...	3	...	...	...	...	...	...	...	...	...	...	...	...	...	...	...	...	...	...	...	...	...
Alahan	21	7	14	...	...	...	...	...	...	...	...	...	...	...	...	...	...	...	...	...	...	...	...	...
Amar	110	110	...	...	...	...	...	...	...	...	...	...	...	...	...	...	...	...	...	...	...	...	...	...
Akhun	147	136	11	...	...	...	...	...	...	...	...	...	...	...	...	...	...	...	...	...	...	...	...	...
Banjo	4	1	3	4	1	3	...	...	...	...	...	...	...	...	...	...	...	...	...	...	...	4	1	3
Bhatti	1,442	802	640	330	196	143	11	6	5	52	23	29	...	...	...	...	...	...	...	...	...	402	225	177
Badhan	3	...	3	3	...	3	...	...	...	...	...	...	...	...	...	...	...	...	...	...	...	3	...	3
Ballan	278	141	137	1	...	1	...	...	...	...	...	...	...	...	...	...	...	...	...	...	...	1	...	1
Bhat	64	39	25	...	...	...	12	4	8	...	...	...	27	13	11	23	22	1	2	...	2	64	39	25
Baina	6,948	3,531	3,417	64	57	7	...	...	...	6,859	3,455	3,404	...	...	...	...	...	...	...	...	...	6,923	3,512	3,411
Baloch	876	715	161	2	1	1	19	15	4	...	...	...	3	2	1	...	...	...	...	...	...	24	18	6
Bakarwal	466	208	258	39	27	12	11	3	8	195	73	122	...	...	...	...	...	...	...	...	...	245	103	143
Bhatra	1	...	1	...	...	...	1	...	1	...	...	...	...	...	...	...	...	...	...	...	...	1	...	1
Baignr	1,248	537	711	...	...	...	340	180	160	418	187	231	256	140	116	222	28	194	12	2	10	1,348	637	711
Bagare	15	...	15	...	...	...	15	...	15	...	...	...	...	...	...	...	...	...	...	...	...	15	...	15
Baldar	1,111	540	571	...	...	...	32	25	7	...	...	...	1,079	515	564	...	...	...	...	...	...	1,111	540	571

PROVINCES WITH DISTRICTS.

Caste, Tribe, Race or Nationality.	Kashmir Province. Khás District. Persons.	Males.	Females.	Muzaffarabad District. Persons.	Males.	Females.	Total Kashmir Province. Persons.	Males.	Females.	Frontier Districts. Ladakh District. Persons.	Males.	Females.	Gilgit District. Persons.	Males.	Females.	Total Frontier Districts. Persons.	Males.	Females.
	26	27	28	29	30	31	32	33	34	35	36	37	38	39	40	41	42	43
Ambor	44	24	20	...	...	...	44	24	20	...	...	...	...	...	...	...	...	...
Aranga	8	...	8	...	...	...	8	...	8	...	...	...	...	...	...	...	...	...
Abju	11	8	3	...	...	...	11	8	3	...	...	...	...	...	...	...	...	...
Aunt	44	22	22	...	...	...	44	22	22	...	...	...	...	...	...	...	...	...
Aopi	20	13	7	...	...	...	20	13	7	...	...	...	...	...	...	...	...	...
Arda	24	15	9	48	48	...	72	63	9	...	...	...	...	...	...	...	...	...
Afa	9	6	3	...	...	...	9	6	3	...	...	...	...	...	...	...	...	...
Ausari	66	59	7	...	...	...	66	59	7	...	...	...	...	...	...	...	...	...
Ashami	53	28	25	...	...	...	53	28	25	...	...	...	...	...	...	...	...	...
Abshwadi	32	12	20	...	...	...	32	12	20	...	...	...	...	...	...	...	...	...
Asbar	10	4	6	...	...	...	10	4	6	...	...	...	...	...	...	...	...	...
Abasho	...	...	...	...	...	...	...	...	...	...	...	...	82	46	36	82	46	36
Afghan	...	...	...	...	...	...	...	...	...	...	...	...	343	296	47	343	296	47
Afridi	...	...	...	...	...	...	...	...	...	...	...	...	19	19	...	19	19	...
Adrash	...	...	...	21	21	...	21	21	...	...	...	...	...	...	...	...	...	...
Achal	...	...	...	9	9	...	9	9	...	...	...	...	...	...	...	...	...	...
Asia	...	...	...	10	10	...	10	10	...	...	...	...	...	...	...	...	...	...
Aghawri	...	...	...	17	17	...	17	17	...	...	...	...	...	...	...	...	...	...
Alaav	454	261	193	6	6	...	460	267	193	132	65	67	...	...	...	132	65	67
Arash	5	5	...	...	...	...	5	5	...	...	...	...	...	...	...	...	...	...
Antmehtor	...	...	...	...	...	...	...	...	...	...	...	...	...	...	...	...	...	...
Agga	96	52	44	...	...	...	96	52	44	...	...	...	...	...	...	...	...	...
Arosy	4	2	2	...	...	...	4	2	2	...	...	...	...	...	...	...	...	...
Andh	3	1	2	...	...	...	3	1	2	...	...	...	...	...	...	...	...	...
Arman	3	1	2	...	...	...	3	1	2	...	...	...	...	...	...	...	...	...
Arkoub	3	...	3	...	...	...	3	...	3	...	...	...	...	...	...	...	...	...
Alahan	21	7	14	...	...	...	21	7	14	...	...	...	...	...	...	...	...	...
Amar	110	110	...	...	...	...	110	110	...	...	...	...	...	...	...	...	...	...
Akhun	147	136	11	...	...	...	147	136	11	...	...	...	...	...	...	...	...	...
Banjo	...	...	...	...	...	...	...	...	...	...	...	...	...	...	...	...	...	...
Bhatti	...	...	...	1,040	577	463	1,040	577	463	...	...	...	...	...	...	...	...	...
Badhan	...	...	...	...	...	...	...	...	...	...	...	...	...	...	...	...	...	...
Ballan	277	141	136	...	...	...	277	141	136	...	...	...	...	...	...	...	...	...
Bhat	...	...	...	...	...	...	...	...	...	...	...	...	...	...	...	...	...	...
Bains	...	...	...	25	19	6	25	19	6	...	...	...	...	...	...	...	...	...
Baloch	...	...	...	852	697	155	852	697	155	...	...	...	...	...	...	...	...	...
Bakarwal	221	105	116	...	...	...	221	105	116	...	...	...	...	...	...	...	...	...
Bhatre	...	...	...	...	...	...	...	...	...	...	...	...	...	...	...	...	...	...
Basigar	...	...	...	...	...	...	...	...	...	...	...	...	...	...	...	...	...	...
Bagaro	...	...	...	...	...	...	...	...	...	...	...	...	...	...	...	...	...	...
Baldar	...	...	...	...	...	...	...	...	...	...	...	...	...	...	...	...	...	...

TABLE XIII.

Caste, Tribe, Race or Nationality.

Caste, Tribe, Race or Nationality.	Total Population.			Provinces with Districts. Jammu Province. Jammu District.			Udhampur District.			Bhimber District			[illegible] District.			Punch Jagir.			Bhadarwah Jagir.			Total Jammu Province.		
	Persons.	Males.	Females.	Persons.	Males.	Females.	Persons.	Males.	Females.	Persons.	Males.	Females.	Persons.	Males.	Females.	Persons.	Males.	Females.	Persons.	Males.	Females.	Persons.	Males.	Females.
1	2	3	4	5	6	7	8	9	10	11	12	13	14	15	16	17	18	19	20	21	22	23	24	25
Bhut	2,431	2,431	...	...	...	...	2,431	2,431	...	...	...	...	...	...	...	...	...	...	...	...	...	2,431	2,431	...
Bharui	451	197	254	...	...	...	12	9	3	118	50	68	321	138	183	...	...	...	...	...	...	451	197	254
Bardar	4	...	4	...	...	...	4	...	4	...	...	...	...	...	...	...	...	...	...	...	...	4	...	4
Boru	3	2	1	...	...	...	3	2	1	...	...	...	...	...	...	...	...	...	...	...	...	3	2	1
Banjara	133	73	60	...	...	...	32	14	18	...	...	...	101	59	42	...	...	...	...	...	...	133	73	60
Barbala	117	58	59	...	...	...	...	...	...	3	...	3	25	12	13	...	...	...	...	...	...	28	12	16
Batwal	15	...	15	...	...	...	...	...	...	15	...	15	...	...	...	...	...	...	...	...	...	15	...	15
Balinds	9,129	5,031	4,098	2,581	1,311	1,270	1,897	981	916	1,670	1,112	558	1,077	607	470	118	78	40	91	39	52	7,434	4,128	3,306
Banial	6	3	3	...	...	...	...	...	...	6	3	3	...	...	...	...	...	...	...	...	...	6	3	3
Bungial	21	6	15	...	...	...	...	...	...	...	...	...	21	6	15	...	...	...	...	...	...	21	6	15
Bhand	4	2	2	...	...	...	...	...	...	...	...	...	...	...	...	...	...	...	4	2	2	4	2	2
Baud	380	165	215	...	...	...	...	...	...	...	...	...	...	...	...	...	...	...	...	...	...	...	...	...
Bodah	201	110	91	...	...	...	...	...	...	...	...	...	...	...	...	...	...	...	...	...	...	...	...	...
Bojal	63	38	25	...	...	...	...	...	...	...	...	...	...	...	...	...	...	...	...	...	...	...	...	...
Baru	477	291	186	...	...	...	...	...	...	...	...	...	...	...	...	...	...	...	...	...	...	...	...	...
Bachn	285	171	114	...	...	...	...	...	...	...	...	...	...	...	...	...	...	...	...	...	...	...	...	...
Badmari	182	95	87	...	...	...	...	...	...	...	...	...	...	...	...	...	...	...	...	...	...	...	...	...
Badra	119	62	57	...	...	...	...	...	...	...	...	...	...	...	...	...	...	...	...	...	...	...	...	...
Baktu	416	201	215	...	...	...	...	...	...	...	...	...	...	...	...	...	...	...	...	...	...	...	...	...
Batta	596	327	269	...	...	...	...	...	...	...	...	...	...	...	...	...	...	...	...	...	...	...	...	...
Bakiar	82	40	42	...	...	...	...	...	...	...	...	...	...	...	...	...	...	...	...	...	...	...	...	...
Bakhsh	467	229	238	...	...	...	...	...	...	...	...	...	...	...	...	...	...	...	...	...	...	...	...	...
Bandi	1,651	745	906	...	...	...	...	...	...	...	...	...	...	...	...	...	...	...	...	...	...	...	...	...
Balgari	566	279	287	...	...	...	...	...	...	...	...	...	...	...	...	...	...	...	...	...	...	...	...	...
Behar	22	16	6	...	...	...	...	...	...	...	...	...	...	...	...	...	...	...	...	...	...	...	...	...
Baugi	204	115	89	...	...	...	...	...	...	...	...	...	...	...	...	...	...	...	...	...	...	...	...	...
Ballu-Baru	270	157	113	...	...	...	...	...	...	...	...	...	...	...	...	...	...	...	...	...	...	...	...	...
Botah	127	79	48	...	...	...	...	...	...	...	...	...	...	...	...	...	...	...	...	...	...	...	...	...
Banko	120	59	61	...	...	...	...	...	...	...	...	...	...	...	...	...	...	...	...	...	...	...	...	...
Bato	305	134	171	...	...	...	...	...	...	...	...	...	...	...	...	...	...	...	...	...	...	...	...	...
Bokra	89	46	43	...	...	...	...	...	...	...	...	...	...	...	...	...	...	...	...	...	...	...	...	...
Barkat	34	17	17	...	...	...	...	...	...	...	...	...	...	...	...	...	...	...	...	...	...	...	...	...
Beragi	13	9	4	...	...	...	...	...	...	...	...	...	...	...	...	...	...	...	...	...	...	...	...	...
Barah	180	118	62	...	...	...	...	...	...	...	...	...	...	...	...	...	...	...	...	...	...	...	...	...
Barkhah	37	30	7	...	...	...	...	...	...	...	...	...	...	...	...	...	...	...	...	...	...	...	...	...
Barari	463	257	206	...	...	...	...	...	...	...	...	...	...	...	...	...	...	...	...	...	...	...	...	...
Bhadar	227	119	108	...	...	...	...	...	...	...	...	...	...	...	...	...	...	...	...	...	...	...	...	...
Bulhal	80	46	34	...	...	...	...	...	...	...	...	...	...	...	...	...	...	...	...	...	...	...	...	...
Bugla	47	20	27	...	...	...	...	...	...	...	...	...	...	...	...	...	...	...	...	...	...	...	...	...
Badian	176	105	71	...	...	...	...	...	...	...	...	...	...	...	...	...	...	...	...	...	...	...	...	...
Benakhur	72	45	27	...	...	...	...	...	...	...	...	...	...	...	...	...	...	...	...	...	...	...	...	...

Caste, Tribe, Race or Nationality.	Kashmir Province. Khas District. Persons.	Males.	Females.	Muzaffarabad District. Persons.	Males.	Females.	Total Kashmir Province. Persons.	Males.	Females.	Frontier Districts. Ladakh District. Persons.	Males.	Females.	Gilgit District. Persons.	Males.	Females.	Total Frontier Districts. Persons.	Males.	Females.
	26	27	28	29	30	31	32	33	34	35	36	37	38	39	40	41	42	43
Bhut	...	...	...	...	...	...	...	...	...	...	...	...	...	...	...	...	...	...
Bharni	...	...	...	...	...	...	...	...	...	...	...	...	...	...	...	...	...	...
Bardar	...	...	...	...	...	...	...	...	...	...	...	...	...	...	...	...	...	...
Boru	...	...	...	...	...	...	...	...	...	...	...	...	...	...	...	...	...	...
Banjara	...	...	...	...	...	...	...	...	...	...	...	...	...	...	...	...	...	...
Barbalu	89	46	43	...	...	...	89	46	43	...	...	...	...	...	...	...	...	...
Batwal	...	...	...	...	...	...	...	...	...	...	...	...	...	...	...	...	...	...
Bafinda	459	320	139	1,122	504	618	1,581	824	757	58	44	14	56	35	21	114	79	35
Banial	...	...	...	...	...	...	...	...	...	...	...	...	...	...	...	...	...	...
Bengial	...	...	...	...	...	...	...	...	...	...	...	...	...	...	...	...	...	...
Bhand	...	...	...	...	...	...	...	...	...	...	...	...	...	...	...	...	...	...
Band	145	73	72	...	...	...	145	73	72	235	92	143	...	...	...	235	92	143
Bodah	201	110	91	...	...	...	201	110	91	...	...	...	...	...	...	...	...	...
Bojal	63	38	25	...	...	...	63	38	25	...	...	...	...	...	...	...	...	...
Baru	477	291	186	...	...	...	477	291	186	...	...	...	...	...	...	...	...	...
Bachu	285	171	114	...	...	...	285	171	114	...	...	...	...	...	...	...	...	...
Badmuri	182	95	87	...	...	...	182	95	87	...	...	...	...	...	...	...	...	...
Badra	119	62	57	...	...	...	119	62	57	...	...	...	...	...	...	...	...	...
Baktu	416	201	215	...	...	...	416	201	215	...	...	...	...	...	...	...	...	...
Batta	470	251	219	...	...	...	470	251	219	126	76	50	...	...	...	126	76	50
Bakiaz	82	40	42	...	...	...	82	40	42	...	...	...	...	...	...	...	...	...
Bakhsh	465	228	237	...	...	...	465	228	237	2	1	1	...	...	...	2	1	1
Bandi	1,249	675	574	...	...	...	1,249	675	574	402	70	332	...	...	...	402	70	332
Batgari	566	279	287	...	...	...	566	279	287	...	...	...	...	...	...	...	...	...
Behar	22	16	6	...	...	...	22	16	6	...	...	...	...	...	...	...	...	...
Bangi	204	115	89	...	...	...	204	115	89	...	...	...	...	...	...	...	...	...
Ballu-Baru	270	157	113	...	...	...	270	157	113	...	...	...	...	...	...	...	...	...
Botah	127	79	48	...	...	...	127	79	48	...	...	...	...	...	...	...	...	...
Banko	120	59	61	...	...	...	120	59	61	...	...	...	...	...	...	...	...	...
Batu	305	134	171	...	...	...	305	134	171	...	...	...	...	...	...	...	...	...
Bokra	89	46	43	...	...	...	89	46	43	...	...	...	...	...	...	...	...	...
Barkat	34	17	17	...	...	...	34	17	17	...	...	...	...	...	...	...	...	...
Beragi	13	9	4	...	...	...	13	9	4	...	...	...	...	...	...	...	...	...
Barah	180	118	62	...	...	...	180	118	62	...	...	...	...	...	...	...	...	...
Barkhah	37	30	7	...	...	...	37	30	7	...	...	...	...	...	...	...	...	...
Barari	463	257	206	...	...	...	463	257	206	...	...	...	...	...	...	...	...	...
Bhador	227	119	108	...	...	...	227	119	108	...	...	...	...	...	...	...	...	...
Bulbal	80	46	34	...	...	...	80	46	34	...	...	...	...	...	...	...	...	...
Bagla	47	20	27	...	...	...	47	20	27	...	...	...	...	...	...	...	...	...
Badian	176	105	71	...	...	...	176	105	71	...	...	...	...	...	...	...	...	...
Banakhur	72	45	27	...	...	...	72	45	27	...	...	...	...	...	...	...	...	...

TABLE XIII.

CASTE, TRIBE, RACE OR NATIONALITY.

Caste, Tribe, Race or Nationality.	Total Population.			Provinces with Districts. — Jammu Province.																				
				Jammu District.			Udhampur District.			Bhimber District.			Jasrota District.			Punch Jágir.			Bhadarwah Jágir.			Total Jammu Province.		
	Persons.	Males.	Females.	Persons.	Males.	Females.	Persons.	Males.	Females.	Persons.	Males.	Females.	Persons.	Males.	Females.	Persons.	Males.	Females.	Persons.	Males.	Females.	Persons.	Males.	Females.
1	2	3	4	5	6	7	8	9	10	11	12	13	14	15	16	17	18	19	20	21	22	23	24	25
Baddu	30	21	18	...	...	...	...	...	...	...	...	...	...	...	...	...	...	...	...	...	...	...	...	...
Badhal	156	125	31	...	...	...	...	...	...	...	...	...	...	...	...	...	...	...	...	...	...	...	...	...
Baralah	5	5	...	...	...	...	...	...	...	...	...	...	...	...	...	...	...	...	...	...	...	...	...	...
Basati	44	33	11	...	...	...	...	...	...	...	...	...	...	...	...	...	...	...	...	...	...	...	...	...
Bedah	47	28	19	...	...	...	...	...	...	...	...	...	...	...	...	...	...	...	...	...	...	...	...	...
Bonjh	5	2	3	...	...	...	...	...	...	...	...	...	...	...	...	...	...	...	...	...	...	...	...	...
Bakarchi	4	4	...	...	...	...	...	...	...	...	...	...	...	...	...	...	...	...	...	...	...	...	...	...
Bal	6	3	3	...	...	...	...	...	...	...	...	...	...	...	...	...	...	...	...	...	...	...	...	...
Barangpa	146	40	106	...	...	...	...	...	...	...	...	...	...	...	...	...	...	...	...	...	...	...	...	...
Barcha	54	54	...	...	...	...	...	...	...	...	...	...	...	...	...	...	...	...	...	...	...	...	...	...
Barupa	138	47	91	...	...	...	...	...	...	...	...	...	...	...	...	...	...	...	...	...	...	...	...	...
Balla	143	80	63	...	...	...	...	...	...	...	...	...	...	...	...	...	...	...	...	...	...	...	...	...
Boshakpa	455	335	120	...	...	...	...	...	...	...	...	...	...	...	...	...	...	...	...	...	...	...	...	...
Barampa	87	39	48	...	...	...	...	...	...	...	...	...	...	...	...	...	...	...	...	...	...	...	...	...
Bagupa	158	64	94	...	...	...	...	...	...	...	...	...	...	...	...	...	...	...	...	...	...	...	...	...
Barjaupa	118	42	76	...	...	...	...	...	...	...	...	...	...	...	...	...	...	...	...	...	...	...	...	...
Batupa	98	28	70	...	...	...	...	...	...	...	...	...	...	...	...	...	...	...	...	...	...	...	...	...
Badkashlapa	23	23	...	...	...	...	...	...	...	...	...	...	...	...	...	...	...	...	...	...	...	...	...	...
Bulakpa	134	66	68	...	...	...	...	...	...	...	...	...	...	...	...	...	...	...	...	...	...	...	...	...
Barganpa	11	3	8	...	...	...	...	...	...	...	...	...	...	...	...	...	...	...	...	...	...	...	...	...
Baroshalpa	57	32	25	...	...	...	...	...	...	...	...	...	...	...	...	...	...	...	...	...	...	...	...	...
Barajpa	86	77	9	...	...	...	...	...	...	...	...	...	...	...	...	...	...	...	...	...	...	...	...	...
Bandarpa	27	14	13	...	...	...	...	...	...	...	...	...	...	...	...	...	...	...	...	...	...	...	...	...
Barghu	36	20	16	...	...	...	...	...	...	...	...	...	...	...	...	...	...	...	...	...	...	...	...	...
Bainkpa	37	18	19	...	...	...	...	...	...	...	...	...	...	...	...	...	...	...	...	...	...	...	...	...
Barancharkpa	6	6	...	...	...	...	...	...	...	...	...	...	...	...	...	...	...	...	...	...	...	...	...	...
Balalpa	10	4	6	...	...	...	...	...	...	...	...	...	...	...	...	...	...	...	...	...	...	...	...	...
Bughchapa	374	166	208	...	...	...	...	...	...	...	...	...	...	...	...	...	...	...	...	...	...	...	...	...
Begampa	78	39	39	...	...	...	...	...	...	...	...	...	...	...	...	...	...	...	...	...	...	...	...	...
Bakarpa	42	24	18	...	...	...	...	...	...	...	...	...	...	...	...	...	...	...	...	...	...	...	...	...
Badanpa	5	3	2	...	...	...	...	...	...	...	...	...	...	...	...	...	...	...	...	...	...	...	...	...
Burkshall	8	...	8	...	...	...	...	...	...	...	...	...	...	...	...	...	...	...	...	...	...	...	...	...
Biahkan	26,583	14,100	12,483	...	...	...	...	...	...	...	...	...	...	...	...	...	...	...	...	...	...	...	...	...
Barol	32	24	8	...	...	...	...	...	...	...	...	...	...	...	...	...	...	...	...	...	...	...	...	...
Baraplang..	284	146	138	...	...	...	...	...	...	...	...	...	...	...	...	...	...	...	...	...	...	...	...	...
Batar	167	95	72	...	...	...	...	...	...	...	...	...	...	...	...	...	...	...	...	...	...	...	...	...
Bosahib	177	97	80	...	...	...	...	...	...	...	...	...	...	...	...	...	...	...	...	...	...	...	...	...
Borikanor	108	62	46	...	...	...	...	...	...	...	...	...	...	...	...	...	...	...	...	...	...	...	...	...
Biska	258	132	126	...	...	...	...	...	...	...	...	...	...	...	...	...	...	...	...	...	...	...	...	...
Banori	104	57	47	...	...	...	...	...	...	...	...	...	...	...	...	...	...	...	...	...	...	...	...	...
Bat	23,857	12,727	11,130	794	433	361	2,543	2,100	443	2,768	1,633	1,135	230	126	104	3,957	884	3,073	...	...	...	10,885	5,170	5,709

PROVINCES WITH DISTRICTS.

Caste, Tribe, Race or Nationality	Kashmir Province. Khas District. Persons.	Males.	Females.	Muzaffarabad District. Persons.	Males.	Females.	Total Kashmir Province. Persons.	Males.	Females.	Frontier Districts. Ladakh District. Persons.	Males.	Females.	Gilgit District. Persons.	Males.	Females.	Total Frontier Districts. Persons.	Males.	Females.
	26	27	28	29	30	31	32	33	34	35	36	37	38	39	40	41	42	43
Baddu	...	...	...	39	21	18	39	21	18	...	...	...	...	...	...	...	...	...
Badhal	...	...	...	156	125	31	156	125	31	...	...	...	...	...	...	...	...	...
Baralah	...	...	...	5	5	...	5	5	...	...	...	...	...	...	...	...	...	...
Basati	...	...	...	44	33	11	44	33	11	...	...	...	...	...	...	...	...	...
Bodah	...	...	...	...	...	...	...	...	...	47	28	19	...	...	...	47	28	19
Bonjh	...	...	...	...	...	...	...	...	...	5	2	3	...	...	...	5	2	3
Bakarchi	...	...	...	...	...	...	...	...	...	4	4	...	...	...	...	4	4	...
Bai	...	...	...	...	...	...	...	...	...	6	3	3	...	...	...	6	3	3
Barangpa	...	...	...	...	...	...	...	...	...	146	40	106	...	...	...	146	40	106
Barcha	...	...	...	...	...	...	...	...	...	54	54	...	...	...	...	54	54	...
Barupa	...	...	...	...	...	...	...	...	...	138	47	91	...	...	...	138	47	91
Balla	...	...	...	...	...	...	...	...	...	143	80	63	...	...	...	143	80	63
Boshakpa	...	...	...	...	...	...	...	...	...	455	335	120	...	...	...	455	335	120
Barampa	...	...	...	...	...	...	...	...	...	87	39	48	...	...	...	87	39	48
Bagupa	...	...	...	...	...	...	...	...	...	158	64	94	...	...	...	158	64	94
Barjanpa	...	...	...	...	...	...	...	...	...	118	42	76	...	...	...	118	42	76
Batupa	...	...	...	...	...	...	...	...	...	98	28	70	...	...	...	98	28	70
Badkashlupa	...	...	...	...	...	...	...	...	...	23	23	...	...	...	...	23	23	...
Bulakpa	...	...	...	...	...	...	...	...	...	134	66	68	...	...	...	134	66	68
Bargonpa	...	...	...	...	...	...	...	...	...	11	3	8	...	...	...	11	3	8
Baroshalpa	...	...	...	...	...	...	...	...	...	67	32	25	...	...	...	57	32	25
Barajpa	...	...	...	...	...	...	...	...	...	86	77	9	...	...	...	86	77	9
Bandarpa	...	...	...	...	...	...	...	...	...	27	14	13	...	...	...	27	14	13
Barghu	...	...	...	...	...	...	...	...	...	36	20	16	...	...	...	36	20	16
Bainkpa	...	...	...	...	...	...	...	...	...	37	18	19	...	...	...	37	18	19
Barnacharkpa ...	...	...	...	...	...	...	...	...	...	6	6	...	...	...	...	6	6	...
Balalpa	...	...	...	...	...	...	...	...	...	10	4	6	...	...	...	10	4	6
Baghchapa	...	...	...	...	...	...	...	...	...	374	166	208	...	...	...	374	166	208
Bagampa	...	...	...	...	...	...	...	...	...	78	39	39	...	...	...	78	39	39
Bakarpa	...	...	...	...	...	...	...	...	...	42	24	18	...	...	...	42	24	18
Badaspa	...	...	...	...	...	...	...	...	...	5	3	2	...	...	...	5	3	2
Burkshali	...	...	...	...	...	...	...	...	...	...	...	...	8	...	8	8	...	8
Bishkan	...	...	...	...	...	...	...	...	...	...	...	...	26,583	14,100	12,483	26,583	14,100	12,483
Barol	...	...	...	...	...	...	...	...	...	...	...	...	32	24	8	32	24	8
Barnplang	...	...	...	...	...	...	...	...	...	...	...	...	284	146	138	284	146	138
Batar	...	...	...	...	...	...	...	...	...	...	...	...	167	95	72	167	95	72
Boashib	...	...	...	...	...	...	...	...	...	...	...	...	177	97	80	177	97	80
Boriknaor	...	...	...	...	...	...	...	...	...	...	...	...	108	62	46	108	62	46
Biako	...	...	...	...	...	...	...	...	...	...	...	...	258	132	126	258	132	126
Banori	...	...	...	...	...	...	...	...	...	...	...	...	104	57	47	104	57	47
Bat	11,721	7,001	4,720	1,251	550	701	12,972	7,551	5,421	...	...	...	...	...	...	...	...	...

TABLE XIII.

Caste, Tribe, Race or Nationality.

Caste, Tribe, Race or Nationality.	Total Population.			Provinces with Districts. Jammu Province. Jammu District.			Chibhal/Chhamper District.			Bhimber District.			Jasrota District.			Punch Jágir.			Bhadarwah Jágir.			Total Jammu Province.		
	Persons.	Males.	Females.	Persons.	Males.	Females.	Persons.	Males.	Females.	Persons.	Males.	Females.	Persons.	Males.	Females.	Persons.	Males.	Females.	Persons.	Males.	Females.	Persons.	Males.	Females.
1	2	3	4	5	6	7	8	9	10	11	12	13	14	15	16	17	18	19	20	21	22	23	24	25
Banay	65	43	22	...	...	...	...	...	...	...	...	...	...	...	...	...	...	...	...	...	...	...	...	...
Baf	19	5	14	...	...	...	...	...	...	...	...	...	...	...	...	...	...	...	...	...	...	...	...	...
Bada	5	2	3	...	...	...	...	...	...	...	...	...	...	...	...	...	...	...	...	...	...	...	...	...
Bachi	22	13	9	...	...	...	...	...	...	...	...	...	...	...	...	...	...	...	...	...	...	...	...	...
Bador	4	1	3	...	...	...	...	...	...	...	...	...	...	...	...	...	...	...	...	...	...	...	...	...
Banda	15	12	3	...	...	...	...	...	...	...	...	...	...	...	...	...	...	...	...	...	...	...	...	...
Bhutli	620	358	262	...	...	...	...	...	...	...	...	...	...	...	...	...	...	...	...	...	...	...	...	...
Beg	5,800	3,063	2,737	...	...	...	...	...	...	...	...	...	...	...	...	...	...	...	...	...	...	...	...	...
Bamnic	55	55	...	...	...	...	...	...	...	...	...	...	...	...	...	...	...	...	...	...	...	...	...	...
Bhobi	18	5	13	...	...	...	...	...	...	...	...	...	...	...	...	...	...	...	...	...	...	...	...	...
Botri	12	6	6	...	...	...	...	...	...	...	...	...	...	...	...	...	...	...	...	...	...	...	...	...
Maha	9,824	4,966	4,858	...	...	...	...	...	...	...	...	...	...	...	...	...	...	...	...	...	...	...	...	...
Bodli	21	1	20	...	...	...	...	...	...	...	...	...	...	...	...	...	...	...	...	...	...	...	...	...
Bathal	3	3	...	...	...	...	...	...	...	...	...	...	...	...	...	...	...	...	...	...	...	...	...	...
Bagla	27	2	25	...	...	...	...	...	...	...	...	...	...	...	...	...	...	...	...	...	...	...	...	...
Boru	30	17	13	...	...	...	...	...	...	...	...	...	...	...	...	...	...	...	...	...	...	...	...	...
Bambu	5	1	4	...	...	...	...	...	...	...	...	...	...	...	...	...	...	...	...	...	...	...	...	...
Bagri	45	31	14	...	...	...	...	...	...	...	...	...	...	...	...	...	...	...	...	...	...	...	...	...
Chamkor	218	97	121	...	...	...	...	...	...	...	...	...	...	...	...	...	...	...	...	...	...	...	...	...
Chocho	311	146	165	...	...	...	...	...	...	...	...	...	...	...	...	...	...	...	...	...	...	...	...	...
Chohlfna	8	2	6	...	...	...	...	...	...	...	...	...	...	...	...	...	...	...	...	...	...	...	...	...
Chomalpa	48	11	37	...	...	...	...	...	...	...	...	...	...	...	...	...	...	...	...	...	...	...	...	...
Cholpa	4	1	3	...	...	...	...	...	...	...	...	...	...	...	...	...	...	...	...	...	...	...	...	...
Chalargarpa	29	2	27	...	...	...	...	...	...	...	...	...	...	...	...	...	...	...	...	...	...	...	...	...
Chandu	64	14	50	...	...	...	...	...	...	...	...	...	...	...	...	...	...	...	...	...	...	...	...	...
Chochallia	86	35	51	...	...	...	...	...	...	...	...	...	...	...	...	...	...	...	...	...	...	...	...	...
Chastampa	31	11	20	...	...	...	...	...	...	...	...	...	...	...	...	...	...	...	...	...	...	...	...	...
Chalanaan	77	30	47	...	...	...	...	...	...	...	...	...	...	...	...	...	...	...	...	...	...	...	...	...
Chopan	522	77	445	8	8	...	...	...	...	...	...	...	...	...	...	...	...	...	...	...	...	8	8	...
Chakarpa	76	19	57	...	...	...	...	...	...	...	...	...	...	...	...	...	...	...	...	...	...	...	...	...
Chhalwan	316	52	264	...	...	...	...	...	...	...	...	...	...	...	...	...	...	...	...	...	...	...	...	...
Chakal	17	12	5	...	...	...	...	...	...	...	...	...	...	...	...	...	...	...	...	...	...	...	...	...
Choh	19	13	6	...	...	...	...	...	...	...	...	...	...	...	...	...	...	...	...	...	...	...	...	...
Chamar	1,854	1,037	817	123	74	40	83	71	12	1,340	628	612	1	1	...	77	...	77	...	...	...	1,521	774	750
Chohdri	1,389	1,174	215	...	...	...	...	...	...	...	...	...	...	...	...	1,327	1,129	198	...	...	...	1,327	1,129	198
Chobra	8,533	4,680	3,853	1,884	1,048	836	992	530	462	2,664	1,332	1,332	109	55	54	1,838	956	882	7	1	6	7,494	3,922	3,572
Chakar	706	303	403	30	13	17	175	96	79	185	...	185	314	161	153	...	...	...	...	...	...	704	270	434
Chorikar	987	586	401	105	90	75	...	...	...	...	...	...	...	...	...	...	...	...	...	...	...	165	90	75
Charwak	230	91	139	121	50	71	...	...	...	...	...	...	...	...	...	...	...	...	...	...	...	121	50	71
Chakwal	25	17	8	...	...	...	...	...	...	...	...	...	...	...	...	...	...	...	...	...	...	...	...	...
Choki	16	10	6	...	...	...	...	...	...	...	...	...	...	...	...	...	...	...	...	...	...	...	...	...

Caste, Tribe, Race or Nationality.	Kashmir Province. — Khas District. Persons.	Males.	Females.	Muzaffarabad District. Persons.	Males.	Females.	Total Kashmir Province. Persons.	Males.	Females.	Frontier Districts. — Ladakh District. Persons.	Males.	Females.	Gilgit District. Persons.	Males.	Females.	Total Frontier Districts. Persons.	Males.	Females.
	26	27	28	29	30	31	32	33	34	35	36	37	38	39	40	41	42	43
Bassy	65	43	22	...	...	...	65	43	42	...	...	...	...	...	...	...	...	...
Baf	19	5	14	...	...	...	19	5	14	...	...	...	...	...	...	...	...	...
Bada	5	2	3	...	...	...	5	2	3	...	...	...	...	...	...	...	...	...
Bachi	22	13	9	...	...	...	22	13	9	...	...	...	...	...	...	...	...	...
Bador	4	1	3	...	...	...	4	1	3	...	...	...	...	...	...	...	...	...
Banda	15	12	3	...	...	...	15	12	3	...	...	...	...	...	...	...	...	...
Bhatli	620	358	262	...	...	...	620	358	262	...	...	...	...	...	...	...	...	...
Beg	5,725	3,002	2,723	...	...	...	5,725	3,002	2,723	...	...	...	75	61	14	75	61	14
Bamoio	55	55	...	...	...	...	55	55	...	...	...	...	...	...	...	...	...	...
Bhobi	18	5	13	...	...	...	18	5	13	...	...	...	...	...	...	...	...	...
Botri	12	6	6	...	...	...	12	6	6	...	...	...	...	...	...	...	...	...
Baba	9,817	4,959	4,858	7	7	...	9,824	4,966	4,858	...	...	...	...	...	...	...	...	...
Bodil	21	1	20	...	...	...	21	1	20	...	...	...	...	...	...	...	...	...
Bathal	3	3	...	...	...	...	3	3	...	...	...	...	...	...	...	...	...	...
Bagiu	27	2	25	...	...	...	27	2	25	...	...	...	...	...	...	...	...	...
Baru	30	17	13	...	...	...	30	17	13	...	...	...	...	...	...	...	...	...
Bambu	5	1	4	...	...	...	5	1	4	...	...	...	...	...	...	...	...	...
Bagri	45	31	14	...	...	...	45	31	14	...	...	...	...	...	...	...	...	...
Chamkor	...	...	...	...	...	...	...	...	...	190	89	101	28	8	20	218	97	121
Chocho	225	113	112	...	...	...	225	113	112	86	33	53	...	...	...	86	33	53
Chohifna	...	...	...	...	...	...	...	...	...	8	2	6	...	...	...	8	2	6
Chomalpa	...	...	...	...	...	...	...	...	...	48	11	37	...	...	...	48	11	37
Chohpa	...	...	...	...	...	...	...	...	...	4	1	3	...	...	...	4	1	3
Chalargarpa	...	...	...	...	...	...	...	...	...	29	2	37	...	...	...	29	2	27
Chandu	...	...	...	...	...	...	...	...	...	64	14	50	...	...	...	64	14	50
Chochallia	...	...	...	...	...	...	...	...	...	86	35	51	...	...	...	86	35	51
Chastampa	...	...	...	...	...	...	...	...	...	31	11	20	...	...	...	31	11	20
Chalanzan	17	9	8	30	12	18	47	21	26	30	9	21	...	...	...	30	9	21
Chopan	...	...	...	409	50	419	469	50	419	45	19	26	...	...	...	45	19	26
Chakarpa	...	...	...	...	...	...	...	...	...	76	19	57	...	...	...	76	19	57
Chhalwan	...	...	...	312	48	264	312	48	264	4	4	...	...	...	...	4	4	...
Chakal	...	...	...	9	9	...	9	9	...	8	3	5	...	...	...	8	3	5
Choh	...	...	...	...	...	...	...	...	...	19	13	6	...	...	...	19	13	6
Chamar	246	212	34	31	25	6	277	237	40	...	...	...	53	26	27	53	26	27
Chohdri	...	...	...	57	40	17	57	40	17	...	...	...	5	5	...	5	5	...
Chohra	417	186	231	620	570	50	1,037	756	281	...	...	...	2	2	...	2	2	...
Chakar	...	...	...	...	...	...	...	...	...	40	20	20	22	13	9	62	33	29
Chorikar	822	496	326	...	...	...	822	406	326	...	...	...	...	...	...	...	...	...
Charwak	...	...	...	...	...	...	...	...	...	97	29	68	12	12	...	109	41	68
Chakwal	...	...	...	21	13	8	21	13	8	...	...	...	4	4	...	4	4	...
Chokhi	...	...	...	...	...	...	...	...	...	16	10	6	...	...	...	16	10	6

TABLE XIII.

Caste, Tribe, Race or Nationality.

Caste, Tribe, Race or Nationality.	Total Population.			Provinces with Districts. — Jammu Province. — Jammu District.			Udhampur District.			Bhimber District.			Jasrota District.			Punch Jágir.			Bhadarwah Jágir.			Total Jammu Province.		
	Persons.	Males.	Females.	Persons.	Males.	Females.	Persons.	Males.	Females.	Persons.	Males.	Females.	Persons.	Males.	Females.	Persons.	Males.	Females.	Persons.	Males.	Females.	Persons.	Males.	Females.
1	2	3	4	5	6	7	8	9	10	11	12	13	14	15	16	17	18	19	20	21	22	23	24	25
Changu	117	60	57	...	...	...	...	...	...	...	...	...	...	...	...	...	...	...	...	...	...	...	...	...
Chalsiay	289	141	148	...	...	...	...	...	...	...	...	...	...	...	...	...	...	...	...	...	...	...	...	...
Chalak	107	70	37	...	...	...	...	...	...	...	...	...	...	...	...	...	...	...	...	...	...	...	...	...
Chala	66	33	33	...	...	...	...	...	...	...	...	...	...	...	...	...	...	...	...	...	...	...	...	...
Charu	276	188	88	...	...	...	...	...	...	...	...	...	...	...	...	...	...	...	...	...	...	...	...	...
Chagal	249	128	121	...	...	...	...	...	...	...	...	...	...	...	...	...	...	...	...	...	...	...	...	...
Chalhkand	125	59	66	...	...	...	...	...	...	...	...	...	...	...	...	...	...	...	...	...	...	...	...	...
Chhadin	45	9	36	...	...	...	...	...	...	...	...	...	...	...	...	...	...	...	...	...	...	...	...	...
Chadan	58	36	22	...	...	...	...	...	...	...	...	...	...	...	...	...	...	...	...	...	...	...	...	...
Chand	309	161	148	...	...	...	...	...	...	...	...	...	...	...	...	...	...	...	...	...	...	...	...	...
Chhasopa	104	58	46	...	...	...	...	...	...	...	...	...	...	...	...	...	...	...	...	...	...	...	...	...
Choghatta	28,676	14,059	14,617	...	...	...	...	...	...	...	...	...	...	...	...	...	...	...	...	...	...	...	...	...
Dagpa	53	23	30	...	...	...	...	...	...	...	...	...	...	...	...	...	...	...	...	...	...	...	...	...
Darvesh	971	490	481	...	...	...	...	...	...	...	...	...	...	...	...	...	...	...	...	...	...	...	...	...
Doarasta	20	10	10	...	...	...	...	...	...	...	...	...	...	...	...	...	...	...	...	...	...	...	...	...
Halalpa	57	18	39	...	...	...	...	...	...	...	...	...	...	...	...	...	...	...	...	...	...	...	...	...
Dalpa	25	10	15	...	...	...	...	...	...	...	...	...	...	...	...	...	...	...	...	...	...	...	...	...
Dadupa	109	67	42	...	...	...	...	...	...	...	...	...	...	...	...	...	...	...	...	...	...	...	...	...
Dahtun	103	76	27	...	...	...	...	...	...	...	...	...	...	...	...	...	...	...	...	...	...	...	...	...
Domba	58	20	38	...	...	...	...	...	...	...	...	...	...	...	...	...	...	...	...	...	...	...	...	...
Daighupa	184	97	87	...	...	...	...	...	...	...	...	...	...	...	...	...	...	...	...	...	...	...	...	...
Damoh	217	108	109	...	...	...	...	...	...	...	...	...	...	...	...	...	...	...	...	...	...	...	...	...
Darpa	10	10	...	...	...	...	...	...	...	...	...	...	...	...	...	...	...	...	...	...	...	...	...	...
Dan	25	10	15	...	...	...	...	...	...	...	...	...	...	...	...	...	...	...	...	...	...	...	...	...
Danpa	26	6	20	...	...	...	...	...	...	...	...	...	...	...	...	...	...	...	...	...	...	...	...	...
Dabapa	34	12	22	...	...	...	...	...	...	...	...	...	...	...	...	...	...	...	...	...	...	...	...	...
Daropa	19	17	2	...	...	...	...	...	...	...	...	...	...	...	...	...	...	...	...	...	...	...	...	...
Doonlpa	28	21	7	...	...	...	...	...	...	...	...	...	...	...	...	...	...	...	...	...	...	...	...	...
Dafojanpa	15	12	3	...	...	...	...	...	...	...	...	...	...	...	...	...	...	...	...	...	...	...	...	...
Darkuchhpa	52	38	14	...	...	...	...	...	...	...	...	...	...	...	...	...	...	...	...	...	...	...	...	...
Dotio	72	64	8	...	...	...	...	...	...	...	...	...	...	...	...	...	...	...	...	...	...	...	...	...
Darjaspa	2	2	...	...	...	...	...	...	...	...	...	...	...	...	...	...	...	...	...	...	...	...	...	...
Dawangpa	12	12	...	...	...	...	...	...	...	...	...	...	...	...	...	...	...	...	...	...	...	...	...	...
Dampa	205	109	96	...	...	...	...	...	...	...	...	...	...	...	...	...	...	...	...	...	...	...	...	...
Darsi	169,293	95,363	73,930	1,820	918	902	618	321	297	11,770	6,545	5,225	585	295	290	26,021	14,795	11,226	195	110	85	41,009	22,984	18,025
Daralitang	795	427	368	...	...	...	...	...	...	...	...	...	...	...	...	...	...	...	...	...	...	...	...	...
Doaskatur	165	86	79	...	...	...	...	...	...	...	...	...	...	...	...	...	...	...	...	...	...	...	...	...
Diniki	256	138	118	...	...	...	...	...	...	...	...	...	...	...	...	...	...	...	...	...	...	...	...	...
Dharpa	1	1	...	...	...	...	...	...	...	...	...	...	...	...	...	...	...	...	...	...	...	...	...	...
Don	21	18	3	...	...	...	...	...	...	...	...	...	...	...	...	...	...	...	...	...	...	...	...	...
Dhobi	1,220	634	586	...	...	...	...	...	...	1,046	520	526	...	...	...	...	...	...	...	...	...	1,046	520	526

Caste, Tribe, Race or Nationality.	Kashmir Province: Khas District. Persons.	Males.	Females.	Muzaffarabad District. Persons.	Males.	Females.	Total Kashmir Province. Persons.	Males.	Females.	Frontier Districts: Ladakh District. Persons.	Males.	Females.	Gilgit District. Persons.	Males.	Females.	Total Frontier Districts. Persons.	Males.	Females.
	26	27	28	29	30	31	32	33	34	35	36	37	38	39	40	41	42	43
Chaugu	37	21	16	19	19	...	56	40	16	61	20	41	...	...	...	61	20	41
Chalsiay	280	141	148	...	...	...	280	141	148	...	...	...	...	...	...	...	...	...
Chalak	90	55	35	17	15	2	107	70	37	...	...	...	...	...	...	...	...	...
Chala	65	32	33	...	...	...	65	32	33	...	...	...	1	1	...	1	1	...
Charu	215	127	88	59	59	...	274	186	88	...	...	...	2	2	...	2	2	...
Chagal	235	114	121	14	14	...	249	128	121	...	...	...	...	...	...	...	...	...
Chahkand	125	59	66	...	...	...	125	59	66	...	...	...	...	...	...	...	...	...
Chhadia	15	7	8	...	...	...	15	7	8	30	2	28	...	...	...	30	2	28
Chadan	...	...	...	58	36	22	58	36	22	...	...	...	...	...	...	...	...	...
Chand	180	91	89	129	70	59	309	161	148	...	...	...	...	...	...	...	...	...
Chaspa	...	...	...	...	...	...	...	...	...	...	...	...	104	58	46	104	58	46
Choghatta	26,998	13,537	13,461	2,578	1,422	1,156	29,576	14,959	14,617	...	...	...	...	...	...	...	...	...
Dagpa	...	...	...	...	...	...	...	...	...	53	23	30	...	...	...	53	23	30
Darvesh	266	102	164	...	...	...	266	102	164	705	388	317	...	...	...	705	388	317
Dourasta	...	...	...	...	...	...	...	...	...	20	10	10	...	...	...	20	10	10
Daladpa	...	...	...	...	...	...	...	...	...	57	18	39	...	...	...	57	18	39
Dalpa	...	...	...	...	...	...	...	...	...	25	10	15	...	...	...	25	10	15
Dadupa	...	...	...	...	...	...	...	...	...	109	67	42	...	...	...	109	67	42
Dubtun	...	...	...	...	...	...	...	...	...	103	76	27	...	...	...	103	76	27
Domba	...	...	...	...	...	...	...	...	...	58	20	38	...	...	...	58	20	38
Daighupa	...	...	...	...	...	...	...	...	...	184	97	87	...	...	...	184	97	87
Damoh	...	...	...	...	...	...	...	...	...	217	108	109	...	...	...	217	108	100
Derpa	...	...	...	...	...	...	...	...	...	10	10	...	...	...	...	10	10	...
Dan	...	...	...	...	...	...	...	...	...	25	10	15	...	...	...	25	10	15
Danpa	...	...	...	...	...	...	...	...	...	26	6	20	...	...	...	26	6	20
Dabapa	...	...	...	...	...	...	...	...	...	34	12	22	...	...	...	34	12	22
Daropa	...	...	...	...	...	...	...	...	...	19	17	2	...	...	...	19	17	2
Donolpa	...	...	...	...	...	...	...	...	...	28	21	7	...	...	...	28	21	7
Dafojanpa	...	...	...	...	...	...	...	...	...	16	13	3	...	...	...	16	13	3
Darkuchhpa	...	...	...	...	...	...	...	...	...	52	38	14	...	...	...	52	38	14
Dotio	...	...	...	...	...	...	...	...	...	72	64	8	...	...	...	72	64	8
Darjaspa	...	...	...	...	...	...	...	...	...	2	2	...	...	...	...	2	2	...
Dawangpa	...	...	...	...	...	...	...	...	...	12	12	...	...	...	...	12	12	...
Dampa	...	...	...	...	...	...	...	...	...	203	107	96	2	2	...	205	109	96
Darzi	120,764	68,882	51,882	6,982	3,336	3,646	127,746	72,218	55,528	172	92	80	366	69	297	538	161	377
Daralitang	...	...	...	...	...	...	...	...	...	...	...	...	795	427	368	795	427	368
Doaskatur	...	...	...	...	...	...	...	...	...	...	...	...	165	86	79	165	86	79
Diniki	...	...	...	...	...	...	...	...	...	...	...	...	256	138	118	256	138	118
Dharpa	...	...	...	...	...	...	...	...	...	...	...	...	1	1	...	1	1	...
Don	...	...	...	...	...	...	...	...	...	...	...	...	21	18	3	21	18	3
Dhobi	...	...	...	148	93	55	148	93	55	...	...	...	26	21	5	26	21	5

TABLE XIII.

CASTE, TRIBE, RACE OR NATIONALITY.

Caste, Tribe, Race or Nationality.	Total Population.			Provinces with Districts. — Jammu Province.																				
				Jammu District.			Udhampur District.			Bhimber District.			Jasrota District.			Punch Jagir.			Bhadarwah Jagir.			Total Jammu Province.		
	Persons.	Males.	Females.	Persons.	Males.	Females.	Persons.	Males.	Females.	Persons.	Males.	Females.	Persons.	Males.	Females.	Persons.	Males.	Females.	Persons.	Males.	Females.	Persons.	Males.	Females.
1	2	3	4	5	6	7	8	9	10	11	12	13	14	15	16	17	18	19	20	21	22	23	24	25
Deo	486	277	209	...	...	...	...	...	...	...	...	...	...	...	...	...	...	...	...	...	...	...	...	...
Dallasake	188	159	29	...	...	...	...	...	...	...	...	...	...	...	...	...	...	...	...	...	...	...	...	...
Darangara	214	136	78	...	...	...	...	...	...	...	...	...	...	...	...	...	...	...	...	...	...	...	...	...
Dollfar	153	123	30	...	...	...	...	...	...	...	...	...	...	...	...	...	...	...	...	...	...	...	...	...
Dalali	4	...	4	...	...	...	...	...	...	...	...	...	...	...	...	...	...	...	...	...	...	...	...	...
Dar	81,207	41,580	39,627	...	...	...	...	...	...	...	...	...	...	...	...	...	...	...	...	...	...	...	...	...
Doom	54,436	25,081	29,355	3,924	1,913	2,011	117	87	30	17,733	9,342	8,391	17	11	6	25,210	11,645	13,565	...	...	...	47,001	22,998	24,003
Daugra	345	203	142	...	...	...	...	...	...	...	...	...	...	...	...	...	...	...	...	...	...	...	...	...
Daptu	21	17	4	...	...	...	...	...	...	...	...	...	...	...	...	...	...	...	...	...	...	...	...	...
Dag	407	253	154	...	...	...	...	...	...	...	...	...	...	...	...	...	...	...	...	...	...	...	...	...
Dodu	40	15	25	...	...	...	...	...	...	...	...	...	...	...	...	...	...	...	...	...	...	...	...	...
Dalchu	16	8	8	...	...	...	...	...	...	...	...	...	...	...	...	...	...	...	...	...	...	...	...	...
Dailu	82	43	39	...	...	...	...	...	...	...	...	...	...	...	...	...	...	...	...	...	...	...	...	...
Daund	528	416	112	...	...	...	...	...	...	...	...	...	...	...	...	...	...	...	...	...	...	...	...	...
Dandar	30	13	17	...	...	...	...	...	...	...	...	...	...	...	...	...	...	...	...	...	...	...	...	...
Danapa	6,204	2,988	3,216	...	...	...	...	...	...	...	...	...	...	...	...	...	...	...	...	...	...	...	...	...
Danglopa	5,460	2,751	2,709	...	...	...	...	...	...	...	...	...	...	...	...	...	...	...	...	...	...	...	...	...
Dalgpa	5,128	2,513	2,615	...	...	...	...	...	...	...	...	...	...	...	...	...	...	...	...	...	...	...	...	...
Doband	1,083	496	587	...	...	...	...	...	...	...	...	...	...	...	...	...	...	...	...	...	...	...	...	...
Doorpa	1,240	623	617	...	...	...	...	...	...	...	...	...	...	...	...	...	...	...	...	...	...	...	...	...
Dant	1,743	812	931	...	...	...	...	...	...	...	...	...	...	...	...	...	...	...	...	...	...	...	...	...
Dangi	641	210	431	...	...	...	...	...	...	...	...	...	...	...	...	...	...	...	...	...	...	...	...	...
Dalu	1,394	515	879	...	...	...	...	...	...	...	...	...	...	...	...	...	...	...	...	...	...	...	...	...
Dhag	5	5	...	...	...	...	...	...	...	...	...	...	...	...	...	...	...	...	...	...	...	...	...	...
Fakku	313	177	136	...	...	...	...	...	...	...	...	...	...	...	...	...	...	...	...	...	...	...	...	...
Faraah	136	70	66	...	...	...	...	...	...	...	...	...	...	...	...	...	...	...	...	...	...	...	...	...
Farah	57	34	23	...	...	...	...	...	...	...	...	...	...	...	...	...	...	...	...	...	...	...	...	...
Fangru	16	7	9	...	...	...	...	...	...	...	...	...	...	...	...	...	...	...	...	...	...	...	...	...
Fandh	9	5	4	...	...	...	...	...	...	...	...	...	...	...	...	...	...	...	...	...	...	...	...	...
Faah	37	25	12	...	...	...	...	...	...	...	...	...	...	...	...	...	...	...	...	...	...	...	...	...
Farid	11	5	6	...	...	...	...	...	...	...	...	...	...	...	...	...	...	...	...	...	...	...	...	...
Fahman	3	3	...	...	...	...	...	...	...	...	...	...	...	...	...	...	...	...	...	...	...	...	...	...
Fatuch	60	38	22	...	...	...	...	...	...	...	...	...	...	...	...	...	...	...	...	...	...	...	...	...
Fakirpa	1,726	853	873	...	...	...	...	...	...	...	...	...	...	...	...	...	...	...	...	...	...	...	...	...
Falupa	28	15	13	...	...	...	...	...	...	...	...	...	...	...	...	...	...	...	...	...	...	...	...	...
Fardpa	60	25	35	...	...	...	...	...	...	...	...	...	...	...	...	...	...	...	...	...	...	...	...	...
Farspa	37	27	10	...	...	...	...	...	...	...	...	...	...	...	...	...	...	...	...	...	...	...	...	...
Fallojpa	67	49	18	...	...	...	...	...	...	...	...	...	...	...	...	...	...	...	...	...	...	...	...	...
Fattahpa	925	442	483	...	...	...	...	...	...	...	...	...	...	...	...	...	...	...	...	...	...	...	...	...
Fopa	21	8	13	...	...	...	...	...	...	...	...	...	...	...	...	...	...	...	...	...	...	...	...	...
Falpa	16	11	5	...	...	...	...	...	...	...	...	...	...	...	...	...	...	...	...	...	...	...	...	...

Caste, Tribe, Race or Nationality.	Khas District. Persons.	Khas District. Males.	Khas District. Females.	Muzaffarabad District. Persons.	Muzaffarabad District. Males.	Muzaffarabad District. Females.	Total Kashmir Province. Persons.	Total Kashmir Province. Males.	Total Kashmir Province. Females.	Ladakh District. Persons.	Ladakh District. Males.	Ladakh District. Females.	Gilgit District. Persons.	Gilgit District. Males.	Gilgit District. Females.	Total Frontier Districts. Persons.	Total Frontier Districts. Males.	Total Frontier Districts. Females.
	26	27	28	29	30	31	32	33	34	35	36	37	38	39	40	41	42	43
Deo	486	277	209	...	...	...	486	277	209	...	...	...	...	...	...	...	...	...
Dellasake	...	...	...	188	159	29	188	159	29	...	...	...	...	...	...	...	...	...
Durangara	...	...	...	214	136	78	214	136	78	...	...	...	...	...	...	...	...	...
Dolifar	...	...	...	153	123	30	153	123	30	...	...	...	...	...	...	...	...	...
Dalali	...	...	...	4	...	4	4	...	4	...	...	...	...	...	...	...	...	...
Dar	78,615	40,739	37,876	2,592	841	1,751	81,207	41,580	39,627	...	...	...	...	...	...	...	...	...
Doom	2,254	1,657	597	4,804	291	4,513	7,058	1,948	5,110	90	40	50	287	95	193	377	135	243
Dangra	345	203	142	...	...	...	345	203	142	...	...	...	...	...	...	...	...	...
Daptu	21	17	4	...	...	...	21	17	4	...	...	...	...	...	...	...	...	...
Dag	407	253	154	...	...	...	407	253	154	...	...	...	...	...	...	...	...	...
Dodu	40	15	25	...	...	...	40	15	25	...	...	...	...	...	...	...	...	...
Dalchu	16	8	8	...	...	...	16	8	8	...	...	...	...	...	...	...	...	...
Dallu	82	43	39	...	...	...	82	43	39	...	...	...	...	...	...	...	...	...
Daund	...	...	...	528	416	112	528	416	112	...	...	...	...	...	...	...	...	...
Dandar	...	...	...	30	13	17	30	13	17	...	...	...	...	...	...	...	...	...
Danapa	...	...	...	...	...	...	...	...	...	6,204	2,988	3,216	...	...	...	6,204	2,988	3,216
Danglepa	...	...	...	...	...	...	...	...	...	5,460	2,751	2,709	...	...	...	5,460	2,751	2,709
Daigpa	...	...	...	...	...	...	...	...	...	5,128	2,513	2,615	...	...	...	5,128	2,513	2,615
Doband	...	...	...	...	...	...	...	...	...	1,083	496	587	...	...	...	1,083	496	587
Doorpa	...	...	...	...	...	...	...	...	...	1,240	623	617	...	...	...	1,240	623	617
Dant	...	...	...	...	...	...	...	...	...	1,743	812	931	...	...	...	1,743	812	931
Daugi	...	...	...	...	...	...	...	...	...	641	210	431	...	...	...	641	210	431
Dalu	1,394	515	879	...	...	...	1,394	515	879	...	...	...	...	...	...	...	...	...
Dhag	5	5	...	...	...	...	5	5	...	...	...	...	...	...	...	...	...	...
Fakku	313	177	136	...	...	...	313	177	136	...	...	...	...	...	...	...	...	...
Farash	136	70	66	...	...	...	136	70	66	...	...	...	...	...	...	...	...	...
Farah	57	34	23	...	...	...	57	34	23	...	...	...	...	...	...	...	...	...
Fangru	16	7	9	...	...	...	16	7	9	...	...	...	...	...	...	...	...	...
Fandh	9	5	4	...	...	...	9	5	4	...	...	...	...	...	...	...	...	...
Fath	37	25	12	...	...	...	37	25	12	...	...	...	...	...	...	...	...	...
Farid	11	5	6	...	...	...	11	5	6	...	...	...	...	...	...	...	...	...
Fahman	3	3	...	...	...	...	3	3	...	...	...	...	...	...	...	...	...	...
Fatuch	...	...	...	...	...	...	...	...	...	60	38	22	...	...	...	60	38	22
Fakirpa	...	...	...	...	...	...	...	...	...	1,726	853	873	...	...	...	1,726	853	873
Falupa	...	...	...	...	...	...	...	...	...	28	15	13	...	...	...	28	15	13
Fardpa	...	...	...	...	...	...	...	...	...	60	25	35	...	...	...	60	25	35
Farspa	...	...	...	...	...	...	...	...	...	37	27	10	...	...	...	37	27	10
Fallepa	...	...	...	...	...	...	...	...	...	67	49	18	...	...	...	67	49	18
Fattehpa	...	...	...	...	...	...	...	...	...	925	442	483	...	...	...	925	442	483
Fopa	...	...	...	...	...	...	...	...	...	21	8	13	...	...	...	21	8	13
Fulpa	...	...	...	...	...	...	...	...	...	16	11	5	...	...	...	16	11	5

TABLE XIII.

Caste, Tribe, Race or Nationality.

Caste, Tribe, Race or Nationality.	Total Population. Persons.	Total Population. Males.	Total Population. Females.	Provinces with Districts. Jammu Province. Jammu District. Persons.	Jammu District. Males.	Jammu District. Females.	Udhampur District. Persons.	Udhampur District. Males.	Udhampur District. Females.	Bhimber District. Persons.	Bhimber District. Males.	Bhimber District. Females.	Jasrota District. Persons.	Jasrota District. Males.	Jasrota District. Females.	Punch Jágír. Persons.	Punch Jágír. Males.	Punch Jágír. Females.	Bhadarwah Jágír. Persons.	Bhadarwah Jágír. Males.	Bhadarwah Jágír. Females.	Total Jammu Province. Persons.	Total Jammu Province. Males.	Total Jammu Province. Females.
1	2	3	4	5	6	7	8	9	10	11	12	13	14	15	16	17	18	19	20	21	22	23	24	25
Fasalpa	55	28	27	...	...	...	...	...	...	...	...	...	...	...	...	...	...	...	...	...	...	...	...	...
Fakkupa	848	421	427	...	...	...	...	...	...	...	...	...	...	...	...	...	...	...	...	...	...	...	...	...
Gurba	62	33	29	...	...	...	...	...	...	...	...	...	...	...	...	...	...	...	...	...	...	...	...	...
Garah	67	42	25	...	...	...	...	...	...	...	...	...	...	...	...	...	...	...	...	...	...	...	...	...
Gutgarh	2,391	835	1,556	...	...	...	92	69	23	...	...	...	...	...	...	...	...	...	...	...	...	92	69	23
Gulial	77	45	32	...	...	...	...	...	...	...	...	...	...	...	...	...	...	...	...	...	...	...	...	...
Galu	153	97	56	...	...	...	...	...	...	...	...	...	...	...	...	...	...	...	...	...	...	...	...	...
Ganale	54,296	21,450	32,846	...	...	...	...	...	...	...	...	...	...	...	...	...	...	...	766	125	641	766	125	641
Galpa	129	59	70	...	...	...	...	...	...	...	...	...	...	...	...	...	...	...	...	...	...	...	...	...
Glodapa	95	46	49	...	...	...	...	...	...	...	...	...	...	...	...	...	...	...	...	...	...	...	...	...
Gosingipa	219	185	34	...	...	...	...	...	...	...	...	...	...	...	...	...	...	...	...	...	...	...	...	...
Galpopa	227	97	130	...	...	...	...	...	...	...	...	...	...	...	...	...	...	...	...	...	...	...	...	...
Garapa	56	26	30	...	...	...	...	...	...	...	...	...	...	...	...	...	...	...	...	...	...	...	...	...
Gochar	16	4	12	...	...	...	...	...	...	...	...	...	...	...	...	...	...	...	...	...	...	...	...	...
Gayangpa	29	16	13	...	...	...	...	...	...	...	...	...	...	...	...	...	...	...	...	...	...	...	...	...
Gokrupa	16	9	7	...	...	...	...	...	...	...	...	...	...	...	...	...	...	...	...	...	...	...	...	...
Garkopa	12	...	12	...	...	...	...	...	...	...	...	...	...	...	...	...	...	...	...	...	...	...	...	...
Ganchandpa	77	52	25	...	...	...	...	...	...	...	...	...	...	...	...	...	...	...	...	...	...	...	...	...
Gammak	24	7	17	...	...	...	...	...	...	...	...	...	...	...	...	...	...	...	...	...	...	...	...	...
Gharpa	15	4	11	...	...	...	...	...	...	...	...	...	...	...	...	...	...	...	...	...	...	...	...	...
Gadholpa	132	110	22	...	...	...	...	...	...	...	...	...	...	...	...	...	...	...	...	...	...	...	...	...
Gashopa	235	194	41	...	...	...	...	...	...	...	...	...	...	...	...	...	...	...	...	...	...	...	...	...
Gangipa	67	48	19	...	...	...	...	...	...	...	...	...	...	...	...	...	...	...	...	...	...	...	...	...
Gobaba	24	3	21	...	...	...	...	...	...	...	...	...	...	...	...	...	...	...	...	...	...	...	...	...
Gujaka	269	150	119	...	...	...	...	...	...	...	...	...	...	...	...	...	...	...	...	...	...	...	...	...
Gorakh	208	140	68	...	...	...	88	24	64	...	...	...	...	...	...	...	...	...	...	...	...	88	24	64
Garam	16	16	...	...	...	...	...	...	...	...	...	...	...	...	...	...	...	...	...	...	...	...	...	...
Gaddi	5,927	2,966	2,961	...	...	...	5,489	2,735	2,754	...	...	...	...	...	...	...	...	...	...	...	...	5,480	2,735	2,754
Gozhani	214	103	111	...	...	...	214	105	111	...	...	...	...	...	...	...	...	...	...	...	...	214	103	111
Gujrati	3	2	1	...	...	...	3	2	1	...	...	...	...	...	...	...	...	...	...	...	...	3	2	1
Total Gujar ...	286,109	156,022	130,087	35,219	18,730	16,489	38,924	15,256	23,690	30,968	16,266	14,702	5,539	3,484	2,055	39,851	22,017	17,834	7,599	3,666	3,933	158,100	79,449	78,651
Gujar	37,126	22,079	15,047	2,150	1,167	983	6,376	3,433	2,943	823	651	172	72	48	24	1,685	960	725	...	...	...	11,106	6,259	4,847
" Awana	2,826	1,684	1,142	75	40	35	66	26	40	193	149	44	...	...	...	475	375	100	...	...	...	809	590	219
" Amau	250	40	210	...	...	...	...	...	...	1	...	1	...	...	...	...	...	...	183	20	163	184	20	164
" Badana	3,291	2,041	1,250	263	102	71	...	...	...	...	...	...	...	...	...	1,731	1,258	473	...	...	...	1,994	1,450	544
" Bokra	727	435	292	...	...	...	...	...	...	14	14	...	...	...	...	...	...	...	...	...	...	14	14	...
" Bajwal	185	139	46	22	18	4	...	...	...	163	121	42	...	...	...	...	...	...	...	...	...	185	139	46
" Badan	610	155	455	6	...	6	...	...	...	...	...	...	...	...	...	439	90	340	...	...	...	445	90	355
" Bachu	1,939	1,546	393	102	93	9	...	...	...	...	...	...	...	...	...	...	...	...	...	...	...	102	93	9

Caste, Tribe, Race or Nationality.	PROVINCES WITH DISTRICTS.																	
	KASHMIR PROVINCE.									FRONTIER DISTRICTS.								
	Khas District.			Muzaffarabad District.			Total Kashmir Province.			Ladakh District.			Gilgit District.			Total Frontier Districts.		
	Persons.	Males.	Females.	Persons.	Males.	Females.	Persons.	Males.	Females.	Persons.	Males.	Females.	Persons.	Males.	Females.	Persons.	Males.	Females.
	26	27	28	29	30	31	32	33	34	35	36	37	38	39	40	41	42	43
Fasalpa	...	...	...	...	...	...	...	...	...	55	28	27	...	...	...	55	28	27
Fakkupa	...	...	...	...	...	...	...	...	...	848	421	427	...	...	...	848	421	427
Gurba	...	...	...	...	...	...	...	...	...	62	33	29	...	...	...	62	33	29
Garah	...	...	...	...	...	...	...	...	...	67	42	25	...	...	...	67	42	25
Gatgarh	...	...	...	2,294	763	1,531	2,294	763	1,531	5	3	2	...	...	...	5	3	2
Galial	...	...	...	...	...	...	...	...	...	77	45	32	...	...	...	77	45	32
Galu	...	...	...	...	...	...	...	...	...	153	97	56	...	...	...	153	97	56
Ganaie	48,259	18,484	29,775	1,694	1,003	691	49,953	19,487	30,466	3,577	1,838	1,739	...	...	...	3,577	1,838	1,739
Galpa	...	...	...	...	...	...	...	...	...	129	59	70	...	...	...	129	59	70
Glodapa	...	...	...	...	...	...	...	...	...	95	46	49	...	...	...	95	46	49
Gosingipa	...	...	...	...	...	...	...	...	...	219	185	34	...	...	...	219	185	34
Galpopa	...	...	...	...	...	...	...	...	...	227	97	130	...	...	...	227	97	130
Garapa	...	...	...	...	...	...	...	...	...	56	26	30	...	...	...	56	26	30
Goohar	...	...	...	...	...	...	...	...	...	16	4	12	...	...	...	16	4	12
Gayangpa	...	...	...	...	...	...	...	...	...	29	16	13	...	...	...	29	16	13
Gokrupa	...	...	...	...	...	...	...	...	...	16	9	7	...	...	...	16	9	7
Garkopa	...	...	...	...	...	...	...	...	...	12	...	12	...	...	...	12	...	12
Gonchandpa	...	...	...	...	...	...	...	...	...	77	52	25	...	...	...	77	52	25
Gammak	...	...	...	...	...	...	...	...	...	24	7	17	...	...	...	24	7	17
Gharpa	...	...	...	...	...	...	...	...	...	15	4	11	...	...	...	15	4	11
Gadholpa	...	...	...	...	...	...	...	...	...	132	110	22	...	...	...	132	110	22
Gashopa	...	...	...	...	...	...	...	...	...	235	194	41	...	...	...	235	194	41
Gangipa	...	...	...	...	...	...	...	...	...	67	48	19	...	...	...	67	48	19
Gobaba	...	...	...	...	...	...	...	...	...	24	3	21	...	...	...	24	3	21
Gajaka	...	...	...	...	...	...	...	...	...	...	...	...	299	150	149	299	150	149
Gorakh	...	...	...	...	...	...	...	...	...	...	...	...	120	116	4	120	116	4
Garam	...	...	...	...	...	...	...	...	...	...	...	...	16	16	...	16	16	...
Gaddi	438	231	207	...	...	...	438	231	207	...	...	...	...	...	...	...	...	...
Goshani	...	...	...	...	...	...	...	...	...	...	...	...	...	...	...	...	...	...
Gujrati	...	...	...	...	...	...	...	...	...	...	...	...	...	...	...	...	...	...
Total Gujar ...	79,006	46,116	32,890	46,644	29,247	17,397	125,650	75,363	50,287	327	110	2,117	2,032	1,100	932	2,359	1,210	1,149
Gujar	15,247	9,209	7,038	8,813	6,574	2,239	24,060	14,783	9,277	11	2	9	1,949	1,035	914	1,960	1,037	923
" Awana	1,240	598	642	717	485	232	1,957	1,083	874	60	11	49	...	...	...	60	11	49
" Aman	63	11	52	9	9	...	72	20	52	...	...	...	...	...	...	...	...	...
" Badana	1,004	494	510	293	97	196	1,297	591	706	...	...	...	...	...	...	...	...	...
" Bokra	...	...	...	713	421	292	713	421	292	...	...	...	...	...	...	...	...	...
" Bajwal	...	...	...	...	...	...	...	...	...	...	...	...	...	...	...	...	...	...
" Badan	...	...	...	165	65	100	165	65	100	...	...	...	...	...	...	...	...	...
" Barhu	1,647	1,453	194	190	...	190	1,837	1,453	384	...	...	...	...	...	...	...	...	...

TABLE XIII.

Caste, Tribe, Race or Nationality.

Caste, Tribe, Race or Nationality.	Total Population.			Provinces with Districts. — Jammu Province. — Jammu District.			Udhampur District.			Bhimber District.			Jasrota District.			Punch Jagir.			Bhadarwah Jagir.			Total Jammu Province.		
	Persons.	Males.	Females.	Persons.	Males.	Females.	Persons.	Males.	Females.	Persons.	Males.	Females.	Persons.	Males.	Females.	Persons.	Males.	Females.	Persons.	Males.	Females.	Persons.	Males.	Females.
1	2	3	4	5	6	7	8	9	10	11	12	13	14	15	16	17	18	19	20	21	22	23	24	25
Gujar Bajral	3,390	2,388	1,002	...	3	...	...	...	...	762	529	233	...	...	...	2,345	1,769	576	...	...	...	3,107	2,298	809
" Bhalsar	1,104	520	584	516	301	215	...	...	...	559	219	340	...	...	...	...	...	...	...	...	...	1,075	520	555
" Bhanday	1,018	623	395	...	...	...	7	7	...	194	193	1	...	...	...	...	...	...	...	...	...	201	200	1
" Balout	475	259	216	...	...	...	...	...	...	254	187	67	...	...	...	...	...	...	...	...	...	254	187	67
" Barwal	1,218	737	481	...	...	...	...	...	...	430	336	94	1	1	...	...	...	...	...	...	...	431	337	94
" Bamua	1,825	960	865	...	...	...	...	...	...	115	57	58	...	...	...	...	...	...	...	...	...	115	57	58
" Bokar	5,812	4,219	1,593	717	383	335	324	226	98	534	262	272	219	123	96	1,285	1,093	192	...	...	...	3,079	2,086	993
" Barkoti	207	100	107	...	...	...	...	...	...	...	...	...	...	...	...	...	...	...	...	...	...	...	...	...
" Baru	820	339	481	2	1	1	...	...	...	125	66	59	...	...	...	...	...	...	...	...	...	127	67	60
" Bajar	10,672	6,248	4,424	1,070	494	576	321	153	168	2,261	1,255	1,006	...	...	...	1,636	789	847	4	3	1	5,292	2,694	2,598
" Rawarwal ...	136	64	72	68	17	51	38	30	8	30	17	13	...	...	...	...	...	...	...	...	...	136	64	72
" Bagray	8,421	4,637	3,784	1,672	826	846	46	21	25	14	14	...	...	...	...	188	55	133	...	...	...	1,920	916	1,004
" Badhal	21	15	6	...	...	...	20	14	6	...	...	...	1	1	...	...	...	...	...	...	...	21	15	6
" Bhulti	8,111	4,059	4,052	76	66	10	11	8	3	499	349	150	...	...	...	1,286	768	518	...	...	...	1,872	1,191	681
" Boogri	933	503	430	14	11	3	3	...	3	...	...	...	67	60	7	...	...	...	...	...	...	84	71	13
" Bajrali	200	102	98	22	18	4	73	49	24	...	...	...	...	...	...	...	...	...	...	...	...	95	67	28
" Chur	58	31	27	...	...	...	...	...	...	...	...	...	...	...	...	...	...	...	...	...	...	...	...	...
" Chak	1,725	1,203	522	...	...	...	1	...	1	...	...	...	...	...	...	...	...	...	...	...	...	1	...	1
" Chaichi	37,314	15,380	21,934	4,352	2,578	1,774	12,519	1,289	11,230	4,861	1,899	2,962	1,533	1,044	489	4,562	2,098	2,464	205	96	109	28,032	9,004	19,028
" Chowhan	25,123	13,161	11,962	2,890	1,358	1,532	1,786	1,010	776	5,396	2,196	3,200	1,119	632	487	4,599	2,534	2,065	86	55	31	15,876	7,785	8,091
" Daidar	9,771	5,553	4,218	1,136	642	494	1,030	467	563	958	636	322	131	75	56	2,398	1,454	944	212	173	39	5,865	3,447	2,418
" Duddi	2,773	1,072	1,701	272	171	101	2,077	1,166	911	...	...	...	20	20	...	...	...	...	2	...	2	2,371	1,357	1,014
" Gowai	11,432	6,049	5,383	1,924	879	1,045	2,885	1,479	1,406	1,086	367	719	400	293	107	...	...	...	192	49	143	7,087	3,067	3,420
" Jakwal	58	24	34	...	...	...	...	...	...	...	...	...	...	...	...	...	...	...	...	...	...	...	...	...
" Jangla	916	483	433	...	...	...	...	...	...	8	7	1	4	4	...	619	402	217	...	...	...	631	413	218
" Jakal	5,466	3,096	2,370	66	36	30	95	48	47	205	18	187	50	34	16	1,307	834	473	...	...	...	1,723	970	753
" Jhookar	1,156	550	606	54	30	24	11	2	9	1	1	...	...	...	...	837	381	456	...	...	...	903	414	489
" Jaral	67	61	6	14	8	6	53	53	...	...	...	...	...	...	...	...	...	...	...	...	...	67	61	6
" Jarah	2,557	1,306	1,251	718	280	438	505	175	330	464	435	29	...	...	...	...	...	...	40	9	31	1,727	899	828
" Janglay	436	229	207	36	27	9	56	16	40	104	76	28	147	110	37	...	...	...	...	...	...	343	229	114
" Kasana	11,521	6,377	5,144	1,387	842	545	4,518	2,197	2,321	1,918	1,377	541	327	194	133	1,602	530	1,073	...	...	...	9,752	5,140	4,612
" Kataria	5,460	3,330	2,130	1,032	367	665	211	112	99	129	67	62	372	218	154	2,009	1,057	952	29	5	24	3,782	1,826	1,956
" Koli	7,506	3,730	3,776	752	233	519	1,088	483	605	519	405	114	...	...	...	2,438	940	1,498	43	22	21	4,840	2,083	2,757
" Kalas	8,403	3,965	4,438	1,139	607	532	659	337	322	2,978	1,062	1,916	...	...	...	...	...	...	...	...	...	4,776	2,006	2,770
" Kalana	20,008	11,417	8,591	5,760	3,445	2,315	634	321	313	...	...	...	...	...	...	4,202	2,307	1,895	...	...	...	10,596	6,073	4,523
" Lali	1,867	917	950	517	236	281	1,108	591	517	64	49	15	1	1	...	177	40	137	...	...	...	1,867	917	950
" Malik	81	58	23	...	...	...	...	...	...	...	...	...	...	...	...	81	58	23	...	...	...	81	58	23
" Parjal	251	216	35	...	...	...	...	...	...	...	...	...	...	...	...	...	...	...	...	...	...	...	...	...
" Paswal	17,838	10,947	6,891	3,901	2,120	1,781	1,443	804	639	2,776	1,645	1,131	458	291	167	3,046	1,562	1,484	3	2	1	11,627	6,424	5,203
" Phambla	2,109	1,071	1,038	57	...	57	...	...	...	1,421	679	742	4	4	...	...	...	...	...	...	...	1,482	683	799
" Pali	184	104	80	...	...	...	...	...	...	...	...	...	...	...	...	...	...	...	...	...	...	...	...	...

PROVINCES WITH DISTRICTS.

Caste, Tribe, Race or Nationality.	Kashmir Province. Khás District. Persons.	Males.	Females.	Muzaffarabad District. Persons.	Males.	Females.	Total Kashmir Province. Persons.	Males.	Females.	Frontier Districts. Ladakh District. Persons.	Males.	Females.	Gilgit District. Persons.	Males.	Females.	Total Frontier Districts. Persons.	Males.	Females.
	26	27	28	29	30	31	32	33	34	35	36	37	38	39	40	41	42	43
Gujar Bajrat	...	...	...	47	...	47	47	...	47	236	90	146	...	...	...	236	90	146
" Bhalsar	...	...	...	29	...	29	29	...	29	...	...	...	...	...	...	...	...	...
" Bhanday	653	358	295	164	65	99	817	423	394	...	...	...	...	...	...	...	...	...
" Balout	...	...	...	221	72	149	221	72	149	...	...	...	...	...	...	...	...	...
" Barwal	627	292	335	160	108	52	787	400	387	...	...	...	...	...	...	...	...	...
" Bamba	437	239	198	1,273	664	609	1,710	903	807	...	...	...	...	...	...	...	...	...
" Bokar	1,072	1,034	38	1,661	1,099	562	2,733	2,133	600	...	...	...	...	...	...	...	...	...
" Barkoti	...	...	...	207	100	107	207	100	107	...	...	...	...	...	...	...	...	...
" Baru	...	...	...	693	272	421	693	272	421	...	...	...	...	...	...	...	...	...
" Bajar	2,058	1,502	556	3,274	2,066	1,208	5,332	3,508	1,824	...	...	...	48	46	2	48	46	2
" Bawarwal	...	...	...	...	...	...	...	...	...	...	...	...	...	...	...	...	...	...
" Bagray	6,501	3,721	2,780	...	...	...	6,501	3,721	2,780	...	...	...	...	...	...	...	...	...
" Badhal	...	...	...	...	...	...	...	...	...	...	...	...	...	...	...	...	...	...
" Bhulti	6,239	2,868	3,371	...	...	...	6,239	2,868	3,371	...	...	...	...	...	...	...	...	...
" Boogri	848	431	417	...	...	...	848	431	417	...	...	...	...	...	...	...	...	...
" Bajrali	58	35	23	47	...	47	105	35	70	...	...	...	...	...	...	...	...	...
" Char	...	...	...	58	31	27	58	31	27	...	...	...	...	...	...	...	...	...
" Chak	1,257	858	399	467	345	122	1,724	1,203	521	...	...	...	...	...	...	...	...	...
" Chaichi	5,269	3,330	1,939	3,908	3,041	867	9,177	6,371	2,806	...	...	...	5	5	...	5	5	...
" Chowhan	5,787	3,292	2,495	3,460	2,084	1,376	9,247	5,376	3,871	...	...	...	...	...	...	...	...	...
" Daidar	2,145	1,242	903	1,752	861	891	3,897	2,103	1,794	...	...	...	9	3	6	9	3	
" Duddi	310	101	209	992	514	478	1,302	615	687	...	...	...	...	...	...	...	...	...
" Gowni	2,605	1,455	1,150	1,740	927	813	4,345	2,382	1,963	...	...	...	...	...	...	...	...	...
" Jakwal	...	...	...	58	24	34	58	24	34	...	...	...	...	...	...	...	...	...
" Jangla	...	...	...	285	70	215	285	70	215	...	...	...	...	...	...	...	...	...
" Jakal	1,474	996	478	2,269	1,130	1,139	3,743	2,126	1,617	...	...	...	...	...	...	...	...	...
" Jhookar	...	...	...	253	136	117	253	136	117	...	...	...	...	...	...	...	...	...
" Jaral	...	...	...	...	...	...	...	...	...	...	...	...	...	...	...	...	...	...
" Jarah	781	387	394	49	20	29	830	407	423	...	...	...	...	...	...	...	...	...
" Janglay	93	...	93	...	...	...	93	...	93	...	...	...	...	...	...	...	...	...
" Kasana	568	223	345	1,201	1,014	187	1,769	1,237	532	...	...	...	...	...	...	...	...	...
" Kataria	...	...	...	1,678	1,504	174	1,678	1,504	174	...	...	...	...	...	...	...	...	...
" Koli	1,394	653	741	1,272	994	278	2,666	1,647	1,019	...	...	...	...	...	...	...	...	...
" Kalas	2,134	1,296	838	1,493	663	830	3,627	1,959	1,668	...	...	...	...	...	...	...	...	...
" Kalana	8,040	4,935	3,105	1,331	391	940	9,371	5,326	4,045	20	7	13	21	11	10	41	18	23
" Lali	...	...	...	...	...	...	...	...	...	...	...	...	...	...	...	...	...	...
" Malik	...	...	...	...	...	...	...	...	...	...	...	...	...	...	...	...	...	...
" Parjal	...	...	...	251	216	35	251	216	35	...	...	...	...	...	...	...	...	...
" Paswal	3,128	2,099	1,029	3,083	2,424	659	6,211	4,523	1,088	...	...	...	...	...	...	...	...	...
" Phambla	...	...	...	627	388	239	627	388	239	...	...	...	...	...	...	...	...	...
" Pali	184	104	80	...	...	...	184	104	80	...	...	...	...	...	...	...	...	...

TABLE XIII.

Caste, Tribe, Race or Nationality.

Caste, Tribe, Race or Nationality.	Total Population.			Provinces with Districts. — Jammu Province. — Jammu District.			Udhampur District.			Bhimber District.			Jasrota District.			Punch Jágir.			Bhadarwah Jágir.			Total Jammu Province.		
	Persons.	Males.	Females.	Persons.	Males.	Females.	Persons.	Males.	Females.	Persons.	Males.	Females.	Persons.	Males.	Females.	Persons.	Males.	Females.	Persons.	Males.	Females.	Persons.	Males.	Females.
1	2	3	4	5	6	7	8	9	10	11	12	13	14	15	16	17	18	19	20	21	22	23	24	25
Gujar Pagal	70	22	48	...	...	...	...	...	...	30	22	8	40	...	40	...	...	...	...	...	...	70	22	48
" Suddan	916	220	696	19	12	7	57	50	7	...	...	...	14	9	5	...	...	...	88	...	88	178	71	107
" Shawali	234	216	18	225	209	16	1	1	...	...	...	...	8	6	2	...	...	...	...	...	...	234	216	18
" Tas	3,070	1,012	1,767	1,123	544	570	77	52	25	...	...	...	207	83	124	856	620	237	95	32	63	2,358	1,340	1,018
" Thakaria	3,201	1,069	1,322	1,069	480	589	825	666	159	479	306	173	344	233	111	...	...	...	17	...	17	2,734	1,685	1,049
" Thakial	257	...	257	...	...	...	...	...	...	...	...	...	...	...	...	...	...	...	...	...	...	...	...	...
" Thakar	5,630	3,363	2,298	1	...	1	...	...	...	...	...	...	...	...	...	48	34	14	...	...	...	49	34	15
Hanspal	791	433	358	...	...	...	...	...	...	...	...	...	...	...	...	...	...	...	...	...	...	...	...	...
Ham hampa	524	300	224	...	...	...	...	...	...	...	...	...	...	...	...	...	...	...	...	...	...	...	...	...
Hanji	2,512	1,278	1,234	...	...	...	...	...	...	...	...	...	...	...	...	...	...	...	...	...	...	...	...	...
Harj	174	48	126	...	...	...	...	...	...	...	...	...	...	...	...	...	...	...	...	...	...	...	...	...
Haidarpa	80	33	47	...	...	...	...	...	...	...	...	...	...	...	...	...	...	...	...	...	...	...	...	...
Hajipa	336	159	177	...	...	...	...	...	...	...	...	...	...	...	...	...	...	...	...	...	...	...	...	...
Hosspa	128	34	94	...	...	...	...	...	...	...	...	...	...	...	...	...	...	...	...	...	...	...	...	...
Hamarpa	293	145	148	...	...	...	...	...	...	...	...	...	...	...	...	...	...	...	...	...	...	...	...	...
Hoarupa	27	15	12	...	...	...	...	...	...	...	...	...	...	...	...	...	...	...	...	...	...	...	...	...
Halipa	70	20	50	...	...	...	...	...	...	...	...	...	...	...	...	...	...	...	...	...	...	...	...	...
Hakoo	32	9	23	...	...	...	...	...	...	...	...	...	...	...	...	...	...	...	...	...	...	...	...	...
Halimpa	92	30	62	...	...	...	...	...	...	...	...	...	...	...	...	...	...	...	...	...	...	...	...	...
Harba	77	39	38	...	...	...	...	...	...	...	...	...	...	...	...	...	...	...	...	...	...	...	...	...
Halupa	40	12	28	...	...	...	...	...	...	...	...	...	...	...	...	...	...	...	...	...	...	...	...	...
Hakupa	18	14	4	...	...	...	...	...	...	...	...	...	...	...	...	...	...	...	...	...	...	...	...	...
Hakim	533	318	215	...	...	...	...	...	...	...	...	...	...	...	...	83	45	38	...	...	...	83	45	38
Haji	1,004	560	444	...	...	...	...	...	...	...	...	...	...	...	...	...	...	...	...	...	...	...	...	...
Hafiz	603	355	248	...	...	...	...	...	...	...	...	...	...	...	...	...	...	...	...	...	...	...	...	...
Hakak	70	32	38	...	...	...	...	...	...	...	...	...	...	...	...	...	...	...	...	...	...	...	...	...
Halla	465	258	207	...	...	...	...	...	...	...	...	...	...	...	...	...	...	...	...	...	...	...	...	...
Hamida	7	5	2	...	...	...	...	...	...	...	...	...	...	...	...	...	...	...	...	...	...	...	...	...
Hakida	60	20	40	...	...	...	...	...	...	...	...	...	...	...	...	...	...	...	...	...	...	...	...	...
Hakka	118	84	34	...	...	...	...	...	...	...	...	...	...	...	...	...	...	...	...	...	...	...	...	...
Husani	18	9	9	...	...	...	...	...	...	...	...	...	...	...	...	...	...	...	...	...	...	...	...	...
Huskas	200	120	80	...	...	...	...	...	...	...	...	...	...	...	...	...	...	...	...	...	...	...	...	...
Ikbal	5	...	5	...	...	...	...	...	...	...	...	...	...	...	...	...	...	...	...	...	...	...	...	...
Ilahi	5	...	5	...	...	...	...	...	...	...	...	...	...	...	...	...	...	...	...	...	...	...	...	...
Jark	224	124	100	...	...	...	...	...	...	...	...	...	...	...	...	...	...	...	...	...	...	...	...	...
Jagdoot	3	1	2	...	...	...	...	...	...	...	...	...	...	...	...	...	...	...	...	...	...	...	...	...
Jarkas	151	61	90	...	...	...	...	...	...	...	...	...	...	...	...	...	...	...	...	...	...	...	...	...
Jat	122,851	64,673	58,178	10,202	5,763	4,439	623	473	150	95,457	48,497	46,960	422	184	238	14,949	9,127	5,822	...	...	...	121,653	64,044	57,609
Janjuha	739	309	430	92	70	22	23	4	19	...	...	...	...	...	...	...	...	...	...	...	...	115	74	41
Jaupa	188	81	107	...	...	...	...	...	...	...	...	...	...	...	...	...	...	...	...	...	...	...	...	...
Joortau	71	38	33	...	...	...	...	...	...	...	...	...	...	...	...	...	...	...	...	...	...	...	...	...

PROVINCES WITH DISTRICTS.

Caste, Tribe, Race or Nationality.	Kashmir Province.									Frontier Districts.								
	Khas District.			Muzaffarabad District.			Total Kashmir Province.			Ladakh District.			Gilgit District.			Total Frontier Districts.		
	Persons.	Males.	Females.	Persons.	Males.	Females.	Persons.	Males.	Females.	Persons.	Males.	Females.	Persons.	Males.	Females.	Persons.	Males.	Females.
	26	27	28	29	30	31	32	33	34	35	36	37	38	39	40	41	42	43
Goortau Pagal	...	...	...	...	...	...	...	...	...	...	...	...	...	...	...	...	...	...
" Suddan	...	...	...	738	140	589	738	140	589	...	...	...	...	...	...	...	...	...
" Shawali	...	...	...	...	...	...	...	...	...	...	...	...	...	...	...	...	...	...
" Tas	721	572	149	...	...	...	721	572	149	...	...	...	...	...	...	...	...	...
" Thakaris	...	...	...	557	284	273	557	284	273	...	...	...	...	...	...	...	...	...
" Thakial	...	...	...	257	...	257	257	...	257	...	...	...	...	...	...	...	...	...
" Thakar	5,423	3,328	2,094	180	...	180	5,611	3,328	2,283	...	...	...	...	...	...	...	...	...
Hanspal	...	...	...	...	...	...	...	...	...	701	433	358	...	...	...	701	433	358
Hamhampa	...	...	...	...	...	...	...	...	...	524	300	224	...	...	...	524	300	224
Hanji	2,512	1,278	1,234	...	...	...	2,512	1,278	1,234	...	...	...	...	...	...	...	...	...
Harj	...	...	...	...	...	...	...	...	...	174	48	126	...	...	...	174	48	126
Haldarpa	...	...	...	...	...	...	...	...	...	80	33	47	...	...	...	80	33	47
Hajipa	...	...	...	...	...	...	...	...	...	336	159	177	...	...	...	336	159	177
Husapa	...	...	...	...	...	...	...	...	...	128	34	94	...	...	...	128	34	94
Hamarpa	...	...	...	...	...	...	...	...	...	293	145	148	...	...	...	293	145	148
Hoarupa	...	...	...	...	...	...	...	...	...	27	15	12	...	...	...	27	15	12
Hallpa	...	...	...	...	...	...	...	...	...	70	20	50	...	...	...	70	20	50
Hakoor	...	...	...	...	...	...	...	...	...	32	9	23	...	...	...	32	9	23
Lalimpa	...	...	...	...	...	...	...	...	...	92	30	62	...	...	...	92	30	62
Harba	...	...	...	...	...	...	...	...	...	77	39	38	...	...	...	77	39	38
Holupa	...	...	...	...	...	...	...	...	...	40	12	28	...	...	...	40	12	28
Hakupa	...	...	...	...	...	...	...	...	...	18	14	4	...	...	...	18	14	4
Hakim	292	150	142	140	118	31	441	268	173	9	5	4	...	...	...	9	5	4
Haji	1,004	560	444	...	...	...	1,004	560	444	...	...	...	...	...	...	...	...	...
Hafiz	603	355	248	...	...	...	603	355	248	...	...	...	...	...	...	...	...	...
Hakák	70	32	38	...	...	...	70	32	38	...	...	...	...	...	...	...	...	...
Halla	271	148	123	115	59	56	386	207	179	79	51	28	...	...	...	79	51	28
Hamida	7	5	2	...	...	...	7	5	2	...	...	...	...	...	...	...	...	...
Hakida	60	20	40	...	...	...	60	20	40	...	...	...	...	...	...	...	...	...
Hakka	118	84	34	...	...	...	118	84	34	...	...	...	...	...	...	...	...	...
Husani	18	9	9	...	...	...	18	9	9	...	...	...	...	...	...	...	...	...
Huskas	...	...	...	...	...	...	...	...	...	3	2	1	200	118	88	200	120	80
Ikbal	...	...	...	5	...	5	5	...	5	...	...	...	...	...	...	...	...	...
Ilahi	5	...	5	...	...	...	5	...	5	...	...	...	...	...	...	...	...	...
Jark	...	...	...	...	...	...	...	...	...	234	124	...	100	...	...	224	124	100
Jagdoot	...	...	...	...	...	...	...	...	...	3	1	...	2	...	...	3	1	2
Jerkas	...	...	...	...	...	...	...	...	...	151	61	90	...	...	...	151	61	90
Jat	580	342	207	386	236	150	925	478	447	240	118	122	33	33	...	273	151	122
Janjuha	119	64	55	505	171	334	624	335	380	...	...	...	...	...	...	...	...	...
Jaspa	...	...	...	...	...	...	...	...	...	188	81	107	...	...	...	188	81	107
Jeortau	...	...	...	...	...	...	...	...	...	71	38	33	...	...	...	71	38	33

TABLE XIII.

Caste, Tribe, Race or Nationality.

Caste, Tribe, Race or Nationality.	Total Population.			Provinces with Districts. Jammu Province. Jammu District.			Udhampur District.			Bhimber District.			Jasrota District.			Punch Jágir.			Bhadarwah Jágir.			Total Jammu Province.		
	Persons.	Males.	Females.	Persons.	Males.	Females.	Persons.	Males.	Females.	Persons.	Males.	Females.	Persons.	Males.	Females.	Persons.	Males.	Females.	Persons.	Males.	Females.	Persons.	Males.	Females.
1	2	3	4	5	6	7	8	9	10	11	12	13	14	15	16	17	18	19	20	21	22	23	24	25
Jamal	89	22	67	...	...	...	...	...	...	...	...	...	...	...	...	...	...	...	...	...	...	...	...	...
Jolah	184	78	106	...	...	...	...	...	...	...	...	...	...	...	...	...	...	...	...	...	...	...	...	...
Jan	38	19	19	...	...	...	...	...	...	...	...	...	...	...	...	...	...	...	...	...	...	...	...	...
Jarka	26	13	13	...	...	...	...	...	...	...	...	...	...	...	...	...	...	...	...	...	...	...	...	...
Jaji	60	25	35	...	...	...	...	...	...	...	...	...	...	...	...	...	...	...	...	...	...	...	...	...
Joddi	88	25	63	...	...	...	...	...	...	...	...	...	...	...	...	...	...	...	...	...	...	...	...	...
Jagral	46	16	30	...	...	...	...	...	...	...	...	...	...	...	...	...	...	...	...	...	...	...	...	...
Jokhar	142	102	40	...	...	...	...	...	...	...	...	...	...	...	...	...	...	...	...	...	...	...	...	...
Jatoor	2,200	1,053	1,147	53	45	8	9	7	2	1,702	774	958	34	16	18	402	241	161	...	...	...	2,200	1,053	1,147
Jagoh	170	35	135	...	...	...	...	...	...	...	...	...	...	...	...	...	...	...	...	...	...	...	...	...
Jalak	486	254	232	...	...	...	...	...	...	...	...	...	...	...	...	...	...	...	...	...	...	...	...	...
Joofa	64	18	46	...	...	...	...	...	...	...	...	...	...	...	...	...	...	...	...	...	...	...	...	...
Jokopa	12	12	...	...	...	...	...	...	...	...	...	...	...	...	...	...	...	...	...	...	...	...	...	...
Jonkpa	22	3	19	...	...	...	...	...	...	...	...	...	...	...	...	...	...	...	...	...	...	...	...	...
Joulpa	7	2	5	...	...	...	...	...	...	...	...	...	...	...	...	...	...	...	...	...	...	...	...	...
Joropa	74	23	51	...	...	...	...	...	...	...	...	...	...	...	...	...	...	...	...	...	...	...	...	...
Jakbalpa	3	3	...	...	...	...	...	...	...	...	...	...	...	...	...	...	...	...	...	...	...	...	...	...
Jotoonpa	10	10	...	...	...	...	...	...	...	...	...	...	...	...	...	...	...	...	...	...	...	...	...	...
Jadarpa	11	4	7	...	...	...	...	...	...	...	...	...	...	...	...	...	...	...	...	...	...	...	...	...
Jalpa	4	1	3	...	...	...	...	...	...	...	...	...	...	...	...	...	...	...	...	...	...	...	...	...
Jakarwar	156	80	76	...	...	...	...	...	...	...	...	...	...	...	...	...	...	...	...	...	...	...	...	...
Jar	514	320	194	...	...	...	...	...	...	...	...	...	...	...	...	...	...	...	...	...	...	...	...	...
Jonda	282	146	136	...	...	...	...	...	...	...	...	...	...	...	...	...	...	...	...	...	...	...	...	...
Janory	485	280	205	...	...	...	...	...	...	...	...	...	...	...	...	...	...	...	...	...	...	...	...	...
Jam	163	35	128	...	...	...	...	...	...	...	...	...	...	...	...	...	...	...	...	...	...	...	...	...
Johar	26	13	13	...	...	...	...	...	...	...	...	...	...	...	...	...	...	...	...	...	...	...	...	...
Jammal	99	38	61	...	...	...	...	...	...	...	...	...	...	...	...	...	...	...	...	...	...	...	...	...
Jalal	60	39	21	...	...	...	...	...	...	...	...	...	...	...	...	...	...	...	...	...	...	...	...	...
Jujepa	4	4	...	...	...	...	...	...	...	...	...	...	...	...	...	...	...	...	...	...	...	...	...	...
Jugta	61	61	...	...	...	...	...	...	...	...	...	...	...	...	...	...	...	...	...	...	...	...	...	...
Jugwal	103	69	34	...	...	...	1	1	...	...	...	...	...	...	...	...	...	...	...	...	...	1	1	...
Jandal	165	91	74	...	...	...	47	18	29	...	...	...	...	...	...	...	...	...	...	...	...	47	18	29
Jaloo	27	19	8	...	...	...	...	...	...	...	...	...	...	...	...	...	...	...	...	...	...	...	...	...
Jagroo	48	37	11	...	...	...	...	...	...	...	...	...	...	...	...	...	...	...	...	...	...	...	...	...
Jugpa	17	8	9	...	...	...	...	...	...	...	...	...	...	...	...	...	...	...	...	...	...	...	...	...
Jatta	36	33	3	...	...	...	...	...	...	...	...	...	...	...	...	...	...	...	...	...	...	...	...	...
Jamdhar	25	25	...	...	...	...	...	...	...	...	...	...	...	...	...	...	...	...	...	...	...	...	...	...
Jantri	240	114	126	...	...	...	...	...	...	...	...	...	...	...	...	...	...	...	...	...	...	...	...	...
Janal	43	33	10	...	...	...	...	...	...	...	...	...	...	...	...	...	...	...	...	...	...	...	...	...
Jagri	2	2	...	...	...	...	...	...	...	...	...	...	...	...	...	...	...	...	...	...	...	...	...	...
Jaddu	2	1	1	...	...	...	...	...	...	...	...	...	...	...	...	...	...	...	...	...	...	...	...	...

Caste, Tribe, Race or Nationality.	Khan District. Persons.	Khan District. Males.	Khan District. Females.	Muzaffarabad District. Persons.	Muzaffarabad District. Males.	Muzaffarabad District. Females.	Total Kashmir Province. Persons.	Total Kashmir Province. Males.	Total Kashmir Province. Females.	Ladakh District. Persons.	Ladakh District. Males.	Ladakh District. Females.	Gilgit District. Persons.	Gilgit District. Males.	Gilgit District. Females.	Total Frontier Districts. Persons.	Total Frontier Districts. Males.	Total Frontier Districts. Females.
	26	27	28	29	30	31	32	33	34	35	36	37	38	39	40	41	42	43
Jarnal	...	...	...	29	15	14	29	15	14	60	7	53	...	...	...	60	7	53
Jolah	41	16	25	...	...	...	41	16	25	143	62	81	...	...	...	143	62	81
Jan	...	...	...	...	...	...	...	...	...	38	19	19	...	...	...	38	19	19
Jarka	...	...	...	...	...	...	...	...	...	26	13	13	...	...	...	26	13	13
Jagi	...	...	...	...	...	...	...	...	...	60	25	35	...	...	...	60	25	35
Joddi	...	...	...	...	...	...	...	...	...	88	25	63	...	...	...	88	25	63
Jagral	...	...	...	32	6	26	32	6	26	14	10	4	...	...	...	14	10	4
Jakhar	...	...	...	...	...	...	...	...	...	75	35	40	67	67	...	142	102	40
Jatoor	...	...	...	...	...	...	...	...	...	...	...	...	...	...	...	...	...	...
Jagoh	...	...	...	...	...	...	...	...	...	170	35	135	...	...	...	170	35	135
Jalak	433	237	196	24	16	8	457	253	204	29	1	28	...	...	...	29	1	28
Joofa	...	...	...	...	...	...	...	...	...	64	18	46	...	...	...	64	18	46
Jokopa	...	...	...	...	...	...	...	...	...	12	12	...	...	...	...	12	12	...
Joutpa	...	...	...	...	...	...	...	...	...	22	3	19	...	...	...	22	3	19
Joulpa	...	...	...	...	...	...	...	...	...	7	2	5	...	...	...	7	2	5
Joropa	...	...	...	...	...	...	...	...	...	74	23	51	...	...	...	74	23	51
Jakbalpa	...	...	...	...	...	...	...	...	...	3	3	...	...	...	...	3	3	...
Jotoonpa	...	...	...	...	...	...	...	...	...	...	...	...	10	10	...	10	10	...
Jadarpa	...	...	...	...	...	...	...	...	...	...	...	...	11	4	7	11	4	7
Jalpa	...	...	...	...	...	...	...	...	...	...	...	...	4	1	3	4	1	3
Jakarwar	104	55	49	...	...	...	104	55	49	52	25	27	...	...	...	52	25	27
Jar	514	320	194	...	...	...	514	320	194	...	...	...	...	...	...	...	...	...
Janda	282	146	136	...	...	...	282	146	136	...	...	...	...	...	...	...	...	...
Janory	485	280	205	...	...	...	485	280	205	...	...	...	...	...	...	...	...	...
Jam	106	34	72	...	...	...	106	34	72	57	1	56	...	...	...	57	1	56
Johar	...	...	...	...	...	...	...	...	...	26	13	13	...	...	...	26	13	13
Jammal	99	38	61	...	...	...	99	38	61	...	...	...	...	...	...	...	...	...
Jalal	52	31	21	8	8	...	60	39	21	...	...	...	...	...	...	...	...	...
Jujepa	...	...	...	...	...	...	...	...	...	4	4	...	...	...	...	4	4	...
Jugta	...	...	...	...	...	...	...	...	...	61	61	...	...	...	...	61	61	...
Jugwal	...	...	...	102	68	34	102	68	34	...	...	...	...	...	...	...	...	...
Jandal	...	...	...	118	73	45	118	73	45	...	...	...	...	...	...	...	...	...
Jaloo	...	...	...	27	19	8	27	19	8	...	...	...	...	...	...	...	...	...
Jagroo	...	...	...	48	37	11	48	37	11	...	...	...	...	...	...	...	...	...
Jugpa	...	...	...	17	8	9	17	8	9	...	...	...	...	...	...	...	...	...
Jatta	...	...	...	36	33	3	36	33	3	...	...	...	...	...	...	...	...	...
Jandhar	...	...	...	25	25	...	25	25	...	...	...	...	...	...	...	...	...	...
Jautri	240	114	126	...	...	...	240	114	126	...	...	...	...	...	...	...	...	...
Jaual	43	33	10	...	...	...	43	33	10	...	...	...	...	...	...	...	...	...
Jagri	2	2	...	...	...	...	2	2	...	...	...	...	...	...	...	...	...	...
Jaddu	2	1	1	...	...	...	2	1	1	...	...	...	...	...	...	...	...	...

TABLE XIII.

CASTE, TRIBE, RACE OR NATIONALITY.

Caste, Tribe, Race or Nationality.	Total Population.			Provinces with Districts. Jammu Province. Jammu District.			Udhampur District.			Bhimber District.			Jasrota District.			Punch Jagir.			Bhadarwah Jagir.			Total Jammu Province.		
	Persons.	Males.	Females.	Persons.	Males.	Females.	Persons.	Males.	Females.	Persons.	Males.	Females.	Persons.	Males.	Females.	Persons.	Males.	Females.	Persons.	Males.	Females.	Persons.	Males.	Females.
1	2	3	4	5	6	7	8	9	10	11	12	13	14	15	16	17	18	19	20	21	22	23	24	25
Javi	9	2	7	...	...	...	...	...	...	...	...	...	...	...	...	...	...	...	...	...	...	...	...	...
Kashmiri	57,454	27,635	29,849	2,021	1,138	883	5,312	2,633	2,679	3,389	1,296	2,093	122	19	103	1,324	354	970	480	250	230	12,648	5,690	6,958
Kanuhora	6	5	1	...	...	...	...	...	...	...	...	...	...	...	...	...	...	...	...	...	...	...	...	...
Karina	8	7	1	...	...	...	...	...	...	...	...	...	...	...	...	...	...	...	...	...	...	...	...	...
Khori	9	3	6	...	...	...	...	...	...	...	...	...	...	...	...	...	...	...	...	...	...	...	...	...
Kolang	40	40	...	...	...	...	...	...	...	...	...	...	...	...	...	...	...	...	...	...	...	...	...	...
Kalotra	12	12	...	...	...	...	...	...	...	...	...	...	...	...	...	...	...	...	...	...	...	...	...	...
Kajil	3	3	...	...	...	...	...	...	...	...	...	...	...	...	...	...	...	...	...	...	...	...	...	...
Karkhal	3	3	...	...	...	...	...	...	...	...	...	...	...	...	...	...	...	...	...	...	...	...	...	...
Kammar	9	9	...	...	...	...	...	...	...	...	...	...	...	...	...	...	...	...	...	...	...	...	...	...
Kanthsylo	113	59	54	...	...	...	...	...	...	...	...	...	...	...	...	...	...	...	...	...	...	...	...	...
Khulang	116	69	47	...	...	...	...	...	...	...	...	...	...	...	...	...	...	...	...	...	...	...	...	...
Kashour	323	184	139	...	...	...	...	...	...	...	...	...	...	...	...	...	...	...	...	...	...	...	...	...
Khapa	41	22	19	...	...	...	...	...	...	...	...	...	...	...	...	...	...	...	...	...	...	...	...	...
Kanwapa	38	8	30	...	...	...	...	...	...	...	...	...	...	...	...	...	...	...	...	...	...	...	...	...
Kangopa	16	8	8	...	...	...	...	...	...	...	...	...	...	...	...	...	...	...	...	...	...	...	...	...
Khotagpa	112	19	93	...	...	...	...	...	...	...	...	...	...	...	...	...	...	...	...	...	...	...	...	...
Karmangpa	25	4	21	...	...	...	...	...	...	...	...	...	...	...	...	...	...	...	...	...	...	...	...	...
Karmakpa	112	85	27	...	...	...	...	...	...	...	...	...	...	...	...	...	...	...	...	...	...	...	...	...
Karjaspa	22	8	14	...	...	...	...	...	...	...	...	...	...	...	...	...	...	...	...	...	...	...	...	...
Katru	5	3	2	...	...	...	...	...	...	...	...	...	...	...	...	...	...	...	...	...	...	...	...	...
Kartupa	18	7	11	...	...	...	...	...	...	...	...	...	...	...	...	...	...	...	...	...	...	...	...	...
Kajapa	19	6	13	...	...	...	...	...	...	...	...	...	...	...	...	...	...	...	...	...	...	...	...	...
Karakpa	6	2	4	...	...	...	...	...	...	...	...	...	...	...	...	...	...	...	...	...	...	...	...	...
Kauparpa	131	66	65	...	...	...	...	...	...	...	...	...	...	...	...	...	...	...	...	...	...	...	...	...
Kotrupa	11	2	9	...	...	...	...	...	...	...	...	...	...	...	...	...	...	...	...	...	...	...	...	...
Kanjupa	20	7	13	...	...	...	...	...	...	...	...	...	...	...	...	...	...	...	...	...	...	...	...	...
Kariohakpa	15	12	3	...	...	...	...	...	...	...	...	...	...	...	...	...	...	...	...	...	...	...	...	...
Kolaypa	2	2	...	...	...	...	...	...	...	...	...	...	...	...	...	...	...	...	...	...	...	...	...	...
Kanpa	8	6	2	...	...	...	...	...	...	...	...	...	...	...	...	...	...	...	...	...	...	...	...	...
Karouk	17	7	10	...	...	...	...	...	...	...	...	...	...	...	...	...	...	...	...	...	...	...	...	...
Kachropa	17	7	10	...	...	...	...	...	...	...	...	...	...	...	...	...	...	...	...	...	...	...	...	...
Kainsopa	8	6	2	...	...	...	...	...	...	...	...	...	...	...	...	...	...	...	...	...	...	...	...	...
Karmpa	1,035	508	527	...	...	...	...	...	...	...	...	...	...	...	...	...	...	...	...	...	...	...	...	...
Kohanpa	31	4	27	...	...	...	...	...	...	...	...	...	...	...	...	...	...	...	...	...	...	...	...	...
Kamopa	151	141	10	...	...	...	...	...	...	...	...	...	...	...	...	...	...	...	...	...	...	...	...	...
Kamaklipa	63	55	8	...	...	...	...	...	...	...	...	...	...	...	...	...	...	...	...	...	...	...	...	...
Karpa	153	134	19	...	...	...	...	...	...	...	...	...	...	...	...	...	...	...	...	...	...	...	...	...
Koharkpa	10	7	3	...	...	...	...	...	...	...	...	...	...	...	...	...	...	...	...	...	...	...	...	...
Karimpa	2,120	1,110	1,010	...	...	...	...	...	...	...	...	...	...	...	...	...	...	...	...	...	...	...	...	...
Kabaolipa	3	3	...	...	...	...	...	...	...	...	...	...	...	...	...	...	...	...	...	...	...	...	...	...

PROVINCES WITH DISTRICTS.

Caste, Tribe, Race or Nationality.	Kashmir Province. Khas District. Persons.	Khas District. Males.	Khas District. Females.	Muzaffarabad District. Persons.	Muzaffarabad District. Males.	Muzaffarabad District. Females.	Total Kashmir Province. Persons.	Total Kashmir Province. Males.	Total Kashmir Province. Females.	Frontier Districts. Ladakh District. Persons.	Ladakh District. Males.	Ladakh District. Females.	Gilgit District. Persons.	Gilgit District. Males.	Gilgit District. Females.	Total Frontier Districts. Persons.	Total Frontier Districts. Males.	Total Frontier Districts. Females.
	26	27	28	29	30	31	32	33	34	35	36	37	38	39	40	41	42	43
Javi	9	2	7	...	...	...	9	2	7	...	...	...	...	...	...	...	...	...
Kashmiri	30,951	14,941	16,010	2,035	1,082	953	32,986	16,023	16,963	11,850	5,922	5,028	...	...	...	11,850	5,922	5,028
Kanchora	...	...	...	...	...	...	...	...	...	...	...	...	6	5	1	6	5	1
Karina	...	...	...	...	...	...	...	...	...	...	...	...	8	7	1	8	7	1
Khori	...	...	...	...	...	...	...	...	...	...	...	...	9	3	6	9	3	6
Kolang	...	...	...	...	...	...	...	...	...	...	...	...	40	40	...	40	40	...
Kalotra	...	...	...	...	...	...	...	...	...	...	...	...	12	12	...	12	12	...
Kajli	...	...	...	...	...	...	...	...	...	...	...	...	3	3	...	3	3	...
Karkhal	...	...	...	...	...	...	...	...	...	...	...	...	3	3	...	3	3	...
Kammar	...	...	...	...	...	...	...	...	...	...	...	...	9	9	...	9	9	...
Kantheylo	...	...	...	...	...	...	...	...	...	...	...	...	113	59	54	113	59	54
Kholang	...	...	...	...	...	...	...	...	...	...	...	...	116	69	47	116	69	47
Kashour	...	...	...	...	...	...	...	...	...	...	...	...	323	184	139	323	184	139
Khapa	...	...	...	...	...	...	...	...	...	41	22	19	...	...	...	41	22	19
Kanwapa	...	...	...	...	...	...	...	...	...	38	8	30	...	...	...	38	8	30
Kangopa	...	...	...	...	...	...	...	...	...	16	8	8	...	...	...	16	8	8
Khotagpa	...	...	...	...	...	...	...	...	...	112	19	93	...	...	...	112	19	93
Karmangpa	...	...	...	...	...	...	...	...	...	25	4	21	...	...	...	25	4	21
Karmakpa	...	...	...	...	...	...	...	...	...	112	85	27	...	...	...	112	85	27
Karjaspa	...	...	...	...	...	...	...	...	...	22	8	14	...	...	...	22	8	14
Katrn	...	...	...	...	...	...	...	...	...	5	3	2	...	...	...	5	3	2
Kartupa	...	...	...	...	...	...	...	...	...	18	7	11	...	...	...	18	7	11
Kajapa	...	...	...	...	...	...	...	...	...	19	6	13	...	...	...	19	6	13
Karakpa	...	...	...	...	...	...	...	...	...	6	2	4	...	...	...	6	2	4
Kanparpa	...	...	...	...	...	...	...	...	...	131	66	65	...	...	...	131	66	65
Katrupa	...	...	...	...	...	...	...	...	...	11	2	9	...	...	...	11	2	9
Kanjupa	...	...	...	...	...	...	...	...	...	20	7	13	...	...	...	20	7	13
Karichakpa	...	...	...	...	...	...	...	...	...	15	12	3	...	...	...	15	12	3
Koloypa	...	...	...	...	...	...	...	...	...	2	2	...	...	...	...	2	2	...
Kanpa	...	...	...	...	...	...	...	...	...	8	6	2	...	...	...	8	6	2
Karouk	...	...	...	...	...	...	...	...	...	17	7	10	...	...	...	17	7	10
Kachropa	...	...	...	...	...	...	...	...	...	17	7	10	...	...	...	17	7	10
Kainsupa	...	...	...	...	...	...	...	...	...	8	6	2	...	...	...	8	6	2
Karmpa	...	...	...	...	...	...	...	...	...	1,035	508	527	...	...	...	1,035	508	527
Kohaupa	...	...	...	...	...	...	...	...	...	31	4	27	...	...	...	31	4	27
Kamspa	...	...	...	...	...	...	...	...	...	151	141	10	...	...	...	151	141	10
Kamakhpa	...	...	...	...	...	...	...	...	...	63	55	8	...	...	...	63	55	8
Karpa	...	...	...	...	...	...	...	...	...	153	134	19	...	...	...	153	134	19
Koharkpa	...	...	...	...	...	...	...	...	...	10	7	3	...	...	...	10	7	3
Karimpa	...	...	...	...	...	...	...	...	...	2,120	1,110	1,010	...	...	...	2,120	1,110	1,010
Kalsechpa	...	...	...	...	...	...	...	...	...	3	3	...	...	...	...	3	3	...

TABLE XIII.

Caste, Tribe, Race or Nationality.

Caste, Tribe, Race or Nationality.	Total Population.			Provinces with Districts. Jammu Province. Jammu District.			Udhampur District.			Bhimber District.			Jasrota District.			Punch Jágir.			Bhadarwah Jágir.			Total Jammu Province.		
	Persons.	Males.	Females.	Persons.	Males.	Females.	Persons.	Males.	Females.	Persons.	Males.	Females.	Persons.	Males.	Females.	Persons.	Males.	Females.	Persons.	Males.	Females.	Persons.	Males.	Females.
1	2	3	4	5	6	7	8	9	10	11	12	13	14	15	16	17	18	19	20	21	22	23	24	25
[illegible]	371	187	184	...	...	...	...	...	...	...	...	...	...	...	...	...	...	...	...	...	...	...	...	...
[illegible]	105	1[illegible]6	79	...	...	...	...	...	...	...	...	...	...	...	...	...	...	...	...	...	...	...	...	...
Kuasa	1,484	844	640	...	...	...	...	...	...	...	...	...	...	...	...	...	...	...	...	...	...	...	...	...
Kolia	61	32	29	...	...	...	...	...	...	...	...	...	...	...	...	...	...	...	...	...	...	...	...	...
Khadipa	125	65	60	...	...	...	...	...	...	...	...	...	...	...	...	...	...	...	...	...	...	...	...	...
Kagapa	62	36	26	...	...	...	...	...	...	...	...	...	...	...	...	...	...	...	...	...	...	...	...	...
Kuwan	9	5	4	...	...	...	...	...	...	...	...	...	...	...	...	...	...	...	...	...	...	...	...	...
Kalai	9	5	4	...	...	...	...	...	...	...	...	...	...	...	...	...	...	...	...	...	...	...	...	...
Kormo	3	...	3	...	...	...	...	...	...	...	...	...	...	...	...	...	...	...	...	...	...	...	...	...
Kambuh	2	...	2	...	...	...	...	...	...	...	...	...	...	...	...	...	...	...	...	...	...	...	...	...
Kokar	13	6	7	...	...	...	...	...	...	...	...	...	...	...	...	...	...	...	...	...	...	...	...	...
Kamhar	11,213	6,194	5,019	2,532	1,460	1,072	1,520	795	725	1,552	858	694	1,454	675	779	997	584	413	730	385	345	8,785	4,757	4,028
Khandi	5,567	3,027	2,540	...	...	...	...	...	...	...	...	...	...	...	...	...	...	...	...	...	...	...	...	...
Komagh	454	229	225	...	...	...	...	...	...	...	...	...	...	...	...	...	...	...	...	...	...	...	...	...
Khokar	575	329	246	3	1	2	...	...	...	...	...	...	...	...	...	...	...	...	...	...	...	3	1	2
Khar	712	423	289	...	...	...	...	...	...	...	...	...	...	...	...	...	...	...	...	...	...	...	...	...
Kambra	496	263	233	...	...	...	...	...	...	...	...	...	...	...	...	...	...	...	...	...	...	...	...	...
Karnawi	588	324	264	...	...	...	...	...	...	...	...	...	...	...	...	...	...	...	...	...	...	...	...	...
Kuka	807	661	146	...	...	...	...	...	...	...	...	...	...	...	...	...	...	...	...	...	...	...	...	...
Karol	484	276	208	...	...	...	...	...	...	...	...	...	...	...	...	...	...	...	...	...	...	...	...	...
Kubi	107	69	38	...	...	...	...	...	...	...	...	...	...	...	...	...	...	...	...	...	...	...	...	...
Katu	546	253	293	...	...	...	...	...	...	...	...	...	...	...	...	...	...	...	...	...	...	...	...	...
Kooh	302	188	114	...	...	...	...	...	...	...	...	...	...	...	...	...	...	...	...	...	...	...	...	...
Kakarsi	541	257	284	...	...	...	...	...	...	...	...	...	...	...	...	...	...	...	...	...	...	...	...	...
Katgru	372	200	172	...	...	...	...	...	...	...	...	...	...	...	...	...	...	...	...	...	...	...	...	...
Kandor	739	353	386	...	...	...	...	...	...	...	...	...	...	...	...	...	...	...	...	...	...	...	...	...
Kaslu	290	182	108	...	...	...	...	...	...	...	...	...	...	...	...	...	...	...	...	...	...	...	...	...
Kumi	1,088	551	537	...	...	...	...	...	...	...	...	...	...	...	...	...	...	...	...	...	...	...	...	...
Kachhil	612	312	300	...	...	...	...	...	...	...	...	...	...	...	...	...	...	...	...	...	...	...	...	...
Katari	45	14	31	...	...	...	...	...	...	...	...	...	...	...	...	...	...	...	...	...	...	...	...	...
Kanoh	1,014	528	486	...	...	...	...	...	...	...	...	...	...	...	...	...	...	...	...	...	...	...	...	...
Kachru	257	148	109	...	...	...	...	...	...	...	...	...	...	...	...	...	...	...	...	...	...	...	...	...
Kanda	395	197	198	...	...	...	...	...	...	...	...	...	...	...	...	...	...	...	...	...	...	...	...	...
Kungu	1	1	...	...	...	...	...	...	...	...	...	...	...	...	...	...	...	...	...	...	...	...	...	...
Kangor	460	352	108	...	...	...	...	...	...	...	...	...	...	...	...	...	...	...	...	...	...	...	...	...
Kanji	8,183	4,152	4,031	...	...	...	...	...	...	...	...	...	...	...	...	...	...	...	...	...	...	...	...	...
Karwai	8,019	4,011	4,008	...	...	...	...	...	...	...	...	...	...	...	...	...	...	...	...	...	...	...	...	...
Kohi	6,192	3,093	3,099	...	...	...	...	...	...	...	...	...	...	...	...	...	...	...	...	...	...	...	...	...
Kand	8,103	4,047	4,056	...	...	...	...	...	...	...	...	...	...	...	...	...	...	...	...	...	...	...	...	...
Kotal	9,056	5,028	4,028	...	...	...	...	...	...	...	...	...	...	...	...	...	...	...	...	...	...	...	...	...
Kahli	6,408	4,244	2,164	...	...	...	...	...	...	...	...	...	...	...	...	...	...	...	...	...	...	...	...	...

PROVINCES WITH DISTRICTS.

Caste, Tribe, Race or Nationality.	Kashmir Province. Khas District. Persons.	Males.	Females.	Muzaffarabad District. Persons.	Males.	Females.	Total Kashmir Province. Persons.	Males.	Females.	Frontier Districts. Ladakh District. Persons.	Males.	Females.	Gilgit District. Persons.	Males.	Females.	Total Frontier Districts. Persons.	Males.	Females.
	26	27	28	29	30	31	32	33	34	35	36	37	38	39	40	41	42	43
Komerpa ...	...	...	...	...	...	...	...	...	...	371	187	184	...	...	...	371	187	184
Kodpa ...	...	...	...	...	...	...	...	...	...	195	116	79	...	...	...	195	116	79
Knasa ...	...	...	...	...	...	...	...	...	...	1,484	844	640	...	...	...	1,484	844	640
Kollu ...	...	...	...	...	...	...	...	...	...	61	32	29	...	...	...	61	32	29
Khadipa ...	...	...	...	...	...	...	...	...	...	125	65	60	...	...	...	125	65	60
Kagapa ...	...	...	...	...	...	...	...	...	...	62	36	26	...	...	...	62	36	26
Kuwan ...	...	...	...	...	...	...	...	...	...	9	5	4	...	...	...	9	5	4
Kalul ...	...	...	...	...	...	...	...	...	...	9	5	4	...	...	...	9	5	4
Karmu ...	...	...	...	...	...	...	...	...	...	3	...	3	...	...	...	3	...	3
Kamboh ...	...	...	...	...	...	...	...	...	...	2	...	2	...	...	...	2	...	2
Kokar ...	...	...	...	...	...	...	...	...	...	13	6	7	...	...	...	13	6	7
Kamhar ...	1,527	982	545	606	261	345	2,133	1,243	890	277	185	92	18	9	9	295	194	101
Khandi ...	5,567	3,027	2,540	...	...	...	5,567	3,027	2,540	...	...	...	...	...	...	...	...	...
Kamagh ...	454	229	225	...	...	...	454	229	225	...	...	...	...	...	...	...	...	...
Khokar ...	572	328	244	...	...	...	572	328	244	...	...	...	...	...	...	...	...	...
Khar ...	657	372	285	55	51	4	712	423	289	...	...	...	...	...	...	...	...	...
Kambru ...	496	263	233	...	...	...	496	263	233	...	...	...	...	...	...	...	...	...
Karnawi ...	125	85	40	...	...	...	125	85	40	463	239	224	...	...	...	463	239	224
Kaka ...	285	171	114	473	467	6	758	638	120	49	23	26	...	...	...	49	23	26
Karol ...	484	276	208	...	...	...	484	276	208	...	...	...	...	...	...	...	...	...
Kobi ...	107	69	38	...	...	...	107	69	38	...	...	...	...	...	...	...	...	...
Kata ...	546	253	293	...	...	...	546	253	293	...	...	...	...	...	...	...	...	...
Koch ...	302	188	114	...	...	...	302	188	114	...	...	...	...	...	...	...	...	...
Kokarsi ...	541	257	284	...	...	...	541	257	284	...	...	...	...	...	...	...	...	...
Kangru ...	372	200	172	...	...	...	372	200	172	...	...	...	...	...	...	...	...	...
Kander ...	739	353	386	...	...	...	739	353	386	...	...	...	...	...	...	...	...	...
Kashu ...	290	182	108	...	...	...	290	182	108	...	...	...	...	...	...	...	...	...
Kami ...	1,088	551	537	...	...	...	1,088	551	537	...	...	...	...	...	...	...	...	...
Kachhi ...	612	312	300	...	...	...	612	312	300	...	...	...	...	...	...	...	...	...
Katari ...	45	14	31	...	...	...	45	14	31	...	...	...	...	...	...	...	...	...
Kawoh ...	1,014	528	486	...	...	...	1,014	528	486	...	...	...	...	...	...	...	...	...
Kachru ...	257	148	109	...	...	...	257	148	109	...	...	...	...	...	...	...	...	...
Kanda ...	395	197	198	...	...	...	395	197	198	...	...	...	...	...	...	...	...	...
Kongu ...	1	1	...	...	...	...	1	1	...	...	...	...	...	...	...	...	...	...
Kangor ...	460	352	108	...	...	...	460	352	108	...	...	...	...	...	...	...	...	...
Kanji ...	8,183	4,152	4,031	...	...	...	8,183	4,152	4,031	...	...	...	...	...	...	...	...	...
Karwal ...	8,019	4,011	4,008	...	...	...	8,019	4,011	4,008	...	...	...	...	...	...	...	...	...
Kohi ...	6,192	3,093	3,099	...	...	...	6,192	3,093	3,099	...	...	...	...	...	...	...	...	...
Kand ...	8,103	4,047	4,056	...	...	...	8,103	4,047	4,056	...	...	...	...	...	...	...	...	...
Kotal ...	9,056	5,028	4,028	...	...	...	9,056	5,028	4,028	...	...	...	...	...	...	...	...	...
Kabli ...	6,408	4,244	2,164	...	...	...	6,408	4,244	2,164	...	...	...	...	...	...	...	...	...

TABLE XIII.

Caste, Tribe, Race or Nationality.

Caste, Tribe, Race or Nationality.	Total Population.			Provinces with Districts. — Jammu Province. Jammu District.			Udhampur District.			Bhimber District.			Jasrota District.			Punch Jágir.			Bhadarwah Jágir.			Total Jammu Province.		
	Persons.	Males.	Females.	Persons.	Males.	Females.	Persons.	Males.	Females.	Persons.	Males.	Females.	Persons.	Males.	Females.	Persons.	Males.	Females.	Persons.	Males.	Females.	Persons.	Males.	Females.
1	2	3	4	5	6	7	8	9	10	11	12	13	14	15	16	17	18	19	20	21	22	23	24	25
Khoru	4,250	2,133	2,117	...	...	...	...	...	...	...	...	...	...	...	...	...	...	...	...	...	...	...	...	...
Kar	1,252	609	643	...	...	...	...	...	...	...	...	...	...	...	...	...	...	...	...	...	...	...	...	...
Kabru	1,629	833	796	...	...	...	...	...	...	...	...	...	...	...	...	...	...	...	...	...	...	...	...	...
Khanna	1,284	640	635	...	...	...	...	...	...	...	...	...	...	...	...	...	...	...	...	...	...	...	...	...
Khatu	2,249	1,127	1,122	...	...	...	...	...	...	...	...	...	...	...	...	...	...	...	...	...	...	...	...	...
Kawar	8,300	5,136	3,164	...	...	...	...	...	...	...	...	...	...	...	...	...	...	...	...	...	...	...	...	...
Khorka	2,100	1,010	1,093	...	...	...	...	...	...	...	...	...	...	...	...	...	...	...	...	...	...	...	...	...
Kasan	169	79	90	...	...	...	...	...	...	...	...	...	...	...	...	...	...	...	...	...	...	...	...	...
Kaltas	175	87	88	...	...	...	...	...	...	...	...	...	...	...	...	...	...	...	...	...	...	...	...	...
Kani	6	3	3	...	...	...	...	...	...	...	...	...	...	...	...	...	...	...	...	...	...	...	...	...
Khoja	14	11	3	...	...	...	...	...	...	...	...	...	...	...	...	...	...	...	...	...	...	...	...	...
Khan	741	435	306	...	...	...	...	...	...	...	...	...	...	...	...	...	...	...	...	...	...	...	...	...
Kureshi	164	106	58	...	...	...	...	...	...	...	...	...	...	...	...	...	...	...	...	...	...	...	...	...
Kasi	150	20	121	...	...	...	...	...	...	...	...	...	...	...	...	...	...	...	...	...	...	...	...	...
Kasab	824	515	309	...	...	...	72	54	18	109	67	42	...	...	...	203	146	57	...	...	...	384	267	117
Kamri	43	10	34	...	...	...	...	...	...	...	...	...	...	...	...	...	...	...	...	...	...	...	...	...
Kasra	78	62	16	...	...	...	...	...	...	...	...	...	...	...	...	...	...	...	...	...	...	...	...	...
Kasid	78	62	16	...	...	...	...	...	...	...	...	...	...	...	...	...	...	...	...	...	...	...	...	...
Kabza	41	25	16	...	...	...	...	...	...	...	...	...	...	...	...	...	...	...	...	...	...	...	...	...
Kalandar	549	303	246	...	...	...	...	...	...	...	...	...	...	...	...	...	...	...	...	...	...	...	...	...
Kanfospa	1,024	512	512	...	...	...	...	...	...	...	...	...	...	...	...	...	...	...	...	...	...	...	...	...
Kalipa	307	158	149	...	...	...	...	...	...	...	...	...	...	...	...	...	...	...	...	...	...	...	...	...
Kampa	22	9	13	...	...	...	...	...	...	...	...	...	...	...	...	...	...	...	...	...	...	...	...	...
Kasampa	65	42	23	...	...	...	...	...	...	...	...	...	...	...	...	...	...	...	...	...	...	...	...	...
Kambor	58	30	28	...	...	...	...	...	...	...	...	...	...	...	...	...	...	...	...	...	...	...	...	...
Kadirpa	287	153	134	...	...	...	...	...	...	...	...	...	...	...	...	...	...	...	...	...	...	...	...	...
Khokhora	249	136	113	...	...	...	...	...	...	...	...	...	...	...	...	...	...	...	...	...	...	...	...	...
Loon	4,356	2,010	2,346	...	...	...	...	...	...	...	...	...	...	...	...	...	...	...	...	...	...	...	...	...
Loi	18	18	...	...	...	...	...	...	...	...	...	...	...	...	...	...	...	...	...	...	...	...	...	...
Lohar	27,845	14,527	13,318	4,795	2,505	2,290	6,037	3,110	2,927	5,907	3,404	2,503	2,404	1,274	1,130	3,869	1,610	2,259	278	139	139	23,502	12,112	11,390
Lahop	434	227	207	...	...	...	...	...	...	...	...	...	...	...	...	...	...	...	...	...	...	...	...	...
Latoo	337	185	152	...	...	...	...	...	...	...	...	...	...	...	...	...	...	...	...	...	...	...	...	...
Lala	44	30	14	...	...	...	...	...	...	...	...	...	...	...	...	...	...	...	...	...	...	...	...	...
Lashkari	78	20	58	...	...	...	...	...	...	...	...	...	...	...	...	...	...	...	...	...	...	...	...	...
Labru	1,403	685	718	...	...	...	...	...	...	...	...	...	...	...	...	...	...	...	...	...	...	...	...	...
Lachu	102	58	44	...	...	...	...	...	...	...	...	...	...	...	...	...	...	...	...	...	...	...	...	...
Lauger	254	125	129	...	...	...	...	...	...	...	...	...	...	...	...	...	...	...	...	...	...	...	...	...
Las	1,491	760	731	...	...	...	...	...	...	...	...	...	...	...	...	...	...	...	...	...	...	...	...	...
Luman	19	6	13	...	...	...	...	...	...	...	...	...	...	...	...	...	...	...	...	...	...	...	...	...
Lawan	307	102	205	...	...	...	...	...	...	...	...	...	...	...	...	...	...	...	...	...	...	...	...	...
Ladhakhi	12	6	6	...	...	...	...	...	...	...	...	...	...	...	...	...	...	...	...	...	...	...	...	...

Caste, Tribe, Race or Nationality.	Kashmir Province. Khás District. Persons.	Khás District. Males.	Khás District. Females.	Muzaffarabad District. Persons.	Muzaffarabad District. Males.	Muzaffarabad District. Females.	Total Kashmir Province. Persons.	Total Kashmir Province. Males.	Total Kashmir Province. Females.	Frontier Districts. Ladakh District. Persons.	Ladakh District. Males.	Ladakh District. Females.	Gilgit District. Persons.	Gilgit District. Males.	Gilgit District. Females.	Total Frontier Districts. Persons.	Total Frontier Districts. Males.	Total Frontier Districts. Females.
	26	27	28	29	30	31	32	33	34	35	36	37	38	39	40	41	42	43
Khoru	4,250	2,133	2,117	...	...	...	4,250	2,133	2,117	...	...	...	...	...	...	...	...	...
Kar	1,252	609	643	...	...	...	1,252	609	643	...	...	...	...	...	...	...	...	...
Kabru	1,629	833	796	...	...	...	1,629	833	796	...	...	...	...	...	...	...	...	...
Khanna	1,284	649	635	...	...	...	1,284	649	635	...	...	...	...	...	...	...	...	...
Khatu	2,249	1,127	1,122	...	...	...	2,249	1,127	1,122	...	...	...	...	...	...	...	...	...
Kawar	8,300	5,136	3,164	...	...	...	8,300	5,136	3,164	...	...	...	...	...	...	...	...	...
Khurka	2,109	1,016	1,093	...	...	...	2,109	1,016	1,093	...	...	...	...	...	...	...	...	...
Kasan	169	79	90	...	...	...	169	79	90	...	...	...	...	...	...	...	...	...
Kakas	175	87	88	...	...	...	175	87	88	...	...	...	...	...	...	...	...	...
Kani	6	3	3	...	...	...	6	3	3	...	...	...	...	...	...	...	...	...
Khoja	14	11	3	...	...	...	14	11	3	...	...	...	...	...	...	...	...	...
Khan	741	435	306	...	...	...	741	435	306	...	...	...	...	...	...	...	...	...
Kurashi	164	106	58	...	...	...	164	106	58	...	...	...	...	...	...	...	...	...
Kazi	150	29	121	...	...	...	150	29	121	...	...	...	...	...	...	...	...	...
Kasab	123	38	85	278	189	89	401	227	174	39	21	18	...	...	...	39	21	18
Kamri	43	19	24	...	...	...	43	19	24	...	...	...	...	...	...	...	...	...
Kasra	78	62	16	...	...	...	78	62	16	...	...	...	...	...	...	...	...	...
Kasid	78	62	16	...	...	...	78	62	16	...	...	...	...	...	...	...	...	...
Kabza	41	25	16	...	...	...	41	25	16	...	...	...	...	...	...	...	...	...
Kalandar	549	303	246	...	...	...	549	303	246	...	...	...	...	...	...	...	...	...
Kanfoopa	1,024	512	512	...	...	...	1,024	512	512	...	...	...	...	...	...	...	...	...
Kalipa	307	158	149	...	...	...	307	158	149	22	9	13	...	...	...	22	9	13
Kampa	...	...	...	...	...	...	...	...	...	65	42	23	...	...	...	65	42	23
Kasampa	...	...	...	...	...	...	...	...	...	58	30	28	...	...	...	58	30	28
Kambor	...	...	...	...	...	...	...	...	...	...	...	...	...	...	...	...	...	...
Kadirpa	...	...	...	...	...	...	...	...	...	387	153	134	...	...	...	287	153	134
Khokhora	...	...	...	...	...	...	...	...	...	...	...	...	249	136	113	249	136	113
Loon	4,356	2,010	2,346	...	...	...	4,356	2,010	2,346	...	...	...	...	...	...	...	...	...
Loi	18	18	...	...	...	...	18	18	...	...	...	...	...	...	...	...	...	...
Lohar	2,553	1,398	1,155	1,663	938	725	4,216	2,336	1,880	...	...	...	127	79	48	127	79	48
Lahup	430	224	206	...	...	...	430	224	206	...	...	...	4	3	1	4	3	1
Latoo	335	185	150	...	...	...	335	185	150	2	...	2	...	...	...	2	...	2
Lala	44	30	14	...	...	...	44	30	14	...	...	...	...	...	...	...	...	...
Lashkari	78	20	58	...	...	...	78	20	58	...	...	...	...	...	...	...	...	...
Labru	239	158	81	...	...	...	239	158	81	1,164	527	637	...	...	...	1,164	527	637
Lachu	83	49	34	...	...	...	83	49	34	19	9	10	...	...	...	19	9	10
Langer	98	51	47	...	...	...	98	51	47	156	74	82	...	...	...	156	74	82
Las	43	22	21	...	...	...	43	22	21	1,448	738	710	...	...	...	1,448	738	710
Luman	19	6	13	...	...	...	19	6	13	...	...	...	...	...	...	...	...	...
Lawan	...	...	...	...	...	...	...	...	...	308	98	205	4	4	...	307	102	205
Ladakhi	...	...	...	...	...	...	...	...	...	12	6	6	...	...	...	12	6	6

TABLE XIII.

CASTE, TRIBE, RACE OR NATIONALITY.

Caste, Tribe, Race or Nationality.	Total Population. Persons.	Males.	Females.	Provinces with Districts. Jammu Province. Jammu District. Persons.	Males.	Females.	Udhampur District. Persons.	Males.	Females.	Bhimber District. Persons.	Males.	Females.	Jasrota District. Persons.	Males.	Females.	Punch Jágír. Persons.	Males.	Females.	Bhadarwah Jágír. Persons.	Males.	Females.	Total Jammu Province. Persons.	Males.	Females.
1	2	3	4	5	6	7	8	9	10	11	12	13	14	15	16	17	18	19	20	21	22	23	24	25
Lasun	8	3	5	...	...	...	...	...	...	...	...	...	...	...	...	...	...	...	...	...	...	...	...	...
Lawa	103	41	62	...	...	...	...	...	...	...	...	...	...	...	...	...	...	...	...	...	...	...	...	...
Musapa	3,290	1,591	1,699	...	...	...	...	...	...	...	...	...	3,053	1,464	1,589	...	...	...	...	...	...	3,053	1,464	1,589
Mughal	14,385	6,935	7,450	706	350	356	683	383	298	30	30	...	...	...	...	2,952	1,954	998	158	24	134	4,529	2,743	1,786
Mochi	36,486	19,145	17,341	764	405	359	789	409	380	4,013	2,326	1,687	775	395	380	2,983	1,456	1,527	199	161	38	9,523	5,152	4,371
Mial	1,160	664	496	...	...	...	...	...	...	...	...	...	...	...	...	...	...	...	...	...	...	...	...	...
Malik	25,817	11,860	13,957	...	...	...	...	...	...	...	...	...	...	...	...	8,007	4,368	3,639	...	...	...	8,007	4,368	3,639
Mali	24,121	13,999	10,122	...	...	...	...	...	...	...	...	...	...	...	...	...	...	...	...	...	...	...	...	...
Mirza	51,314	29,817	21,497	12,268	7,311	4,957	8,664	4,892	3,772	10,336	5,615	4,721	5,780	3,695	2,085	11,713	6,922	4,791	2,417	1,312	1,105	51,178	29,747	21,431
Musalli	1,553	764	789	54	35	19	...	...	...	931	488	443	...	...	...	282	96	186	3	3	...	1,270	622	648
Mangu	51,730	29,443	22,287	6,178	3,656	2,522	10,615	5,919	4,696	17,303	9,656	7,647	192	190	2	13,483	7,541	5,942	1,652	1,107	545	49,423	28,069	21,354
Mandu	43,906	28,322	15,584	2,311	634	1,677	10,202	9,284	918	13,569	7,036	6,533	1,000	..	1,000	15,208	10,249	4,959	1,202	797	405	43,452	28,000	15,452
Magh	55,333	22,864	32,469	4,888	2,317	2,571	311	209	102	19,532	9,875	9,657	85	40	45	24,083	9,372	14,711	...	...	...	48,899	21,813	27,086
Maliar	51,645	28,701	22,944	13,515	7,246	6,269	411	195	216	7,226	4,118	3,108	2,024	1,061	963	527	74	453	312	201	111	24,015	12,895	11,120
Machhi	809	471	338	590	265	325	6	3	3	145	135	10	...	...	...	66	66	...	...	...	...	807	469	338
Mir	70,603	38,850	31,753	...	...	...	...	...	...	12	...	12	...	...	...	...	...	...	...	...	...	12	...	12
Mirasi	6,235	3,470	2,765	2,163	1,332	831	672	468	204	2,368	1,147	1,221	...	...	...	...	...	...	9	9	...	5,212	2,956	2,256
Mulla	227	143	84	165	102	63	28	18	10	23	19	4	...	...	...	...	...	...	...	...	...	216	139	77
Nanbai	969	623	346	...	...	...	...	...	...	...	...	...	...	...	...	...	...	...	...	...	...	...	...	...
Nai	13,022	7,950	5,072	2,153	1,182	971	1,335	724	611	1,272	712	560	1,042	562	480	805	413	392	375	193	182	6,982	3,786	3,196
Naddaf	467	318	149	...	...	...	2	1	1	...	...	...	4	2	2	...	...	...	...	...	...	6	3	3
Nandagri	54	28	26	...	...	...	...	...	...	...	...	...	...	...	...	...	...	...	...	...	...	...	...	...
Nagu	130	82	48	...	...	...	...	...	...	...	...	...	...	...	...	...	...	...	...	...	...	...	...	...
Nawach	241	131	110	...	...	...	...	...	...	...	...	...	...	...	...	...	...	...	...	...	...	...	...	...
Nandwal	197	99	98	...	...	...	...	...	...	...	...	...	...	...	...	...	...	...	...	...	...	...	...	...
Nairpa	27	...	27	...	...	...	27	...	27	...	...	...	...	...	...	...	...	...	...	...	...	27	...	27
Nanak	26	5	21	...	...	...	11	5	6	...	...	...	...	...	...	...	...	...	...	...	...	11	5	6
Pagwapa	71	26	45	...	...	...	...	...	...	...	...	...	...	...	...	...	...	...	...	...	...	...	...	...
Pastapa	136	60	76	...	...	...	...	...	...	...	...	...	...	...	...	...	...	...	...	...	...	...	...	...
Pathipal	30	12	18	...	...	...	...	...	...	...	...	...	...	...	...	...	...	...	...	...	...	...	...	...
Partimpa	3	3	...	...	...	...	...	...	...	...	...	...	...	...	...	...	...	...	...	...	...	...	...	...
Paropa	27	12	15	...	...	...	...	...	...	...	...	...	...	...	...	...	...	...	...	...	...	...	...	...
Palupa	31	10	21	...	...	...	...	...	...	...	...	...	...	...	...	...	...	...	...	...	...	...	...	...
Parshipa	15	7	8	...	...	...	...	...	...	...	...	...	...	...	...	...	...	...	...	...	...	...	...	...
Pachipa	78	30	48	...	...	...	...	...	...	...	...	...	...	...	...	...	...	...	...	...	...	...	...	...
Panarpa	127	42	85	...	...	...	...	...	...	...	...	...	...	...	...	...	...	...	...	...	...	...	...	...
Potampa	134	49	85	...	...	...	...	...	...	...	...	...	...	...	...	...	...	...	...	...	...	...	...	...
Pahlwan	81	53	28	...	...	...	...	...	...	...	...	...	...	...	...	...	...	...	...	...	...	...	...	...
Pashkhore	132	67	65	...	...	...	...	...	...	...	...	...	...	...	...	...	...	...	...	...	...	...	...	...
Pajar	608	386	222	...	...	...	...	...	...	...	...	...	...	...	...	...	...	...	...	...	...	...	...	...
Parmi	6	2	4	...	...	...	...	...	...	...	...	...	...	...	...	...	...	...	...	...	...	...	...	...

Caste, Tribe, Race or Nationality.	Provinces with Districts.																	
	Kashmir Province.									Frontier Districts.								
	Khas District.			Muzaffarabad District.			Total Kashmir Province.			Ladakh District.			Gilgit District.			Total Frontier Districts.		
	Persons.	Males.	Females.	Persons.	Males.	Females.	Persons.	Males.	Females.	Persons.	Males.	Females.	Persons.	Males.	Females.	Persons.	Males.	Females.
	26	27	28	29	30	31	32	33	34	35	36	37	38	39	40	41	42	43
Lasun	...	...	...	...	...	...	...	...	...	8	3	5	...	...	...	8	3	5
Lawa	...	...	...	...	...	...	...	...	...	103	41	62	...	...	..	103	41	62
Musapa	...	...	...	...	...	...	...	...	...	237	127	110	...	...	...	237	127	110
Mughal	2,815	1,002	1,813	5,677	2,491	3,186	8,492	3,493	4,999	1,304	699	605	...	...	...	1,304	699	605
Mochi	8,962	4,678	4,284	933	487	446	9,895	5,165	4,730	17,068	8,828	8,240	...	...	...	17,068	8,828	8,240
Mial	...	...	...	...	...	...	...	...	...	1,160	664	496	...	...	...	1,160	664	496
Malik	13,684	7,373	6,311	...	...	...	13,684	7,373	6,311	4,126	119	4,007	...	...	...	4,126	119	4,007
Mali	...	...	...	...	...	...	...	...	...	24,121	13,999	10,122	...	...	...	24,121	13,999	10,122
Mirza	...	...	...	...	...	...	...	...	...	136	70	66	...	...	...	136	70	66
Musalli	...	...	...	159	122	37	159	122	37	124	20	104	...	...	...	124	20	104
Mangu	1,274	625	649	734	563	171	2,008	1,188	820	299	186	113	...	...	...	299	186	113
Mandu	...	..	...	...	...	...	...	...	...	454	322	132	...	...	...	454	322	132
Megh	1,592	941	651	4,576	17	4,559	6,168	958	5,210	74	42	32	192	51	141	266	93	173
Maliar	22,318	12,601	9,717	5,312	3,205	2,107	27,630	15,806	11,824	...	...	...	...	...	...	...	...	...
Machbi	...	...	...	...	...	...	...	...	...	...	...	...	2	2	...	2	2	...
Mir	65,814	36,648	29,166	4,777	2,202	2,575	70,591	38,850	31,741	...	...	...	...	...	...	...	...	...
Mirasi	392	287	105	628	224	404	1,020	511	509	...	...	...	3	3	...	3	3	...
Mulla	...	...	...	...	...	...	...	...	...	...	...	...	11	4	7	11	4	7
Nanbai	590	287	303	379	336	43	969	623	346	...	...	...	...	...	...	...	...	...
Nai	5,839	3,135	2,704	201	129	72	6,040	3,264	2,776	...	...	...	...	...	...	...	...	...
Naddaf	461	315	146	...	...	...	461	315	146	...	...	...	...	...	...	...	...	...
Nandagri	54	28	26	...	...	...	54	28	26	...	...	...	...	...	...	...	...	...
Nagu	130	82	48	..	...	...	130	82	48	...	...	...	...	...	...	...	...	...
Nawach	241	131	110	...	...	...	241	131	110	...	...	...	...	...	...	...	...	...
Nandwal	96	57	39	...	...	...	96	57	39	101	42	59	...	...	...	101	42	59
Nairpa	...	...	..	...	...	...	...	...	...	...	...	...	...	...	...	...	...	...
Nanak	...	...	...	...	...	...	...	...	...	15	...	15	...	...	...	15	...	15
Pagwapa	...	...	...	...	...	...	...	...	...	71	26	45	...	...	...	71	26	45
Pastapa	...	...	...	...	...	...	...	...	...	136	60	76	...	...	...	136	60	76
Pathipa	..	...	...	...	...	...	...	...	...	30	12	18	...	...	...	30	12	18
Partimpa	...	...	...	...	...	...	...	...	...	3	3	...	...	...	...	3	3	...
Paropa	...	...	...	...	...	...	...	...	...	27	12	15	...	...	...	27	12	15
Palupa	..	...	...	...	...	...	...	...	...	31	10	21	...	...	..	31	10	21
Parshipa	...	...	..	...	...	...	...	...	...	15	7	8	...	...	...	15	7	8
Pachipa	..	...	...	...	...	...	...	...	...	78	30	48	...	...	...	78	30	48
Panarpa	..	..	...	...	...	...	...	...	...	127	42	85	...	...	...	127	42	85
Potampa	..	...	...	...	...	...	...	...	...	134	49	85	...	..	...	134	49	85
Pahlwan	...	...	...	..	...	...	...	...	...	81	53	28	...	...	...	81	53	28
Poshkhore...	...	...	...	...	...	...	...	...	...	...	...	...	132	67	65	132	67	65
Papar	...	...	...	451	281	170	451	281	170	...	...	...	157	105	52	157	105	52
Parmi	...	...	...	...	...	...	...	...	...	...	...	...	6	2	4	6	2	4

TABLE XIII.

Caste, Tribe, Race or Nationality.

Caste, Tribe, Race or Nationality.	Total Population.			Provinces with Districts. Jammu Province. Jammu District.			Udhampur District.			Bhimber District.			Jasrota District.			Punch Jágir.			Bhadarwah Jágir.			Total Jammu Province.		
	Persons.	Males.	Females.	Persons.	Males.	Females.	Persons.	Males.	Females.	Persons.	Males.	Females.	Persons.	Males.	Females.	Persons.	Males.	Females.	Persons.	Males.	Females.	Persons.	Males.	Females.
1	2	3	4	5	6	7	8	9	10	11	12	13	14	15	16	17	18	19	20	21	22	23	24	25
Palolory	6	2	4	...	...	...	...	...	...	...	...	...	...	...	...	...	...	...	...	...	...	...	...	...
Patwari	338	164	174	...	...	...	...	...	...	...	...	...	...	...	...	...	...	...	...	...	...	...	...	...
Patti	309	168	141	...	...	...	...	...	...	...	...	...	2	2	...	...	...	...	...	...	...	2	2	...
Pailn	2,463	1,865	598	...	...	...	...	...	...	...	...	...	...	...	...	1,533	1,358	175	...	...	...	1,533	1,358	175
Parimo	275	143	132	...	...	...	...	...	...	...	...	...	...	...	...	...	...	...	...	...	...	...	...	...
Pari	12,017	6,208	6,700	...	...	...	...	...	...	...	...	...	...	...	...	...	...	...	...	...	...	...	...	...
Phamnu	116	62	54	...	...	...	...	...	...	...	...	...	...	...	...	...	...	...	...	...	...	...	...	...
Palsa	184	146	138	...	...	...	...	...	...	...	...	...	...	...	...	...	...	...	...	...	...	...	...	...
Paikhali	23	14	9	...	...	...	...	...	...	...	...	...	...	...	...	...	...	...	...	...	...	...	...	...
Pala	2,436	1,294	1,142	...	...	...	...	...	...	...	...	...	...	...	...	...	...	...	...	...	...	...	...	...
Potu	240	150	90	...	...	...	...	...	...	...	...	...	...	...	...	...	...	...	...	...	...	...	...	...
Pistu	287	121	166	...	...	...	...	...	...	...	...	...	...	...	...	...	...	...	...	...	...	...	...	...
Patoie	50	16	34	7	6	1	...	...	...	...	...	...	15	10	5	28	...	28	...	...	...	50	16	34
Pandi	163	88	75	...	...	...	19	8	11	...	...	...	...	...	...	...	...	...	...	...	...	19	8	11
Padiar	11	5	6	...	...	...	11	5	6	...	...	...	...	...	...	...	...	...	...	...	...	11	5	6
Paharu	104	...	104	...	...	...	...	...	...	104	...	104	...	...	...	...	...	...	...	...	...	104	...	104
Pinjn	169	86	83	...	...	...	...	...	...	...	...	...	...	...	...	...	...	...	...	...	...	...	...	...
Padar	170	81	89	...	...	...	...	...	...	...	...	...	...	...	...	...	...	...	...	...	...	...	...	...
Pirzadah	1,246	717	529	...	...	...	...	...	...	...	...	...	...	...	...	...	...	...	...	...	...	...	...	...
Pinjawal	25	25	...	...	...	...	...	...	...	...	...	...	...	...	...	...	...	...	...	...	...	...	...	...
Pugal	30	30	...	...	...	...	...	...	...	...	...	...	...	...	...	...	...	...	...	...	...	...	...	...
Pakwali	27	24	3	...	...	...	...	...	...	...	...	...	...	...	...	...	...	...	...	...	...	...	...	...
Paral	22	22	...	...	...	...	...	...	...	...	...	...	...	...	...	...	...	...	...	...	...	...	...	...
Para	101	72	29	...	...	...	...	...	...	...	...	...	...	...	...	...	...	...	...	...	...	...	...	...
Panwal	8	...	8	...	...	...	...	...	...	...	...	...	...	...	...	...	...	...	...	...	...	...	...	...
Total Pathan ...	45,131	26,631	18,500	1,920	1,151	779	1,236	791	445	1,444	823	651	288	229	59	12,817	8,385	4,432	597	311	286	18,302	11,690	6,612
Pathan	24,048	13,624	11,024	564	276	268	929	539	390	579	327	252	124	113	11	2,020	1,107	802	512	280	232	4,737	2,709	2,085
" Abakhel ...	42	31	11	20	20	0	13	11	2	...	...	...	...	...	...	...	...	...	...	...	...	42	31	11
" Abanzai ...	189	109	80	29	11	18	...	...	...	...	...	...	...	...	...	...	...	...	...	...	...	29	11	18
" Akhunzadah ...	88	45	43	21	20	1	...	...	...	...	...	...	...	...	...	...	...	...	67	25	42	88	45	43
" Adamkhel ...	51	49	2	51	40	2	...	...	...	...	...	...	...	...	...	...	...	...	...	...	...	51	40	2
" Amirankhel ...	298	168	130	298	168	130	...	...	...	...	...	...	...	...	...	...	...	...	...	...	...	298	168	130
" Alikhel ...	439	219	220	...	...	...	...	...	...	...	...	...	...	...	...	...	...	...	...	...	...	...	...	...
" Abaskhel ...	16	15	1	16	15	1	...	...	...	...	...	...	...	...	...	...	...	...	...	...	...	16	15	1
" Bahuri	22	17	5	22	17	5	...	...	...	...	...	...	...	...	...	...	...	...	...	...	...	22	17	5
" Bakri	240	124	116	22	18	4	...	...	...	36	18	18	...	...	...	...	...	...	...	...	...	58	36	22
" Basikhel ...	40	20	20	40	20	20	...	...	...	...	...	...	...	...	...	...	...	...	...	...	...	40	20	20
" Daudzai ...	35	27	8	34	26	8	...	...	...	...	...	...	1	1	...	...	...	...	...	...	...	35	27	8
" Danakhel ...	354	260	94	14	4	10	...	...	...	...	...	...	...	...	...	...	...	...	...	...	...	14	4	10

PROVINCES WITH DISTRICTS.

Caste, Tribe, Race or Nationality.	Kashmir Province.									Frontier Districts.								
	Khas District.			Muzaffarabad District.			Total Kashmir Province.			Ladakh District.			Gilgit District.			Total Frontier Districts.		
	Persons.	Males.	Females.	Persons.	Males.	Females.	Persons.	Males.	Females.	Persons.	Males.	Females.	Persons.	Males.	Females.	Persons.	Males.	Females.
	26	27	28	29	30	31	32	33	34	35	36	37	38	39	40	41	42	43
Palolory	...	...	...	...	...	...	...	...	...	...	...	...	6	2	4	6	2	4
Patwari	338	164	174	...	...	...	338	164	174	...	...	...	...	...	...	...	...	...
Patti	307	166	141	...	...	...	307	166	141	...	...	...	6	6	...	6	6	...
Pailu	924	501	423	...	...	...	924	501	423	...	...	...	...	...	...	...	...	...
Parimo	275	143	132	...	...	...	275	143	132	...	...	...	...	...	...	...	...	...
Pari	12,607	6,088	6,609	220	120	100	12,917	6,208	6,709	...	...	...	...	...	...	...	...	...
Phamnu	116	62	54	...	...	...	116	62	54	...	...	...	...	...	...	...	...	...
Paisa	184	146	138	...	...	...	184	146	138	...	...	...	...	...	...	...	...	...
Palkhali	23	14	9	...	...	...	23	14	9	...	...	...	...	...	...	...	...	...
Pala	2,436	1,294	1,142	...	...	...	2,436	1,294	1,142	...	...	...	...	...	...	...	...	...
Potu	249	150	99	...	...	...	249	150	99	...	...	...	...	...	...	...	...	...
Pistu	287	121	166	...	...	...	287	121	166	...	...	...	...	...	...	...	...	...
Patoie	...	...	...	...	...	...	...	...	...	...	...	...	...	...	...	...	...	...
Pandi	144	80	64	...	...	...	144	80	64	...	...	...	...	...	...	...	...	...
Padiar	...	...	...	...	...	...	...	...	...	...	...	...	...	...	...	...	...	...
Paharu	...	...	...	...	...	...	...	...	...	...	...	...	...	...	...	...	...	...
Pinju	169	86	83	...	...	...	169	86	83	...	...	...	...	...	...	...	...	...
Padar	170	81	89	...	...	...	170	81	89	...	...	...	...	...	...	...	...	...
Pirzadah	1,246	717	529	...	...	...	1,246	717	529	...	...	...	...	...	...	...	...	...
Pinjawal	...	...	...	25	25	...	25	25	...	...	...	...	...	...	...	...	...	...
Pagal	...	...	...	30	30	...	30	30	...	...	...	...	...	...	...	...	...	...
Pakwall	...	...	...	27	24	3	27	24	3	...	...	...	...	...	...	...	...	...
Paral	...	...	...	22	22	...	22	22	...	...	...	...	...	...	...	...	...	...
Para	...	...	...	101	72	29	101	72	29	...	...	...	...	...	...	...	...	...
Panwal	...	...	...	8	...	8	8	...	8	...	...	...	...	...	...	...	...	...
Total Pathans ...	**20,560**	**10,818**	**9,742**	**5,646**	**3,743**	**1,903**	**26,206**	**14,561**	**11,645**	**282**	**188**	**94**	**341**	**192**	**149**	**623**	**380**	**243**
Pathan	17,799	9,660	8,139	1,649	961	688	19,448	10,621	8,827	282	188	94	181	113	68	463	301	162
" Abakhel ...	...	...	...	...	...	...	...	...	...	...	...	...	...	...	...	...	...	...
" Abauzai ...	...	...	...	100	98	62	100	98	62	...	...	...	...	...	...	...	...	...
" Akhunzadah ...	...	...	...	...	...	...	...	...	...	...	...	...	...	...	...	...	...	...
" Adamkhel ...	...	...	...	...	...	...	...	...	...	...	...	...	...	...	...	...	...	...
" Amirankhe ...	...	...	...	...	...	...	...	...	...	...	...	...	...	...	...	...	...	...
" Allikhel ...	...	...	...	430	210	220	430	210	220	...	...	...	...	...	...	...	...	...
" Abaakhel ...	...	...	...	...	...	...	...	...	...	...	...	...	...	...	...	...	...	...
" Bahuri ...	...	...	...	...	...	...	...	...	...	...	...	...	...	...	...	...	...	...
" Bakri ...	...	...	...	182	88	94	182	88	94	...	...	...	...	...	...	...	...	...
" Basikhel ...	...	...	...	...	...	...	...	...	...	...	...	...	...	...	...	...	...	...
" Dandmai ...	...	...	...	...	...	...	...	...	...	...	...	...	...	...	...	...	...	...
" Danakhol ...	...	...	...	340	256	84	340	256	84	...	...	...	...	...	...	...	...	...

TABLE XIII.

CASTE, TRIBE, RACE OR NATIONALITY.

Caste, Tribe, Race or Nationality.	Total Population.			Provinces with Districts — Jammu Province. Jammu District.			Udhampur District.			Bhimber District.			Jasrota District.			Punch Jágir.			Bhadarwah Jágir.			Total Jammu Province.		
	Persons.	Males.	Females.	Persons.	Males.	Females.	Persons.	Males.	Females.	Persons.	Males.	Females.	Persons.	Males.	Females.	Persons.	Males.	Females.	Persons.	Males.	Females.	Persons.	Males.	Females.
1	2	3	4	5	6	7	8	9	10	11	12	13	14	15	16	17	18	19	20	21	22	23	24	25
Pathan Durrani ...	866	427	439	...	...	...	2	2	...	...	...	...	1	1	...	...	...	...	...	...	...	3	3	...
Pathan Paridkhel ...	54	10	44	...	...	...	...	...	...	...	...	...	...	...	...	54	10	44	...	...	...	54	10	44
Pathan Ghazi ...	781	276	505	...	...	...	...	...	...	...	...	...	...	...	...	...	...	...	...	...	...	...	...	...
Pathan Ghilzai ...	68	42	26	48	32	16	2	2	...	...	...	...	8	8	...	...	...	...	...	...	...	58	42	16
Pathan Hassanzai ...	506	477	29	22	12	10	1	1	...	...	...	...	...	...	...	...	...	...	...	...	...	23	13	10
Pathan Isabzai ...	770	489	281	53	25	28	2	1	1	74	60	14	118	98	20	330	194	136	...	...	...	577	378	199
Pathan Israiel ...	260	149	111	21	19	2	...	...	...	95	54	41	...	...	...	...	...	...	...	...	...	116	73	43
Pathan Isakhel ...	50	49	1	35	34	1	15	15	...	...	...	...	...	...	...	...	...	...	...	...	...	50	49	1
Pathan Jahangiri ...	130	66	64	...	...	...	...	...	...	...	...	...	...	...	...	...	...	...	...	...	...	...	...	...
Pathan Kheri ...	190	104	86	15	15	...	1	...	1	14	10	4	...	...	...	...	...	...	...	...	...	30	25	5
Pathan Khan ...	259	79	180	...	...	...	3	3	...	...	...	...	...	...	...	256	76	180	...	...	...	259	79	180
Pathan Khilji ...	29	22	7	...	...	...	...	...	...	...	...	...	12	5	7	...	...	...	...	...	...	12	5	7
Pathan Kakakhel ...	1,501	781	720	17	12	5	12	9	3	8	6	2	...	...	...	...	...	...	...	...	...	37	27	10
Pathan Kakazai ...	611	348	263	...	...	...	1	1	...	232	115	117	9	1	8	151	25	126	...	...	...	393	142	251
Pathan Lodhi ...	443	179	264	86	52	34	...	...	...	154	73	81	5	2	3	145	52	93	...	...	...	390	179	211
Pathan Madadkhel ...	403	240	163	181	103	78	...	...	...	...	...	...	...	...	...	78	20	58	...	...	...	259	123	136
Pathan Mohamandi ...	160	78	82	7	4	3	5	5	...	15	11	4	...	...	...	60	37	23	...	...	...	87	57	30
Pathan Qazikhel ...	494	367	127	...	...	...	113	112	...	6	3	3	...	...	...	...	...	...	...	...	...	118	115	3
Pathan Qazalbash ...	24	17	7	24	17	7	...	...	...	...	...	...	...	...	...	...	...	...	...	...	...	24	17	7
Pathan Rohilla ...	9,005	6,409	2,596	...	...	...	8	7	1	...	...	...	...	...	...	8,997	6,402	2,595	...	...	...	9,005	6,409	2,596
Pathan Salarzai ...	21	9	12	21	9	12	...	...	...	...	...	...	...	...	...	...	...	...	...	...	...	21	9	12
Pathan Salarkhel ...	14	10	4	14	10	4	...	...	...	...	...	...	...	...	...	...	...	...	...	...	...	14	10	4
Pathan Salamankhel ...	649	365	284	12	7	5	...	...	...	...	...	...	...	...	...	366	117	249	...	...	...	378	124	254
Pathan Suwati ...	205	99	106	10	10	...	...	...	...	...	...	...	...	...	...	...	...	...	...	...	...	10	10	...
Pathan Shahkhel ...	141	121	20	...	...	...	11	9	2	...	...	...	...	...	...	...	...	...	...	...	...	11	9	2
Pathan Waziri ...	67	35	32	26	20	6	...	...	...	36	15	21	5	...	5	...	...	...	...	...	...	67	35	32
Pathan Yusafzai ...	968	675	293	188	126	62	119	74	45	195	131	64	5	...	5	351	285	66	18	6	12	876	622	254
Rajput	67,809	30,812	36,997	3,438	1,657	1,781	21	10	11	21,204	10,692	10,512	25	16	9	25,643	10,751	14,892	...	...	...	50,331	23,126	27,205
Ratar	4,241	2,152	2,089	...	...	...	...	...	...	...	...	...	...	...	...	...	...	...	...	...	...	...	...	...
Rishi	6,735	3,218	3,517	...	...	...	...	...	...	...	...	...	...	...	...	...	...	...	...	...	...	...	...	...
Rathi	13	2	11	...	...	...	...	...	...	...	...	...	...	...	...	...	...	...	...	...	...	...	...	...
Rajgan	243	144	99	...	...	...	...	...	...	...	...	...	...	...	...	...	...	...	...	...	...	...	...	...
Rangroz	998	459	539	320	158	162	57	33	24	...	...	...	211	94	117	...	...	...	...	...	...	588	285	303
Rana	4,025	1,865	2,160	12	5	7	...	...	...	...	...	...	...	...	...	...	...	...	...	...	...	12	5	7
Rab	446	231	215	...	...	...	...	...	...	...	...	...	...	...	...	...	...	...	...	...	...	...	...	...
Rania	3,070	1,439	1,631	...	...	...	...	...	...	...	...	...	...	...	...	...	...	...	...	...	...	...	...	...
Rasam	44	15	29	...	...	...	...	...	...	...	...	...	...	...	...	...	...	...	...	...	...	...	...	...
Ragh	64	39	25	...	...	...	...	...	...	...	...	...	...	...	...	...	...	...	...	...	...	...	...	...
Rafugar	121	60	61	...	...	...	...	...	...	...	...	...	...	...	...	...	...	...	...	...	...	...	...	...
Rashu	225	156	69	...	...	...	...	...	...	...	...	...	...	...	...	...	...	...	...	...	...	...	...	...
Rawat	88	45	43	...	...	...	...	...	...	...	...	...	...	...	...	...	...	...	...	...	...	...	...	...

Caste, Tribe, Race or Nationality.	Provinces with Districts.																	
	Kashmir Province.									Frontier Districts.								
	Khas District.			Muzaffarabad District.			Total Kashmir Province.			Ladakh District.			Gilgit District.			Total Frontier Districts.		
	Persons.	Males.	Females.	Persons.	Males.	Females.	Persons.	Males.	Females.	Persons.	Males.	Females.	Persons.	Males.	Females.	Persons.	Males.	Females.
	26	27	28	29	30	31	32	33	34	35	36	37	38	39	40	41	42	43
Rawat Durrani	784	375	409	79	49	30	863	424	439	...	...	...	...	...	...	...	...	...
" Faridkhel	...	...	...	...	...	...	...	...	...	...	...	...	...	...	...	...	...	...
" Ghazi	781	276	505	...	...	...	781	276	505	...	...	...	...	...	...	...	...	...
" Ghilzai	...	...	...	10	...	10	10	...	10	...	...	...	...	...	...	...	...	...
" Hassanzai	...	...	...	483	464	19	483	464	19	...	...	...	...	...	...	...	...	...
" Isahzai	...	...	...	193	111	82	193	111	82	...	...	...	...	...	...	...	...	...
" Israiel	...	...	...	144	76	68	144	76	68	...	...	...	...	...	...	...	...	...
" Isakhel	...	...	...	...	...	...	...	...	...	...	...	...	...	...	...	...	...	...
" Jahangiri	...	...	...	130	66	64	130	66	64	...	...	...	...	...	...	...	...	...
" Khori	...	...	...	...	...	...	...	...	...	...	...	...	160	79	81	160	79	81
" Khan	...	...	...	...	...	...	...	...	...	...	...	...	...	...	...	...	...	...
" Khilji	...	...	...	17	17	...	17	17	...	...	...	...	...	...	...	...	...	...
" Kakakhel	1,187	503	684	277	251	26	1,464	754	710	...	...	...	...	...	...	...	...	...
" Kakazai	...	...	...	218	206	12	218	206	12	...	...	...	...	...	...	...	...	...
" Lodhi	...	...	...	53	...	53	53	...	53	...	...	...	...	...	...	...	...	...
" Madudkhel	...	...	...	144	117	27	144	117	27	...	...	...	...	...	...	...	...	...
" Mohamadi	...	...	...	73	21	52	73	21	52	...	...	...	...	...	...	...	...	...
" Qazikhel	...	...	...	376	252	124	376	252	124	...	...	...	...	...	...	...	...	...
" Qazalbash	...	...	...	...	...	...	...	...	...	...	...	...	...	...	...	...	...	...
" Rohilla	...	...	...	...	...	...	...	...	...	...	...	...	...	...	...	...	...	...
" Salarzai	...	...	...	...	...	...	...	...	...	...	...	...	...	...	...	...	...	...
" Salarkhel	...	...	...	...	...	...	...	...	...	...	...	...	...	...	...	...	...	...
" Sulemankhel	...	...	...	271	241	30	271	241	30	...	...	...	...	...	...	...	...	...
" Suwati	...	...	...	195	89	106	195	89	106	...	...	...	...	...	...	...	...	...
" Shahkhel	...	...	...	130	112	18	130	112	18	...	...	...	...	...	...	...	...	...
" Waziri	...	...	...	...	...	...	...	...	...	...	...	...	...	...	...	...	...	...
" Yusufzai	9	4	5	83	49	34	92	53	39	...	...	...	...	...	...	...	...	...
Rajput	14,186	6,705	7,481	3,292	981	2,311	17,478	7,686	9,792	...	...	...	...	...	...	...	...	...
Ratar	3,818	1,920	1,898	420	229	191	4,238	2,149	2,089	...	...	...	3	3	...	3	3	...
Rishi	6,505	3,008	3,497	230	210	20	6,735	3,218	3,517	...	...	...	...	...	...	...	...	...
Rathi	13	2	11	...	...	...	13	2	11	...	...	...	...	...	...	...	...	...
Rajgan	148	83	65	92	59	33	240	142	98	3	2	1	...	...	...	3	2	1
Rangrez	310	131	179	...	...	...	310	131	179	100	43	57	...	...	...	100	43	57
Rana	...	...	...	4,013	1,860	2,153	4,013	1,860	2,153	...	...	...	...	...	...	...	...	...
Rab	446	231	215	...	...	...	446	231	215	...	...	...	...	...	...	...	...	...
Rania	2,617	1,299	1,318	411	100	311	3,028	1,399	1,629	...	...	...	42	40	2	42	40	2
Rasam	44	15	29	...	...	...	44	15	29	...	...	...	...	...	...	...	...	...
Ragh	64	39	25	...	...	...	64	39	25	...	...	...	...	...	...	...	...	...
Rafugar	121	60	61	...	...	...	121	60	61	...	...	...	...	...	...	...	...	...
Rashu	225	156	69	...	...	...	225	156	69	...	...	...	...	...	...	...	...	...
Rawat	55	22	33	...	...	...	55	22	33	...	...	...	33	23	10	33	23	10

TABLE XIII.

Caste, Tribe, Race or Nationality.

Caste, Tribe, Race or Nationality.	Total Population. Persons.	Total Population. Males.	Total Population. Females.	Jammu District. Persons.	Jammu District. Males.	Jammu District. Females.	Chenani District. Persons.	Chenani District. Males.	Chenani District. Females.	Bhimber District. Persons.	Bhimber District. Males.	Bhimber District. Females.	Jasrota District. Persons.	Jasrota District. Males.	Jasrota District. Females.	Punch Jágir. Persons.	Punch Jágir. Males.	Punch Jágir. Females.	Bhadarwah Jágir. Persons.	Bhadarwah Jágir. Males.	Bhadarwah Jágir. Females.	Total Jammu Province. Persons.	Total Jammu Province. Males.	Total Jammu Province. Females.
1	2	3	4	5	6	7	8	9	10	11	12	13	14	15	16	17	18	19	20	21	22	23	24	25
Rasah	37	16	21	...	...	...	...	...	...	...	...	...	...	...	...	...	...	...	...	...	...	...	...	...
Rainchu	24	10	14	...	...	...	...	...	...	...	...	...	...	...	...	...	...	...	...	...	...	...	...	...
Rada	48	25	23	...	...	...	...	...	...	...	...	...	...	...	...	...	...	...	...	...	...	...	...	...
Rawal	27	13	14	3	...	3	5	3	2	...	...	...	...	...	...	...	...	...	...	...	...	8	3	5
Ratni	29	18	11	...	...	...	...	...	...	...	...	...	...	...	...	...	...	...	...	...	...	...	...	...
Ralloo	28	24	4	...	...	...	...	...	...	...	...	...	...	...	...	...	...	...	...	...	...	...	...	...
Rangar	66	37	29	...	...	...	...	...	...	...	...	...	...	...	...	...	...	...	...	...	...	...	...	...
Rais	1,605	945	660	...	...	...	...	...	...	...	...	...	...	...	...	...	...	...	...	...	...	...	...	...
Rangin	59	48	11	...	...	...	...	...	...	...	...	...	...	...	...	...	...	...	...	...	...	...	...	...
Raktan	25	3	22	...	...	...	...	...	...	...	...	...	...	...	...	...	...	...	...	...	...	...	...	...
Rasaygn	297	152	145	...	...	...	...	...	...	...	...	...	...	...	...	...	...	...	...	...	...	...	...	...
Rabsandpa	67	35	32	...	...	...	...	...	...	...	...	...	...	...	...	...	...	...	...	...	...	...	...	...
Ranjupa	19	19	...	...	...	...	...	...	...	...	...	...	...	...	...	...	...	...	...	...	...	...	...	...
Raklopa	33	20	13	...	...	...	...	...	...	...	...	...	...	...	...	...	...	...	...	...	...	...	...	...
Ralpa	133	112	21	...	...	...	...	...	...	...	...	...	...	...	...	...	...	...	...	...	...	...	...	...
Rafnapa	100	60	40	...	...	...	...	...	...	...	...	...	...	...	...	...	...	...	...	...	...	...	...	...
Ratpa	125	87	38	...	...	...	...	...	...	...	...	...	...	...	...	...	...	...	...	...	...	...	...	...
Roma	533	456	77	...	...	...	...	...	...	...	...	...	...	...	...	...	...	...	...	...	...	...	...	...
Railpa	195	84	111	...	...	...	...	...	...	...	...	...	...	...	...	...	...	...	...	...	...	...	...	...
Rolupa	76	20	56	...	...	...	...	...	...	...	...	...	...	...	...	...	...	...	...	...	...	...	...	...
Roman	24	9	15	...	...	...	...	...	...	...	...	...	...	...	...	...	...	...	...	...	...	...	...	...
Rachn	199	105	94	...	...	...	...	...	...	...	...	...	...	...	...	...	...	...	...	...	...	...	...	...
Rabar	10	9	1	...	...	...	...	...	...	...	...	...	...	...	...	...	...	...	...	...	...	...	...	...
Sial	26	24	2	...	...	...	...	...	...	...	...	...	...	...	...	...	...	...	...	...	...	...	...	...
Showl	483	229	254	...	...	...	...	...	...	...	...	...	...	...	...	...	...	...	...	...	...	...	...	...
Sheikh	66,279	33,277	33,002	1,961	1,108	858	1,280	525	705	3,290	1,608	1,682	335	264	71	6,730	1,911	4,819	1,621	891	730	15,217	6,352	8,865
Sarin	228	32	196	...	...	...	...	...	...	...	...	...	...	...	...	...	...	...	...	...	...	...	...	...
Sapash	286	113	173	...	...	...	...	...	...	...	...	...	...	...	...	...	...	...	...	...	...	...	...	...
Saraj	95	51	44	...	...	...	...	...	...	...	...	...	...	...	...	...	...	...	...	...	...	...	...	...
Sarwan	150	103	47	...	...	...	...	...	...	...	...	...	...	...	...	...	...	...	...	...	...	...	...	...
Sandari	1,221	705	516	4	...	4	...	...	...	24	19	5	20	9	11	41	26	15	...	...	...	89	58	31
Sultani	817	555	262	...	...	...	...	...	...	...	...	...	...	...	...	...	...	...	...	...	...	...	...	...
Sakka	140	94	46	...	...	...	...	...	...	...	...	...	...	...	...	...	...	...	...	...	...	...	...	...
Sardar	169	63	106	...	...	...	...	...	...	...	...	...	...	...	...	...	...	...	...	...	...	...	...	...
Salas	327	140	187	...	...	...	...	...	...	...	...	...	...	...	...	...	...	...	...	...	...	...	...	...
Sarham	93	46	47	...	...	...	...	...	...	...	...	...	...	...	...	...	...	...	...	...	...	...	...	...
Sonyara	9,563	5,022	4,541	2,404	1,328	1,130	1,227	654	573	1,359	725	634	979	480	499	693	279	414	85	43	42	6,707	3,509	3,198
Sallapa	148	62	86	...	...	...	...	...	...	...	...	...	...	...	...	...	...	...	...	...	...	...	...	...
Skitpa	471	230	241	...	...	...	...	...	...	...	...	...	...	...	...	...	...	...	...	...	...	...	...	...
Sharpa	210	91	119	...	...	...	...	...	...	...	...	...	...	...	...	...	...	...	...	...	...	...	...	...
Sikapa	313	187	126	...	...	...	...	...	...	...	...	...	...	...	...	...	...	...	...	...	...	...	...	...

(Provinces with Districts — Jammu Province.)

PROVINCES WITH DISTRICTS.

Caste, Tribe, Race or Nationality.	Kashmir Province. Khas District. Persons.	Khas District. Males.	Khas District. Females.	Muzaffarabad District. Persons.	Muzaffarabad District. Males.	Muzaffarabad District. Females.	Total Kashmir Province. Persons.	Total Kashmir Province. Males.	Total Kashmir Province. Females.	Frontier Districts. Ladakh District. Persons.	Ladakh District. Males.	Ladakh District. Females.	Gilgit District. Persons.	Gilgit District. Males.	Gilgit District. Females.	Total Frontier Districts. Persons.	Total Frontier Districts. Males.	Total Frontier Districts. Females.
	26	27	28	29	30	31	32	33	34	35	36	37	38	39	40	41	42	43
Razah	37	16	21	...	...	...	37	16	21	...	...	...	...	...	...	...	...	...
Rainchu	24	10	14	...	...	...	24	10	14	...	...	...	...	...	...	...	...	...
Radu	48	25	23	...	...	...	48	25	23	...	...	...	...	...	...	...	...	...
Rawal	19	10	9	...	...	...	19	10	9	...	...	...	...	...	...	...	...	...
Ratni	29	18	11	...	...	...	29	18	11	...	...	...	...	...	...	...	...	...
Railoo	6	2	4	22	22	...	28	24	4	...	...	...	...	...	...	...	...	...
Rangar	66	37	29	...	...	...	66	37	29	...	...	...	...	...	...	...	...	...
Rala	...	...	...	1,665	945	660	1,665	945	660	...	...	...	...	...	...	...	...	...
Rangin	...	...	...	...	...	...	...	...	...	59	48	11	...	...	...	59	48	11
Raktau	...	...	...	...	...	...	...	...	...	25	3	22	...	...	...	25	3	22
Raznqpa	...	...	...	...	...	...	...	...	...	207	152	145	...	...	...	207	152	145
Rabaandpa	...	...	...	...	...	...	...	...	...	67	35	32	...	...	...	67	35	32
Ranjupa	...	...	...	...	...	...	...	...	...	19	19	...	...	...	...	19	19	...
Raklopa	...	...	...	...	...	...	...	...	...	33	20	13	...	...	...	33	20	13
Ralpa	...	...	...	...	...	...	...	...	...	133	112	21	...	...	...	133	112	21
Rafnapa	...	...	...	...	...	...	...	...	...	100	60	40	...	...	...	100	60	40
Ratpa	...	...	...	...	...	...	...	...	...	125	87	38	...	...	...	125	87	38
Rome	...	...	...	...	...	...	...	...	...	533	456	77	...	...	...	533	456	77
Railpa	...	...	...	...	...	...	...	...	...	195	84	111	...	...	...	195	84	111
Rolupa	...	...	...	...	...	...	...	...	...	76	20	56	...	...	...	76	20	56
Roman	...	...	...	...	...	...	...	...	...	24	9	15	...	...	...	24	9	15
Ruchu	...	...	...	...	...	...	...	...	...	199	105	94	...	...	...	199	105	94
Rahar	...	...	...	10	9	1	10	9	1	...	...	...	...	...	...	...	...	...
Sial	26	24	2	...	...	...	26	24	2	...	...	...	...	...	...	...	...	...
Showl	483	229	254	...	...	...	483	229	254	...	...	...	...	...	...	...	...	...
Shaikh	48,515	25,134	23,381	2,401	1,370	1,031	50,916	26,504	24,412	599	315	284	147	106	41	740	421	325
Sadu	228	32	196	...	...	...	228	32	196	...	...	...	...	...	...	...	...	...
Sapsah	286	113	173	...	...	...	286	113	173	...	...	...	...	...	...	...	...	...
Saraj	95	51	44	...	...	...	95	51	44	...	...	...	...	...	...	...	...	...
Sarwan	150	103	47	...	...	...	150	103	47	...	...	...	...	...	...	...	...	...
Sundori	1,132	647	485	...	...	...	1,132	647	485	...	...	...	...	...	...	...	...	...
Sultani	817	555	262	...	...	...	817	555	262	...	...	...	...	...	...	...	...	...
Sakka	140	94	46	...	...	...	140	94	46	...	...	...	...	...	...	...	...	...
Sardar	169	63	106	...	...	...	169	63	106	...	...	...	...	...	...	...	...	...
Salas	327	140	187	...	...	...	327	140	187	...	...	...	...	...	...	...	...	...
Sarham	93	46	47	...	...	...	93	46	47	...	...	...	...	...	...	...	...	...
Sunyarn	1,673	898	775	...	...	...	1,673	898	775	914	436	478	269	179	90	1,183	615	568
Salispa	...	...	...	...	...	...	...	...	...	148	62	86	...	...	...	148	62	86
Akltpa	...	...	...	...	...	...	...	...	...	471	230	241	...	...	...	471	230	241
Skarpa	...	...	...	...	...	...	...	...	...	210	91	119	...	...	...	210	91	119
Sikipa	...	...	...	...	...	...	...	...	...	313	187	126	...	...	...	313	187	126

TABLE XIII.

Caste, Tribe, Race or Nationality.

Caste, Tribe, Race or Nationality.	Total Population.			Provinces with Districts. — Jammu Province. — Jammu District.			Udhampur District.			Bhimber District.			Jasrota District.			Punch Jagir.			Bhadarwah Jagir.			Total Jammu Province.		
	Persons.	Males.	Females.	Persons.	Males.	Females.	Persons.	Males.	Females.	Persons.	Males.	Females.	Persons.	Males.	Females.	Persons.	Males.	Females.	Persons.	Males.	Females.	Persons.	Males.	Females.
1	2	3	4	5	6	7	8	9	10	11	12	13	14	15	16	17	18	19	20	21	22	23	24	25
Sangpa	586	374	212	...	...	...	...	...	...	...	...	...	...	...	...	...	...	...	...	...	...	...	...	...
Satripa	96	57	39	...	...	...	...	...	...	...	...	...	...	...	...	...	...	...	...	...	...	...	...	...
Sangara	126	81	45	...	...	...	...	...	...	...	...	...	...	...	...	...	...	...	...	...	...	...	...	...
Shari	118	62	56	...	...	...	...	...	...	...	...	...	...	...	...	...	...	...	...	...	...	...	...	...
Saugi	405	405	...	...	...	...	...	...	...	...	...	...	...	...	...	...	...	...	...	...	...	...	...	...
Sasi	261	105	156	...	...	...	...	...	...	...	...	...	...	...	...	...	...	...	...	...	...	...	...	...
Samanpa	311	161	150	...	...	...	...	...	...	...	...	...	...	...	...	...	...	...	...	...	...	...	...	...
Soui	392	243	149	...	...	...	...	...	...	...	...	...	...	...	...	...	...	...	...	...	...	...	...	...
Sahal	205	205	...	...	...	...	...	...	...	...	...	...	...	...	...	...	...	...	...	...	...	...	...	...
Saryal	25	25	...	...	...	...	...	...	...	...	...	...	...	...	...	...	...	...	...	...	...	...	...	...
Saryara	984	285	699	...	...	...	676	193	483	53	26	27	244	55	189	...	...	...	...	...	...	973	274	699
Skaj	55	55	...	...	...	...	...	...	...	...	...	...	...	...	...	...	...	...	...	...	...	...	...	...
Sikm	9	3	6	...	...	...	...	...	...	...	...	...	...	...	...	...	...	...	...	...	...	...	...	...
Sadhan	114	107	7	10	3	7	104	101	...	...	...	...	...	...	...	...	...	...	...	...	...	114	107	7
Total Sayed ...	53.991	29,039	24.952	2,712	1.474	1.239	735	430	305	6.599	3.611	2.988	127	75	52	9.744	5.444	4.300	88	30	58	20.006	11.064	8.942
Sayed Abusi ...	259	219	40	13	6	7	6	4	2	100	185	5	...	...	...	50	24	26	...	...	...	259	219	40
Bakhari	7,187	4,088	3,099	676	366	310	134	223	211	2,087	1,487	1,200	36	26	10	2,272	1,255	1,017	...	...	...	6,105	3,297	2,808
Gilani	2,810	1,400	1,110	410	204	208	...	...	...	1,017	399	618	10	10	9	1,121	577	544	...	...	...	2,567	1,190	1,377
Hadi	1,085	896	789	123	49	74	...	...	...	110	54	56	...	...	...	...	...	...	...	...	...	233	103	130
Gilani	2,974	1,595	1,379	125	64	61	2	1	1	41	24	17	...	...	...	2,473	1,193	1,280	...	...	...	2,041	1,282	1,359
Kadri	389	141	248	32	15	17	18	6	13	293	112	181	...	...	...	46	0	37	...	...	...	389	141	248
Kalamdani ...	164	136	28	...	...	...	1	1	...	110	100	10	...	...	...	...	...	...	...	...	...	111	101	10
Mashhadi	4,156	2,422	1,734	317	158	159	...	...	...	1,095	535	507	17	12	5	1,845	959	886	...	...	...	3,274	1,664	1,610
... ...	32,416	17,135	15,281	142	112	30	255	181	74	767	653	114	30	15	15	1,214	1,069	145	88	30	58	2,498	2,000	486
Shirazi	807	451	356	310	178	132	5	6	...	151	73	78	3	3	...	322	192	130	...	...	...	701	151	340
Trimzi	1,144	556	588	685	322	243	14	10	4	138	49	89	22	9	13	401	166	235	...	...	...	1,140	566	584
Shala	693	399	294	...	...	...	...	...	...	...	...	...	...	...	...	...	...	...	...	...	...	...	...	...
Shan	227	109	118	...	...	...	...	...	...	...	...	...	...	...	...	...	...	...	...	...	...	...	...	...
Shalbaf	250	126	124	...	...	...	...	...	...	...	...	...	...	...	...	...	...	...	...	...	...	...	...	...
Shagu	234	151	83	...	...	...	...	...	...	...	...	...	...	...	...	...	...	...	...	...	...	...	...	...
Shah	750	456	294	...	...	...	...	...	...	...	...	...	...	...	...	...	...	...	...	...	...	...	...	...
Shakhsaz	240	112	128	...	...	...	...	...	...	...	...	...	...	...	...	...	...	...	...	...	...	...	...	...
Shaai	88	49	39	...	...	...	...	...	...	...	...	...	...	...	...	...	...	...	...	...	...	...	...	...
Sharu	2,184	1,099	1,085	...	...	...	...	...	...	...	...	...	...	...	...	...	...	...	...	...	...	...	...	...
Shardpa	56	19	37	...	...	...	...	...	...	...	...	...	...	...	...	...	...	...	...	...	...	...	...	...
Shakhupa	376	211	165	...	...	...	...	...	...	...	...	...	...	...	...	...	...	...	...	...	...	...	...	...

Caste, Tribe, Race or Nationality.	PROVINCES WITH DISTRICTS.																	
	KASHMIR PROVINCE.									FRONTIER DISTRICTS.								
	Khas District.			Muzaffarabad District.			Total Kashmir Province.			Ladakh District.			Gilgit District.			Total Frontier Districts.		
	Persons.	Males.	Females.	Persons.	Males.	Females.	Persons.	Males.	Females.	Persons.	Males.	Females.	Persons.	Males.	Females.	Persons.	Males.	Females.
	26	27	28	29	30	31	32	33	34	35	36	37	38	39	40	41	42	43
Sangpa	...	...	...	...	...	...	...	...	...	586	374	212	...	...	...	586	374	212
Satripa	...	...	...	...	...	...	...	...	...	96	57	39	...	...	...	96	57	39
Sangara	...	...	...	...	...	...	...	...	...	126	81	45	...	...	...	126	81	45
Sahri	...	...	...	...	...	...	...	...	...	118	62	56	...	...	...	118	62	56
Sangi	...	...	...	...	...	...	...	...	...	405	405	...	...	...	...	405	405	...
Sasi	...	...	...	...	...	...	...	...	...	261	105	156	...	...	...	261	105	156
Samanpa	...	...	...	...	...	...	...	...	...	311	161	150	...	...	...	311	161	150
Soni	...	...	...	...	...	...	...	...	...	...	...	...	392	243	149	392	243	149
Sahal	...	...	...	...	...	...	...	...	...	...	...	...	205	205	...	205	205	...
Saryal	...	...	...	...	...	...	...	...	...	...	...	...	25	25	...	25	25	...
Saryara	...	...	...	...	...				...	...	...	...	11	11	...	11	11	...
Skaj									...	...	...	...	55	55	...	55	55	...
Sikm	...	...	...	...	...	...	...	...	...	...	...	...	9	3	6	9	3	6
Sadhun	...	...	...	...	...	...	...	...	...	...	...	...	...	...	...	...	...	...
Total Sayed	30,218	16,130	14,088	3,082	1,511	1,571	33,300	17,641	15,659	...	...	...	685	334	351	685	334	351
Sayed Abasi	...	...	...	...	...	...	...	...	...	...	...	...	...	...	...	...	...	...
" Bukhari	605	572	33	477	219	258	1,082	791	291	...	...	...	...	...	...	...	...	...
" Gilani	...	...	...	243	210	33	243	210	33	...	...	...	...	...	...	...	...	...
" Hadi	342	342	...	1,110	451	659	1,452	793	659	...	...	...		...	...	...	...	...
" Jilani	333	313	20	...	...	...	333	313	20	...	...	...	...	...	...	...	...	...
" Kadri	...	...	...	...	...	...	...	...	...	...	...	...	...	...	...	...	...	...
" Kulandari	53	35	18	...	...	...	53	35	18	...	...	...	...	...	...	...	...	...
" Mashhedi	656	640	16	226	118	108	882	758	124	...	...	...	...	...	...	...	...	...
" Sayad	28,229	14,228	14,001	1,006	513	493	29,235	14,741	14,494	...	...	...	685	334	351	685	334	351
" Shirazi	...	...	...	16	...	16	16	...	16	...	...	...	...	...	...	...	...	...
" Trimzi	...	...	...	4	...	4	4	...	4	...	...	...	...	...	...	...	...	...
Shala	693	399	294	...	...	...	693	399	294	...	...	...		...	...	...	...	...
Sham	227	109	118	...	...	...	227	109	118	...	...	...		...	...	...	...	...
Shalbaf	217	122	95		...	...	217	122	95	33	4	29	...	...	...	33	4	29
Shagu	234	151	83	...	...	...	234	151	83	...	...	...	...	...	...	...	...	...
Shah	750	456	294	...	...	...	750	456	294	...	...	...	...	...	...	...	...	...
Shakhsas	240	112	128	...	...	...	240	112	128	...	...	...	...	...	...	...	...	...
Shani	88	49	39	...	...	...	88	49	39	...	...	...	...	...	...	...	...	...
Sharu	2,184	1,099	1,085	...	...	...	2,184	1,099	1,085	...	...	...	...	...	...	...	...	...
Shardpa	...	...	...	...	...	...	...	...	...	56	19	37	...	...	...	56	19	37
Shakhupa	...	...	...	...	...	...	...	...	...	376	211	165	...	...	...	376	211	165

TABLE XIII.

Caste, Tribe, Race or Nationality.

Caste, Tribe, Race or Nationality.	Total Population.			Provinces with Districts. Jammu Province. Jammu District.			Udhampur District.			Bhimber District.			Jasrota District.			Punch Jágir.			Bhadarwah Jagir.			Total Jammu Province.		
	Persons.	Males.	Females.	Persons.	Males.	Females.	Persons.	Males.	Females.	Persons.	Males.	Females.	Persons.	Males.	Females.	Persons.	Males.	Females.	Persons.	Males.	Females.	Persons.	Males.	Females.
1	2	3	4	5	6	7	8	9	10	11	12	13	14	15	16	17	18	19	20	21	22	23	24	25
Shoripa	38	29	9	...	...	...	...	...	...	...	...	...	...	...	...	...	...	...	...	...	...	...	...	...
Sharaipa	41	26	15	...	...	...	...	...	...	...	...	...	...	...	...	...	...	...	...	...	...	...	...	...
Sharnurpa	154	78	76	...	...	...	...	...	...	...	...	...	...	...	...	...	...	...	...	...	...	...	...	...
Shakurpa	70	38	32	...	...	...	...	...	...	...	...	...	...	...	...	...	...	...	...	...	...	...	...	...
Shalipa	130	40	90	...	...	...	...	...	...	...	...	...	...	...	...	...	...	...	...	...	...	...	...	...
Sharaipa	53	49	4	...	...	...	...	...	...	...	...	...	...	...	...	...	...	...	...	...	...	...	...	...
Sharn	40	40	...	...	...	...	...	...	...	...	...	...	...	...	...	...	...	...	...	...	...	...	...	...
Sharahpa	41	27	14	...	...	...	...	...	...	...	...	...	...	...	...	...	...	...	...	...	...	...	...	...
Sharinnapa	52	20	32	...	...	...	...	...	...	...	...	...	...	...	...	...	...	...	...	...	...	...	...	...
Shagapa	53	15	38	...	...	...	...	...	...	...	...	...	...	...	...	...	...	...	...	...	...	...	...	...
Shampa	57	15	42	...	...	...	...	...	...	...	...	...	...	...	...	...	...	...	...	...	...	...	...	...
Shokpa	129	36	93	...	...	...	...	...	...	...	...	...	...	...	...	...	...	...	...	...	...	...	...	...
Sherbal	43	10	33	...	...	...	...	...	...	...	...	...	...	...	...	...	...	...	...	...	...	...	...	...
Shake	80	33	47	...	...	...	...	...	...	...	...	...	...	...	...	...	...	...	...	...	...	...	...	...
Shilpa	124	30	94	...	...	...	...	...	...	...	...	...	...	...	...	...	...	...	...	...	...	...	...	...
Shalanpa	386	160	226	...	...	...	...	...	...	...	...	...	...	...	...	...	...	...	...	...	...	...	...	...
Sharal	107	26	81	...	...	...	...	...	...	...	...	...	...	...	...	...	...	...	...	...	...	...	...	...
Shamadpa	87	45	42	...	...	...	...	...	...	...	...	...	...	...	...	...	...	...	...	...	...	...	...	...
Shauni	30	15	15	...	...	...	...	...	...	...	...	...	...	...	...	...	...	...	...	...	...	...	...	...
Shalu	18	5	13	...	...	...	...	...	...	...	...	...	...	...	...	...	...	...	...	...	...	...	...	...
Shurduki	367	191	176	...	...	...	...	...	...	...	...	...	...	...	...	...	...	...	...	...	...	...	...	...
Shamshari	82	53	29	...	...	...	...	...	...	...	...	...	...	...	...	...	...	...	...	...	...	...	...	...
Shikukas	184	95	89	...	...	...	...	...	...	...	...	...	...	...	...	...	...	...	...	...	...	...	...	...
Shardink	130	71	59	...	...	...	...	...	...	...	...	...	...	...	...	...	...	...	...	...	...	...	...	...
Shetutang	388	202	186	...	...	...	...	...	...	...	...	...	...	...	...	...	...	...	...	...	...	...	...	...
Shanal	152	74	78	...	...	...	...	...	...	...	...	...	...	...	...	...	...	...	...	...	...	...	...	...
Shin	7,733	4,303	3,430	...	...	...	...	...	...	...	...	...	...	...	...	...	...	...	...	...	...	...	...	...
Sufi	22,407	11,516	10,891	...	...	...	...	...	...	...	...	...	...	...	...	...	...	...	...	...	...	...	...	...
Sargar	256	127	129	...	...	...	...	...	...	...	...	...	...	...	...	...	...	...	...	...	...	...	...	...
Saika	533	298	235	...	...	...	...	...	...	...	...	...	...	...	...	...	...	...	...	...	...	...	...	...
Sadarpa	12	12	...	...	...	...	...	...	...	...	...	...	...	...	...	...	...	...	...	...	...	...	...	...
Salipa	14	4	10	...	...	...	...	...	...	...	...	...	...	...	...	...	...	...	...	...	...	...	...	...
Sufupa	13	13	...	...	...	...	...	...	...	...	...	...	...	...	...	...	...	...	...	...	...	...	...	...
Sadigpa	186	127	59	...	...	...	...	...	...	...	...	...	...	...	...	...	...	...	...	...	...	...	...	...
Swati	315	162	153	...	...	...	...	...	...	...	...	...	...	...	...	...	...	...	...	...	...	...	...	...
Safi	45	...	45	...	...	...	...	...	...	...	...	...	...	...	...	...	...	...	...	...	...	...	...	...
Sadiki	403	256	147	3	2	1	...	...	...	...	...	...	...	...	...	...	...	...	...	...	...	3	2	1
Saddal	93	63	30	93	63	30	...	...	...	...	...	...	...	...	...	...	...	...	...	...	...	93	63	30
Thari	360	207	153	...	...	...	...	...	...	...	...	...	...	...	...	...	...	...	...	...	...	...	...	...
Tas	94	61	33	...	...	...	...	...	...	...	...	...	...	...	...	...	...	...	...	...	...	...	...	...
Tomboris	80	47	33	...	...	...	...	...	...	...	...	...	...	...	...	...	...	...	...	...	...	...	...	...

PROVINCES WITH DISTRICTS.

Caste, Tribe, Race or Nationality.	Kashmir Province. Khás District. Persons.	Males.	Females.	Muzaffarabad District. Persons.	Males.	Females.	Total Kashmir Province. Persons.	Males.	Females.	Frontier Districts. Ladakh District. Persons.	Males.	Females.	Gilgit District. Persons.	Males.	Females.	Total Frontier Districts. Persons.	Males.	Females.
	26	27	28	29	30	31	32	33	34	35	36	37	38	39	40	41	42	43
Sheripa	...	...	...	...	...	...	...	...	...	38	29	0	...	...	...	38	20	0
Sharalpa	...	...	...	...	...	...	...	...	...	41	26	15	...	...	...	41	26	15
Sharnarpa	...	...	...	...	...	...	...	...	...	154	78	76	...	...	...	154	78	76
Shakurpa	...	...	...	...	...	...	...	...	...	70	38	32	...	...	...	70	38	32
Shulipa	...	...	...	...	...	...	...	...	...	136	46	90	...	...	...	136	46	90
Sharafpa	...	...	...	...	...	...	...	...	...	53	49	4	...	...	...	53	49	4
Shura	...	...	...	...	...	...	...	...	...	40	40	...	...	...	...	40	40	...
Sharalipa	...	...	...	...	...	...	...	...	...	41	27	14	...	...	...	41	27	14
Sharmapa	...	...	...	...	...	...	...	...	...	52	20	32	...	...	...	52	20	32
Shagapa	...	...	...	...	...	...	...	...	...	53	15	38	...	...	...	53	15	38
Shampa	...	...	...	...	...	...	...	...	...	57	15	42	...	...	...	57	15	42
Shokpa	...	...	...	...	...	...	...	...	...	129	36	93	...	...	...	129	36	93
Sherbal	...	...	...	...	...	...	...	...	...	43	10	33	...	...	...	43	10	33
Shako	...	...	...	...	...	...	...	...	...	80	33	47	...	...	...	80	33	47
Shilpa	...	...	...	...	...	...	...	...	...	124	30	94	...	...	...	124	30	94
Shalanpa	...	...	...	...	...	...	...	...	...	386	160	226	...	...	...	386	160	296
Sharal	...	...	...	...	...	...	...	...	...	107	26	81	...	...	...	107	26	81
Shamadpa	...	...	...	...	...	...	...	...	...	...	...	...	87	45	42	87	45	42
Shami	...	...	...	...	...	...	...	...	...	...	...	...	30	15	15	30	15	15
Shalu	...	...	...	...	...	...	...	...	...	...	...	...	18	5	13	18	5	13
Shurduki	...	...	...	...	...	...	...	...	...	...	...	...	307	191	176	307	191	176
Shamshari	...	...	...	...	...	...	...	...	...	...	...	...	82	53	29	82	53	29
Shikukas	...	...	...	...	...	...	...	...	...	...	...	...	184	95	89	184	95	89
Shardink	...	...	...	...	...	...	...	...	...	...	...	...	130	71	59	130	71	59
Shetutang	...	...	...	...	...	...	...	...	...	...	...	...	388	202	186	388	202	186
Shauul	...	...	...	...	...	...	...	...	...	...	...	...	152	74	78	152	74	78
Shin	...	...	...	...	...	...	...	...	...	...	...	...	7,733	4,303	3,430	7,733	4,303	3,430
Sul	12,636	6,527	6,109	7,967	4,179	3,788	20,603	10,706	9,807	1,804	810	994	...	...	...	1,804	810	994
Sargar	250	127	123	...	...	...	250	127	123	533	268	265	...	...	...	533	268	265
Salka	...	...	...	...	...	...	...	...	...	12	12	...	...	...	...	12	12	...
Sadarpa	...	...	...	...	...	...	...	...	...	14	4	10	...	...	...	14	4	10
Salipa	...	...	...	...	...	...	...	...	...	13	13	...	...	...	...	13	13	...
Sufupa	...	...	...	...	...	...	...	...	...	186	127	59	...	...	...	186	127	59
Sadigpa	...	...	...	...	...	...	...	...	...	315	162	153	...	...	...	315	162	153
Swati	...	...	...	45	...	45	45	...	45	...	...	...	...	...	...	...	...	...
Safi	...	...	...	400	254	146	400	254	146	...	...	...	...	...	...	...	...	...
Sadiki	...	...	...	...	...	...	...	...	...	...	...	...	...	...	...	...	...	...
Suddal	...	...	...	...	...	...	...	...	...	...	...	...	...	...	...	...	...	...
Thari	300	207	153	...	...	...	300	207	153	...	...	...	...	...	...	...	...	...
Tas	94	61	33	...	...	...	94	61	33	...	...	...	...	...	...	...	...	...
Toshoria	80	47	33	...	...	...	80	47	33	...	...	...	...	...	...	...	...	...

TABLE XIII.

Caste, Tribe, Race or Nationality.

Caste, Tribe, Race or Nationality.	Total Population.			Provinces with Districts. Jammu Province. Jammu District.			Udhampur District.			Bhimber District.			Jasrota District.			Punch Jágir.			Bhadarwah Jágir.			Total Jammu Province.		
	Persons.	Males.	Females.	Persons.	Males.	Females.	Persons.	Males.	Females.	Persons.	Males.	Females.	Persons.	Males.	Females.	Persons.	Males.	Females.	Persons.	Males.	Females.	Persons.	Males.	Females.
1	2	3	4	5	6	7	8	9	10	11	12	13	14	15	16	17	18	19	20	21	22	23	24	25
Tulpipah	55	40	15	...	...	...	...	...	...	...	...	...	...	...	...	...	...	...	...	...	...	...	...	...
Tukdilpa	75	45	30	...	...	...	...	...	...	...	...	...	...	...	...	...	...	...	...	...	...	...	...	...
Tolu	388	206	182	...	...	...	...	...	...	...	...	...	...	...	...	...	...	...	...	...	...	...	...	...
Tark	2,453	1,051	1,402	...	...	...	18	12	6	...	...	...	...	...	...	...	...	...	...	...	...	18	12	6
Tell	21,560	11,528	10,032	3,000	1,670	1,330	956	528	428	4,376	2,447	1,929	2,544	1,383	1,161	2,558	1,638	920	1	1	...	13,435	7,667	5,768
Taripa	250	126	124	...	...	...	...	...	...	...	...	...	...	...	...	...	...	...	...	...	...	...	...	...
Thakupa	250	90	160	...	...	...	...	...	...	...	...	...	...	...	...	...	...	...	...	...	...	...	...	...
Taslipa	66	15	51	...	...	...	...	...	...	...	...	...	...	...	...	...	...	...	...	...	...	...	...	...
Tappa	215	72	143	...	...	...	...	...	...	...	...	...	...	...	...	...	...	...	...	...	...	...	...	...
Tumapa	92	32	60	...	...	...	...	...	...	...	...	...	...	...	...	...	...	...	...	...	...	...	...	...
Toutary	11,525	6,685	4,840	...	...	...	...	...	...	...	...	...	...	...	...	4,995	3,412	1,583	...	...	...	4,995	3,412	1,583
Tharkhan	22,440	12,261	10,179	2,417	1,400	1,017	633	353	280	7,056	3,978	3,078	124	38	86	2,719	1,622	1,097	61	34	27	13,010	7,425	5,585
Tarn	597	506	91	...	...	...	5	5	...	...	...	...	...	...	...	...	...	...	...	...	...	5	5	...
Thaploo	179	108	71	...	...	...	...	...	...	...	...	...	...	...	...	...	...	...	...	...	...	...	...	...
Thallah	189	95	94	...	...	...	...	...	...	...	...	...	...	...	...	...	...	...	...	...	...	...	...	...
Tirimbon	166	84	82	...	...	...	...	...	...	...	...	...	...	...	...	...	...	...	...	...	...	...	...	...
Tamokoq	82	53	29	...	...	...	...	...	...	...	...	...	...	...	...	...	...	...	...	...	...	...	...	...
Tamohi	207	104	103	...	...	...	...	...	...	...	...	...	...	...	...	...	...	...	...	...	...	...	...	...
Tanje	29	14	15	...	...	...	...	...	...	...	...	...	...	...	...	...	...	...	...	...	...	...	...	...
Tarhavanang	436	230	206	...	...	...	...	...	...	...	...	...	...	...	...	...	...	...	...	...	...	...	...	...
Tarkish	25	25	...	...	...	...	...	...	...	...	...	...	...	...	...	...	...	...	...	...	...	...	...	...
Tarmal	3	3	...	...	...	...	3	3	...	...	...	...	...	...	...	...	...	...	...	...	...	3	3	...
Tibili	3	2	1	...	...	...	3	2	1	...	...	...	...	...	...	...	...	...	...	...	...	3	2	1
Timboli	200	80	120	...	...	...	...	...	...	...	...	...	...	...	...	...	...	...	...	...	...	...	...	...
Tajhal	10	10	...	...	...	...	...	...	...	...	...	...	...	...	...	...	...	...	...	...	...	...	...	...
Talul	157	35	122	...	...	...	...	...	...	...	...	...	...	...	...	...	...	...	...	...	...	...	...	...
Taroj	824	304	520	...	...	...	...	...	...	...	...	...	...	...	...	...	...	...	...	...	...	...	...	...
Turmasi	45	17	28	...	...	...	...	...	...	...	...	...	...	...	...	...	...	...	...	...	...	...	...	...
Tarind	23	20	3	...	...	...	...	...	...	...	...	...	...	...	...	...	...	...	...	...	...	...	...	...
Tukual	239	63	176	...	...	...	...	...	...	...	...	...	...	...	...	...	...	...	...	...	...	...	...	...
Takarpa	39	6	33	...	...	...	...	...	...	...	...	...	...	...	...	...	...	...	...	...	...	...	...	...
Takhakpa	30	13	17	...	...	...	...	...	...	...	...	...	...	...	...	...	...	...	...	...	...	...	...	...
Thaus	90	40	50	...	...	...	...	...	...	...	...	...	...	...	...	...	...	...	...	...	...	...	...	...
Turkpa	63	18	45	...	...	...	...	...	...	...	...	...	...	...	...	...	...	...	...	...	...	...	...	...
Tahaya	19	14	5	...	...	...	...	...	...	...	...	...	...	...	...	...	...	...	...	...	...	...	...	...
Tonedar	45	6	39	...	...	...	...	...	...	...	...	...	...	...	...	...	...	...	...	...	...	...	...	...
Takay	184	131	53	...	...	...	...	...	...	...	...	...	...	...	...	...	...	...	...	...	...	...	...	...
Thadu	108	66	42	...	...	...	...	...	...	...	...	...	...	...	...	...	...	...	...	...	...	...	...	...
Tanko	23	16	7	...	...	...	...	...	...	...	...	...	...	...	...	...	...	...	...	...	...	...	...	...
Wahpapa	33	21	12	...	...	...	...	...	...	...	...	...	...	...	...	...	...	...	...	...	...	...	...	...
Wani	4,281	2,142	2,139	...	...	...	...	...	...	...	...	...	...	...	...	...	...	...	...	...	...	...	...	...

PROVINCES WITH DISTRICTS.

Caste, Tribe, Race or Nationality.	Kashmir Province. Khas District. Persons.	Males.	Females.	Muzaffarabad District. Persons.	Males.	Females.	Total Kashmir Province. Persons.	Males.	Females.	Frontier Districts. Ladakh District. Persons.	Males.	Females.	Gilgit District. Persons.	Males.	Females.	Total Frontier Districts. Persons.	Males.	Females.
	26	27	28	29	30	31	32	33	34	35	36	37	38	39	40	41	42	43
Tulpipah	...	...	...	...	...	...	...	...	...	55	40	15	...	...	...	55	40	15
Takdilpa	7	...	...	...	...	...	...	...	...	75	45	30	...	...	...	75	45	30
Tolu	...	...	...	...	...	...	...	...	...	388	206	182	...	...	...	388	206	182
Turk	1,093	478	615	1,341	560	781	2,434	1,038	1,396	1	1	...	...	...	...	1	1	...
Toli	7,507	3,658	3,939	524	199	325	8,121	3,857	4,264	1	1	...	3	3	...	4	4	...
Taripa	...	...	...	...	...	...	...	...	...	250	126	124	...	...	...	250	126	124
Thakupa	...	...	...	...	...	...	...	...	...	259	90	169	...	...	...	259	90	169
Tualipa	...	...	...	...	...	...	...	...	...	66	15	51	...	...	...	66	15	51
Taggpa	...	...	...	...	...	...	...	...	...	215	72	143	...	...	...	215	72	143
Tumapa	...	...	...	...	...	...	...	...	...	93	33	60	...	...	...	93	33	60
Toutary	6,427	3,218	3,209	103	55	48	6,530	3,273	3,257	...	...	...	...	...	...	...	...	...
Tharkhan	8,567	4,350	4,217	863	486	377	9,450	4,836	4,594	...	...	...	...	...	...	...	...	...
Taru	592	501	91	...	...	...	592	501	91	...	...	...	...	...	...	...	...	...
Thaploo	179	108	71	...	...	...	179	108	71	...	...	...	...	...	...	...	...	...
Thallah	189	95	94	...	...	...	189	95	94	...	...	...	...	...	...	...	...	...
Tirimboo	166	84	82	...	...	...	166	84	82	...	...	...	...	...	...	...	...	...
Tamokoo	82	53	29	...	...	...	82	53	29	...	...	...	...	...	...	...	...	...
Tamebi	207	104	103	...	...	...	207	104	103	...	...	...	...	...	...	...	...	...
Tanjo	29	14	15	...	...	...	29	14	15	...	...	...	...	...	...	...	...	...
Tarbavanang	...	...	...	...	...	...	...	...	...	...	...	...	436	230	206	436	230	206
Tarkisb	...	...	...	...	...	...	...	...	...	...	...	...	25	25	...	25	25	...
Tarmal	...	...	...	...	...	...	...	...	...	...	...	...	...	...	...	...	...	...
Tibili	...	...	...	...	...	...	...	...	...	...	...	...	...	...	...	...	...	...
Timboli	...	...	...	200	80	120	200	80	120	...	...	...	...	...	...	...	...	...
Tajhal	...	...	...	10	10	...	10	10	...	...	...	...	...	...	...	...	...	...
Talal	...	...	...	157	35	122	157	35	122	...	...	...	...	...	...	...	...	...
Tarej	...	...	...	824	304	520	824	304	520	...	...	...	...	...	...	...	...	...
Turmasi	...	...	...	45	17	28	45	17	28	...	...	...	...	...	...	...	...	...
Tarind	...	...	...	23	20	3	23	20	3	...	...	...	...	...	...	...	...	...
Tukhal	...	...	...	239	63	176	239	63	176	...	...	...	...	...	...	...	...	...
Takarpa	39	6	33	...	...	...	39	6	33	...	...	...	...	...	...	...	...	...
Takhakpa	...	...	...	...	...	...	...	...	...	30	13	17	...	...	...	30	13	17
Thans	33	22	11	...	...	...	33	22	11	57	18	39	...	...	...	57	18	39
Turkpa	...	...	...	...	...	...	...	...	...	63	18	45	...	...	...	63	18	45
Takaya	...	...	...	...	...	...	...	...	...	19	14	5	...	...	...	19	14	5
Touedar	42	8	39	...	...	...	42	8	39	...	...	...	3	3	...	3	3	...
Takay	184	131	53	...	...	...	184	131	53	...	...	...	...	...	...	...	...	...
Thadu	108	66	42	...	...	...	108	66	42	...	...	...	...	...	...	...	...	...
Tanku	22	15	7	...	...	...	22	15	7	...	...	...	...	...	...	...	...	...
Wahpapa	...	...	...	...	...	...	...	...	...	33	21	12	...	...	...	33	21	12
Wani	...	...	...	...	...	...	...	...	...	4,281	2,142	2,139	...	...	...	4,281	2,142	2,139

TABLE XIII.

Caste, Tribe, Race or Nationality.

Caste, Tribe, Race or Nationality.	Total Population.			Provinces with Districts. Jammu Province. Jammu District.			Udhampur District.			Bhimber District.			Jasrota District.			Punch Jagir.			Bhadarwah Jagir.			Total Jammu Province.		
	Persons.	Males.	Females.	Persons.	Males.	Females.	Persons.	Males.	Females.	Persons.	Males.	Females.	Persons.	Males.	Females.	Persons.	Males.	Females.	Persons.	Males.	Females.	Persons.	Males.	Females.
1	2	3	4	5	6	7	8	9	10	11	12	13	14	15	16	17	18	19	20	21	22	23	24	25
Wanjanpa	504	247	257	...	...	...	...	...	...	...	...	...	...	...	...	...	...	...	...	...	...	...	...	...
Waji	1,313	649	664	...	...	...	...	...	...	...	...	...	...	...	...	...	...	...	...	...	...	...	...	...
Warzab	6	2	4	...			4	1	3	...	...	...	...	...	...	...	...	...	...	...	...	4	1	3
Wain ...	47,747	25,148	22,599	...	...		...	...	...	...	...	...	...	...	...	...	...	...	...	...	...	...	...	...
Wangroo	11,584	10,963	621	...	...	...	...	...	...	...	...	...	...	...	...	...	...	...	...	...	...	...	...	...
Yajho	23	11	12	...	...	...	...	...	...	...	...	...	...	...	...	...	...	...	...	...	...	...	...	...
Yousi	47	47	...	...	...	...	...	...	...	...	...	...	...	...	...	...	...	...	...	...	...	...	...	...
Yoghmapa	10	7	3	...	...	...	...	...	...	...	...	...	...	...	...	...	...	...	...	...	...	...	...	...
Yonsafa	16	12	4	...	...	...	...	...	...	...	...	...	...	...	...	...	...	...	...	...	...	...	...	...
Zaru	402	207	195	...	...	...	...	...	...	...	...	...	...	...	...	...	...	...	...	...	...	...	...	...
Zookals	84	39	45	...	...	...	...	...	...	...	...	...	...	...	...	...	...	...	...	...	...	...	...	...
Zabid	185	75	110	...	...	...	...	...	...	...	...	...	...	...	...	...	...	...	...	...	...	...	...	...
Zakair	15	9	6	...	...	...	...	...	...	...	...	...	...	...	...	...	...	...	...	...	...	...	...	...
Zatah	4	2	2	...	...	...	...	...	...	...	...	...	...	...	...	...	...	...	...	...	...	...	...	...
Zoba	28	10	18	...	...	...	...	...	...	...	...	...	...	...	...	...	...	...	...	...	...	...	...	...
Zaindar	38	18	20	...	...	...	...	...	...	...	...	...	...	...	...	...	...	...	...	...	...	...	...	...
Zarandaty	101	51	50	...	...	...	...	...	...	...	...	...	...	...	...	...	...	...	...	...	...	...	...	...
Zok	3	...	3	...	...	...	...	...	...	...	...	...	...	...	...	...	...	...	...	...	...	...	...	...
Total Christians ...	422	236	186	134	80	56	2	2	...	1	1	...	...	...	...	7	3	4	2	2	...	146	88	58
European	197	106	91	6	5	1	...	...	...	1	1	...	...	...	...	5	1	4	2	2	...	14	9	5
Eurasian ...	23	10	13	4	1	3	1	1	...	...	...	...	...	...	...	...	...	...	...	...	...	5	2	3
Native Christians ...	202	120	82	124	74	50	1	1	...	...	...	...	...	...	...	2	2	...	...	...	...	127	77	50
Unspecified ...	60	36	24	3	...	3	...	...	...	...	...	...	...	...	...	...	...	...	...	...	...	3	...	3

Caste, Tribe, Race or Nationality.	PROVINCES WITH DISTRICTS.																	
	KASHMIR PROVINCE.									FRONTIER DISTRICTS.								
	Khas District.			Muzaffarabad District.			Total Kashmir Province.			Ladakh District.			Gilgit District.			Total Frontier Districts.		
	Persons.	Males.	Females.	Persons.	Males.	Females.	Persons.	Males.	Females.	Persons.	Males.	Females.	Persons.	Males.	Females.	Persons.	Males.	Females.
	26	27	28	29	30	31	32	33	34	35	36	37	38	39	40	41	42	43
Wanjanpa ...	...	...	...	...	...	...	...	...	...	504	247	257	...	...	...	504	247	257
Waji	...	...	...	...	...	...	...	...	...	1,318	649	664	...	...	...	1,313	649	664
Warsab	...	...	...	...	...	...	...	...	...	...	...	...	2	1	1	2	1	1
Wain	47,504	25,058	22,446	243	89	154	47,747	25,148	22,599	...	...	...	...	...	...	...	...	...
Wangroo	980	573	407	10,604	10,300	214	11,584	10,963	621	...	...	...	...	...	...	...	...	...
Yajbo	23	11	12	...	...	...	23	11	12	...	...	...	...	...	...	...	...	...
Youai	47	47	...	...	...	...	47	47	...	...	...	...	...	...	...	...	...	...
Yoghmapa	...	...	...	...	...	...	...	...	...	10	7	3	...	...	...	10	7	[illegible]
Yousafia	...	...	...	...	...	...	...	...	...	16	12	4	...	...	...	16	12	[illegible]
Zaru	402	207	195	...	...	...	402	207	195	...	...	...	...	...	...	...	...	...
Zonkala	84	39	45	...	...	...	84	39	45	...	...	...	...	...	...	...	...	...
Zahid	185	75	110	...	...	...	185	75	110	...	...	...	...	...	...	...	...	...
Zakair	15	9	6	...	...	...	15	9	6	...	...	...	...	...	...	...	...	...
Zatab	4	2	2	...	...	...	4	2	2	...	...	...	...	...	...	...	...	...
Zoba	28	10	18	...	...	...	28	10	18	...	...	...	...	...	...	...	...	...
Zaindar	38	18	20	...	...	...	38	18	20	...	...	...	...	...	...	...	...	...
Zarandaty	...	...	...	...	...	...	...	...	...	...	...	...	101	51	50	101	51	50
Zok	...	...	...	...	...	...	...	...	...	...	...	...	8	...	8	8	...	8
Total Christians ...	235	122	113	8	5	3	243	127	116	5	2	3	28	19	9	33	21	12
European	156	82	74	...	...	...	156	82	74	5	2	3	22	18	9	27	15	12
Eurasion	14	4	10	...	...	...	14	4	10	...	...	...	4	4	...	4	4	...
Native Christians ...	65	36	29	8	5	3	73	41	32	...	...	...	2	2	...	2	2	...
Unspecified ...	44	26	18	8	5	3	52	31	21	3	3	...	2	2	...	5	5	...

TABLE XIV.

CIVIL CONDITION BY AGE FOR SELECTED CASTES.

TABLE XIV.

CIVIL CONDITION BY AGE FOR SELECTED CASTES.

SELECTED CASTE.	UNMARRIED.																			
	TOTAL.		0—5.		5—12.		12—15.		15—20.		20—40.		40 and over.		TOTAL.		0—5.		5—12.	
	Males.	Females.	Males.	Females.	Males.	Females.	Males.	Females.	Males.	Females.	Males.	Females.	Males.	Females.	Males.	Females.	Males.	Females.	Males.	Females.
HINDUS.																				
Brahman ...	44.518	40.524	15,018	15,000	10,507	10,157	11,583	7,989	6,197	5,521	824	1,648	304	208	43.139	37.703	5	10	236	5,155
Fakir ..	3.268	3.007	768	964	873	728	945	810	652	499	...	...	...	...	4.185	4.464	...	...	...	..
Khatri ..	9.523	7.007	2,531	1,668	2,358	1,758	2,316	2,243	2,069	1.338	132		87	.	11.994	9,030	...	..	133	224
Mahajan ...	6.032	5.743	658	2.527	1.719	2,626	343	321	294	259	18	16	..		6,237	6.047	...	...	9	11
Rajput ..	22.018	19.629	10,662	9,567	4,622	4,352	4,249	4,150	2,144	1,560	184	..	217	..	46,727	43.106	...	...	3,230	2.716
MUHAMMADANS.																				
Arab ...	2.351	1.957	668	442	981	853	586	537	171	128	...	...	...	..	3,101	2.805	...	..	5	7
Awan ...	5.062	4.671	1,781	3,183	1,062	723	1,011	688	368	75	152	...	88	..	4.793	4,952	3	...	2	28
Bat ..	4.322	3.949	1,569	1,216	1,613	1,473	985	1,058	150	156	10	16	.	...	5.963	4.631	...	...	41	11
Hashkan ..	4.511	4.301	2,421	2,072	1,681	1,721	317	405	92	103	..	...	.	.	6.322	7,109	...	..	...	...
Chogata ...	4.521	4.313	1.785	2,139	1,200	907	941	852	535	416	...	...	..	...	7.916	7.521	...	...	3	7
Dar	11.511	10 412	4,629	4,313	4,615	3,717	2,283	2.101	293	283	.	...		..	21 291	19,371	..	...	101	115
Kashmiri	8.665	8.894	5,967	6,084	1,865	1.772	621	636	382	399	..	...	...	...	12.811	13.965	..	...	...	..
Mali ...	4.651	4.217	2,170	2,078	2,001	1,686	292	231	131	161	57	51	...	.	8.522	4.991	...	.	...	2
Maliar ..	11 344	9.789	5,388	4,006	2,558	3,513	2,051	1.219	1,023	416	324	5	.	...	13.203	10.224	..	..	12	47
Sayad ...	9,818	8.445	2,867	1.862	3,505	3,366	2,306	2,202	1,137	952	1	...	.	...	14.299	13.277	..	..	187	150
Shaikh ...	10.150	9,260	6,967	4,854	1,625	2,596	920	1,245	606	518	32	44	..	...	16.239	17.091	...	.	108	92
Tain ...	8.313	7.161	3,828	3,307	2,387	2,102	1,447	1,217	495	383	156	142	...	.	12 686	10,701	...	...	9	11

TABLE XIV.

Civil Condition by Age for Selected Castes.

Married 12–15		Married 15–20		Married 20–40		Married 40 and over		Widowed Total		Widowed 0–5		Widowed 5–12		Widowed 12–15		Widowed 15–20		Widowed 20–40		Widowed 40 and over	
Males	Females	Males	Females	Males	Females	Males	Females	Males	Females	Males	Females	Males	Females	Males	Females	Males	Females	Males	Females	Males	Females
HINDUS																					
2,369	3,305	10,438	[illegible]	[illegible]	10,789	15,186	12,578	10.502	9.483	...	...	[illegible]	[illegible]	320	[illegible]	1,065	1,191	2,722	2,464	6,065	4,925
831	797	1,010	1,081	797	717	[illegible]	[illegible]	1.863	1.280		...		...	94	106	146	326	614	652	712	492
332	384	1,168	912	3,447	3,269	[illegible]	[illegible]	6.412	3.921	...	...		...	28	36	1,173	1.035	1,775	1,436	3,436	1,411
1,550	1,318	1,117	627	[illegible]	[illegible]	2,174	[illegible]	1.562	1.598		...		...	7	1	620	725	526	617	310	555
3,425	5,249	8,082	6,053	9,760	8,61	20,223	19,77	17.147	17.920	..	...	167	148	1.023	868	2,626	2,222	3,548	3,212	6,780	11,470
MUHAMMADANS																					
181	145	257	261	671	502	1,987	1,890	883	857	...	..	.	..	71	42	232	197	315	325	255	208
16	679	718	959	2,122	1,095	1,342	1,071	2.446	656		...	..	...	...	1	11	5	718	144	1,717	506
284	270	518	530	2,039	1,021	2,081	1,897	2.442	2 550	..	...	...	...	26	132	122	351	204	185	2,000	1,582
187	197	297	667	1,547	1,031	4,291	1,974	3 267	1.073	...	...	...	...	83	97	547	287	961	512	1,676	177
122	114	1,915	1,803	2,579	2,305	3,247	3,287	2,522	2 783	...	..	...	...	35	21	355	813	907	504	625	1,445
1,247	1,127	3,572	3,117	11,417	9,522	4,954	5,036	8.475	9.544	..	..	...	.	126	113	1,735	1,657	3,213	2,922	3,431	5,152
510	567	1,595	1,713	3,516	3,727	7,181	7,338	5.959	6.990	...	...	...	...	6	1	717	773	1,285	1,464	3,951	4,752
210	187	1,102	651	2,017	1,307	2,184	1,918	826	914	.		...	...	7	5	67	82	302	297	420	580
1,012	1,328	2,008	1,822	3,932	3,620	5,003	3,467	4 154	2 931		..	..	...	532	347	769	537	1,028	1,094	1,825	958
719	547	1,413	1,274	6,575	5,586	6,065	5,791	4.322	3.230	.	..	5	5	148	91	898	748	957	798	2,279	1,586
410	372	1,078	1,062	6,906	6,079	7,728	9,482	6.888	7.251	.	...	23	21	119	110	424	439	1,592	1,682	4,730	8,099
2,211	1,007	2,113	1,502	4,411	4,305	3,942	2,976	4 149	4.737	..	...	...	...	547	413	963	803	1,102	947	1,537	2,574

TABLE XV.

OCCUPATION OR MEANS OF LIVELIHOOD.

TABLE XV.

Occupation or Means of Livelihood.

Class.	Order.	Occupation or Means of Livelihood	TOTAL STATE. Total workers and dependents.	Actual workers. Total. Males.	Actual workers. Total. Females.	Actual workers. Partially agriculturists. Males.	Actual workers. Partially agriculturists. Females.	Dependents both Sexes.
1	2	3	4	5	6	7	8	9
		GRAND TOTAL	2,905.578	823.535	79,002	11.096	341	2,002,741
A.—GOVERNMENT.	I.—ADMINISTRATION.	TOTAL ORDER I.—ADMINISTRATION ...	15.429	6.092	106	275	...	9.291
		Total Sub-order 1	37	21	...	1	..	16
		Service of the Imperial Government and Local Administration.						
		1. Agent to the Governor-General	...	..	.	...	...	---
		2. Officers of Government and their families	...	...	...	...	..	...
		3. Clerks, Inspectors, etc., and their families	...	...	...	...	...	..
		4. Constables, messengers, warders, and unspecified	37	21	..	1		16
		Total Sub-order 1—A.	4.524	1.710	..	70		2.814
		Service of the Tabulating State						
		a. Chiefs, nobles and their families	311	3	..	...	–	308
		b. Darbar officials, Inspectors and Deputy Inspectors. Police.	283	98	...	...		185
		c. Wazir Wazárats and Tahsildárs	370	133		8	..	237
		d. Police Constables	3,560	1.476	...	62	...	2,084
		Total Sub-order 2	2 198	1.117	106	46	...	975
		Service of Local and Municipal Bodies.						
		5. Inspecting and supervising officials	43	30	...	...	...	13
		6. Clerical establishment	533	429	...	19	...	404
		7. Menials other than scavengers	1,322	658	106	27	...	558
		Total Sub-order 3 ..	8.670	3.184	...	158	..	5.486
		Village Service						
		8. Head men not shown as agriculturists	785	406	...	1	...	379
		9. Accountants not shown as agriculturists	18	11	...	..	...	7
		10. Watchmen and other village servants	7.887	2,787		157	...	5.100
	II.—DEFENCE.	TOTAL ORDER II—DEFENCE	11.722	7.625	161	264	3	3.936
		Total Sub-order 4	1.436	452	161	22	3	523
		Army (Imperial).						
		11. Military Officers	65	8	.	...	...	57
		12. Non-Commissioned Officers and Privates...	3	3	..	...	...	...
		13. Followers	201	34	161	4	3	6
		14. Military administrative establishment			..	..	...	...
		15. Military Police, etc.	452	32	...		...	420
		16. Military service unspecified	715	375	...	18	..	340
		Total Sub-order 4 A	10.286	7 173	..	242		3.113
		Army (Tabulating State).						
		a. Imperial Service Troops. — Officers	235	127	..	...	..	108
		Imperial Service Troops. — Non-Commissioned Officers, Private, etc.	7.432	5.409	...	123	.	2.023
		b. State Troops other than Imperial Service Troops — Officers	1.672	1.054	...	93	...	618
		State Troops other than Imperial Service Troops — Non-Commissioned Officers, Private, etc	947	583	...	26		364
		Total Sub-order 5	...	..	...	..	...	...
		Navy and Marine						
		17. Naval Officers	...	...	...	...	...	...
		18. Naval Engineers, Warrant Officers and Seamen ...	...		...	..	...	...
		19. Naval Administrative Staff	...		...	...	...	... -

TABLE XV.

OCCUPATION OR MEANS OF LIVELIHOOD.

JAMMU PROVINCE.						KASHMIR PROVINCE					
Total workers and dependents.	Actual workers. Total.		Actual workers. Partially agriculturists.		Dependents both sexes.	Total workers and dependents.	Actual workers. Total.		Actual workers. Partially agriculturists.		Dependents both sexes.
	Males.	Females.	Males.	Females.			Males.	Females.	Males.	Females.	
10	11	12	13	14	15	16	17	18	19	20	21
1,521,307	431.712	36.305	8,260	165	1,053.290	11.57.394	3.34.038	41.018	2.739	150	722.338
6,727	2.843	33	223	...	3.851	7.854	2.725	73	51		5,056
37	21	...	1	...	16	..			...	..	...
...	...	...	...	...	...		..	...	..	..	...
...	...	...	...	...	...	...	...	...	...	..	...
...	...	...	...	...	...	...	...	..	...	..	...
37	21	...	1	...	16	...	...	.	..	..	...
2,272	958	..	63	...	1.314	2.215	724	...	7	..	1,491
311	3	...	...	...	308	...			...	.	...
210	64	...	..	...	146	71	32	...	...	..	89
156	52	...	6	...	104	212	79	...	3	.	133
1,595	830	...	58	...	756	1,932	613	..	4	...	1,819
1.179	586	33	44	..	560	1.018	531	73	2	...	414
43	30	...	...	...	13	...	...	..	..	...	...
290	120	...	17	...	170	542	309	...	2	...	233
846	436	33	27	...	377	476	222	73	..	...	181
3,239	1.278	...	115		1,981	4.621	1.470	.	42	.	3,151
35	19	...	1	...	16	...	...	...	...	...	...
18	11	...	...	...	7	...	...	...	...	...	...
3,186	1,248	...	114	...	1,938	4,621	1,470	..	42	...	3,151
8,109	4,795	159	245	3	3.155	1.505	821	.	15	...	684
1.429	450	159	22	3	820	..	...	.	..	..	..
60	6	...	...	..	54	..	...	...	...	...	...
3	3	..	...	...	...	...	..	...	...	..	...
199	84	159	4	3	6	...	..	...	...	...	...
...	...	...	...	...	...	...	..	...	...	...	...
452	32	...	...	...	420	..				...	
715	375	..	15	...	340	...					
6,650	4.345	..	223	...	2.335	1.505	821	..	15	...	684
150	65	...	...	...	85	36	23	..	..	...	12
4,065	2,701	...	105	...	1,324	1,392	767	...	14	...	625
1,529	959	...	92	...	570	62	24	.	1	...	36
916	560	...	26	...	356	15	7	..	...	..	8
...	...	..	..	...	...		...	...	..	...	...
...	...	...	...	...	...	.	..	..	...	...	...
...	...	...	...	...	...	...	...	...	.	.	...
...	...	...	...	...	...	...	...	...	...	...	...

TABLE XV.

Occupation or Means of Livelihood.

Class.	Order.	Occupation or means of livelihood.	FRONTIER DISTRICTS. Total workers and dependents.	Actual workers. Total. Males.	Actual workers. Total. Females.	Actual workers. Partially agriculturists. Males.	Actual workers. Partially agriculturists. Females.	Dependents both sexes.
1	2	3	22	23	24	25	26	27
		GRAND TOTAL	226.877	58.065	1.679	97	6	167,113
A.—GOVERNMENT.	I.—ADMINISTRATION.	TOTAL ORDER I.—ADMINISTRATION	848	464	.	1	...	384
		TOTAL SUB-ORDER 1.	...	...	...	...	...	...
		Service of the Imperial Government and Local Administration.						
		1. Agent to the Governor-General	...	...	...	...	...	...
		2. Officers of Government and their families	...	...	...	...	...	...
		3. Clerks, Inspectors, etc., and their families ...	...	...	...	...	...	...
		4. Constables, messengers, warders and unspecified ...	...	...	.	...	...	...
		TOTAL SUB-ORDER 1 A.	37	28	...	...	...	9
		Service of Tabulating State.						
		a. Chiefs, nobles and their families	...	...	...	...	...	...
		b. Darbar officials, Inspectors and Deputy Inspectors, Police.	2	2	...	...	...	...
		c. Wazir Wazárats and Tahsildars	2	2	...	...	...	..
		d. Police Constables	33	24	...	...	...	9
		TOTAL SUB-ORDER 2	1	...	...	...	...	1
		Service of Local and Municipal Bodies.						
		5. Inspecting and supervising officials	...	...	...	...	...	...
		6. Clerical establishment	1	...	...	..	...	1
		7. Menials other than scavengers	...	...	...	...	...	...
		TOTAL SUB-ORDER 3	810	436	...	1	...	374
		Village Service.						
		8. Head men not shown as agriculturists	750	387	...	..	...	363
		9. Accountants not shown as agriculturists	...	..	...	...	...	...
		10. Watchmen and other village servants	60	49	...	1	...	11
	II.—DEFENCE.	TOTAL ORDER II.—DEFENCE	2.108	2,009	2	4	...	97
		TOTAL SUB-ORDER 4	7	2	2	...	...	3
		Army—Imperial.						
		11. Military Officers	5	2	...	...	...	3
		12. Non-Commissioned Officers and Privates...	...	...	...	...	...	...
		13. Followers	2	...	2	...	...	...
		14. Military administrative establishment	...	...	...	..	...	...
		15. Military Police, etc.	...	...	..	...	...	...
		16. Military Service unspecified	...	...	...	...	...	...
		TOTAL SUB-ORDER 4 A	2.101	2,007	..	4	...	94
		Army (Tabulating State).						
		a. Imperial Service Troops. { Officers	40	39	...	...	...	10
		{ Non-Commissioned Officers, Private, etc.	1,955	1,681	...	4	...	74
		b. State Troops other than Imperial Service Troops. { Officers	81	71	..	...	...	10
		{ Non-Commissioned Officers, Private, etc.	16	16	...	...	...	...
		TOTAL SUB-ORDER	...	...	...	...	...	...
		Navy and Marine.						
		17. Naval Officers	...	...	...	...	...	...
		18. Naval Engineers, Warrant Officers and Seamen ...	...	...	...	...	...	...
		19. Naval Administrative Staff	...	...	...	..	...	...

TABLE XV.

OCCUPATION OR MEANS OF LIVELIHOOD.

JAMMU CITY.						SRINAGAR CITY.					
Total workers and dependents.	ACTUAL WORKERS.				Dependents both sexes.	Total workers and dependents.	ACTUAL WORKERS.				Dependents both sexes.
	Total.		Partially agriculturists.				Total.		Partially agriculturists.		
	Males.	Females.	Males.	Females.			Males.	Females.	Males.	Females.	
28	29	30	31	32	33	34	35	36	37	38	39
36,130	**16,519**	**1,556**	**479**	**3**	**18,055**	**1.22.618**	**40.226**	**14,559**	**103**	**3**	**67.833**
947	**389**	...	**27**	..	**558**	**2,936**	**1.029**	**54**	**5**	...	**1.853**
...	..	...	...	...	..	..	...	...	...	...	...
...	...	...	...	...	...	...	..	..	...	...	...
...	...	...	...	...	...	...	...	...	...	...	...
...	..	...	...	...	...	...	...	...	..	...	...
..	...	..	...	...	...	...	...	...	...	...	...
591	**301**	...	**26**	...	**290**	**1,678**	**427**	...	**3**	...	**1,251**
... 13	... 5	..	...	...	... 8	... 53	... 24	...	...	...	... 29
5	2	...	...	...	3	135	47	...	...	...	88
573	294	...	26	...	270	1,450	356	...	3	...	1,134
307	**68**	...	...	...	**239**	**775**	**432**	**54**	**2**	.	**289**
... 138	... 40	...	...	...	... 98	... 333	... 218	...	...	...	... 115
160	28	...	...	...	141	442	214	54	2	...	174
49	**20**	...	**1**	...	**29**	**483**	**170**	..	...	...	**313**
...	...	...	...	...	...	...	...	...	...	...	...
...	...	...	...	...	...	...	...	...	...	...	...
49	20	...	1	...	29	483	170	...	...	...	313
3,062	**2,463**	...	**28**	...	**599**	**1,239**	**662**	...	**14**	...	**577**
229	**107**	...	**4**	...	**122**	.	...	...	...	...	...
...	...	...	...	...		...	..	...	...	..	...
...	...	...	...	...	...	..	..	...	.	...	...
...	...	...	...	...	...	...	...	...	...	..	...
...	...	...	...	...	...	..	...	...	.	..	...
...	...	...	...	...	...	...	...	...	...	..	...
220	107	...	4	...	122	..	...	...	...	...	...
2,833	**2,356**	...	**24**	...	**477**	**1,239**	**662**		**14**	.	**577**
...	...	...	...	...	...	3	2	...	..	...	1
1,484	1,108	...	24	...	376	1,236	660	..	14	...	576
2	2	...	...	...	...	...		...	...	..	...
1,347	1,216	...	...	...	101	..	..	...	...	...	...
...	...	...	..	...	...	...		..	..	...	...
...	...	...	...	...	...	...	...	...	...	...	...
...	...	...	...	...	...	...	...	...	...	...	...
...	...	...	...	...	...	...	...	...	...	...	...

TABLE XV.

Occupation or Means of Livelihood

Class.	Order.	Occupation or means of livelihood.	TOTAL STATE. Total workers and dependants.	Actual workers. Total. Males.	Actual workers. Total. Females.	Actual workers. Partially agriculturists. Males.	Actual workers. Partially agriculturists. Females.	Dependants both sexes.
1	2	3	4	5	6	7	8	9
A.—GOVERNMENT—concld.	III.—Service of Native and Foreign States.	TOTAL ORDER III.—SERVICE OF NATIVE AND FOREIGN STATES.	21,194	8,641	4	276	...	12,549
		Total Sub-order 6	20,743	8,443	4	275	...	12,296
		Civil Officers of State other than the Tabulating State						
		20. Darbār officials, etc.	20,743	8,443	4	275	...	12,296
		Total Sub-order 7	451	198	...	1	...	253
		Military Service of States other than the Tabulating State.						
		a. Imperial Service Troops Officers	17	10	...	...	...	7
		Non-Commissioned Officers, privates, etc.	430	186	...	1	...	244
		b. State Troops other than Imperial Service Troops Officers.	...	...	...	...	...	...
		Non-Commissioned Officers, privates, etc. ..	4	2	...	...	...	2
B.—PASTURE AND AGRICULTURE.	IV.—Provision and care of animals.	TOTAL ORDER IV.—PROVISION AND CARE OF ANIMALS.	34,483	11,253	1,401	421	15	21,799
		Total Sub-order 8	34,347	11,229	1,400	421	15	21,718
		Stock Breeding and Dealing.						
		25. Horse, mule and ass breeders, dealers and attendants ...	756	202	...	1	...	554
		26. Cattle breeders and dealers and commissariat farm establishment.	8,235	2,303	234	157	8	5,698
		27. Herdsmen	11,363	4,280	765	126	6	6,338
		28 Elephant catchers	...	...	...	...	...	...
		29 Camel breeders and attendants	200	77	1	2	..	122
		30. Sheep and goat breeders and dealers	6,297	1,824	269	33	...	4,204
		31. Shepherds and goat herds	7,469	2,539	131	102	1	4,799
		32. Pig breeders and dealers and swine herds	7	4	...	...	...	3
		Total Sub-order 9	136	54	1	...	...	81
		Training and care of Animals.						
		33. Veterinary Surgeons, farriers, etc	30	10	...	...	...	20
		34. Horse and elephant trainers, etc.	105	44	.	...	...	61
		35 Vermin and animal catchers	1	...	1	...	.	...
	V.—Agriculture.	TOTAL ORDER V.—AGRICULTURE	2,184,860	585,368	24,386	359	17	1,575,106
		Total Sub-order 10	2,162,371	575,103	23,323	175	..	1,563,945
		Landholders and Tenants.						
		36. 1. Owners (cultivating)	313,579	101,251	4,031	99	...	208,597
		2. Owners (rent receivers)	124,879	22,350	294	12	..	102,235
		3 Mortgagees (cultivating)	1,060	636	11	2	...	413
		4. Mortgagees (rent receivers)	74	5	21	..	...	48
		5. Occupancy tenants (rent receivers)	417	82	89	...	..	246
		37. 1. Occupancy tenants (cultivating)	941,586	260,539	10,784	3	...	670,263
		2. Tenants-at-will	336,184	75,191	2,973	4	...	258,020
		3. Tenants-at-will (rent receivers)	9,668	7,438	21	...	...	2,209
		4. Partners in cultivation	3,304	504	11	...	...	2,789
		5. Sub-tenants as Lichbaits, etc.	431,320	107,107	5,088	55	.	319,125
		Total Sub-order 11	17,901	8,764	858	132	17	8,279
		Agricultural Labourers						
		38. Farm servants	7,443	4,803	509	12	5	2,131
		39. Field labourers	10,458	3,961	349	120	12	6,148
		40. Taungya or jhum cultivators	..	...	...	...	...	...
		Total Sub-order 12	2,934	851	205	39	...	1,678
		Growers of special products.						
		41. Cinchona plantations, owners, managers and superior staff	..	...	...	...	...	...
		42. Cinchona plantations, labourers and other subordinate,	...	...	...	...	...	...
		43. Coffee plantations, owners, managers and superior staff	...	...	...	...	...	...
		44. Coffee plantations, labourers and other subordinates ...	...	...	...	...	...	...
		45. Indigo factories, owners, managers and superior staff ...	...	...	...	...	...	...
		46. Indigo factories, labourers and other subordinates ...	...	...	...	...	...	...
		47. Tea plantations, owners, managers and superior staff ...	...	...	...	...	...	...

TABLE XV.

OCCUPATION OR MEANS OF LIVELIHOOD

JAMMU PROVINCE.						KASHMIR PROVINCE.					
Total workers and dependents.	Actual workers.				Dependents both sexes.	Total workers and dependents.	Actual workers.				Dependents both sexes.
	Total.		Partially agriculturists.				Total.		Partially agriculturists.		
	Males.	Females.	Males.	Females.			Males.	Females.	Males.	Females.	
10	11	12	13	14	15	16	17	18	19	20	21
13,172	**5,910**	...	**207**	...	**7,262**	**7,473**	**2,403**	...	**55**	...	**5,070**
12,891	**5,798**	...	**206**	...	**7,093**	**7,303**	**2,317**	...	**55**	...	**4,986**
12,891	5,798	..	206	...	7,093	7,303	2,317	...	55	...	4,986
281	**112**	...	**1**	...	**169**	**170**	**86**	...	...	...	**84**
16	9	...	...	...	7	1	1	...	...	...	...
261	101	...	1	...	160	169	85	..	...	...	84
...	...	...	...	..	..	..	...	...	...	...	...
4	2	...	...	...	2	...	...	...	...	...	...
20,949	**7,450**	**626**	**209**	**3**	**12,873**	**12,589**	**3,588**	**727**	**200**	**9**	**8,274**
20,840	**7,407**	**625**	**209**	**3**	**12,808**	**12,562**	**3,577**	**727**	**209**	**9**	**8,258**
682	164	...	...	...	518	74	38	...	1	...	36
1,765	523	143	28	2	1,099	6,460	1,771	91	129	6	4,508
7,105	3,049	310	74	1	3,746	3,345	997	407	49	2	1,941
...	...	...	...	...	...	...	...	...	...	...	...
199	77	1	2	...	121	1	...	...	...	...	1
4,875	1,562	60	26	..	3,253	1,422	262	209	7	...	951
6,207	2,028	111	79	...	4,068	1,260	509	20	23	1	731
7	4	...	...	...	3	...	...	...	...	...	...
109	**43**	**1**	...	...	**65**	**27**	**11**	...	...	...	**16**
27	9	..	...	...	18	3	1	..	..	...	2
81	34	...	...	...	47	24	10	...	...	..	14
1	...	1	...	...	..	.	...	...	...	..	...
1,151,690	**305,358**	**14,939**	**334**	**17**	**831,393**	**820,298**	**229,510**	**8,899**	**25**	...	**581,889**
1,132,760	**296,235**	**14,104**	**175**	.	**822,421**	**816,576**	**228,493**	**8,692**		.	**579,391**
255,813	75,849	3,899	99	..	176,065	2,842	1,073	24	...	...	1,745
15,775	4,966	200	12	.	10,609	26	8	.	...	...	18
1,060	636	11	2	...	413	...	...	...	...	..	...
74	5	21	...		48	..	...	.	...	...	...
417	82	89	...	...	246	...	...	...	...	...	...
206,836	50,861	2,439	3	.	153,536	734,750	209,678	8,345	..	...	516,727
208,533	48,797	2,316	4	..	157,420	79,218	17,724	323		...	61,171
9,628	7,428	21	...	..	2,179	40	10	...	..	...	30
3,304	504	11	...	..	2,789	...	...	...	.	...	...
431,320	107,107	5,088	55	...	319,125	...	...	..	.	...	...
17,673	**8,645**	**827**	**130**	**17**	**8,201**	**175**	**80**	**19**	**2**	...	**76**
7,215	4,684	478	10	5	2,053	175	80	19	2	...	76
10,458	3,961	349	120	12	6,148	..	..	..	...	...	...
...	...	..	...	...	...	...	...	..	...	...	...
361	**119**	**8**	**16**	...	**234**	**2,489**	**706**	**188**	**23**	...	**1,595**
...	...	...	...	...	...	...	...	...	...	...	...
...	...	...	...	...	...	...	...	...	...	...	...
...	...	...	...	...	...	...	...	...	...	...	...
...	...	...	...	...	...	...	...	...	...	...	...
...	...	...	...	...	...	...	...	...	...	...	...
...	...	...	...	...	...	...	...	...	...	...	...
...	...	...	...	...	...	...	...	...	...	...	...

TABLE XV.

Occupation or Means of Livelihood.

Class.	Order.	Occupation or Means of Livelihood.	FRONTIER DISTRICTS. Total workers and dependents.	Actual Workers. Total. Males.	Actual Workers. Total. Females.	Actual Workers. Partially agriculturists. Males.	Actual Workers. Partially agriculturists. Females.	Dependents both sexes.
1	2	3	22	23	24	25	26	27
A.—GOVERNMENT—concld.	III.—Service of Native and Foreign States.	TOTAL ORDER III.—SERVICE OF NATIVE AND FOREIGN STATES.	549	328	4	14	..	217
		Total Sub-order 6	549	328	4	14	...	217
		Civil Officers of State other than the Tabulating State.						
		20. Darbár officials, etc.	549	328	4	14	...	217
		Total Sub-order 7	...	...	..		...	...
		Military Service of States other than the Tabulating State.						
		a. Imperial Service Troops Officers	...	...	...	...	...	...
		Non-Commissioned Officers, privates, etc.... ...	...	...	..	...	...	...
		b. State Troops other than Imperial Service Troops Officers.	...	...	...	...	...	...
		Non-Commissioned Officers, privates, etc.... ...	...	...	...	...	...	...
B.—PASTURE AND AGRICULTURE.	IV.—Provision and care of animals.	TOTAL ORDER IV.—PROVISION AND CARE OF ANIMALS	945	245	48	3	3	652
		Total Sub-order 8	945	245	48	3	3	652
		Stock Breeding and Dealing.						
		25. Horse, mule and ass breeders, dealers and attendants ...	...	...	...	...	...	...
		26. Cattle breeders and dealers and commissariat farm establishment.	10	9	...	..	...	1
		27. Herdsmen	933	234	48	3	3	651
		28. Elephant catchers	...	...	...	...	...	...
		29. Camel breeders, dealers and attendants	...	...	...	...	...	...
		30. Sheep and goat breeders and dealers	...	...	...	...	...	...
		31. Shepherds and goat herds	2	2	...	...	...	...
		32. Pig breeders and dealers and swine herds	...	...	...	...	...	...
		Total Sub-order 9	...	...	...	...	...	...
		Training and care of animals.						
		33. Veterinary Surgeons, farriers, etc.	...	...	...	..	...	....
		34. Horses and elephant trainers, etc.	...	...	...	..	...	...
		35. Vermin and animal catchers	...	..	...	...	...	...
	V.—Agriculture.	TOTAL ORDER V.—AGRICULTURE	212,572	50,440	548	..	...	161,884
		Total Sub-order 10	212,735	50,375	527	...	.	161,833
		Landholders and Tenants.						
		36. 1. Owners (cultivating)	55,224	24,329	108	...	..	30,787
		2. Owners (rent receivers)	109,078	17,376	85	...	..	91,617
		3. Mortgagees (cultivating)	...	...	...	...	...	...
		4. Mortgagees (rent receivers)	...	...	...	...	...	...
		5. Occupancy tenants (rent receivers)	...	...	...	...	...	...
	37. 1. Occupancy tenants (cultivating)		...	...	...	...	..	...
		2. Tenants-at-will	48,433	8,670	334	...	..	39,429
		3. Tenants-at-will (rent receivers)	...	...	...	...	...	.
		4. Partners in cultivation	...	...	..	...	...	...
		5. Sub-tenants as Lichhains etc.	...	...	...	...	...	...
		Total Sub-order 11	53	39	12	..	...	2
		Agricultural Labourers.						
		38. Farm servants	53	39	12	.	..	2
		39. Field labourers	...	...	...		...	...
		40. Taungya or jhum cultivators	...	...	...	...	...	...
		Total Sub-order 12 ...	84	26	9	..	...	49
		Growers of special products.						
		41. Cinchona plantations, owners, managers and superior staff	...	...	.	...	.	...
		42. Cinchona plantations, labourers and other subordinates	...	...	...	...	...	...
		43. Coffee plantations, owners, managers and superior staff	...	...	...	...	...	...
		44. Coffee plantations, labourers and other subordinates ...	...	...	...	...	...	...
		45. Indigo factories; owners managers and superior staff ...	...	...	...	...	..	...
		46. Indigo factories, labourers and other subordinates ...	...	...	...	...	...	...
		47. Tea plantations, owners, managers and superior staff ...	..	...	...	...	...	...

TABLE XV.

Occupation or Means of Livelihood.

JAMMU CITY.						SRINAGAR CITY.					
Total workers and dependents.	Actual workers. Total. Males.	Actual workers. Total. Females.	Actual workers. Partially agriculturists. Males.	Actual workers. Partially agriculturists. Females.	Dependents both sexes.	Total workers and dependents.	Actual workers. Total. Males.	Actual workers. Total. Females.	Actual workers. Partially agriculturists. Males.	Actual workers. Partially agriculturists. Females.	Dependents both sexes.
28	29	30	31	32	33	34	35	36	37	38	39
8,006	3,483	...	153		4,522	5,142	1,403	...	23		3,739
8,006	3,483		153	...	4,522	5,142	1,403	...	23	...	3,739
8,005	3,483		153	...	4,522	5,142	1,403		23	...	3,739
						...					...
...			...	...		...		...	...	...	...
...	...	...	...	...		...	...	...		...	...
...	...	...	...	...	...						...
175	35	90	3	1	50	41	21	2		...	18
121	17	90	3	1	14	33	18	2	...	...	13
...		...	...	...		31	16	...		...	13
11	8	...	1	...	3	...	...	...	...	...	...
99	5	90	...	1	4	2	...	2	...	...	...
11	4	...	2	...	7	...	...	...	...	...	...
...		...	...	...			...	...	...	...	...
...	...	...	...	...		...	...		...	...	...
...	...	...	...	...			...			...	...
54	18	...	...	...	36	8	3	...		...	5
14	7			...	7	3	1	...			3
40	11		...	...	29	5	2	...			8
	...	...		...			...	...			...
1,398	958	27	89	...	413	4,506	1,553	368	3		2,565
1,300	926	24	86	...	350	2,722	1,045	213	...	...	1,464
819	637	6	86	...	176	123	48	4		...	71
2	...	2	...	...	...	...		...	...	...	...
1	1	...	...	...					...	...	...
...	...	...	...	...		...	...		...	...	...
34	5	...	...	...	29	...	...	...	...	...	...
435	274	16	...	...	145	2,509	997	209	...	...	1,898
...	...	...	...	...	...	...	...	...	...	...	...
9	9	...	...	...	...	...	...	...	...	...	...
3	...	3	...	...		...		...		...	...
3	...	3	...	...	...	...	...	...	...		...
...	...	...		...	...	...		...	...		...
30	15	...		...	15	1,275	350	155	3	...	770
...	...	...	...	...	...	...	...	...	...	...	...
...	...	...	...	...	...	...	...	...	...	...	...
...	...	...	...	...	...	...	...	...	...	...	...
...	...	...	...	...	...	...	...	...	...	...	...
...	...	...	...	...	...	...	...	...	...	...	...

TABLE XV.

OCCUPATION OR MEANS OF LIVELIHOOD.

Class.	Order.	Occupation or means of livelihood.	TOTAL STATE. Total workers and dependants.	Actual workers. Total. Males.	Actual workers. Total. Females.	Actual workers. Partially agriculturists. Males.	Actual workers. Partially agriculturists. Females.	Dependants both sexes.
1	2	3	4	5	6	7	8	9
B.—PASTURE AND AGRICULTURE—concld.	V.—AGRICULTURE—concld.	48. Tea plantations, labourers and other subordinate staff	1	...	1	...		...
		49. Betel, vine and areca-nut growers	19	3	...	...	...	16
		50. Cardamom and pepper growers	...	...	...	...	...	...
		51. Cocoanut growers	...	...	...	...	...	...
		52. Fruit and vegetable growers	2.493	746	175	39	...	1.572
		53. Miscellaneous	421	102	29	...	...	290
		TOTAL SUB-ORDER 13	1,654	650	...	13	...	1.004
		Agricultural training and supervision and forests.						
		54. Directors of agriculture and their staff	125	74	...	...	...	51
		55. Agricultural chemists and experts	2	1	...	...	...	1
		56. Agents and managers of landed estates (not planters)	...	...	...	...	...	...
		57. Clerks, bailiffs, petty rent collectors, etc.	...	...	...	...	...	...
		58. Forest officers	115	52	...	1	...	63
		59. Forest rangers, guards, peons	1.412	523	...	12	...	889
C.—PERSONAL SERVICE.	VI.—PERSONAL HOUSEHOLD AND SANITARY SERVICE.	TOTAL ORDER VI.—PERSONAL, HOUSEHOLD AND SANITARY SERVICES.	58.427	22.758	3.195	952	23	32.474
		TOTAL SUB-ORDER 14	55,627	21.925	2.799	906	23	30.903
		Personal and Domestic Services.						
		60. Barbers	14.342	4.768	165	509	14	9,409
		61. Cooks	1.577	808	78	1	...	691
		62. Door-keepers, etc.	113	59	...	...	...	54
		63. Grooms, coachmen, dog-boys, etc.	432	220	1	7	...	211
		64. Indoor servants	26.046	11.731	1.592	178	5	12,723
		65. Washermen	5.388	1,823	239	158	3	3.326
		66. Water carriers	7.202	2.291	707	51	1	4.204
		67. Shampooers	8	4	...	...	...	4
		68. Miscellaneous and unspecified	519	221	17	2	...	281
		TOTAL SUB-ORDER 15	85	26	...	...	...	59
		Non-domestic entertainment.						
		69. Hotel, lodging-house, bar, or refreshment-room keepers		...	...	...	...	
		70. Rest-house, Serai, bath-house, etc., owners and managers	5	1	...	...	...	4
		71. Club Secretaries, Managers, Stewards, etc.	80	25	...	...	...	55
		TOTAL SUB-ORDER 16	2.715	807	396	46	...	1.512
		Sanitation.						
		72. Sanitary officers of Government and establishments	30	3	4	...	...	23
		73. Sanitary Inspectors, Local and Municipal	10	1	...	...	...	9
		74. Sweepers and scavengers	2.562	762	388	46	...	1.412
		75. Dust and sweeping contractors	113	41	4	...	...	68
D.—PREPARATION AND SUPPLY OF MATERIAL SUBSTANCES.	VII.—FOOD, DRINK AND STIMULANTS.	TOTAL ORDER VII.—FOOD, DRINK AND STIMULANTS.	76.784	24.319	3.270	1.238	26	49.195
		TOTAL SUB-ORDER 17	29.208	8.407	1.092	412	8	19.709
		Provision of Animal Food						
		76. Butchers and slaughterers	899	288	9	1	...	602
		77. Cheese makers and sellers	...	...	...	...	...	...
		78. Cow and buffalo keepers, and milk and butter sellers	17.672	5.061	833	170	8	11.778
		79. Fishermen and fish-curers	2,558	666	57	86	...	1.835
		80. Fish dealers	173	54	48	...	...	71
		81. Fowl and egg dealers	33	7	1	...	...	25
		82. Ghee preparers and sellers	5.430	1.538	141	143	...	3.751
		83. Collectors of edible birds' nests	...	...	...	...	...	...
		84. Miscellaneous	2.443	793	3	12	...	1.647
		TOTAL SUB-ORDER 18	38.679	12.616	2.082	744	14	24.081
		Provision of vegetable food.						
		85. Biscuit factories; owners, managers, and superior staff		...	...	...	...	...
		86. Biscuit factories; operatives and other subordinates	...	...	...	...	...	...
		87. Flour mills; owners, managers and superior staff	...	...	...	...	...	...
		88. Flour mills: operatives and other subordinates	...	...	...	...	...	...
		89. Oil mills: owners, managers and superior staff	...	...	...	...	...	...
		90. Oil mills: operatives and other subordinates	...	...	...	...	...	...

TABLE XV.

OCCUPATION OR MEANS OF LIVELIHOOD.

JAMMU PROVINCE.						KASHMIR PROVINCE.					
Total workers and dependants.	ACTUAL WORKERS.				Dependants both sexes.	Total workers and dependants.	ACTUAL WORKERS.				Dependants both sexes.
	Total.		Partially agriculturists.				Total.		Partially agriculturists.		
	Males.	Females.	Males.	Females.			Males.	Females.	Males.	Females.	
10	11	12	13	14	15	16	17	18	19	20	21
1	...	1	...	...		...	...	...	...	...	...
...	...	...	..	...	...	19	3	..	...	...	16
...	...	...	...	...	..	...	.	...	..	...	...
...	...	...	...	...	..	..	...	..	..	...	...
360	119	7	16	...	234	2,114	618	160	23	...	1,236
...	..	..	...	..	..	356	85	28	...	..	248
898	359	...	13	...	537	758	291	...	...	...	487
105	69	..	...	...	36	20	5	..	...	...	15
2	1	..	...	..	1	.	...	..	...	...	...
...	..	..	...	..		..	...	..	...	.	...
...	..	..	...	...	...	...	...	..	...	...	...
69	17	...	1	...	52	46	35	...	...	...	11
720	272	...	12	...	448	692	251	..	..		441
33,095	13,375	2,186	740	14	17,464	23,752	8,587	704	206	7	14,461
30,924	12,703	1,888	694	14	16,333	23,126	8,454	610	206	7	14,062
7,266	2,206	132	355	8	4,928	7,031	2,532	33	152	6	4,466
587	350	48	1	...	189	927	398	27	...	...	502
118	59	...	...	...	54	...	...	..	...	...	...
181	113	1	7	...	67	251	107	...	...	...	144
13,565	6,605	965	136	2	4,995	12,066	4,491	332	38	1	7,248
3,364	1,121	64	142	3	2,179	2,003	684	175	16	...	1,144
6,820	2,028	661	51	1	3,640	840	208	43	...	..	559
..	...	...	...	...	...	8	4	...	...	...	4
519	221	17	2	...	281	...	...	...	...	..	...
25	10	...	..	...	15	59	15	...	..	..	44
...	..	...	...	...	...	...	...	.	..	...	...
5	1	...	...	...	4	..	...	...	..	...	...
20	9	...	...	...	11	59	15	...	..	...	44
2,076	682	298	46	...	1,116	567	118	94	..	..	355
1	...	...	..	...	1	29	3	4	..	..	22
10	1	...	..	...	9	...	..	...	..	...	...
2,024	647	298	46	...	1,079	538	115	90	...	...	333
41	14	...	..	...	27	...	...	..	..	..	...
26,835	12,161	1,714	695	15	22,980	29,661	12,043	1,549	529	11	2,089
10,652	2,999	263	97	.	7,370	18,403	5,378	808	303	8	12,217
76	33	1	...	..	42	833	255	8	1	...	560
...	...	...	...	...	...	...	..	...	..		...
5,143	1,352	146	29	..	3,645	12,444	3,695	686	131	8	8,062
27	19	..	...	..	8	2,531	647	57	86	...	1,827
8	1	1	...	...	6	165	53	47	...	...	65
7	1	1	...	...	5	28	6	...	..	...	20
4,665	1,361	134	62	...	3,190	745	177	7	61	...	561
...	...	..	..	...	...	...	...	...	..	...	..
706	232	...	6	...	474	1,669	545	3	4	...	1,121
20,510	6,971	1,409	532	11	12,130	18,086	5,597	619	210	3	11,870
...	...	...	...	...	...	..	...	...	...	...	...
...	...	...	...	...	...	...	...	...	...	...	...
...	...	...	...	...	...	...	...	...	...	...	...
...	...	...	...	...	...	...	...	...	...	...	...
...	...	...	...	...	...	...	...	...	...	...	...
...	...	...	...	...	...	...	...	...	...	...	...

TABLE XV.

OCCUPATION OR MEANS OF LIVELIHOOD.

Class.	Order.	Occupation or means of livelihood.	Frontier Districts: Total workers and dependents.	Actual workers: Total: Males.	Actual workers: Total: Females.	Actual workers: Partially agriculturists: Males.	Actual workers: Partially agriculturists: Females.	Dependents both sexes.
1	2	3	22	23	24	25	26	27
B.—PASTURE AND AGRICULTURE—concld.	V.—AGRICULTURE—concld.	48. Tea plantations, labourers and other subordinate staff ...	...					
		49. Betel, vine and areca-nut growers	...	...	...	...	..	...
		50. Cardamom and pepper growers	...	...	...	...	...	...
		51. Cocoanut growers	...	...	...	...	..	...
		52. Fruit and vegetable growers	19	9	8	...	...	2
		53. Miscellaneous ...	65	17	1	...	...	47
		TOTAL SUB-ORDER 13	...	...	...	...	...	...
		Agricultural training and supervision and forests.						
		54. Directors of agriculture and their staff	...	...	...	...	...	...
		55. Agricultural chemists and experts	...	...	...	...	...	...
		56. Agents and Managers of landed estates (not planters) ...	...	...	...	...	...	...
		57. Clerks, bailiffs, petty rent collectors, etc.	...	...	...	...	...	...
		58. Forest officers	...	...	...	...	...	...
		59. Forest rangers, guards, peons	...	...	...	...	...	...
C.—PERSONAL SERVICE.	VI.—PERSONAL, HOUSEHOLD AND SANITARY SERVICES.	TOTAL ORDER VI.—PERSONAL, HOUSE, HOLD AND SANITARY SERVICES.	1,650	796	305	6	2	549
		TOTAL SUB-ORDER 14	1,577	768	301	6	2	508
		Personal and Domestic Services.						
		60. Barbers	45	30	.	2	..	15
		61. Cooks ...	63	60	3	...	..	...
		62. Door-keepers, etc.	...	...	..	...	..	...
		63. Grooms, coachmen, dog-boys, etc	...	...	...	...	.	...
		64. Indoor servants	1,415	635	295	4	2	485
		65. Washermen	21	18	...	...	...	3
		66. Water carriers	33	25	3	...	...	5
		67. Shampooers	...	...	...	...	...	...
		68. Miscellaneous and unspecified	...	...	...	...	...	...
		TOTAL SUB-ORDER 15	1	1	.	..	.	..
		Non-domestic entertainment.						
		69. Hotel, lodging-house, bar, or refreshment-room keepers	...	..	..	...	...	...
		70. Rest-house, Serai, bath-house, etc., owners and Managers	...	...	..	...	..	.
		71. Club Secretaries, Managers, Stewards, etc.	1	1	...	...	.	...
		TOTAL SUB-ORDER 16	72	27	4	...	...	4
		Sanitation.						
		72. Sanitary officers of Government and establishments	..	...	..	...	...	...
		73. Sanitary Inspectors, Local and Municipal	..	...	...	...	...	...
		74. Sweepers and Scavengers ...	...	...	...	...	..	...
		75. Dust and sweeping contractors	72	27	4	...	..	41
D.—PREPARATION AND SUPPLY OF MATERIAL SUBSTANCES.	VII.—FOOD, DRINK AND STIMULANTS.	TOTAL ORDER VII.—FOOD, DRINK AND STIMULANTS.	288	115	7	14	..	166
		TOTAL SUB-ORDER 17	153	30	1	12	...	122
		Provision of Animal Food.						
		76. Butchers and slaughterers ...	...		...	...	...	...
		77. Cheese makers and sellers ...	...	..	..	...	...	...
		78. Cow and buffalo keepers, and milk and sellers	85	14	1	10	...	70
		79. Fishermen and fish-curers	..	...	..	...	..	...
		80. Fish dealers ...	...	...	...	...	...	...
		81. Fowl and egg dealers	...	..	...	...	...	...
		82. Ghee preparers and sellers ...	...	...	...	...	...	...
		83. Collectors of edible birds' nests	...	...	...	...	...	...
		84. Miscellaneous	68	16	...	2	...	52
		TOTAL SUB-ORDER 18	83	48	4	2	..	31
		Provision of vegetable food.						
		85. Biscuit factories; owners, managers, and superior staff...	...	...	...	...	...	...
		86. Biscuit factories; operatives and other subordinates	...	...	...	...	...	...
		87. Flour mills: owners, managers and superior staff	...	...	...	...	...	...
		88. Flour mills: operatives and other subordinates	...	...	...	...	...	...
		89. Oil mills: owners, managers and superior staff ...	...	...	...	...	...	...
		90. Oil mills: operatives and other subordinates	...	...	...	...	...	...

TABLE XV.

OCCUPATION OR MEANS OF LIVELIHOOD

JAMMU CITY.						SRINAGAR CITY.					
Total workers and dependents.	ACTUAL WORKERS.				Dependents both sexes.	Total workers and dependents.	ACTUAL WORKERS.				Dependents both sexes.
	Total		Partially agriculturists.				Total.		Partially agriculturists.		
	Males.	Females.	Males.	Females.			Males.	Females.	Males.	Females.	
28	29	30	31	32	33	34	35	36	37	38	39
...	...	...	...	...	...	...	...	...	...	...	...
...	...	...	...	...	...	...	...	...	...	...	...
...	...	...	...	...	...	...	...	...	...	...	...
...	...	...	...	...	...	...	...	...	...	...	...
30	15	...	...	...	15	1,275	350	155	3	...	770
...	...	...	...	...			...	...	...	...	...
65	17	...	3	...	48	509	158	...	...	...	351
...	...	...	...	...	...	...	...	...	...	...	...
...	...	...	...	...	...	...	...	...	...	...	...
...	...	...	...	...	...		...	...	...	...	...
...	...	...	...	...		46	35	...	...	...	11
65	17	...	3	...	48	463	123	...	...	...	340
2,820	1,243	315	67	1	1,282	9,039	3,130	346	20	...	5,563
2,028	930	128	67	1	970	8,700	3,062	268	20	...	5,370
329	122	1	1	...	206	1,432	800	...	...	...	633
156	130	...	...	...	26	457	190	2	...	...	265
53	21	...	...		32	...	...	...	...	...	...
85	34	...	6		1	102	34	...	...	...	68
610	297	30	59	1	283	5,280	1,572	128	20	...	3,580
232	74	12	...	...	146	695	254	100	...	...	341
615	252	85	1	...	276	725	212	38	...	...	475
...	...	...	...	...				...	...	...	...
		...	...	...		...	...	...	...	...	...
25	10		...	...	15		...	...	...	...	...
...	...	...	...	...	...	...	...	...	...	...	...
5	1	...	...	...	4		...	...	...	...	...
20	9		...	...	11		...		...	...	...
767	303	187	...		277	339	68	78	...	...	193
1	...	...	...	...	1	...	...	...	...	...	...
6	1	...	...		5	...	...	...	...	...	...
700	302	187	...	...	271	330	68	78	...	...	193
...	...	...	...	...	...		...	...	...		...
2,456	765	60	2	...	1,631	9,123	3,120	493	6	...	5,510
237	65	1		...	171	3,558	1,202	290	...	...	2,086
...	...	...	...	...	...	...	...	...	...	...	...
...	...	...	...	...	...	...	...	...	...	...	...
59	16	1	...	...	42	2,184	774	265	...	...	1,145
15	9	...	...	...	6	109	18	16	...	...	75
		...	...	...	...	96	39	8	...	...	49
		...	...	...	...	26	6	...	...	...	20
16	6	...	...	...	10	...	...	...	...	...	...
...	...	...	...	...	...	...	...	...	...	...	...
147	34	...	...	...	113	1,143	365	1	...	...	777
1,921	608	59	2		1,254	4,944	1,650	200	1		3,092
...	...	...	...	...	...	...	...	...	...	...	...
...	...	...	...	...	...	...	...	...	...	...	...
...	...	...	...	...	...	...	...	...	...	...	...
...	...	...	...	...	...	...	...	...	...	...	...
...	...	...	...	...	...	...	...	...	...	...	...
...	...	...	...	...	...	...	...	...	...	...	...

TABLE XV.

OCCUPATION OR MEANS OF LIVELIHOOD.

Class.	Order.	Occupation or means of livelihood.	TOTAL STATE. Total workers and dependents.	Actual workers. Total. Males.	Actual workers. Total. Females.	Actual workers. Partially agriculturists. Males.	Actual workers. Partially agriculturists. Females.	Dependents both sexes.
1	2	3	4	5	6	7	8	9
D.—PREPARATION AND SUPPLY OF MATERIAL SUBSTANCES—contd.	VII.—Food, Drink and Stimulants—concld.	92. Rice mills: operatives and other subordinates ...	2	..	1	...	...	1
		94. Sugar factories: operatives and other subordinates	9	1	2	...	...	6
		95. Bakers...	4.730	1.524	179	4	...	3.027
		96. Flour grinders	7.791	3.154	895	79	2	3.742
		97. Grain and pulse dealers	3.323	1.111	13	69	2	2.199
		98. Grain parchers	165	55	5		...	105
		99. Makers of sugar, molasses and gur by hand	10	2	..		...	8
		100. Oil pressers	11.129	3.376	942	353	5	7.411
		101. Oil sellers	1.511	382	27	27	..	1.102
		102. Rice pounders and huskers...	1.462	262	210	5	1	990
		103. Sweetmeat-makers	2.033	729	1	1	...	1.303
		104. Sweetmeat sellers	510	138	1	3		371
		105. Vegetable and fruit sellers	4.872	1.551	348	128	4	2.973
		106. Miscellaneous	1.085	317	8	47	...	760
		TOTAL SUB-ORDER 19	8.944	3.310	146	82	4	5.468
		Provision of drink, Condiments and Stimulants.						
		107. Ærated water factories: owners, managers and superior staff.	5	1	.	...	..	4
		112. Distilleries: operatives and other subordinates	40	11		...		29
		116. Ice factories: workmen and other subordinates	2	2	..	..		..
		121. Water-works: managers and superior staff	15	15		..		...
		122. Water-works-workmen and other subordinates	74	15	..	5	...	59
		123. Cardamom, betel leaf and areca nut sellers	2	1				1
		124. Grocers and general condiment dealers	3.455	1.137	82	40	2	2.236
		125. Opium, bhang, gânja, etc., preparers	48	33	2		...	13
		126. Opium, bhang, gânja, etc., sellers	94	18	.			76
		128. Salt sellers	3.868	1.583	14	37	2	2.271
		130. Tobacco and snuff sellers	1.230	403	48		...	779
		132. Toddy-sellers	22	15	...			7
		133. Wine and spirit distillers	12	12	.	..	..	
		134. Wine and spirit-sellers	61	61		..	...	...
		135. Miscellaneous	16	3	..	.		13
	VIII.—Light, Firing and Forage.	TOTAL ORDER VIII.—LIGHT, FIRING AND FORAGE ...	8.218	2.568	1.207	43	8	4.443
		TOTAL SUB-ORDER 20	216	53	.	..	.	163
		Lighting.						
		145. Match, candle, torch, lamp, lantern makers and sellers, etc.	216	53	..		...	163
		TOTAL SUB-ORDER 20	8.002	2.515	1.207	43	8	4.280
		Fuel and Forage.						
		147. Collieries: miners and other subordinates	8	4	...		..	4
		148. Coal dealers, brokers, company managers, etc. ...	23	8	...		.	15
		149. Hay, grass, and fodder sellers	2.927	896	504	32	7	1.527
		150. Firewood, charcoal and cow-dung sellers	5,044	1.607	703	11	1	2.734
	IX.—Buildings.	TOTAL ORDER IX.—BUILDINGS	4.755	1.498	58	18	..	3.199
		TOTAL SUB-ORDER 22	1.783	475	43	2	...	1.265
		Building Materials.						
		151. Brick and tile factories: owners, managers and superior staff.	111	14	20	..	...	77
		154. Stone and marble works: labourers and other subordinates.	13	5	...	.	...	7
		155. Brick and tile makers	1.379	337	22	1	.	1,020
		156. Brick and tile sellers	21	6	1	...	...	14
		157. Lime, chunam and shell burners	217	111	..	1	...	106
		158. Lime, chunam and shell sellers	43	2	...	...	..	41
		TOTAL SUB-ORDER 23	2,912	1.023	15	16	..	1,934
		Artificers in Buildings.						
		162. Building contractors	221	71	...	...	...	150
		163. Masons and builders	2.182	857	14	16	..	1.291
		164. Painters, plumbers and glaziers	443	54	1	..	...	388
		165. Thatchers	3	1	...	...	..	2
		166. Stone and marble workers ...	143	40	..	...	...	103

TABLE XV.

Occupation or Means of Livelihood.

Jammu Province.						Kashmir Province.					
Total workers and dependents.	Actual workers. Total. Males.	Actual workers. Total. Females.	Partially agriculturists. Males.	Partially agriculturists. Females.	Dependents both sexes.	Total workers and dependents.	Actual workers. Total. Males.	Actual workers. Total. Females.	Partially agriculturists. Males.	Partially agriculturists. Females.	Dependents both sexes.
10	11	12	13	14	15	16	17	18	19	20	21
...	...	...	...	...	...	2	...	1	...	..	1
9	1	2	...	...	6	...	...	..	.	..	...
458	193	10	1	...	246	4,252	1,322	158	2	..	2,772
7,061	2,954	875	77	2	3,232	692	182	10	1	..	491
2,964	977	11	69	2	1,076	359	134	2	...		228
91	38	5	...	...	48	74	17	...		...	57
10	2	...	...	...	8	...	...	..	...	..	
4,638	1,229	101	202	2	3,303	6,493	2,144	241	181	3	4,108
624	196	3	5	...	425	887	186	24	22	..	677
847	114	131	2	1	632	615	148	79	3	...	388
769	365	1	1	...	423	1,238	359	..	...	..	879
508	136	1	3	...	371	2	2	..	...	..	
1,560	508	259	125	4	793	2,296	1,030	88	1	...	2,178
948	254	1	47	...	693	137	63	7	.	...	67
5,681	**2.195**	**22**	**66**	**4**	**3.464**	**3.211**	**1.078**	**122**	**16**	..	**2,011**
5	1	...	...	...	1	.	...	...			...
1	1	...	..	...	...	39	10		...	...	29
2	2	...	...	...	...	...		...		...	...
6	6	...	...	...	...	9	9	...		...	...
12	...	...	...	..	12	62	15	...	5	...	47
1	...	...	...	...	1	1	1	...	..	...	..
1.398	490	3	20	2	605	2,057	647	79	11	...	1,331
...		...	...	...	...	...	..		..	.	.
77	11	...	...		66	17	7	..	..		10
3.720	1,549	14	37	2	2,157	148	34	.		...	114
383	78	5	...	...	300	843	321	43	..		479
22	15	...	...	.	7	...	...	..		..	...
4	4	..	..	..	.	8	8	...		..	.
35	35	...	...	..	..	26	26	...	..	.	.
15	3	..	...		12	1	...	..	..	...	1
5,120	**1,621**	**978**	**29**	**4**	**2.521**	**2.910**	**768**	**226**	**12**	**4**	**1.916**
..	...	..	...	..	..	**216**	**53**	...		...	**163**
...	...	...	...	...	...	216	53	.			163
5.120	**1,621**	**978**	**29**	**4**	**2.521**	**2.694**	**715**	**226**	**12**	**4**	**1.753**
8	4	..	...	..	4	..	..	..	...	.	
18	7	...	...	...	11	5	1	..		.	4
1,973	656	362	24	3	955	954	240	142	8	1	572
3,121	954	616	5	1	1,551	1,785	474	84	1	.	1,177
1.880	**816**	**8**	**13**	.	**1.034**	**2.853**	**661**	**50**	**5**	...	**2.142**
319	**218**	**2**	**2**		**99**	**1,464**	**257**	**41**	...		**1.166**
...	...	...	...	...	...	111	34	20	...	.	77
12	5	...	...	..	7	.	...	.	...	..	.
153	102	1	1	...	50	1.226	235	21	..	..	970
21	6	1	...	..	14	..	...	..	..	..	
120	103	...	1	...	17	97	8	...	...	..	69
18	2	...	...		11	30	..		...	..	30
1.541	**600**	**6**	**11**	...	**935**	**1.389**	**404**	**9**	**5**	..	**976**
178	55	...	...	...	118	38	11	..	...	..	27
1.200	498	5	11	...	697	980	345	9	5	...	576
22	6	1	..	...	15	421	48	.	...	...	578
3	1	..	...	...	2	...	...	...	...	...	...
143	40	...	...	...	108	...	...	...	...	...	

TABLE XV.

Occupation or Means of Livelihood.

Class	Order	Occupation or Means of Livelihood	FRONTIER DISTRICTS.					
			Total workers and dependents.	Actual workers. Total.		Actual workers. Partially agriculturists.		Dependents both sexes.
				Males.	Females.	Males.	Females.	
1	2	3	22	23	24	25	26	27
D.—PREPARATION AND SUPPLY OF MATERIAL SUBSTANCES—contd.	VII.—Food, Drink and Stimulants—concld.	92. Rice mills: operatives and other subordinates	...	...	...	...	...	...
		94. Sugar factories: operatives and other subordinates	...	...	...	...	...	...
		95. Bakers	20	9	2	1	...	9
		96. Flour grinders	38	18	1	1	...	19
		97. Grain and pulse dealers	...	...	...	...	...	...
		98. Grain parchers	...	...	...	...	...	...
		99. Makers of sugar, molasses and gur by hands	...	...	...	...	...	...
		100. Oil pressers	3	3	...	...	...	...
		101. Oil sellers	...	...	...	...	...	...
		102. Rice pounders and huskers	...	...	...	...	...	...
		103. Sweetmeat makers	6	5	...	...	...	1
		104. Sweetmeat sellers	...	...	...	...	...	...
		105. Vegetable and fruit sellers	16	13	1	...	...	2
		106. Miscellaneous	...	...	...	...	...	...
		Total Sub-order 19	52	37	2	...	...	13
		Provision of drink Condiments and Stimulants.						
		107. Ærated water factories: owners, managers and superior staff.	...	...	...	...	...	...
		112. Distilleries: operatives and other subordinates	...	...	...	...	...	...
		116. Ice factories: workmen and other subordinates	...	...	...	...	...	...
		121. Water-works: managers and superior staff	...	...	...	...	...	...
		122. Water-works: workmen and other subordinates	...	...	...	...	...	...
		123. Cardamom, betel leaf and areca nut sellers	...	...	...	...	...	...
		124. Grocers and general condiment dealers	...	...	...	...	...	...
		125. Opium, bhang, gánja, etc., preparers	48	33	2	...	...	13
		126. Opium, bhang, gánja, etc., sellers	...	...	...	...	...	...
		128. Salt sellers	...	...	...	...	...	...
		130. Tobacco and snuff sellers	4	4	...	...	...	...
		132. Toddy sellers	...	...	...	...	...	...
		133. Wine and spirit distillers	...	...	...	...	...	...
		134. Wine and spirit sellers	...	...	...	...	...	...
		135. Miscellaneous	...	...	...	...	...	...
	VIII.—Light, Firing and Forage.	TOTAL ORDER VIII.—LIGHT, FIRING AND FORAGE	188	179	3	2	...	6
		Total Sub-order 20	...	...	...	...	...	...
		Lighting.						
		145. Match, candle, torch, lamp lantern makers and sellers, etc	...	...	...	...	...	...
		Total Sub-order 21	188	179	3	2	...	6
		Fuel and Forage.						
		147. Collieries, miners and other subordinates	...	...	...	...	...	...
		148. Coal dealers, brokers, company managers, etc	...	...	...	...	...	...
		149. Hay, grass and fodder sellers	...	...	...	...	...	...
		150. Firewood, charcoal and cow-dung sellers	188	179	3	2	...	6
	IX.—Buildings.	TOTAL ORDER IX.—BUILDINGS	42	19	...	...	...	23
		Total Sub-order 22	...	...	...	...	...	...
		Building Materials						
		151. Brick and tile factories: owners, managers and superior staff.	...	...	...	...	...	...
		154. Stone and marble works: labourers and other subordinates	...	...	...	...	...	...
		155. Brick and tile makers	...	...	...	...	...	...
		156. Brick and tile sellers	...	...	...	...	...	...
		157. Lime, chunam and shell burners	...	...	...	...	...	...
		158. Lime, chunam and shell sellers	...	...	...	...	...	...
		Total Sub-order 23	42	19	...	...	...	23
		Artificers in Buildings						
		162. Building contractors	10	5	...	...	...	5
		163. Masons and builders	32	14	...	...	...	18
		164. Painters, plumbers and glaziers	...	...	...	...	...	...
		165. Thatchers	...	...	...	...	...	...
		166. Stone and marble workers	...	...	...	...	...	...

TABLE XV.

Occupation or Means of Livelihood.

JAMMU CITY.						SRINAGAR CITY.					
Total workers and dependents.	Actual workers.				Dependents both sexes.	Total workers and dependents.	Actual workers.				Dependents both sexes.
	Total.		Partially agriculturists.				Total.		Partially agriculturists.		
	Males.	Females.	Males.	Females.			Males.	Females.	Males.	Females.	
28	29	30	31	32	33	34	35	36	37	38	39
...	...	..	...	...	..	...		..	..	..	..
234	111	2	...	...	121	1,471	562	74	...	...	835
402	145	11	...		246	209	30	...	...	.	179
287	9	...		..	278		.	...	...	...	...
19	11		..	..	3	74	17		...	...	57
...		..	..	..	8	...	...	..	..	...	...
4		...	...	..	4	408	142	15	...	...	251
3	1	...	..	...	2	..	...	...	...	...	...
160	25	36	1	...	99	434	115	70	...	..	249
287	145	...	...	...	142	1,008	276	.	...	.	732
247	50	...	...	..	197		..	...	...	..	...
278	111	10	1	.	157	1,310	508	41	1	..	791
..	...	..	...	...	..		..	.	...	...	...
298	**92**		...		**206**	**621**	**268**	**3**	**5**	...	**350**
5	1	...	...	..	4	...	...	...	...	...	...
...	...	...	...	..	...	1	...	..	...	...	1
2	2	...	...	...	...	...	...	...	...	..	...
6	6	...	..	.	..	9	9	...	...	...	...
12	...	...	...	...	12	58	12	..	5	...	46
...	..		...	..	...	1	1	...	...	..	...
170	43		...	...	127	..	...	...	...	...	...
...	...	...	...	...	...	...	..	...	...	...	...
15	6	...	...	..	9	16	7	...	...	..	9
13	...	...	..	...	13	..	..	...	...	...	...
68	27	...	...	..	41	536	239	3	...	...	294
...	..	...	...	..		..	...	...	..	...	...
...	...	...	...	..		..	...	...	...	...	..
7	7	...	..	...	.	.	..	...	...	...	...
...	...	...	..			..	..	...	...	...	..
226	**85**	**11**	**3**	...	**130**	**1,590**	**404**	**64**	**4**	..	**1,122**
...	...	...		...		**213**	**50**	...	..	...	**163**
...	.	...	...	..	...	213	50	...	...	..	163
226	**85**	**11**	**3**	...	**130**	**1,377**	**354**	**64**	**4**	...	**959**
8	4	...	..		4	..	...	...	...	...	...
8	2	...	.	...	6	.	...	..	...	...	...
21	15	.	3	...	6	293	86	16	...	...	191
189	64	11		...	114	1,084	268	48	4	...	768
954	**450**	**2**	**4**	...	**502**	**1,713**	**371**	**1**	**5**	...	**1,341**
168	**112**	**1**	**1**	...	**55**	**714**	**107**	...	..	...	**607**
...	...	...	...	...	..	...	...	..	...	...	...
12	5	.	.	..	7	...	..	..	..	...	...
139	98	1	1	...	40	684	107	...	...	...	577
8	...	..	...	..	8	.	..	...	...	...	...
9	9	..	..	...	..	...	...	..	...	...	...
...	...		...	...	...	30	...	...	...	...	30
786	**338**	**1**	**3**	...	**447**	**999**	**264**	**1**	**5**	...	**734**
91	8	...	...	...	83	...	...	..	...	...	...
681	324	...	3	...	357	578	216	1	5	...	361
14	6	1	...	...	7	421	48	...	...	...	378
...	...	...	...	...	...	...	...	...	...	...	...
...	...	...	...	...	...	...	...	..	...	...	...

TABLE XV.

OCCUPATION OR MEANS OF LIVELIHOOD.

Class.	Order.	Occupation or means of livelihood.	TOTAL STATE. Total workers and dependents.	Actual workers. Total. Males.	Actual workers. Total. Females.	Actual workers. Partially agriculturists. Males.	Actual workers. Partially agriculturists. Females.	Dependents both sexes.
1	2	3	4	5	6	7	8	9
D.—PREPARATION AND SUPPLY OF MATERIAL SUBSTANCES—*contd.*	X.—VEHICLES AND VESSELS.	TOTAL ORDER X.—VEHICLES AND VESSELS	8	4	...	...	...	4
		TOTAL SUB-ORDER 24	1	1	...	...	...	...
		Railway and Tramway Plant.						
		167. Railway and Tramway factories: owners, managers and superior staff.	1	1	...	...	...	...
		TOTAL SUB-ORDER 25	6	2	..	...	...	4
		Carts, Carriages, etc.						
		173. Painters of carriages, etc.	6	2	..	...	..	4
		TOTAL SUB-ORDER 26	1	1	...	...	...	...
		Ships and Boats.						
		175. Ship wrights, boat builders, etc.	1	1	...	...	...	...
	XI.—SUPPLEMENTARY REQUIREMENTS.	TOTAL ORDER XI.—SUPPLEMENTARY REQUIREMENTS.	18,759	6,202	290	669	9	12,297
		TOTAL SUB-ORDER 27	334	140	1	1	...	193
		Paper.						
		181. Paper makers and sellers	322	134	1	1	...	187
		182. Stationers	12	6	...	...	...	6
		TOTAL SUB-ORDER 28	519	130	1	1	...	388
		Books and Prints.						
		184. Printing Press: workmen and other subordinates ...	11	2	...	1	..	9
		185. Hand-press: proprietors, lithographers and printers ...	225	47	..	...	...	178
		186. Book-binders	209	57	1	...	...	151
		187. Book sellers, book agents and publishers	74	24	...	...	...	50
		TOTAL SUB-ORDER 29	61	17	.	...	...	44
		Watches, Clocks and Scientific Instruments.						
		190. Watch and clock makers	52	16	...	...	...	36
		191. Watch and clock sellers and opticians	9	1	...	..	...	8
		TOTAL SUB-ORDER 30	1,035	319	29	14	...	687 [?]
		Carving and Engraving.						
		194. Wood and ebony carvers	2	1	...	...	...	1
		196. Cotton stamp makers and sellers	63	16	..	1	...	47
		197. Turners and lacquerers	644	176	29	12	..	439
		198. Die-sinkers and seal, etc., engravers	232	89	...	1	...	143
		200. Mica, flint talc workers and sellers	24	10	..	...	...	14
		201. Mosaic and alabaster workers and sellers	70	27	...	...	...	43
		TOTAL SUB-ORDER 31	334	62	2	...	...	270
		Toys and Curiosities.						
		202. Toy, kite and cage makers and sellers	10	1	2		...	7
		203. Hukka-stem makers and sellers	243	49	...	..	...	194
		204. Papier-mache workers and sellers	81	12	...		...	69
		TOTAL SUB-ORDER 32	12	2	4	...	...	6
		Music and Musical Instruments.						
		206. Music and musical instrument makers	12	2	4	...	...	6
		TOTAL SUB-ORDER 33	995	250	24	26	1	691
		Bangles, necklaces, beads, sacred threads, etc.						
		208. Makers of bangles, other than glass	3	1	...	...	...	2
		210. Makers of glass bangles	338	121	2	18	...	215
		211. Sellers of glass bangles	539	141	6	8	...	392
		212. Imitation and pewter jewellery makers	5	2	...	...	...	3
		214. Rosary, bead and necklace makers	1	...	...	...	...	1
		215. Rosary, bead and necklace sellers	28	7	...	...	...	21
		216. Flower garland makers and sellers	81	8	16	...	1	57

TABLE XV.

Occupation or Means of Livelihood.

Jammu Province.						Kashmir Province.					
Total workers and dependents.	Actual workers.				Dependents both sexes.	Total workers and dependents.	Actual workers.				Dependents both sexes.
	Total.		Partially agriculturists.				Total.		Partially agriculturists.		
	Males.	Females.	Males.	Females.			Males.	Females.	Males.	Females.	
10	11	12	13	14	15	16	17	18	19	20	21
8	4	...	...	...	4	...	..	..	...	...	...
1	1	...	..	...	...	...	...	...	.	...	...
1	1	...	...	...	...	..	...	...	...	...	..
6	2	..	...	...	4	...	...	...	...	...	...
6	2	...	...	...	4	...	...	...	...	...	...
1	1	...	...	...	...	...	...	...	...	...	...
1	1	...	...	..	...	...	...	...	...	...	...
15,622	5,039	283	662	9	10,300	3,080	1,116	7	7	...	1,957
14	7	1	...	...	6	320	133	...	1	...	187
3	1	1	...	...	1	319	133	..	1	...	186
11	6	..	.	...	5	1	..	...	..	...	1
154	34	1	1	...	119	365	96	...	...	...	269
11	2	..	1	...	9	...	..	...	...	...	..
...	...	...	...	..	...	225	47	...		...	178
117	25	1	.	..	91	92	32	...	..	...	60
26	7	...	...	...	19	48	17	...	..	...	81
19	6		.	...	13	42	11	...	..	...	31
19	6	..	...	.	13	33	10	..	...	...	23
...	..	..	..	...	...	9	1	...	...	...	8
485	108	29	10	...	348	547	209	...	4	...	338
2	1			...	1	..	...	..	...	...	...
63	16	..	1	..	47	...	...	.	.	..	...
412	88	29	9	...	295	232	88	..	3	...	144
7	3	...	.	.	4	225	86	..	1	...	139
...	...	...	.	.	...	24	10	..	..	...	14
1	...	..	...	...	1	66	25	...	...	...	41
163	24	2	...	...	137	171	38	...	..	.	133
10	1	2	..		7	...	...		...	...	...
153	23	..	...	.	130	90	26	...	...	..	64
...	..	...	...	...		81	12	..	...	...	69
12	2	4	...	...	6	...	..	...	...	..	...
12	2	4	...	...	6	..	...	..	...	...	...
506	120	20	24	1	366	488	159	4	2	...	325
3	1	...	...	...	2	...	...	...	...	..	...
215	71	1	18	...	143	123	50	1	...	...	72
215	43	3	6	...	169	324	98	3	2	...	223
5	2	...	...	...	3	...	...	...	...	...	—
1	...	...	...	...	1	...	...	...	...	...	...
1	1	...	...	...	...	28	5	...	...	...	21
66	2	16	...	1	48	15	6	...	...	...	8

TABLE XV.

OCCUPATION OR MEANS OF LIVELIHOOD.

Class.	Order.	Occupation or means of livelihood.	FRONTIER DISTRICTS. Total workers and dependents.	Actual workers. Total. Males.	Actual workers. Total. Females.	Actual workers. Partially agriculturists. Males.	Actual workers. Partially agriculturists. Females.	Dependents both sexes.
1	2	3	22	23	24	25	26	27
D.—PREPARATION AND SUPPLY OF MATERIAL SUBSTANCES—contd.	X.—Vehicles and Vessels.	TOTAL ORDER X.—VEHICLES AND VESSELS	...	...	...	...	...	...
		TOTAL SUB-ORDER 24	...	...	...	...	...	...
		Railway and Tramway Plant.						
		167. Railway and Tramway Factories: owners, managers and superior staff.	...	...	...	...	...	...
		TOTAL SUB-ORDER 25	...	...	...	...	...	...
		Carts, Carriages, etc.						
		173. Painters of carriages, etc.	...	...	...	...	...	...
		TOTAL SUB-ORDER 26	...	...	...	...	...	...
		Ships and Boats.						
		175. Ship wrights, boat builders, etc.	...	...	...	...	...	...
	XI.—Supplementary Requirements.	TOTAL ORDER XI.—SUPPLEMENTARY REQUIREMENTS.	87	47	...	...	...	40
		TOTAL SUB-ORDER 27	...	...	...	...	...	...
		Paper.						
		181. Paper makers and sellers	...	...	...	...	...	...
		182. Stationers	...	...	...	...	...	...
		TOTAL SUB-ORDER 28	...	...	...	...	...	...
		Books and Prints.						
		184. Printing Press: workmen and other subordinates ...	...	...	...	...	...	...
		185. Hand-press proprietors, lithographers and printers ...	...	...	...	...	...	...
		186. Book binders	...	...	...	...	...	...
		187. Book-sellers, book agents and publishers	...	...	...	...	...	...
		TOTAL SUB-ORDER 29	...	...	...	...	...	...
		Watches, Clocks and Scientific Instruments.						
		190. Watch and clock makers	...	...	...	...	...	...
		191. Watch and clock sellers and opticians	...	...	...	...	...	...
		TOTAL SUB-ORDER 30	3	2	...	...	...	1
		Carving and Engraving.						
		194. Wood and ebony carvers	...	...	...	...	...	...
		196. Cotton stamp makers and sellers	...	...	...	...	...	...
		197. Turners and lacquerers	...	...	...	...	...	...
		198. Die-sinkers and seal, etc., engravers	...	...	...	...	...	...
		200. Mica, flint talc workers, etc., sellers	...	...	...	...	...	...
		201. Mosaic and alabaster workers and sellers	3	2	...	...	...	1
		TOTAL SUB-ORDER 31	...	...	...	...	...	...
		Toys and Curiosities.						
		202. Toy, kite and cage makers and sellers	...	...	...	...	...	...
		203. Hukka-stem makers and sellers	...	...	...	...	...	...
		204. Papier-maché workers and sellers	...	...	...	...	...	...
		TOTAL SUB-ORDER 32	...	...	...	...	...	...
		Music and Musical Instruments.						
		206. Music and musical instrument makers	...	...	...	...	...	...
		TOTAL SUB-ORDER 33	1	1	...	...	...	...
		Bangles, necklaces, beads, sacred threads, etc.						
		208. Makers of bangles, other than glass	...	...	...	...	...	...
		210. Makers of glass bangles	...	...	...	...	...	...
		211. Sellers of glass bangles	...	...	...	...	...	...
		212. Imitation and pewter jewellery makers	...	...	...	...	...	...
		214. Rosary, bead and necklace sellers	...	...	...	...	...	...
		215. Rosary, bead, and necklace makers	1	1	...	...	...	...
		216. Flower garland makers and sellers	...	...	...	...	...	...

TABLE XV.

Occupation or Means of Livelihood.

JAMMU CITY.						SRINAGAR CITY.					
Total workers and dependents.	Actual workers. Total. Males.	Actual workers. Total. Females.	Actual workers. Partially agriculturists. Males.	Actual workers. Partially agriculturists. Females.	Dependents both sexes.	Total workers and dependents.	Actual workers. Total. Males.	Actual workers. Total. Females.	Actual workers. Partially agriculturists. Males.	Actual workers. Partially agriculturists. Females.	Dependents both sexes.
28	29	30	31	32	33	34	35	36	37	38	39
6	2	...	...	...	4	.	.	-	...	...	...
...	...			..	...	..	..	...	...	...	...
...	...	...	..	...	..	...	...	..	...	...	...
6	2	..	...	..	4	..	.	...	...	..	...
6	2	...	..	.	4	..		..	..	.	..
...	...	...	..		..	...	..	...	...	...	...
...	.	..	..	...	..	..	..	..	...	...	..
423	106	26	1	1	291	2,044	732	5	...	...	1,307
7	2	...	...		5	20	1	...	...	...	19
...	..	...				20	1	.	...	...	19
7	2	...	...	...	5	...	...	...	.	..	..
63	14	...		..	49	343	87	..	.	...	286
6	..	.	..	..	8	...	..	.	...	..	...
...	...	.	..	...	...	225	47	.	.	..	178
33	9	...		...	24	82	28	..	..	...	54
22	5	...		...	17	36	12		..	..	84
9	4	...	..	...	5	40	11	...	...	...	29
9	4	...	.	...	5	31	10	..	..	...	21
...	...	...	...	...	.	9	1	..	.	...	6
11	4	...	...	..	7	200	76	...	...	...	124
...	...	...	...	...	...	.	...	..	..	...	...
...	...	...	...	..		...	...	..	..	.	...
8	2	...	..	...	6	48	3	..	...	...	45
3	3	...	..	...	1	128	63	...	...	...	65
...	...	..	...	...	...	24	10	...	...	...	14
..	...	...	..	..		...	...	..	...	...	...
45	13	...	...	...	32	171	38	...	.	...	133
3	1	...	...	...	2	..	.	..	...	...	...
43	12	...	..	...	30	90	26	...	..	...	64
..	...	...	...	...	..	81	12	...	...	...	69
10	...	4	...	...	6	...	...	...	...	...	...
10	...	4	...	...	6	...	..	...	...	...	...
36	4	10	...	1	22	172	62	2	..	...	108
...	...	...	..	...	...	...	...	...	..	...	...
7	3	1	...	...	3	165	59	2	...	...	104
...	...	..	...	...	...	...	...	...	...	...	...
...	...	...	...	...	...	...	...	...	...	...	...
...	...	...	...	...	...	7	3	...	...	...	4
29	1	9	...	1	10	...	...	...	...	...	...

TABLE XV.

Occupation or Means of Livelihood.

Class.	Order.	Occupation or Means of Livelihood.	TOTAL STATE. Total workers and dependents.	Actual workers. Total. Males.	Actual workers. Total. Females.	Actual workers. Partially agriculturists. Males.	Actual workers. Partially agriculturists. Females.	Dependents both sexes.
1	2	3	4	5	6	7	8	9
D.—Preparation and Supply of Material Substances—contd.	XI.—Supplementary Requirements—concld.	Total Sub-order 35	1.171	449	8	...		714
		Harness.						
		223. Saddlers cloth makers, embroiderers and sellers	582	255	8	...	..	319
		224. Whip, goad and walking sticks, etc. makers	589	194	...	...	..	395
		Total Sub-order 36	13,354	4.485	214	557	8	8.655
		Tools and Machinery.						
		227. Knife and tool makers	684	234	3	28	...	447
		228. Knife and tool sellers	15	...	...	...	...	15
		229. Knife and tool grinders	15	5	...	...	...	10
		230. Plough and agricultural implement makers	10,728	2.793	182	421	8	7.753
		231. Looms and loom-comb makers and sellers	1,903	1,444	29	138		430
		232. Mechanics other than railway mechanics	2	2	...	...	..	..
		234 Sugar-press makers	7	7	..	...	...	...
		Total Sub-order 37	974	318	7	40	.	649
		Arms and Ammunition.						
		238. Arsenals: operatives and other subordinates	624	203	...	39	...	451
		243. Gun makers, menders and sellers	75	54	...	..	..	21
		244. Ammunition, gunpowder and firework makers	144	43	1	1	..	100
		245. Ammunition, gunpowder and firework sellers	52	11	6	...	..	35
		246. Makers of swords, spears and other weapons	19	7	..	.	...	12
	XII.—Textile, Fabrics and Dress.	TOTAL ORDER XII.—TEXTILE, FABRICS AND DRESS	134.561	36.888	28.667	1.520	132	69.006
		Total Sub-order 38	23.301	9,946	148	318	...	13.207
		Wool and Fur.						
		248. Carpet weavers	3,691	1,031	33	...	.	2.627
		249. Shawl weavers	18.517	8.556	46	293	...	9.915
		250. Felt and pashami workers	199	55	46	.	..	98
		251. Persons occupied with blankets, woollen cloth and yarn, fur, feathers and natural wool.	790	259	21	25	...	510
		252. Wool carders	14	2	..	...	...	12
		253. Wool dyers	22	8	...	...	...	14
		254. Dealers in woollen goods, fur and feathers	68	35	2	...	...	31
		Total Sub-order 39	3 031	1.123	118	10	...	1.790
		Silk.						
		255. Silk filatures: owners, managers and superior staff	1	1	...	...	...	.
		256. Silk filatures: operatives and other subordinates	193	54	...	1	...	139
		257. Silk mills: owners, managers and superior staff	9	7	...	...	...	2
		258. Silk mills: operatives and other subordinates	1.017	403	...	...	...	534
		259. Silk worm rearers and cocoon-gatherers	412	132	10	3	...	270
		260. Silk carders, spinners and weavers: makers of silk braid and thread	1.280	352	99	6	...	799
		261. Sellers of raw silk, silk cloth, braid and thread	113	63	9	...	.	41
		262. Silk dyers	6	1	...	..	..	5
		Total Sub-order 40	78.322	14.769	27.778	1,074	112	35,775
		Cotton.						
		268. Cotton spinning, weaving and other mills: operatives and other subordinates.	3	1	...	...	...	2
		271. Cotton cleaners, pressers and ginners	3.229	933	135	32	1	2.161
		272. Cotton weavers, hand industry	39.719	11.874	965	999	19	26.880
		273. Cotton carpet and rug makers	1	1	...	...	...	...
		275. Cotton spinners, sizers and yarn beaters	31.615	769	26,628	8	92	4.198
		276. Cotton yarn and thread sellers	120	33	13	...	...	74
		277. Calenderers, fullers and printers	638	241	6	1	...	391
		278. Cotton dyers	2,499	766	29	34	...	1.704
		279. Tape makers	480	131	2	...	...	347
		281. Tent makers	18	...	...	...	...	18

TABLE XV.

Occupation or Means of Livelihood.

JAMMU PROVINCE.						KASHMIR PROVINCE.					
Total workers and dependents.	Actual workers.				Dependents both sexes.	Total workers and dependents.	Actual workers.				Dependents both sexes.
	Total.		Partially agriculturists.				Total.		Partially agriculturists.		
	Males.	Females.	Males.	Females.			Males.	Females.	Males.	Females.	
10	11	12	13	14	15	16	17	18	19	20	21
116	**37**	**5**	...	...	**74**	**1,055**	**412**	**3**	...	...	**840**
116	37	5	...	...	74	466	218	3	...	...	245
...	...	...	...	...		589	194	...	...	...	395
13,277	**4,445**	**214**	**557**	**8**	**8,618**	**1**	...	...	...	...	**1**
684	234	3	28	...	447	...	...	...	...	...	...
15	...	...	...	...	15	...	...	...	...	...	...
14	5	...	...	...	9	1	...	...	...	...	1
10,652	2,753	182	421	...	7,717	...	...	...	...	...	...
1,003	1,414	29	138	...	430	...	...	...	...	...	...
2	2	...	...	...		...	...	...	...	...	...
7	7	...	...	...		...	...	...	...	...	...
876	**256**	**7**	**40**		**613**	**91**	**58**	...			**38**
684	203	...	30	...	451	...	...	...	...	...	...
3	2	...	...	...	1	72	52	...	...	...	20
141	42	1	1	...	98	3	1	...	...	...	2
48	9	6	...	...	33	4	2	...	...	...	3
...	...	...	...	...	...	12	3	...	...	...	9
44.918	**12.013**	**4 557**	**998**	**50**	**23.349**	**88,933**	**24.701**	**23.968**	**520**	**82**	**40.264**
747	**238**	**64**	**25**	...	**445**	**22.350**	**9.698**	**76**	**293**	...	**12.606**
...	...	...	...	...	...	3,691	1,031	33	...	...	3,627
67	26	1	...	...	40	18,293	8,527	41	293	...	9,725
56	2	42	...	...	12	126	46	...	...	...	80
588	200	21	25	...	367	202	59	...	...	...	143
14	2	...	...	...	12	...	...	...	...	...	...
22	8	...	...	...	14	...	...	...	...	...	...
...	...	...	...	...	...	68	35	2	...	...	21
433	**115**	**66**	**3**	...	**252**	**2.596**	**1.006**	**52**	**7**		**1.539**
...	...	...	...	...	...	1	1	...	...	...	...
...	...	...	...	...	...	193	54	...	1	...	159
...	...	...	...	...	...	9	7	...	...	...	2
...	...	...	...	...	...	1,015	481	...	...	...	534
...	...	...	...	...	...	412	182	10	3	...	270
314	51	57	3	...	206	968	331	42	3	...	509
113	63	9	...	...	41	...	...	...	...	...	...
6	1	...	...	...	5	...	...	...	...	...	...
37.252	**9,660**	**4.145**	**913**	**30**	**23.477**	**40.657**	**5.020**	**23.501**	**160**	**82**	**12.136**
3	1	...	...	...	2	...	...	...	...	...	...
1,061	466	128	12	1	1,067	1,564	464	7	20	...	1,098
28,314	6,103	894	877	15	19,317	11,252	3,686	68	121	4	7,498
...	...	...	...	...	...	1	1	...	...	...	...
5 406	568	3.083	...	14	1,847	25,892	220	23,416	8	78	2,236
120	33	13	...	...	74	...	...	...	...	...	...
94	27	4	1	...	63	544	214	2	...	...	329
1,592	462	23	23	...	1,107	908	304	6	11	...	806
...	...	...	...	...	...	480	131	2	...	...	247
...	...	...	...	...	...	18	...	...	...	...	14

TABLE XV.

Occupation or Means of Livelihood.

Class.	Order.	Occupation or means of livelihood.	FRONTIER DISTRICTS. Total workers and dependents.	Actual workers. Total. Males.	Actual workers. Total. Females.	Actual workers. Partially agriculturists. Males.	Actual workers. Partially agriculturists. Females.	Dependents both sexes.
1	2	3	22	23	24	25	26	27
D.—PREPARATION AND SUPPLY OF MATERIAL SUBSTANCES—contd.	XI.—Supplementary Requirements—concld.	Total Sub-order 35	...	...	...	...	...	...
		Harness.						
		223. Saddlers, cloth makers, embroiderers and sellers ...	...	...	..	..	...	..
		224. Whip, goad and walking sticks, etc., makers	...	...	...	...	...	...
		Total Sub-order 36	76	40	...	...	...	36
		Tools and Machinery.						
		227. Knife and tool makers	...		...	..	...	...
		228. Knife and tool sellers	...	..	...	...	...	...
		229. Knife and tool grinders	...	...	..	...	...	...
		230. Plough and agricultural implement makers	76	40	...	...	...	36
		231. Looms and loom-comb makers and sellers ...	..	..	...	...	...	...
		232. Mechanics other than railway mechanics	..		...	...	...	...
		234. Sugar-press makers	...	...	...	..	...	...
		Total Sub-order 37	7	4	...	..	...	3
		Arms and Ammunition.						
		238. Arsenals: operatives and other subordinates	..	..	..	...	...	...
		243. Gun makers, menders and sellers	...		...	...	...	...
		244. Ammunition, gunpowder and firework makers	..		...	...	...	...
		245. Ammunition, gunpowder and firework sellers	..	...	..	...	...	...
		246. Makers of swords, spears and other weapons	7	4	..	...	...	3
	XII.—Textile, Fabrics and Dress.	TOTAL ORDER XII.—TEXTILE, FABRICS AND DRESS	732	186	143	2	...	403
		Total Sub-order 38	174	10	8	...	...	156
		Wool and Fur.						
		248. Carpet weavers	...	...	...	...	...	..
		249. Shawl weavers	157	3	4	...	...	150
		250. Felt and pasham workers	17	7	4	...	...	6
		251. Persons occupied with blankets, woollen cloth and yarn, fur, feathers and natural wool.	...	...	...	..	...	...
		252. Wool carders	...	...	...	...	...	...
		253. Wool dyers	...	...	...	...	..	..
		254. Dealers in woollen goods, fur and feathers	...	...	..	...	...	...
		Total Sub-order 39	2	2	..	...	...	...
		Silk.						
		255. Silk filatures: owners, managers and superior staff	...		...	...		...
		256. Silk filatures: operatives and other subordinates ...	..	..	...	...	...	...
		257. Silk mills: owners, managers and superior staff ...	.	...	...	...	...	...
		258. Silk mills: operatives and other subordinates	2	2	...	...	...	..
		259. Silk worm rearers and cocoon gatherers	...	..	...	...	...	...
		260. Silk carders, spinners and weavers; makers of silk braid and thread.	...	..	...	...	...	...
		261. Sellers of raw silk, silk cloth, braid and thread	..	...	...	...	...	..
		262. Silk dyers	..	..	...	...	...	...
		Total Sub-order 40	353	89	132	1	...	182
		Cotton.						
		268. Cotton spinning, weaving and other mills: operatives and other subordinates	...	...	...	...	...	...
		271. Cotton cleaners, pressers and ginners	4	3	...	...	...	1
		272. Cotton weavers, hand industry	153	85	3	1	...	65
		273. Cotton carpet and rug makers	...	...	...	...	...	...
		275. Cotton spinners, sizers and yarn beaters	225	1	129	...	...	96
		276. Cotton yarn and thread sellers	...	...	...	...	...	
		277. Calenderers, fullers and printers	...	...	...	...	...	...
		278. Cotton dyers	1	...	...	...	...	...
		279. Tape makers		...	...	...	...	1
		281. Tent makers	...	...	...	...	...	...

TABLE XV.

OCCUPATION OR MEANS OF LIVELIHOOD.

JAMMU CITY.						SRINAGAR CITY.					
Total workers and dependents.	Actual workers. Total. Males.	Actual workers. Total. Females.	Actual workers. Partially agriculturists. Males.	Actual workers. Partially agriculturists. Females.	Dependents both sexes.	Total workers and dependents.	Actual workers. Total. Males.	Actual workers. Total. Females.	Actual workers. Partially agriculturists. Males.	Actual workers. Partially agriculturists. Females.	Dependents both sexes.
28	29	30	31	32	33	34	35	36	37	38	39
116	37	5		...	74	1,019	402	3	...	..	614
116	37	5	...	...	74	465	217	3	...	...	245
...	...	...	...	...	...	554	185	...	...	...	369
22	6	...	...	...	16	...	...	..	...	...	..
14	...	...	...	...	14	...	...	...	...	..	.
..	...	...	...	...	...	...	...	...	...	...	...
1	1	...	...	...	...	...	...	...	...	...	.
4	2	...	...	...	2	...	...	...	...	...	..
1	1	...	...	...	..	...	...	...	...	...	..
2	2	...	...	...	...	...	...	...	...	..	..
...	...	..	...	...	..	...	..	...	...	...	...
104	22	7	1	..	75	79	56	...	...	...	24
...	...	...	...	...	...	...	...	...	...	...	...
3	2	...	..	...	1	72	52	...	...	...	20
71	20	1	1	...	50	...	...	...	...	...	...
30	...	6	...	...	24	4	2	...	...	...	2
...	...	...	..	...	...	3	1	...	...	...	2
2,174	685	307	1	...	1,182	43,552	13,535	12,073	14	3	17,944
35	3	23	...	...	9	12,259	6,093	45	11	...	6,121
...	..	...	..	...	...	3,660	1,022	33	...	...	2,605
...	...	...	...	...	...	8,473	5,025	12	11	...	3,436
29	1	23	...	...	5	126	46	...	...	...	80
...	...	...	...	..	...	...	...	..	...	...	...
..	...	...	...	..	...	...	...	.	...	.	...
6	2	...	...	.	4	...	...	..	..	...	...
...	...	...	.	.	...	...	...	.	...	.	..
245	75	66	..		104	1,367	564	27	...	...	776
...	...	..	...	..	...	...	...	..	...	...	..
...	...	...	...	..	...	..	...	..	...	..	..
...	...	...	...	..	...	9	7	...	...	...	2
...	...	..	...	..	..	723	331	..	...	...	392
...	...	...	...	..	...	44	15	..	...	...	29
160	34	57			89	591	211	27	...	...	358
65	41	9	..	.	15	..	...			...	
..	...	...			..	...	...		...		
655	142	146	...	..	367	14,907	870	11,769	1	3	2,268
...			...	..	...	...	...	..	...	...	
32	14	.	...	.	18	228	71	2	...	...	15
148	58	4	...	..	86	787	338	6	1	..	448
...	...	...	...	...	..	..	...	...	...	...	...
157	...	127	...	.	30	12,713	75	11,758	..	3	880
52	...	18	...	...	30	...	...	...	...	...	..
...	...	.	...	...	...	289	123		...	...	166
266	70	2	...	...	194	392	132	1	...	...	259
...	...	...	...	...	...	480	131	2	...	...	347
...	...	...	...	...	...	18	...	...	...	...	18

TABLE XV.

OCCUPATION OR MEANS OF LIVELIHOOD.

Class	Order	Occupation or means of livelihood	Total workers and dependents	Actual workers — Total — Males	Actual workers — Total — Females	Actual workers — Partially agriculturists — Males	Actual workers — Partially agriculturists — Females	Dependents both sexes
1	2	3	4	5	6	7	8	9
D.—PREPARATION AND SUPPLY OF MATERIAL SUBSTANCES—contd.	XII.—TEXTILE, FABRICS AND DRESS—concld.	TOTAL SUB-ORDER 41	363	96	148	...	...	119
		Jute, Hemp, Flax, Coir, etc						
		289. Dealers in raw fibres ...	6	1	1	...	...	4
		290. Rope, sacking and net makers	83	23	8	...	...	52
		291. Rope, sacking and net sellers	26	5	...	...	...	21
		292. Fibre matting and bag makers	244	64	139	...	...	41
		293. Fibre matting and bag sellers	4	3	...	...	...	1
		TOTAL SUB-ORDER 42	29,554	10,954	475	118	20	18,125
		Dress.						
		301. Embroiderers and lace and muslin makers	1,152	502	3	1	...	647
		302. Hat, cap, turban makers, binders and sellers	698	406	7	...	...	285
		303. Hosiers and haberdashers	313	38	63	...	...	212
		304. Piece-goods dealers ...	3,445	1,118	6	11	...	2,321
		306. Tailors, milliners, dress-makers and darners	23,946	8,890	396	106	20	14,860
	XIII.—METAL AND PRECIOUS STONES.	TOTAL ORDER XIII.—METAL AND PRECIOUS STONES	18,993	6,835	65	431	1	12,093
		TOTAL SUB-ORDER 43	10,455	3,759	25	76	...	6,671
		Gold, Silver and precious Stones.						
		312. Goldsmiths' dust washers	64	27	1	...	...	36
		313. Enamellers	153	52	...	...	...	101
		314. Electro-platers	102	47	...	...	...	55
		315. Dealers in plate and plate ware	117	27	...	...	...	90
		316. Gold and silver wire drawers and braid makers	1,359	513	1	10	...	845
		317. Workers in gold, silver and precious stones	6,984	2,619	20	47	...	4,345
		318. Dealers in gold, silver and precious stones	1,676	474	3	19	...	1,199
		TOTAL SUB-ORDER 44	1,441	567	3	25	...	871
		Brass, Copper and Bell Metal.						
		322. Brass, copper and bell metal workers	1,206	389	3	1	...	814
		323. Brass, copper and bell metal sellers	235	178	...	24	...	57
		TOTAL SUB-ORDER 45	179	57	...	...	...	122
		Tin, Zinc, Quicksilver and Lead.						
		324. Workers in tin, zinc, quicksilver and lead	177	55	...	...	...	122
		325. Sellers of tin, zinc and lead goods	2	2	...	...	...	...
		TOTAL SUB-ORDER 46	6,918	2,452	37	330	1	4,429
		Iron and Steel.						
		327. Iron foundries, operatives and other subordinates	8	6		...	...	2
		328. Workers in iron and hardware	6,792	2,399	37	330	1	4,356
		329. Sellers of iron and hardware	118	47	...	...	...	71
	XIV.—GLASS, EARTHEN AND STONEWARE.	TOTAL ORDER XIV.—GLASS, EARTHEN AND STONE-WARE.	13,642	3,856	506	328	24	9,280
		TOTAL SUB-ORDER 47	15	3	..	..	...	12
		Glass and Chinaware						
		333. Sellers of glass and Chinaware other than bangles	15	3	...	...	...	12
		TOTAL SUB-ORDER 48	13,627	3,853	506	328	24	9,268
		Earthen and Stoneware.						
		336. Potters and pot and pipe-bowl makers ...	13,246	3,724	504	328	24	9,018
		337. Sellers of pottery ware	2	2	...	...	...	...
		338. Grindstone and millstone makers and menders ...	377	127	2	..	...	248
		339. Grindstone and millstone sellers ...	2	...	...	...	...	2

TABLE XV.

Occupation or Means of Livelihood.

JAMMU PROVINCE.						KASHMIR PROVINCE.					
Total workers and dependents.	Actual workers. Total. Males.	Actual workers. Total. Females.	Actual workers. Partially agriculturists. Males.	Actual workers. Partially agriculturists. Females.	Dependents both sexes.	Total workers and dependents.	Actual workers. Total. Males.	Actual workers. Total. Females.	Actual workers. Partially agriculturists. Males.	Actual workers. Partially agriculturists. Females.	Dependents both sexes.
10	11	12	13	14	15	16	17	18	19	20	21
65	29	2		...	54	278	67	146			65
6	1	1		...	4	...	...	...		...	
34	13		...		21	49	10	8		...	31
23	4	...		...	19	3	1	...			2
22	11	1	...	...	10	222	53	138	...		31
...	...	...	...			1	3	...	...		1
6.359	1.959	279	57	20	4.121	23.022	8.910	193	60		13.919
13	11	1			1	1,065	469	1	1	...	595
57	19	2	...	...	37	641	388	5		...	248
...	...	...	...		...	313	38	63	...	...	212
2,248	699	5	11		1,544	1,164	401	1			763
4,041	1,231	271	46	20	2,539	19,839	7,614	123	59		12,102
8,553	2,950	39	257	1	5,594	10,136	3.703	26	142	...	6.407
5.471	1.793	13	49		3.665	4 791	1.822	12	27	...	2.957
64	27	1	...	...	36				...	...	...
4	3	...	...	...	1	149	49	...	...	...	100
78	39	...	...	...	39	24	8	...	...	...	16
24	11	...	...	...	13	93	16		...	...	77
619	172	1	6		445	635	235	...	4	...	400
3,233	1,125	8	24	...	2,100	3,673	1,460	12	23		2,201
1,450	416	3	19	...	1,031	217	54	...	...	...	163
345	132	3		...	210	1,096	435		25		661
254	87	3	...		164	952	302	...	1		650
91	45	...	...	...	46	144	133	...	24		11
2	2			...	...	167	53				114
...		...		...	...	167	53		...	...	114
2	2	...		...	...	...					...
2.765	1.023	23	238	1	1.719	4.082	1.393	14	90	...	2.675
...	...	...	...	...	...	8	6	...		...	2
2,744	1,019	23	238	1	1,702	3,977	1,344	14	90	...	2,619
21	4	...		...	17	97	43	...		...	54
7.170	2.116	127	225	5	4 927	6,460	1.733	379	103	19	4.348
	...	...	...		...	15	3		...		12
...		...	...	...		15	3	...	...		12
7.170	2 116	127	225	5	4.927	6.445	1.730	379	103	19	4.336
7,140	2,110	126	225	5	4,904	6,094	1,607	378	103	19	4,109
2	2	...	...	...	...	...	...	...	...	...	...
26	4	1	...	...	21	351	123	1	...	...	227
2	...	...	...	...	2	...	...	...	...	...	...

TABLE XV.

Occupation or Means of Livelihood.

Class.	Order.	Occupation or Means of Livelihood.	Frontier Districts. Total workers and dependents.	Actual workers. Total. Males.	Actual workers. Total. Females.	Actual workers. Partially agriculturists. Males.	Actual workers. Partially agriculturists. Females.	Dependents (both sexes).
1	2	3	22	23	24	25	26	27
D.—Preparation and Supply of Material Substances—contd.	XII.—Textile, Fabrics and Dress—concld.	Total Sub-order 41	...	...	..	...	...	...
		Jute, Hemp, Flax, Coir, etc.						
		289. Dealers in raw fibres	...	...	...	...	...	..
		290. Rope, sacking and net makers	...	...	...	...	...	..
		291. Rope, sacking and net sellers	...	...	...	...	...	...
		292. Fibre matting and bag makers	...	...	...	...	...	...
		293. Fibre matting and bag sellers	...	...	...	...	...	...
		Total Sub-order 43	173	85	3	1	...	85
		Dress.						
		301. Embroiderers and lace and muslin makers	74	22	1	...	...	51
		302. Hat, cap, turban makers, binders and sellers	...	...	..	...	...	...
		303. Hosiers and haberdashers	...	...	..	...	...	...
		304. Piece-goods dealers	33	18	...	...	...	15
		306. Tailors, milliners, dress-makers and darners	66	45	2	1	...	19
	XIII.—Metal and Precious Stones.	TOTAL ORDER XIII.—METAL AND PRECIOUS STONES	274	182	...	2	...	92
		Total Sub-order 43 ...	193	144	...	...	...	49
		Gold, Silver and precious Stones.						
		312. Goldsmiths' dust washers	...	...	...	...	...	...
		313. Enamellers	...	...	...	...	...	...
		314. Electro-platers	...	...	...	...	...	...
		315. Dealers in plate and plate ware	...	...	...	...	...	...
		316. Gold and silver wire drawers and braid makers	106	106	...	...	...	...
		317. Workers in gold, silver and precious stones	78	34	...	...	...	44
		318. Dealers in gold, silver and precious stones	9	4	...	...	...	5
		Total Sub-order 44 ..	...	...	...	...	...	
		Brass, Copper and Bell Metal.						
		322. Brass, copper and bell metal workers	...	..	...	...	..	..
		323. Brass, copper and bell metal sellers	...	...	...	...	...	..
		Total Sub-order 45	10	2	...	...	...	8
		Tin, Zinc, Quicksilver and Lead.						
		324. Workers in tin, zinc, quicksilver and lead	10	2	..	...	..	8
		325. Sellers of tin, zinc and lead goods	..		...	...	..	...
		Total Sub-order 46 ...	71	36	...	2	...	35
		Iron and Steel.						
		327. Iron foundries: operatives and other subordinates			..	..	...	
		328. Workers in iron and hardware	71	36	...	2	...	35
		329. Sellers of iron and hardware	...	..	...	..	...	
	XIV.—Glass, Earthen and Stoneware.	TOTAL ORDER XIV.—GLASS, EARTHEN AND STONE-WARE.	12	7	...	..	...	5
		Total Sub-order 47 ...		...	..	..	...	...
		Glass and Chinaware.						
		333. Sellers of glass and Chinaware other than bangles	...				..	...
		Total Sub-order 48 ..	12	7			...	5
		Earthen and Stoneware.						
		336. Potters and pot and pipe-bowl makers	12	7	..	..	...	5
		337. Sellers of pottery ware	...	.	...	...	...	..
		338. Grindstone and millstone makers and menders	...	...	...	...	...	..
		339. Grindstone and millstone sellers	...	...	...	...	...	...

TABLE XV.

Occupation or Means of Livelihood.

Jammu City: Total workers and dependents	Jammu City: Actual workers, Total, Males	Jammu City: Actual workers, Total, Females	Jammu City: Partially agriculturists, Males	Jammu City: Partially agriculturists, Females	Jammu City: Dependents both sexes	Srinagar City: Total workers and dependents	Srinagar City: Actual workers, Total, Males	Srinagar City: Actual workers, Total, Females	Srinagar City: Partially agriculturists, Males	Srinagar City: Partially agriculturists, Females	Srinagar City: Dependents both sexes
28	29	30	31	32	33	34	35	36	37	38	39
21	11				10	270	38	133			99
...			...	...	...						...
...	...	...	...	...	...	3	1	...	...	...	2
21	11	...	...		10	267	37	133	...	...	97
1,218	464	73	1		692	14,749	5,970	99	2		8,680
12	10	1	...	...	1	1,057	465	1	1	...	591
3	2		...	...	1	628	388	5	...	...	235
...	...	...	...			306	31	63	...		212
347	102	...			245	953	330	1	...		622
826	310	71	1	...	445	11,805	4,756	29	1	...	7,020
1,061	411	2	2		648	3,578	1,634	8	...	...	1,936
777	264	...			513	2,472	1,127	2	...		1,343
...	...	...	...		...	...	...	...			...
75	36	...		...	39	1	1	...	...	...	...
24	11	...	...	...	13	86	14	...	...	...	72
37	2	...	...	...	35	476	195	...	...	...	281
368	100	...	...	...	268	1,870	908	2	...	...	960
42	22				20	37	9		...	...	28
85	35		...	...	50	516	178			...	338
83	33		...		50	516	178	...			338
2	2	...	...	...		...		...			
	...	...	...			151	43				108
...	...	...	...	...	...	151	43	...			108
199	112	2	2	...	85	739	226	6	...		507
185	106	2	2	...	77	739	226	6	...	...	507
14	6	...			8		...		...	...	...
151	48	3	...	...	100	311	165	20		...	126
	...	...	...	...	...	15	3	...		...	12
	...					15	3		...	...	12
151	48	3	...	...	100	296	100	20	...	...	176
150	47	3	...	...	100	296	102	20	...	...	174
1	1	...	...	...	...	...	...	...	...	...	...
...	...	...	...	...	...	...	...	...	...	...	...

TABLE XV.

Occupation or Means of Livelihood.

Class.	Order.	Occupation or means of livelihood	Total State: Total workers and dependents.	Actual workers: Total: Males.	Actual workers: Total: Females.	Actual workers: Partially agriculturists: Males.	Actual workers: Partially agriculturists: Females.	Dependents (not workers).
1	2	3	4	5	6	7	8	9
D.—Preparation and supply of material substances—concld.	XV.—Wood, Cane, and Leaves, etc.	TOTAL ORDER XV.—WOOD, CANE AND LEAVES, etc. ...	20,354	6,552	258	555	7	13,514
		Total Sub-order 49	14,359	4,760	106	470	5	9,493
		Wood and Bamboo.						
		340. Carpentry works, owners, managers and superior staff	7	1	...	...	..	6
		341. Carpentry works, operatives and other subordinates ...	3	2	...	...	..	1
		343. Saw mills; workmen and other subordinates	1	1	...	...	...	
		344. Carpenters	11,691	3,655	33	453	5	7,503
		345. Dealers in timber and bamboos	320	99	7	5	.	214
		346. Wood cutters and sawyers	2,337	802	66	12	...	1,469
		Total Sub-order 50	5,995	1,622	152	85	2	4,021
		Cane works, matting and leaves, etc.						
		347. Baskets, mats, fans, screens, brooms, etc., makers and sellers.	4,782	1,591	126	82	2	3,065
		348. Comb and tooth stick makers and sellers	158	43	..	...	...	115
		349. Leaf plate makers and sellers	1,055	188	26	3	...	841
	XVI.—Drugs, Gums, Dyes, etc.	TOTAL ORDER XVI.—DRUGS, GUMS, DYES, etc. ...	1,001	263	57	5	...	681
		Total Sub-order 51	24	...	17	...	...	7
		Gums, Wax, Resins, and similar Forest produce.						
		360. Wax, honey and forest produce collectors and sellers ...	24	...	17	.	...	7
		Total Sub-order 52	977	263	40	5	...	654
		Drugs, Dyes and Pigments, etc.						
		364. Soap factories operatives and other subordinates ...	354	99	40	5	...	215
		369. Chemists and druggists	460	151	...	...	...	309
		370. Borax refiners	1	1	...	...	...	...
		372. Soap sellers	27	8	...	...	...	19
		373. Antimony preparers and sellers	47	9	...	...	...	38
		374. Madder, saffron and logwood workers and dealers ...	34	5	...	...	..	29
		375. Ink makers and sellers	3	1	...	...	...	2
		376. Perfume, incense and sandal wood preparers	1	...	...	...	...	1
		377. Perfume, incense and sandal wood sellers	24	7	..	...	...	17
		379. Persons occupied with miscellaneous dyes	26	2	...	...	..	24
	XVII.—Leather, etc.	TOTAL ORDER XVII.—LEATHER, etc.	31,566	9,085	680	1,064	9	21,501
		Total Sub-order 53	31,566	9,085	680	1,064	9	21,501
		Leather, Horn and Bones.						
		386. Leather dyers	538	207	6	..	...	325
		387. Shoe, boot and sandal makers	26,594	7,705	437	1,018	7	18,452
		388. Tanners and curriers	3,536	953	226	41	2	2,357
		389. Sellers of manufactured leather goods	492	128	6	5	...	358
		390. Sellers of hides, horns, bristles and bones	391	87	5	..	...	299
		391. Water bag, well bag, bucket and ghee pot makers ...	15	5	...	...	...	10
E.—Commerce, Transport, Storage.	XVIII.—Commerce.	TOTAL ORDER XVIII.—COMMERCE	56,515	18,165	543	588	14	37,757
		Total Sub-order 54	11,363	3,249	196	275	3	7,936
		Money and securities.						
		392. Bankers, money-lenders, etc	10,649	2,946	195	271	3	7,508
		394. Money changers and testers	656	251	3	4	..	402
		395. Bank clerks, cashiers, bill collectors, accountants, etc. ...	78	52	..	.	...	26
		Total Sub-order 55	8,917	2,911	85	84	9	5,921
		General Merchandise.						
		396. General Merchants	8,917	2,911	85	84	9	5,921

TABLE XV.

Occupation or Means of Livelihood.

Jammu Province: Total workers and dependents.	Jammu Province: Actual workers, Total, Males.	Jammu Province: Actual workers, Total, Females.	Jammu Province: Actual workers, Partially agriculturists, Males.	Jammu Province: Actual workers, Partially agriculturists, Females.	Jammu Province: Dependents both sexes.	Kashmir Province: Total workers and dependents.	Kashmir Province: Actual workers, Total, Males.	Kashmir Province: Actual workers, Total, Females.	Kashmir Province: Actual workers, Partially agriculturists, Males.	Kashmir Province: Actual workers, Partially agriculturists, Females.	Kashmir Province: Dependents both sexes.
10	11	12	13	14	15	16	17	18	19	20	21
7,431	2,723	151	334	1	4,557	12.855	3,524	103	216	6	8,928
4.909	1.784	83	274	1	3,042	9,352	2.941	19	191	4	6,422
7	1	...		...	6	...	...	...	...	...	...
3	2	...	...	...	1	...	...	...	...	...	...
1	1	...	...			...	...	...	...	...	...
3,963	1,476	15	263	1	2,475	7,657	2,344	14	185	4	5,299
320	99	7	5	...	214	...	...		...	...	...
612	205	61	6	...	346	1,725	597	5	6	...	1,128
2,523	939	68	60		1,515	3,473	853	84	25	2	2,506
1,816	751	42	57		1,023	2,968	840	84	25	2	2,048
93	24	...	...	...	69	65	19	...	...	...	46
613	164	26	3	...	423	412	24	...	...	...	418
244	72	17	...	...	155	757	211	40	5	...	506
24	...	17	...		7	...	...	...	...	...	...
24	...	17	...	...	7	...	...	...	...	...	...
220	72	...	...	...	148	757	211	40	5	...	506
1	...	...	...	...	1	353	99	40	5	...	214
158	68	...	...	...	100	302	93	...	...	...	209
1	1	...	...	...		...	...	...	...	...	...
27	8	...	...	...	10	...	...	...	...	...	...
4	3	...	...	...	1	41	6	...	...	...	37
...	...	...	...	...	...	34	5	...	...	...	29
2	...	...	...	...	2	1	1	...	...	...	...
1	...	...	...	...	1	...	...	...	...	...	...
...	...	...	...	...	...	24	7	...	...	...	17
26	2	...	...	...	24	...	...	...	...	...	...
21,102	6,118	401	950	9	14,583	10,423	2.945	278	114	...	7.20
21,102	6,118	401	950	9	14,583	10.423	2.945	278	114	...	7,200
304	120	5	...	...	179	234	87	1		...	146
18,134	5,406	316	917	7	12,412	8,420	2,277	120	104	...	6,023
1,992	464	73	29	2	1,455	1,544	480	153	12	...	902
406	68	4	4	...	334	86	60	2	1	.	24
251	55	3	.	...	193	[illegible]	32	2			105
15	5	...	...		10			...	...		...
31.523	10.415	441	487	4	20.667	24.063	7.364	87	94	10	16,612
9.488	2.594	191	264	3	6.701	1.860	638	6	11		1.216
9,268	2,522	191	264	3	6,555	1,368	[illegible]	3	7	...	942
205	69	...	...	...	136	451	182	3	4	...	206
15	3	...		...	12	[illegible]	[illegible]	...	...	...	[illegible]
3,397	1,251	52	51		2,094	4.965	1.417	27	31	9	[illegible]
3,397	1,251	52	51	...	2,094	[illegible]	1,417	27	31	9	[illegible]

TABLE XV.

Occupation or Means of Livelihood.

Class	Order	Occupation or Means of Livelihood	Frontier Districts. Total workers and dependents	Actual Workers — Total — Males	Actual Workers — Total — Females	Actual Workers — Partially agriculturists — Males	Actual Workers — Partially agriculturists — Females	Dependents both sexes
1	2	3	22	23	24	25	26	27
II.—PREPARATION AND SUPPLY OF MATERIAL SUBSTANCES.—concld.	XV.—Wood, Cane and Leaves, etc.	TOTAL ORDER XV.—WOOD, CANE AND LEAVES, etc.	68	35	4	5	..	29
		Total Sub-order 49	68	35	4	5		29
		Wood and Bamboo.						
		340. Carpentry works, owners, managers and superior staff	..	.	...	...	...	
		341. Carpentry works, operatives and other subordinates	..	..	...	..	..	...
		343. Saw mills · workmen and other subordinates	..		...	..	...	.
		344. Carpenters	68	35	4	5	..	29
		345. Dealers in timber and bamboos	.	.		...	...	
		346. Wood cutters and sawyers	.	..		...	..	...
		Total Sub-order 50	.			..	...	...
		Cane works, matting and leaves, etc.						
		347. Baskets, mats, fans, screens, brooms, etc., makers and sellers.	..	...	.	..	..	...
		348. Comb and tooth stick makers and sellers	.	..	...	...		...
		349. Leaf-plate makers and sellers	.	..	...	.	...	...
	XVI.—Drugs, Gums, Dyes, etc.	TOTAL ORDER XVI.—DRUGS, GUMS, DYES, etc.	.	..			...	...
		Total Sub-order 51		.	.	.	...	...
		Gums, Wax, Resins and similar Forest produce.						
		360. Wax, honey and forest produce collectors and sellers	...		..	..	...	...
		Total Sub-order 52	.	...	.	..	...	..
		Drugs, Dyes and Pigments, etc.						
		361. Soap factories operatives and other subordinates		...	...	..	...	
		369. Chemists and druggists	..	.	..	...	...	..
		370. Borax refiners	..	.	.	.	..	..
		372. Soap sellers	..	..	..	...	..	..
		373. Antimony preparers and sellers	..	...	..	...	...	..
		374. Madder, saffron and logwood worker and dealers		...	.		...	..
		375. Ink makers and sellers	..	.	..		..	..
		376. Perfume, incense and sandal wood preparers	..	...	...	...	.	...
		377. Perfume, incense and sandal wood sellers	...	..	..	..	..	..
		379. Persons occupied with miscellaneous dyes	...	..	..	.	..	...
	XVII.—Leather, etc.	TOTAL ORDER XVII.—LEATHER, etc.	41	22	1		..	18
		Total Sub-order 53	41	22	1		.	18
		Leather, Horn and Bones.						
		386. Leather dyers	...	.	..	...	.	...
		387. Shoe, boot and sandal makers	40	22	1	...	..	17
		388. Tanners and curriers	...	...	.	.	..	...
		389. Sellers of manufactured leather goods	...	...	...	..	..	...
		390. Sellers of hides, horns, bristles and bones	1	..	..	...	...	1
		391. Water bag, well bag, bucket and ghee-pot makers	..	..	.		.	...
III.—COMMERCE, TRANSPORT, STORAGE.	XVIII.—Commerce	TOTAL ORDER XVIII.—COMMERCE	929	406	15	7		508
		Total Sub-order 54	37	17	1	..		19
		Money and securities.						
		392. Bankers, money-lenders, etc.	15	1	1	...	.	13
		394. Money changers and testers	.	..			.	...
		395. Bank clerks, cashiers, bill collectors, accountants, etc.	22	16		.	..	6
		Total Sub-order 55	555	243	6	2	...	308
		General Merchandise.						
		396. General Merchants	555	243	6	2	...	306

TABLE XV.

Occupation or Means of Livelihood.

Jammu City						Srinagar City					
Total workers and dependents.	Actual workers. Total. Males.	Actual workers. Total. Females.	Actual workers. Partially agriculturists. Males.	Actual workers. Partially agriculturists. Females.	Dependants both sexes.	Total workers and dependents.	Actual workers. Total. Males.	Actual workers. Total. Females.	Actual workers. Partially agriculturists. Males.	Actual workers. Partially agriculturists. Females.	Dependants both sexes.
28	29	30	31	32	33	34	35	36	37	38	39
541	245	...	6	...	296	3,113	952	24	2	...	2,137
491	226	...	6	...	265	2,449	865	2	2	...	1,582
7	1	...	...	...	6	...	...	...	...	...	...
2	1	...	...	...	1	...	...	...	...	...	...
428	200	...	6	...	228	1,688	553	1	...	...	1,134
54	24	...	...	...	30	761	312	1	2	...	448
50	19	...	...	...	31	664	57	22	...	...	585
11	4	...	...	...	7	158	45	22	...	...	91
2	1	...	...	...	1	64	18	...	...	...	46
37	14	...	...	...	23	442	24	...	...	...	418
113	39	...	...	...	74	425	106	34	...	...	285
...	...	...	...	...	...	...	...	...	...	...	...
...	...	...	...	...	...	...	...	...	...	...	...
113	39	...	...	...	74	425	106	34	...	...	285
...	...	...	...	...	...	129	26	34	...	...	69
71	34	...	...	...	37	223	66	...	...	...	155
22	5	...	...	...	17	...	...	...	...	...	...
...	...	...	...	...	...	33	...	...	...	...	33
...	...	...	...	...	...	16	5	...	...	...	11
2	...	...	...	...	2	...	...	...	...	...	...
1	...	...	...	...	1	24	7	...	...	...	17
17	...	...	...	...	17	...	...	...	...	...	...
728	262	7	1	...	459	1,090	431	4	...	...	655
728	262	7	1	...	459	1,090	431	4	...	...	655
47	15	...	...	...	32	234	87	1	...	...	146
612	230	7	1	...	375	814	338	3	...	...	473
4	...	...	...	...	4	...	...	...	...	...	...
30	16	...	...	...	14	...	...	...	...	...	...
28	...	...	...	...	28	42	6	...	...	...	36
7	1	...	...	...	6	...	...	...	...	...	...
3,179	1,276	10	20	...	1,893	8,637	2,853	18	...	...	5,766
919	305	7	8	...	607	1,012	333	1	...	...	678
720	240	7	8	...	473	1,012	333	1	...	...	678
197	64	...	...	...	133	...	...	...	...	...	...
2	1	...	...	...	1	...	...	...	...	...	...
427	184	...	...	...	243	2,439	635	15	...	...	1,789
427	184	...	...	...	243	2,439	635	15	...	...	1,789

TABLE XV.

Occupation or Means of Livelihood.

Class.	Order.	Occupation or Means of Livelihood.	TOTAL STATE. Total workers and dependants.	Actual workers. Total. Males.	Actual workers. Total. Females.	Actual workers. Partially agriculturists. Males.	Actual workers. Partially agriculturists. Females.	Dependants both sexes.
1	2	3	4	5	6	7	8	9
8.—Commerce, Transport, Storage—concld.	XVIII.—Commerce—concld.	Total Sub-order 56 ...	34,513	11,478	252	214	2	22,783
		Dealing Unspecified.						
		398. Shop-keepers, otherwise unspecified	29,599	9,552	171	185	...	19,576
		399. Shop-keepers' clerks, salesmen, etc.	14	...	..	..	...	14
		400. Shop-keepers and money lenders' servants	550	171	21	1	...	358
		401. Pedlars, hawkers, etc.	4,350	1,455	60	18	...	2,835
		Total Sub-order 57	1,702	547	8	15	...	1,147
		Middlemen, Brokers and Agents.						
		402. Brokers and agents	537	110	5	..	...	422
		405. Farmers of liquor, opium, etc.	11	6	1	...	...	4
		407. Contractors, otherwise unspecified	1,154	431	2	15	..	721
	XIX.—Transport and Storage.	TOTAL ORDER XIX.—TRANSPORT AND STORAGE ...	24,791	8,918	1,365	289	4	14,508
		Total Sub-order 58	256	106	...	3	..	150
		Railway.						
		411. Clerical staff on Railways	139	52	..	...	...	87
		412. Station masters, and assistants, inspectors, overseers, etc.	22	7	...	...	...	15
		413. Guards, drivers, fireman, etc.	20	1	...	...	...	19
		414. Pointsmen, shunters, porters, signallers, etc.	31	4	...	...	...	27
		415. Railway service unspecified	44	42	-	3	...	2
		Total Sub-order 59 ...	9,937	3,823	33	259	3	6,081
		Road.						
		418. Livery stable-keeper, etc.	6	1	...	...	...	5
		419. Drivers, stable boys, etc., not private servants	210	114	7	5	...	89
		420. Pálki, etc., bearers, and owners	31	20	...	1	...	11
		421. Pack bullock owners, drivers, etc.	5,442	1,828	22	160	3	3,597
		422. Pack camel, elephant, mule, etc., owners and drivers ...	4,248	1,865	6	98	1	2,379
		Total Sub-order 60 ...	12,658	4,267	1,315	17	...	7,076
		Water.						
		424. Shipping clerks, supercargoes and stevedores	52	13	...	..	..	39
		425. Boat and barge owners, etc.	2	..	...	...	...	2
		429. Boat and barge men	12,530	4,234	1,308	16	...	6,988
		430. Pilots	28	8	...	...	...	20
		431. Lock-keepers, etc., and canal service	51	17	7	1	...	27
		Total Sub-order 61 ...	1,289	531	2	10	1	756
		Messages.						
		433. Post Office : officers and superior staff	182	91	2	...	...	89
		434. Post Office : clerks, messengers, runners and other subordinates.	925	365	...	10	1	560
		435. Telegraph : officers and superior staff	7	5	...	...	...	2
		436. Telegraph : clerks, signallers, messengers and other subordinates	175	70	...	..	...	105
		Total Sub-order 62	651	191	15	...	...	445
		Storage and Weighing.						
		441. Porters	437	109	14	...	...	314
		442. Weighmen and measurers	207	80	1	..	...	126
		443. Watchmen employed at stores	7	2	...	...	...	5

TABLE XV.

OCCUPATION OR MEANS OF LIVELIHOOD.

JAMMU PROVINCE						KASHMIR PROVINCE					
Total workers and dependents.	Actual workers. Total. Males.	Actual workers. Total. Females.	Actual workers. Partially agriculturists. Males.	Actual workers. Partially agriculturists. Females.	Dependents both sexes.	Total workers and dependents.	Actual workers. Total. Males.	Actual workers. Total. Females.	Actual workers. Partially agriculturists. Males.	Actual workers. Partially agriculturists. Females.	Dependents both sexes.
10	11	12	13	14	15	16	17	18	19	20	21
17,778	**6,257**	**194**	**158**	**1**	**11,327**	**16,426**	**5,100**	**50**	**51**	**1**	**11,276**
16,208	5,835	111	144	1	10,229	13,052	3,893	32	46	1	9,167
14	...	...	...		14		...	..	...	..	...
147	64	2		..	81	403	107	19	1	..	277
1,409	355	61	14	.	1,003	2,941	1,100	9	4	...	1,832
862	**313**	**4**	**14**	.	**545**	**812**	**209**	**4**	**1**	.	**599**
86	20	1	...	.	59	457	90	4	..		302
3	...	1	..		2	8	6	..	...	...	2
779	293	2	14	..	481	347	113	..	1		234
6,461	**2,470**	**21**	**203**	**3**	**3,970**	**17,994**	**6,203**	**1,334**	**78**	..	**10,457**
256	**106**		**8**	..	**150**	..	...	...	..	..	...
139	62	...	...	..	87	...	...	...	.	.	...
22	7	...	...	...	15	...		...	.	...	...
20	1	..	..	...	19	..	...	...	.	...	...
31	4	...	..	..	27	...	...		...	...	...
44	42	...	3	.	2	..		..	..	...	...
5,317	**1,986**	**21**	**195**	**2**	**3,900**	**4,455**	**1,652**	**12**	**64**	...	**2,781**
5	1	...	.	..	4	1	..	...	...	...	1
131	73	6	5	...	52	70	41	1	...	...	37
31	20	...	1	...	11	...	..	...		...	...
3,627	1,319	14	122	2	2,294	1,815	504	8	38	...	1,208
1,523	583	1	67	.	939	2,560	1,187	8	26	...	1,480
329	**97**	...	**3**	...	**232**	**12,284**	**4,142**	**1,207**	**13**	...	**6,815**
52	18	..		.	39	...	..	..		...	...
2	..	...	.	...	2		...	...	.	...	
275	84	...	3	...	191	12,190	4,122	1,300	12		6,769
	.	...	...	..		23	3	...	...	..	20
	...	...	.		..	51	17	7	1		27
388	**197**	...	**5**	**1**	**191**	**795**	**362**	...	**1**	...	**583**
11	4	...	.	...	7	156	74		...	...	82
344	179	...	5	1	165	519	148	...	1		376
..		..	.	...		7	5	.	...		2
38	14	...	...	...	19	113	40		...	...	73
171	**74**	...		...	**97**	**480**	**117**	**15**	...		**268**
21	21	...	...	...	...	416	88	14	...	...	316
159	63	...	...	...	97	57	27	1	...	...	25
...	...	...	...	...	...	7	2	...	...	...	5

TABLE XV.

Occupation or Means of Livelihood.

Class.	Order.	Occupation or means of livelihood.	Frontier Districts. Total workers and dependents.	Actual workers. Total. Males.	Actual workers. Total. Females.	Partially agriculturists. Males.	Partially agriculturists. Females.	Dependents both sexes.
1	2	3	22	23	24	25	26	27
X.—Commerce, Transport, Storage—concld.	XVIII.—Commerce—concld.	Total Sub-order 56 ...	309	121	8	5	...	180
		Dealing Unspecified.						
		398. Shop-keepers, otherwise unspecified	309	121	8	5	...	180
		399. Shop-keepers' clerks, salesmen, etc.	...	...	...	...	...	...
		400. Shop-keepers and money-lenders' servants ...	...	...	...	...	...	...
		401. Pedlars, hawkers, etc.	...	...	...	...	...	...
		Total Sub-order 57	28	25	...	...	...	3
		Middlemen, Brokers and Agents.						
		402. Brokers and agents	...	...	...	...	...	...
		405. Farmers of liquor, opium, etc.	...	...	...	...	...	...
		407. Contractors, otherwise unspecified	28	25	...	...	...	3
	XIX.—Transport and Storage.	TOTAL ORDER XIX.—TRANSPORT AND STORAGE ...	336	245	10	5	1	81
		Total Sub-order 58	...	...	...	...	...	...
		Railway.						
		411. Clerical staff on Railways	...	...	...	...	...	...
		412. Station masters and assistants, inspectors, overseers, etc.	...	...	...	...	...	...
		413. Guards, drivers, firemen, etc.	...	...	...	...	...	...
		414. Pointsmen, shunters, porters, signallers, etc.	...	...	...	...	...	...
		415. Railway service unspecified	...	...	...	...	...	...
		Total Sub-order 59	165	145	...	...	1	20
		Road.						
		418. Livery stable-keeper, etc	...	...	...	...	...	...
		419. Drivers, stable boys, etc., not private servants	...	...	...	...	...	...
		420. Palki, etc., bearers and owners	...	...	...	...	...	...
		421. Pack bullock owners, drivers, etc.	...	...	...	...	...	...
		422. Pack camel, elephant, mule, etc., owners and drivers ..	165	145	...	...	1	20
		Total Sub-order 60	65	28	8	1	...	29
		Water.						
		424. Shipping clerks, supercargoes and stevedores	...	...	...	...	...	...
		425. Boat and barge owners, etc.	...	...	...	...	...	...
		429. Boat and barge men	65	28	8	1	...	29
		430. Pilots	...	...	...	...	...	...
		431. Lock-keepers, etc., and canal service	...	...	...	...	...	...
		Total Sub-order 61	106	72	2	4	...	32
		Messages.						
		433. Post Office : officers and superior staff	15	13	2	...	...	...
		434. Post Office : clerks, messengers, runners and other subordinates.	62	43	...	4	...	19
		435. Telegraph : officers and superior staff	...	...	...	...	...	...
		436. Telegraph : clerks, signallers, messengers and other subordinates.	20	16	...	...	...	13
		Total Sub-order 62	...	...	...	...	...	...
		Storage and Weighing.						
		441. Porters	...	...	...	...	...	...
		442. Weighmen and measurers	...	...	...	...	...	...
		443. Watchmen employed at stores	...	...	...	...	...	...

TABLE XV.

Occupation or Means of Livelihood.

Jammu City.						Srinagar City.					
Total workers and dependents.	Actual workers. Total.		Actual workers. Partially agriculturists.		Dependents both sexes.	Total workers and dependents.	Actual workers. Total.		Actual workers. Partially agriculturists.		Dependents both sexes.
	Males.	Females.	Males.	Females.			Males.	Females.	Males.	Females.	
28	29	30	31	32	33	34	35	36	37	38	39
1.352	**663**	**3**	**12**		**686**	**4.562**	**1.736**	**2**	..	..	**2.824**
1,081	611	2	12	..	468	4,360	1,626	2	...	...	2,732
14	...	...	...	.	14	..	..	...	...	..	...
10	...	...	..	..	10	...				...	...
247	52	1	..	..	194	202	110	..		...	92
381	**124**	...	...	.	**257**	**624**	**149**	..	...	..	**475**
5	3	...	..	..	2	392	75		...	...	313
...	...	...		...	..	8	6	..	...	...	2
376	121	...	...	...	255	224	64	...	...	..	160
536	**248**	...	**9**	...	**288**	**6.252**	**2.298**	**491**	**1**	...	**3.463**
158	**73**	..	**3**	...	**85**	...	..	...	...	...	...
122	47	..	...		75	...	...	...	...	...	...
2	...	...	...	...	2	...	...	...	...	...	...
1	...	...	...	...	1	...	...	...	...	...	...
8	1	...	...	...	7	...	...	...	...	...	...
25	25	...	3	...	...	...	...	...	...	...	...
240	**101**	...	**6**		**139**	**465**	**137**	...	...	...	**328**
4	1	...	...	..	3	...	..	...	...	..	...
105	61	...	5	...	44	...	...	...	...	...	...
12	8	...	1	...	4	...	...	...	...	...	...
38	1	...	...	...	37	...		...	...	..	...
81	30	...	..	...	51	465	137	...	...	...	328
18	**5**	...	...	...	**13**	**5.084**	**2.006**	**476**	**1**	...	**2.602**
...	...	...	...	...	...	...	..	...	..	...	...
...	...	...	..	...	...		...	...	..	...	...
18	5	...	...	...	13	5,061	2,003	476	1	...	2,582
...	...	...	...	...	...	23	3	...	.	...	20
...	...	...	...	...	...	...	...	...	..	...	...
59	**29**	...	...	...	**30**	**385**	**78**	...		..	**307**
1	1	...	...	...	...	3	1	...	...	...	2
50	27	..	...		23	329	63	...	...	...	266
..	...	...	...	...	..	7	5	...	...	...	2
8	1	...	...	...	7	46	9	...	...	...	37
61	**40**	...	...	...	**21**	**318**	**77**	**15**	..	...	**226**
...	...	...	..	...	...	261	50	14	...	...	197
61	40	...	...	...	21	57	27	1	...	...	29
...	...	...	...	...	...	...	...	...	...	...	...

TABLE XV.

Occupation or Means of Livelihood.

Class.	Order.	Occupation or means of livelihood.	TOTAL STATE. Total workers and dependents.	Actual workers. Total. Males.	Actual workers. Total. Females.	Actual workers. Partially agriculturists. Males.	Actual workers. Partially agriculturists. Females.	Dependents both sexes.
1	2	3	4	5	6	7	8	9
F.—PROFESSIONS.	XX.—Learned and Artistic Professions.	TOTAL ORDER XX.—LEARNED AND ARTISTIC PROFESSIONS.	48,816	16,873	1,368	762	11	30,575
		Total Sub-order 63	36,828	12.114	1.209	654	11	23.505
		Religion.						
		444. Priests, ministers, etc., ...	21,997	7,265	875	403	2	13,857
		445. Catechists, readers, church and mission service, etc. ...	3,415	1,103	21	43	...	2.291
		446. Religious mendicants, inmates of monasteries, convents, etc.	2,997	1,065	95	52	...	1,537
		447. Church, temple, burial or burning ground service, pilgrim conductors, undertakers, etc.	8.084	2,567	218	156	9	5.299
		448. Circumcisors	13	9	...	...	...	4
		449. Astrologers, divines, horoscope makers, etc.	322	105	..	...	...	217
		Total Sub-order 64	1.780	692	17	11	..	1.071
		Education.						
		452. Principals, professors, and teachers	1,204	537	15	9	...	652
		453. Clerks and servants connected with education	576	156	2	2	...	419
		Total Sub-order 65	2.932	1.428	3	27	...	1,501
		Literature.						
		454. Authors, editors, journalists, etc.	11	3	..	...	...	8
		456. Writers (unspecified) and private clerks	44	4	...	...	...	40
		457. Public scribes and copyists	2,612	1,282	...	12	...	1,330
		458. Service in libraries and literary institutions	265	139	3	15	...	123
		Total Sub-order 66	1.284	394	...	5	...	890
		Law.						
		459. Barristers, advocates and pleaders	433	108	...	1	...	325
		460. Solicitors and attorneys	42	18	...		...	24
		461. Law agents, mukhtiárs, etc.	32	5	...	...	..	27
		462. Kázis	19	5	...	..	...	14
		463. Articled clerks and other lawyers' clerks	91	35	...	...	...	56
		464 Petition-writers, touts, etc., ...	394	155	..	4	...	239
		465. Stamp-vendors	273	68	...	...	...	205
		Total Sub-order 67	2.559	873	95	40	..	1.591
		Medicine.						
		467. Practitioners with diploma, license or certificate ..	16	8	1	..	...	7
		468. Practitioners without diploma	1.804	618	37	37	...	1.149
		470. Oculists	2	2	...	1	..	...
		472. Midwives	78	4	47			27
		473. Compounders, matrons, nurses and hospital asylum and dispensary service	659	241	10	2	...	408
		Total Sub-order 68	211	82		9	...	129
		Engineering and survey.						
		475. Civil engineers and architects	67	29	...	6	..	38
		477. Draughtsmen and operators in survey offices, overseers, etc.	143	52	...	3		91
		478. Clerks, etc., in offices of the above	1	1	...	...	...	...
		Total Sub-order 69	5		..	...	...	5
		Natural Science.						
		481. Metallurgists	5	..	...	...	...	5

TABLE XV.

OCCUPATION OR MEANS OF LIVELIHOOD.

JAMMU PROVINCE.						KASHMIR PROVINCE.					
Total workers and dependents.	Actual workers. Total. Males.	Actual workers. Total. Females.	Actual workers. Partially agriculturists. Males.	Actual workers. Partially agriculturists. Females.	Dependents both sexes.	Total workers and dependents.	Actual workers. Total. Males.	Actual workers. Total. Females.	Actual workers. Partially agriculturists. Males.	Actual workers. Partially agriculturists. Females.	Dependents both sexes.
10	11	12	13	14	15	16	17	18	19	20	21
26,752	9,276	1,102	604	11	16,374	20,484	6,505	216	133	...	13,763
21,933	7,033	1,001	527	11	13,899	13,680	4,234	159	108	...	9,287
14,535	5,150	799	345	2	8,606	7,349	2,072	76	58	...	5,201
149	41	...	7		108	3,099	1,018	15	36	...	2,066
987	340	28	42	...	619	2,010	725	67	10	...	1,218
6,213	1,493	174	133	9	4,544	932	326	1	4	..	605
...	...	...	...	..	..	..	...	..	...	..	...
29	9	...	...	...	20	290	93	..	...	...	197
570	288	9	9	...	273	1,155	392	8	1	...	785
330	263	9	7	...	258	640	262	6	1	...	381
40	25	...	2	...	15	536	130	2	...	...	404
1,420	920	3	21	...	497	1,404	429	...	2	...	
...	...	...	...	..	...	11	3	..	...	...	8
11	4	...	...	...	7	33	...	...	...	...	33
1,144	777	...	6	...	367	1,360	420	...	2	...	934
265	139	3	15	...	123	...	...	..	...	...	...
876	305	...	5	...	571	407	88	...	..	..	319
268	73	..	1	...	195	165	35		...	.	130
42	18	...	..	..	24	...	...	...	..	..	..
...	...	...	.	...	..	32	5	...	..	..	27
11	5	...	...	...	6	8	...	...	...	..	8
81	32	...	...	..	49	10	3	...	.	...	7
389	151	..	4	...	238	4	3	...	..	...	1
85	26	...	...	..	59	188	12	...	...	...	140
834	304	49	18	..	461	1,608	478	46	21	...	1,084
11	4	1	...	...	6	5	4	..	...	..	1
568	223	5	17	...	335	1,217	379	32	20	..	406
2	2	..	1	...		..	...	..	.	...	...
71	4	42	...	...	25	7	...	5	...	...	2
187	71	1	...	...	115	479	95	9	1	...	375
79	21	..	9	...	58	32	61	...	..	...	11
30	9	...	6	..	21	37	20	...	...	...	17
48	11	...	3	..	37	95	41	..	..	...	54
1	1	...	...	...	...	...	...	...	.	...	...
...	...	..	...	...	...	5	...	..	...	...	5
...	...	...	...	...	...	5	...	...	...	...	5

TABLE XV.

Occupation or Means of Livelihood.

Class	Order	Occupation or means of livelihood	Frontier Districts. Total workers and dependents	Actual workers: Total: Males	Actual workers: Total: Females	Actual workers: Partially agriculturists: Males	Actual workers: Partially agriculturists: Females	Dependents both sexes
1	2	3	22	23	24	25	26	27
F.—PROFESSIONS	XX.—Learned and Artistic Professions.	TOTAL ORDER XX.—LEARNED AND ARTISTIC PROFESSIONS.	1,580	1,092	50	25	.	438
		Total Sub-order 63	1,215	847	49	19	...	319
		Religion						
		444. Priests, ministers, etc.	93	43	...	...	...	50
		445. Catechists, readers, church and mission service, etc. ..	167	44	6	...	...	117
		446. Religious mendicants, inmates of monasteries, convents, etc.	...		..	...	...	...
		447. Church, temple, burial or burning ground service, pilgrim conductors, undertakers, etc.	939	748	43	19	...	148
		448. Circumcisors	13	9	...	...	...	4
		449. Astrologers, divines, horoscope makers, etc	3	3	...	...	...	...
		Total Sub-order 64	25	12	...	1	...	13
		Education.						
		452. Principals, professors and teachers	25	12	...	1	...	13
		453. Clerks and servants connected with education	...	...	...	...	...	...
		Total Sub-order 65	108	79	...	4	..	29
		Literature						
		454. Authors, editors, journalists, etc.	...	...	...	...	...	...
		456. Writers (unspecified) and private clerks	...	...	...	...	...	...
		457. Public scribes and copyists	108	79	...	4	...	29
		458. Service in libraries and literary institutions	...	...	...	...	...	...
		Total Sub-order 66 ...	1	1	...	...	...	...
		Law.						
		459. Barristers, advocates and pleaders	..	...	...	...	...	...
		460. Solicitors and attorneys	..	...	...	...	...	...
		461. Law agents, mukhtiárs etc., ...	...	...	...	...	...	...
		462. Kázís	...	...	...	...	...	...
		463. Articled clerks and other laywers' clerks	...	...	..	...	...	...
		464. Petition-writers, touts, etc.	1	1	...	...	...	...
		465. Stamp-vendors	...	...	...	...	...	...
		Total Sub-order 67	117	91	...	1	...	26
		Medicine.						
		467. Practitioners with diploma, license or certificate ..	...	...	...	...	...	...
		468. Practitioners without diploma	24	16	...	...	...	8
		470. Oculists	...	...	...	...	...	...
		472. Midwives	...	...	...	...	...	...
		473. Compounders, matrons, nurses and hospital asylum and dispensary service.	93	75	...	1	...	18
		Total Sub-order 68	...	...	...	...	.	...
		Engineering and survey.						
		475. Civil engineers and architects	...	...	...	...	...	...
		477. Draughtsmen and operators in survey offices, overseers, etc.	...	...	...	...	...	...
		478. Clerks, etc., in offices of the above	...	..	...	...	...	...
		Total Sub-order 69	...	...	...	...	...	...
		Natural Science.						
		481. Metallurgists	...	...	...	...	...	...

TABLE XV.

Occupation or Means of Livelihood.

JAMMU CITY.						SRINAGAR CITY.					
Total workers and dependents.	Actual workers. Total		Actual workers. Partially agriculturists.		Dependents both sexes.	Total workers and dependents	Actual workers. Total.		Actual workers. Partially agriculturists.		Dependents both sexes.
	Males.	Females.	Males.	Females.			Males.	Females.	Males.	Females.	
28	29	30	31	32	33	34	35	36	37	38	39
2,735	1,154	144	26	...	1,437	8,574	2,873	65	1	...	5,636
1,832	695	127	14	...	810	4,404	1,566	31	.	...	2,807
1,541	671	127	14	...	743	2,490	834	28	...	...	1,628
...	...	...	...	...	...	60	2	...	...	...	58
8	7	...	...	...	1	1,391	569	3	...	...	819
67	12	...	...	...	55	325	132	...	...	...	193
16	5	...	...	...	11	138	29	...	..	...	109
82	41		3	...	41	619	173	6	1		440
42	16	...	1	...	26	83	43	4	1	...	36
40	25	...	2	..	15	536	130	2	...	...	404
66	53	2	..	..	11	923	229	...	..	...	694
...	...	..	...	.	...	...	...		...	...	...
...	...	...	..	...	...	...	...	...	...	..	...
59	52	.	...	...	7	923	229	...	...	.	694
7	1	2	...	...	4	...	...	..	...	...	...
393	142	..	2	...	251	343	70	...	...	..	273
154	36	...	1	...	118	164	34	...	...	...	130
40	18	...	..	...	22	...	...	...	..	..	...
...	...	...	.	...	...	7	1	...	...	...	6
...	...	..	...	...	..	8	..	...	..	...	8
87	26	...	...	..	81	..	...	...	..	...	...
117	54	...	1	...	63	...	...	...	..	...	...
25	8	...	...	...	17	164	35	..	...	..	129
175	78	10	.	...	87	763	214	26	.	...	523
...	...	...	...	...		3	3		...	...	...
85	41	1	...	...	43	520	156	19	...	..	345
...	...	...	...	...	..	...		...	...	...	...
9	...	8	...	...	1	...	...	...	...	...	...
81	37	1	...	..	43	240	55	7	...	..	178
67	16	...	6	...	51	75	25	...	...	..	50
29	8	...	6	...	21	4	2	...	...	..	2
37	7	...	..	...	30	71	23	...	...	...	48
1	1	...	..	...	..	..	...	...	...	..	...
..	...	...	...	...	...	...	...	...	.	...	...
...	...	...	...	...	...	...	...	...	...	...	...

TABLE XV.

OCCUPATION OR MEANS OF LIVELIHOOD.

Class.	Order.	Occupation or means of livelihood.	Total workers and dependents.	Actual workers. Total. Males.	Actual workers. Total. Females.	Actual workers. Partially agriculturists. Males.	Actual workers. Partially agriculturists. Females.	Dependents both sexes.
1	2	3	4	5	6	7	8	9
		TOTAL STATE.						
F.—PROFESSIONS—concld.	XX.—LEARNED AND ARTISTIC PROFESSIONS—concld.	TOTAL SUB-ORDER 70 ...	1,615	675	2	1	...	938
		Pictorial Art and Sculpture.						
		483. Painters, superintendents of schools of art, etc. ...	1,177	520	1	.	...	656
		484. Sculptors	420	145	1	1	...	274
		485. Photographers	18	10	...	...	...	8
		TOTAL SUB-ORDER 71	1,602	615	42	15	...	945
		Music, Acting, Dancing, etc.						
		487. Music composers and teachers	2	1	...		...	1
		488. Band masters and players (not military)	155	76		...	...	79
		489. Piano-tuners	4	2	...		...	2
		490. Actors, singers and dancers and their accompanists	1,441	536	42	15	...	863
	XXI.—SPORT.	TOTAL ORDER XXI.—SPORT ...	731	257	13	9	...	461
		TOTAL SUB-ORDER 72	160	75	3	5	...	82
		Sports.						
		492. Shikaris, falconers, bird-catchers	145	69	3	5	...	73
		493. Huntsmen, whippers-in	15	6	...		...	9
		TOTAL SUB-ORDER 73	571	182	10	4	...	379
		Games and Exhibitions.						
		494. Owners and managers of places of public entertainment	5	1	...	.	...	4
		495. Persons engaged in service of place of public entertainment.	11	3	...	...	...	8
		496. Exhibitors of trained animals	1	1	...	...	...	..
		498. Conjurors, buffoons, reciters, fortune tellers, etc. ...	135	35	1	4	...	99
		499. Tumblers, acrobats, wrestlers, professional cricketers, etc.	419	142	9	...	...	268
G.—UNSKILLED LABOUR, NOT AGRICULTURAL.	XXII.—EARTHWORK AND GENERAL LABOUR.	TOTAL ORDER XXII.—EARTHWORK AND GENERAL LABOUR.	47,273	15,044	4,765	320	9	27,464
		TOTAL SUB-ORDER 74	1,746	775	119	12	...	852
		Earthwork, etc.						
		500. Well-sinkers	96	24	4	8	..	68
		501. Tank-diggers and excavators	213	83	...	.	...	130
		502. Road, canal and Railway labour	1,437	718	115	4	..	604
		TOTAL SUB-ORDER 75	45,527	14,269	4,646	308	9	26,612
		General Labour.						
		504. General labour	45,527	14,269	4,646	308	9	26,612
	XXIII.—INDEFINITE AND DISREPUTABLE OCCUPATIONS.	TOTAL ORDER XXIII.—INDEFINITE AND DISREPUTABLE OCCUPATIONS.	689	143	240	...	...	306
		TOTAL SUB-ORDER 76 ...	246	131	5	...	...	110
		Indefinite.						
		505. Uncertain or not returned	246	131	5	...	...	110
		TOTAL SUB-ORDER 77	443	12	235	..	...	196
		Disreputable.						
		506. Prostitutes including saqins and nauchis	438	11	235	...	...	192
		508. Receivers of stolen goods	4	1	..	...	...	3
		509. Witches, wizards, cow-poisoners, etc	1	...	..	...	...	1

TABLE XV.

Occupation or Means of Livelihood.

JAMMU PROVINCE.						KASHMIR PROVINCE					
Total workers and dependants.	Actual workers. Total. Males.	Actual workers. Total. Females.	Actual workers. Partially agriculturists. Males.	Actual workers. Partially agriculturists. Females.	Dependants both sexes.	Total workers and dependants.	Actual workers. Total. Males.	Actual workers. Total. Females.	Actual workers. Partially agriculturists. Males.	Actual workers. Partially agriculturists. Females.	Dependants both sexes.
10	11	12	13	14	15	16	17	18	19	20	21
356	140	...	1	...	216	1,256	532	2	..	..	722
1	1				...	1,173	516	1	...	..	656
349	135		1	...	214	71	10	1			60
6	4	...			2	12	6				6
624	265	40	14	..	319	807	291	1	1	...	515
2	1	..	..		1						...
56	26			...	32	...		...		...	...
4	2				2						
620	236	40	14	.	344	807	291	1	1		515
410	136	8		..	268	321	121	5	9		195
35	19		...		16	125	56	3	5	...	66
20	13	...	...	...	7	125	56	3	5	...	66
15	6	...		...	9	...	..		..		...
375	117	8	...	...	250	196	65	2	4		129
5	1	...	..		4		...			...	..
11	3	...			8						...
1	1	...	..	..	...			...			...
11	1		...	...	10	124	34	1	4	..	89
347	111	8			228	72	31	1			40
30.973	9.114	3.901	288	9	17.958	15.043	5 376	697	30	...	8,970
1.500	656	109	12	...	735	246	119	10	...		117
21	12		8	.	9	75	12	1	..	..	59
202	24	...			178	11	9			...	2
1.277	620	109	4	.	548	160	98	6			56
29.473	8.456	3,792	276	9	17.223	14.797	5,257	687	30	...	8,853
29,473	8,456	3,792	276	9	17.223	14 797	5,257	687	30	...	8,853
351	33	142		..	176	316	97	95	...		124
87	29			..	58	151	97	5		...	49
87	29	...	...	.	58	151	97	5	...	...	49
264	4	142	..		118	165		90		..	75
262	3	142	...	...	117	162	...	90	...		72
1	1	...	...		...	3	..		...	...	3
1	...	..	..		1	...		..	...	...	...

TABLE XV.

OCCUPATION OR MEANS OF LIVELIHOOD.

Class.	Order	Occupation or means of livelihood	FRONTIER DISTRICTS. Total workers and dependents.	Actual workers. Total. Males.	Actual workers. Total. Females.	Partially agriculturists. Males.	Partially agriculturists. Females.	Dependents both sexes.
1	2	3	22	23	24	25	26	27
F.—PROFESSIONS—concld.	XX.—LEARNED AND ARTISTIC PROFESSIONS—concld.	TOTAL SUB-ORDER 70	3	3	...	...	...	...
		Pictorial Art and Sculpture.						
		483. Painters, superintendents of schools of art, etc.	3	3	..	...	...	...
		484. Sculptors	...		...	...	...	...
		485. Photographers			...	...	...	...
		TOTAL SUB-ORDER 71	111	59	1	...	...	51
		Music, Acting, Dancing, etc						
		487. Music composers and teachers	97	50	..	...	...	47
		488. Band masters and players (not military)	...	..	...	...	..	...
		489. Piano-tuners	14	9	1	...	..	4
		490. Actors, singers and dancers and their accompanists						
	XXI.—SPORT.	TOTAL ORDER XXI.—SPORTS	..		..	...	..	.
		TOTAL SUB-ORDER 72	..	..	...	...	...	...
		Sports.						
		492. Shikaries, falconers, bird-catchers	...	..	...	...	...	...
		493. Huntsmen, whippers-in	..	...	...	...	...	...
		TOTAL SUB-ORDER 73	...	..	...	..	...	...
		Games and Exhibitions						
		494. Owners and managers of places of public entertainment		..	...	...	...	..
		495. Persons engaged in service of place of public entertainment.	.	...	...	...	...	...
		496. Exhibitors of trained animals	..	...	...	...	...	...
		498. Conjurors, buffoons, reciters, fortune-tellers, etc.	..	...	...	...	...	...
		499. Tumblers, acrobats, wrestlers, professional cricketers, etc.	..	...	...	...	..	..
G.—UNSKILLED LABOUR, NOT AGRICULTURAL.	XXII.—EARTHWORK AND GENERAL LABOUR.	TOTAL ORDER XXII.—EARTHWORK AND GENERAL LABOUR.	1,257	554	167	2	..	536
		TOTAL SUB-ORDER 74	..		..	..	...	...
		Earthwork, etc						
		500. Well-sinkers	...	...	...	...	..	...
		501. Tank-diggers and excavators	...	...	...	...	...	...
		502 Road, canal and Railway labourers		...	...	...	..	...
		TOTAL SUB-ORDER 75	1,257	554	167	2	...	536
		General Labour.						
		504 General labour	1,257	554	167	2	...	536
	INDEFINITE AND DISREPUTABLE OCCUPATIONS.	TOTAL ORDER XXIII.—INDEFINITE AND DISREPUTABLE OCCUPATIONS.	22	13	3	...	...	6
		TOTAL SUB-ORDER 76	8	5	...	...	...	3
		Indefinite						
		505. Uncertain or not returned	8	5	...	...	...	3
		TOTAL SUB-ORDER 77	14	8	3	...	...	3
		Disreputable.						
		506. Prostitutes including saqins and naauchis	14	8	3	...	...	3
		508. Receivers of stolen goods	...	...	...	...	...	...
		509. Witches, wizards, cow-poisoners, etc.	...	...	...	...	...	...

TABLE XV.

Occupation or Means of Livelihood.

Jammu City						Srinagar City					
Total workers and dependents.	Actual workers — Total — Males.	Actual workers — Total — Females.	Actual workers — Partially agriculturists — Males.	Actual workers — Partially agriculturists — Females.	Dependents both sexes.	Total workers and dependents.	Actual workers — Total — Males.	Actual workers — Total — Females.	Actual workers — Partially agriculturists — Males.	Actual workers — Partially agriculturists — Females.	Dependents both sexes.
28	29	30	31	32	33	34	35	36	37	38	39
225	92	...	1	..	133	1,218	527	2	..	..	689
1	1	...	...	...		1,173	516	1	...	...	656
228	90	...	1	...	133	34	6	1	...	..	27
1	1	..		...	...	11	5	.	...	..	6
95	37	5			53	229	69	...	..		160
2	1	.	.		1	...	...	..	...	.	...
38	16	...	...		23	...	...	...	...	..	...
...	..	...	...	...		..	...	...	...		...
55	20	5	...	..	30	229	69	..	...	..	160
30	13	...	.	..	17	171	60	4	1	.	105
20	7	...	...	...	13	54	35	3	1	..	46
19	6	...	..	...	13	84	35	3	1	...	40
1	1	...	..	...	.	.	.	...	..	...	...
10	6	...	..	...	4	87	27	1	..	..	59
5	1	...	...	..	4				...	...	
1	1	...	...	.	.	...	...	.	...	..	...
..	...	...	..	...	.	..	..	...	...	...	..
...	...	...	...	...	...	87	27	1	...	...	59
4	4	...	...	...	..	..	..	...	...	...	...
3,032	1,469	315	28	..	1,248	4,972	1,686	278	1	...	3,008
53	37	...	...	..	16	13	3	4	.	..	6
...	...	...	...	.	...	13	3	4	...	..	6
...	...	...	...	...	...	...	...	...	...	...	...
53	37	...	...	...	16	...	...	...	...	...	...
2,979	1,432	315	28	...	1,232	4,959	1,683	274	1		3,002
2,979	1,432	315	28	...	1,232	4,959	1,683	274	1	..	3,002
95	3	83	..	...	9	158	26	68	..	...	64
5	3	...	...	...	2	29	26	..	...	..	3
5	3	...	..	...	2	29	26	.	...	.	3
90	...	83	.	...	7	129	...	68	...	...	61
90	...	83	..	...	7	129	...	68	...	...	61
...	...	...	...	...	...	...	...	...	...	...	...
...	...	...	...	...	...	...	...	...	...	...	...

TABLE XV.

Occupation or Means of Livelihood.

Class.	Order.	Occupation or means of livelihood	Total State. Total workers and dependants.	Actual workers. Total. Males.	Actual workers. Total. Females.	Actual workers. Partially agriculturists. Males.	Actual workers. Partially agriculturists. Females.	Dependants both sexes.
1	2	3	4	5	6	7	8	9
II.—Means of subsistence independent of occupation.	XXIV.—Independent.	TOTAL ORDER XXIV.—INDEPENDENT	71,967	24,588	6,397	710	29	40,962
		Total Sub-order 78 ..	63,522	21,754	6,052	547	12	35,888
		Property and alms.						
		510. House-rent shares, and other property not being land ..	1,749	498	60	14	...	1,191
		511. Allowances from patrons or relatives	212	31	10	...	...	171
		(A). In Africa	1	...	...	..	...	1
		512. Educational or other endowments, scholarships, etc. ...	1,286	460	331	1	...	495
		513. Mendicancy (not in connection with a religious order) ...	60,274	20,795	5,651	532	12	33,528
		Total Sub-order 79 .	8,445	2,804	345	163	17	5,298
		At the State Expense.						
		514. Pensions, civil services	435	152	9	3	...	274
		515. Pension, military services	374	98	12	18	...	266
		516. Pension unspecified	7,096	2,035	307	142	17	4,754
		518. Prisoners under trial	104	94	10	...	...	...
		519. Prisoners for debt	1	1	..	...	..	...
		520. Prisoners convicted or in reformatories, etc. . ..	435	428	7	...	..	2

Note.—There were no entries under the groups of occupations

TABLE XV.

Occupation or Means of Livelihood.

Jammu Province.						Kashmir Province.					
Total workers and dependents.	Actual workers.				Dependents both sexes.	Total workers and dependents.	Actual workers.				Dependents both sexes.
	Total.		Partially agriculturists.				Total.		Partially agriculturists.		
	Males.	Females.	Males.	Females.			Males.	Females.	Males.	Females.	
10	11	12	13	14	15	16	17	18	19	20	21
42,272	**14,903**	**4,472**	**524**	**27**	**22,897**	**27,646**	**8,964**	**1,556**	**181**	**2**	**17,105**
36,470	**12,902**	**4,164**	**399**	**12**	**19,404**	**25,161**	**8,240**	**1,524**	**143**		**15,897**
85	...	38		..	47	1,582	495	22	14	...	1,065
4	...	3		...	1	20	8	3		...	9
1	...	...	...	...	1	...		..	...	...	...
12	2	2	..	...	8	13	13	...	..	...	...
36,368	12,000	4,121	399	12	19,347	23,546	7,724	1,499	129		14,333
5,802	**2,001**	**308**	**125**	**15**	**3,493**	**2,455**	**744**	**32**	**88**	**2**	**1,709**
231	82	1	8	...	138	203	65	8			
374	96	12	18	...	206	...	...	...	..	..	130
4,818	1,451	278	104	15	3,089	2,135	634	24	38	2	1,577
86	76	10	..		..	18	18	...	...	...	...
...	...	..	...	...	...	..	...	...	...	...	...
303	296	7	...	...	...	129	127	...	...	...	2

which have been omitted from the table

TABLE XV.

OCCUPATION OR MEANS OF LIVELIHOOD.

Class	Order	Occupation or means of livelihood	FRONTIER DISTRICTS. Total workers and dependents.	Actual workers. Total. Males.	Females.	Partially agriculturists. Males.	Females.	Dependents both sexes.
1	2	3	22	23	24	25	26	27
II.—MEANS OF SUBSISTENCE INDEPENDENT OF OCCUPATION.	XXIV.—INDEPENDENT.	TOTAL ORDER XXIV.—INDEPENDENT	2,049	701	369	5	..	979
		TOTAL SUB-ORDER 78	1,891	642	364	5	.	855
		Property and alms						
		510 House-rent, shares, and other property not being land ..	82	8		...	..	79
		511 Allowances from patrons or relatives	188	23	4	..	...	161
		(A). In Africa	..	...			...	...
		512 Educational or other endowments, scholarships, etc. ...	1,201	445	329	1	...	487
		513 Mendicancy (not in connection with a religious order) .	360	171	31	1	..	158
		TOTAL SUB-ORDER 79	158	59	5	...	..	94
		At the State Expense.						
		514 Pensions, civil services .. -	11	5		...	...	6
		515. Pension, military services	143	50	5	...	...	88
		516. Pension unspecified ... -	...			...	...	...
		518. Prisoners under trial	..		...	...	...	...
		519. Prisoners for debt	1	1	...	...	...	...
		520. Prisoners, convicted or in reformatories, etc.	3	3	...	...	...	...

NOTE.—There were no entries under the groups of occupations

TABLE XV.

Occupation or Means of Livelihood.

JAMMU CITY.						SRINAGAR CITY.					
Total workers and dependents.	Actual workers. Total. Males.	Actual workers. Total. Females.	Actual workers. Partially agriculturists. Males.	Actual workers. Partially agriculturists. Females.	Dependents both sexes.	Total workers and dependents.	Actual workers. Total. Males.	Actual workers. Total. Females.	Actual workers. Partially agriculturists. Males.	Actual workers. Partially agriculturists. Females.	Dependents both sexes.
[illegible]	29	30	31	32	33	34	35	36	37	38	39
1,283	687	154	9		442	4,112	1,240	139	3	...	2,73[illegible]
740	324	113	1		203	3,097	953	128	3	...	2,016
73		[illegible]	...		...	1,47[illegible]	[illegible]	20	2		993
...	...	...	...			20	8	3			9
13	3	2	...	...	8	...	...		...	...	...
[illegible]	321	[illegible]	1		[illegible]	1,604	[illegible]	[illegible]	[illegible]	...	1,01[illegible]
543	363	41	8		139	1,015	287	11			717
47	11		2	...	[illegible]	[illegible]	[illegible]	[illegible]			[illegible]
38	14	...	4	...	24						...
145	42	21	2		[illegible]	[illegible]	[illegible]	[illegible]			[illegible]
14	1	10				15	[illegible]				...
... [illegible]	[illegible]	7			...	[illegible]	[illegible]			...	[illegible]

which have been omitted from the table

TABLE XV.

JAMMU AND SRINAGAR CITIES.

TABLE XV.

Occupation or Means of Livelihood.

JAMMU CITY.

Class.	Order.	Occupation or means of livelihood.	Table for the City. Total workers and dependents.	Actual workers. Total. Males.	Actual workers. Total. Females.	Actual workers. Partially agriculturists. Males.	Actual workers. Partially agriculturists. Females.	Dependents both sexes.
1	2	3	4	5	6	7	8	9
A.—GOVERNMENT.		**TOTAL JAMMU CITY**	**36.130**	**18,519**	**1,556**	**479**	**3**	**18,055**
		TOTAL CLASS A.—GOVERNMENT	**12,014**	**6,335**	...	**208**	...	**5,679**
	1. A.	TOTAL ORDER I	**947**	**389**		**27**	...	**558**
		TOTAL SUB-ORDER 1 A	**591**	**301**	...	**26**	...	**290**
		Service of the Tabulating State.						
		b. Darbar officials, Inspectors and Deputy Inspectors, Police.	13	5	...	...	...	6
		c. Wa ir Wazárats and Tahsildárs	5	2	...	...	...	3
		d. Pol e Constables	573	294	...	26	...	279
	2.	TOTAL SUB-ORDER 2	**307**	**68**	...	...	...	**239**
		Service of Local and Municipal Bodies.						
		6. Clerical establishment	138	40	...	...	...	98
		7. Menials other than scavengers	169	28	...	...	...	141
	3.	TOTAL SUB-ORDER 3	**49**	**20**	...	**1**	...	**29**
		Village Service.						
		10. Watchmen and other village servants	49	20	...	1	...	29
	4. II.—DEFENCE.	TOTAL ORDER II	**3,062**	**2,463**	...	**28**	...	**599**
		TOTAL SUB-ORDER 4	**229**	**107**	...	**4**	...	**122**
		Army—Imperial.						
		16. Military service unspecified	229	107	...	4	...	122
	4 A.	TOTAL SUB-ORDER 4 A	**2,833**	**2,356**	...	**24**	...	**477**
		Army (Tabulating State).						
		a. Non-Commissioned Officers, Privates, etc.... ...	1,484	1,108	...	24	...	376
		b. State Troops other than Imperial Service Troops...	2	2	...	...	...	...
		Non-Commissioned Officers, Privates, etc. ...	1,347	1,246	...	...	...	101
	III.—SERVICE OF FOREIGN NATIVE STATES.	TOTAL ORDER III	**8,005**	**3,483**	...	**153**	...	**4,522**
		TOTAL SUB-ORDER 6	**8,005**	**3,483**	...	**153**	...	**5,422**
		Civil Officers of State other than the Tabulating State.						
		20. Darbár officials, etc.	8,005	3,483	...	153	...	4,522
B.—PASTURE AND AGRICULTURE.		TOTAL CLASS B.—PASTURE AND AGRICULTURE ...	**1,573**	**993**	**117**	**92**	**1**	**463**
	IV.—PROVISION AND CARE OF ANIMALS.	TOTAL ORDER IV.—PROVISION AND CARE OF ANIMALS.	**175**	**35**	**90**	**3**	**1**	**50**
		TOTAL SUB-ORDER 8	**121**	**17**	**90**	**3**	**1**	**14**
		Stock Breeding and Dealing.						
		26. Cattle breeders and dealers and commissariat farm establishment.	11	8	...	1	...	3
		27. Herdsmen	99	5	90	...	1	4
		29 Camel breeders, dealers and attendants	11	4	...	2	...	7
		TOTAL SUB-ORDER 9	**54**	**18**	...	...	...	**36**
		Training and care of Animals.						
		33. Veterinary Surgeons, farriers, etc.	14	7	...	...	...	7
		34. Horse and elephant trainers, etc.	40	11	...	...	...	29

TABLE XV.

Occupation or Means of Livelihood.

JAMMU CITY.

Class.	Order.	Occupation or means of livelihood.	Total workers and dependants.	Actual workers. Total. Males.	Actual workers. Total. Females.	Actual workers. Partially agriculturists. Males.	Actual workers. Partially agriculturists. Females.	Dependants both sexes.
1	2	3	4	5	6	7	8	9
B.—PASTURE AND AGRICULTURE—concld.	V.—Agriculture.	TOTAL ORDER V.—AGRICULTURE	1,398	958	27	89	...	413
		Total Sub-order 10	1,300	926	24	86	...	350
		Landholders and Tenants.						
		36. 1. Owners ...	819	637	6	86	...	176
		2. Owners (rent receivers) ...	2	...	2	...	...	...
		3. Mortgagees (cultivating) ...	1	1	...	...	...	...
		37. 1. Occupancy tenants (cultivating) ...	34	5	...	...	...	29
		2. Tenants-at-will ...	435	274	16	...	...	145
		5. Sub-tenants as Lichhains, etc. ...	9	9	...	...	..	...
		Total Sub-order 11	3	...	3	...	...	...
		Agricultural Labourers.						
		39. Field labourers ...	3	...	3	...	...	...
		Total Sub-order 12	30	15	...	...	...	15
		Growers of special products.						
		52. Fruit and vegetable growers ...	30	15	...	...	...	15
		Total Sub-order 13	65	17	...	3	...	48
		Agricultural training and supervision and forests.						
		59. Forest rangers, guards and peons ...	65	17	...	3	...	48
C.—PERSONAL SERVICES.		TOTAL CLASS C.—PERSONAL SERVICES	2,820	1,243	315	67	1	1,860
	VI.—Personal Household and Sanitary Services.	TOTAL ORDER VI.—PERSONAL, HOUSEHOLD AND SANITARY SERVICES.	2,820	1,243	315	67	1	1,262
		Total Sub-order 14	2,028	930	128	67	1	970
		Personal and Domestic Services.						
		60. Barbers ...	329	122	1	1	...	206
		61. Cooks ...	156	130	...	...	...	26
		62. Door-keepers, etc. ...	53	21	...	...	...	32
		63. Grooms, coachmen, dog boys, etc. ...	35	34	...	6	...	1
		64. Indoor servants ...	610	297	30	59	...	283
		65. Washermen ...	232	74	12	...	...	146
		66. Water-carriers ...	613	252	85	1	...	276
		Total Sub-order 15	25	10	...	...	...	15
		Non-domestic entertainment.						
		70. Rest-house, Serai, bath-house, etc., owners and managers	5	1	...	...	...	4
		71. Club Secretaries, Managers, Stewards, etc.	20	9	...	...	...	11
		Total Sub-order 16	767	303	187	..	...	277
		Sanitation.						
		72. Sanitary officers of Government and establishment ...	1	..	...	...	...	1
		73. Sanitary Inspectors, Local and Municipal ...	6	1	...	...	...	5
		74. Sweepers and scavengers ...	700	302	187	...	...	271
D.—PREPARATION AND SUPPLY OF MATERIAL SUBSTANCES.		TOTAL CLASS D.—PREPARATION AND SUPPLY OF MATERIAL SUBSTANCES.	8,833	3,098	418	20	1	5,317
	VII.—Food, Drink and Stimulants.	TOTAL ORDER VII.—FOOD, DRINK AND STIMULANTS.	2,456	765	60	2	...	1,631
		Total Sub-order 17	237	65	1	...	...	171
		Provision of Animal Food.						
		78. Cow and buffalo keepers, and milk and butter sellers ...	59	16	1	...	...	42
		79. Fishermen and fish-curers ...	15	9	...	...	...	6
		82. Ghee preparers and sellers ...	16	6	...	...	...	10
		84. Miscellaneous ...	147	34	...	...	...	113

TABLE XV.

Occupation or Means of Livelihood.

JAMMU CITY.

Class.	Order.	Occupation or means of livelihood.	TABLE FOR THE CITY. Total workers and dependents.	Actual workers. Total. Males.	Actual workers. Total. Females.	Actual workers. Partially agriculturists. Males.	Actual workers. Partially agriculturists. Females.	Dependents both sexes.
1	2	3	4	5	6	7	8	9
D.—Preparation and Supply of Material Substances—contd.	VII.—Food, Drink and Stimulants—concld.	Total Sub-order 18	1.921	608	59	2	...	1.254
		Provision of vegetable food.						
		95. Bakers	234	111	2	..	...	121
		96. Flour grinders	402	145	11		...	246
		97. Grain and pulse dealers	287	9		...	...	278
		98. Grain parchers	19	11	...	...	...	8
		100. Oil pressers	4	...	...	...	...	4
		101. Oil sellers	3	1	...	...	...	2
		102. Rice pounders and huskers	160	25	36	1	...	99
		103. Sweetmeat makers	287	145	...	...	...	142
		104. Sweetmeat sellers	247	50	...	...	...	197
		105. Vegetable and fruit sellers	278	111	10	1	...	157
		Total Sub-order 19	298	92	...	...	...	206
		Provision of drink Condiments and Stimulants.						
		107. Ærated water factories: owners, managers and superior staff.	5	1	...	...	...	
		116. Ice factories: workmen and other subordinates ...	2	3	...	...	...	...
		121. Water-works: managers and superior staff	6	6	...	...	...	...
		122. Water-works: workmen and other subordinates ...	12	...	...	...	...	12
		124. Grocers and general condiment dealers and staff ...	170	43	...	...	...	127
		126. Opium, bhang, gánja, etc., sellers	15	6	...	...	...	9
		128. Salt sellers	13	...	...	...	...	13
		130. Tobacco and snuff sellers	68	27	...	...	...	41
		134. Wine and spirit sellers	7	7	...	...	...	...
	VIII.—Light, Firing and Forage.	TOTAL ORDER VIII.—LIGHT, FIRING AND FORAGE ...	226	85	11	3	...	130
		Total Sub-order 21	226	85	11	3	...	130
		Fuel and Forage.						
		147. Collieries, miners and other subordinates	8	4	...	...	...	4
		148. Coal dealers, brokers, company managers, etc.	8	2	...	...	...	6
		149. Hay, grass and fodder sellers	21	15	...	3	...	6
		150. Firewood, charcoal and cow-dung sellers	189	64	11	...	...	114
	IX.—Buildings.	TOTAL ORDER IX.—BUILDINGS	954	450	2	4	...	502
		Total Sub-order 22	168	112	1	1	...	55
		Building Materials.						
		154. Stone and marble works: labourers and other subordinates.	12	5	...	...	...	7
		155. Brick and tile makers	139	98	1	1	...	40
		156. Brick and tile sellers	8	...	...	...	...	8
		157. Lime, chunam and shell burners	9	9	...	...	...	...
		Total Sub-order 23	786	338	1	3	...	447
		Artificers in Buildings.						
		162. Building contractors	91	8	...	...	...	83
		163. Masons and builders...	681	324	...	3	...	357
		164. Painters, plumbers and glaziers	14	6	1	...	...	7
	X.—Vehicles and Vessels.	TOTAL ORDER X.—VEHICLES AND VESSELS	6	2	...	...	...	4
		Total Sub-order 25	6	2	...	...	...	4
		Carts, Carriages, etc.						
		173. Painters of carriages, etc.	6	2	...	...	...	4

TABLE XV.

OCCUPATION OR MEANS OF LIVELIHOOD.

JAMMU CITY.

Class.	Order.	Occupation or means of livelihood	Table for the city. Total workers and dependents.	Actual workers. Total. Males.	Actual workers. Total. Females.	Actual workers. Partially agriculturists. Males.	Actual workers. Partially agriculturists. Females.	Dependents both sexes.
1	2	3	4	5	6	7	8	9
B.—PREPARATION AND SUPPLY OF MATERIAL SUBSTANCES—contd.	XI.—Supplementary requirements.	TOTAL ORDER XI.—SUPPLEMENTARY REQUIREMENTS.	423	106	26	1	1	291
		Total Sub-order 27	7	2	..	...	...	5
		Paper.						
		182. Stationers	7	2	...	...	..	5
		Total Sub-order 28	63	14	...	...	...	49
		Books and Prints.						
		184. Printing Presses: workmen and other subordinates ...	8	...	...	...	...	8
		186. Book-binders	33	9	...	...	..	24
		187. Book sellers, book agents and publishers	22	5	...	..	...	17
		Total Sub-order 29	9	4	...	..	...	5
		Watches, Clocks and Scientific Instruments.						
		190. Watch and clock makers	9	4	..	...	...	5
		Total Sub-order 30	11	4	...	...	...	7
		Carving and Engraving.						
		197. Turners and lacquerers	8	2	...	...	...	6
		198. Dye-sinkers and seal, etc., engravers	3	2	...	...	...	1
		Total Sub-order 31 ...	45	13	...	...	...	32
		Toys and Curiosities.						
		202. Toy, kite and cage makers and sellers	3	1	...	..	...	2
		203. Hukka-stem makers and sellers	42	12	.	..	...	30
		Total Sub-order 32	10	.	4	...	...	6
		Music and Musical Instruments.						
		206. Music and musical instrument makers	10	...	4	...	..	6
		Total Sub-order 33	36	4	10	...	1	22
		Bangles, necklaces, beads, sacred threads, etc.						
		210. Makers of glass bangles	7	3	1	..	..	3
		216. Flower garland makers and sellers	29	1	9	...	1	19
		Total Sub-order 35	116	37	5	..	...	74
		Harness.						
		223. Saddler, cloth makers, embroiderers and sellers ...	116	37	5	...	...	74
		Total Sub-order 36	22	6	...	...	...	16
		Tools and Machinery.						
		227. Knife and tool makers	14	...	...	...	...	14
		229. Knife and tool grinders	1	1	...	...	...	...
		230. Plough and agricultural implement makers	4	2	...	...	...	2
		231. Looms and loom-comb makers and sellers	1	1	...	...	...	...
		232. Mechanics other than railway mechanics...	2	2	...	...	...	...
		Total Sub-order 37	104	42	7	1	...	75
		Arms and Ammunition.						
		243. Gun makers, menders and sellers	3	2	...	...	...	1
		244. Ammunition, gunpowder and firework makers	71	20	1	1	...	50
		245. Ammunition, gunpowder and firework sellers	30	...	6	...	...	24

TABLE XV.

Occupation or Means of Livelihood.

JAMMU CITY

Class.	Order.	Occupation or means of livelihood.	TABLE FOR THE CITY.					
			Total workers and dependents.	Actual workers.				Dependents both sexes.
				Total.		Partially agriculturists.		
				Males.	Females.	Males.	Females.	
1	2	4	4	5	6	7	8	9
D.—Preparation and supply of material substances—contd.	XII.—Textile, Fabrics and Dress	TOTAL ORDER XII.—TEXTILE, FABRICS AND DRESS	2,174	685	307	1	...	1,182
		Total Sub-order 38	35	3	23	...	...	9
		Wool and Fur.						
		250. Felt and pasham workers	29	1	23	...	...	5
		253. Wool dyers	6	2	...	...	...	4
		Total Sub-order 39	245	75	66	...	..	104
		Silk.						
		260. Silk carders, spinners and weavers; makers of silk braid and thread.	180	34	57	...	...	89
		261. Sellers of raw silk, silk cloth, braid and thread	65	41	9	...	...	15
		Total Sub-order 40	655	142	146	...	...	367
		Cotton.						
		271. Cotton cleaners, pressers and ginners	32	14	...	...	...	18
		272. Cotton weavers, hand industry	148	58	4	...	...	86
		275. Cotton spinners, sizers and yarn beaters	157	...	127	...	...	30
		276. Cotton yarn and thread sellers	52	...	13	...	...	39
		278 Cotton dyers	266	70	2	...	...	194
		Total Sub-order 41	21	11	...	...	...	10
		Jute, Hemp, Flax, Coir. etc.						
		292 Fibre matting and bag makers	21	11	...	...	...	10
		Total Sub-order 42	1,218	454	72	1	...	692
		Dress.						
		301 Embroiderers and lace and muslin makers	12	10	1	...	...	1
		302 Hat, cap, and turban makers, binders and sellers ...	3	2	...	...	...	1
		304. Piece-goods dealers	347	102	...	...	...	245
		306. Tailors, milliners, dress-makers and darners	856	340	71	1	...	445
	XIII.—Metal and Precious Stones	TOTAL ORDER XIII.—METAL AND PRECIOUS STONES	1,061	411	2	2	...	648
		Total Sub-order 43	777	264	...	...	...	513
		Gold, Silver and Precious Stones						
		314. Electro-platers	75	36	...	...	...	39
		315. Dealers in plate and plate ware	24	11	...	...	...	13
		316. Gold and silver wire drawers and braid makers	37	2	...	...	...	35
		317. Workers in gold, silver and precious stones	559	193	...	...	...	366
		318. Dealers in gold, silver and precious stones	62	22	...	...	...	60
		Total Sub-order 44	85	35	...	...	...	50
		Brass, Copper and Bell Metal.						
		322. Brass, copper and bell metal workers	83	33	...	...	...	50
		323. Brass, copper and bell metal sellers	2	2	...	...	...	...
		Total Sub-order 46	199	112	2	2	...	85
		Iron and Steel.						
		328. Workers in iron and hardware	185	106	2	2	...	77
		329. Sellers of iron and hardware	14	6	...	...	...	8
	XIV.—Glass, Earthen and Stoneware.	TOTAL ORDER XIV.—GLASS, EARTHEN AND STONE-WARE.	151	48	3	...	...	100
		Total Sub-order 48	151	48	3	...	...	100
		Earthen and Stoneware.						
		336. Potters and pot and pipe-bowl makers	150	47	3	...	...	100
		338. Grindstone and millstone makers and menders	1	1	...	...	...	...

TABLE XV.

Occupation or Means of Livelihood.

JAMMU CITY.

Class.	Order.	Occupation or means of livelihood.	Total workers and dependants.	Actual workers. Total. Males.	Actual workers. Total. Females.	Actual workers. Partially agriculturists. Males.	Actual workers. Partially agriculturists. Females.	Dependants both sexes.
1	2	3	10	11	12	13	14	15
D.—PREPARATION AND SUPPLY OF MATERIAL SUBSTANCES—concld.	XV.—Wood, Cane and Leaves, etc.	TOTAL ORDER XV.—WOOD, CANE AND LEAVES, etc. ...	541	245	...	6	...	296
		Total Sub-order 49	491	226	.	6	..	265
		Wood and Bamboos.						
		340. Carpentry works, owners, managers and superior staff	7	1	.		.	6
		341. Carpentry works, operatives and other subordinates ...	2	1	...	..	.	1
		344. Carpenters	428	200	...	6	...	228
		346. Wood cutters and sawyers	54	24	.	...	...	30
		Total Sub-order 50 .	50	19	. .		..	31
		Cane works, matting and leaves, etc.						
		347. Baskets, mats, fans, screens, brooms, etc., makers and sellers.	11	4	..	...	...	7
		348. Comb and tooth stick makers and sellers . ..	2	1	...	...	...	1
		349. Leaf-plate makers and sellers	37	14	...	...	...	23
	XVI.—Drugs, Gums, Dyes, etc.	TOTAL ORDER XVI.—DRUGS, GUMS, DYES, etc. ...	113	39	...	...	.	74
		Total Sub-order 52	113	39	...	..		74
		Drugs, Dyes and Pigments, etc.						
		369. Chemists and druggists	71	34			.	37
		372. Soap sellers	22	5	..	.	...	17
		375. Ink makers and sellers	2	...	...	...	..	2
		376. Perfume, incense and sandal wood preparers . ..	1	...	...	.	..	1
		379. Persons occupied with miscellaneous dyes	17	...	.	...	.	17
	XVII.—Leather, etc.	TOTAL ORDER XVII.—LEATHER, etc. ...	728	262	7	1		459
		Total Sub-order 53	728	262	7	1	..	459
		Leather, Horn and Bones.						
		386. Leather dyers	47	15	...	.	.	32
		387. Shoe, boot and sandal makers	612	230	7	1	...	375
		388. Tanners and curriers	4	...	...	.	...	4
		389. Sellers of manufactured leather goods	30	16	...	..	...	14
		390. Sellers of hides, horns, bristles and bones ...	28	..	...	...	.	28
		391. Water bag, well bag, bucket and ghee-pot makers ...	7	1	...	.	..	6
E.—COMMERCE, TRANSPORT, STORAGE.		TOTAL CLASS E.—COMMERCE, TRANSPORT, STORAGE.	3,715	1,524	10	29	.	2,181
	XVIII.—Commerce.	TOTAL ORDER XVIII.—COMMERCE	3,179	1,276	10	20		1,893
		Total Sub-order 54 ..	919	305	7	8	...	607
		Money and Securities.						
		392. Bankers, money-lenders, etc	720	240	7	8	..	473
		394. Money changers and testers	197	64	...	..	...	133
		395. Bank clerks, Cashiers, bill Collectors, accountants, etc.	2	1	...	..	...	1
		Total Sub-order 55	527	184	...		...	343
		General Merchandise.						
		396. General merchants	527	184	..		...	343
		Total Sub-order 56 .	1,352	663	3	12	..	689
		Dealing, Unspecified.						
		398. Shopkeepers, otherwise unspecified	1,081	611	2	12	...	468
		399. Shopkeepers' clerks, salesmen, etc. .. .	14	...	...	...	...	14
		400. Shopkeepers and money-lenders' servants	10	...	...	...	...	10
		401. Pedlars, hawkers, etc.	247	52	1	...	...	194
		Total Sub-order 57	381	124	...	.	...	257
		Middlemen, Brokers and Agents.						
		402. Brokers and agents	5	3	...	...	...	2
		407. Contractors, otherwise unspecified	376	121	...	...	...	255

TABLE XV.

OCCUPATION OR MEANS OF LIVELIHOOD.

JAMMU CITY.

Class.	Order.	Occupations or means of livelihood.	Table for the City. Total workers and dependents.	Actual workers. Total. Males.	Actual workers. Total. Females.	Actual workers. Partially agriculturists. Males.	Actual workers. Partially agriculturists. Females.	Dependants both sexes.
1	2	3	4	5	6	7	8	9
E.—COMMERCE, TRANSPORT, STORAGE—concld.	XIX.—TRANSPORT AND STORAGE.	TOTAL ORDER XIX.—TRANSPORT AND STORAGE ...	536	248		9	..	288
		TOTAL SUB-ORDER 58	158	73	...	3	...	85
		*Railway.**						
		411. Clerical staff on Railways	122	47	...	...	...	75
		412. Station masters and assistants, inspectors, overseers, etc.	2	...	...	...	...	2
		413. Guards, drivers, firemen, etc.	1	...	...	...	...	1
		414. Pointsmen, shunters, porters, signallers, etc.	8	1	...	...	...	7
		415. Railway service unspecified	25	25		3	...	...
		TOTAL SUB-ORDER 59	240	101	...	6	...	139
		Road.						
		416. Livery stable-keepers, etc.	4	1	..	..	..	3
		419. Drivers, stable boys, etc., not private servants	105	61		5	...	44
		420. Pálki, etc., bearers, and owners	12	8	...	1	...	4
		421. Pack bullock owners, drivers, etc.	38	1	...	...	..	37
		422. Pack camel, elephant, mule, etc., owners and drivers ...	81	30	...	...	...	51
		TOTAL SUB-ORDER 60	18	5	...	...	..	13
		Water.						
		429. Boat and barge men	18	5	...	...	...	13
		TOTAL SUB-ORDER 61	59	29	...	...	...	30
		Messages.						
		433. Post Office: officers and superior staff	1	1	...	...	...	...
		434. Post Office: clerks, messengers, runners and other subordinates.	50	27	...	...	...	23
		436. Telegraph: clerks, signallers, messengers and other subordinates.	8	1	...	...	...	7
		TOTAL SUB-ORDER 62	61	40	..	...	...	21
		Storage and Weighing.						
		442. Weighmen and measurers	61	40	...	...	...	21
F.—PROFESSIONS.		TOTAL CLASS F.—PROFESSIONS	2,765	1,167	144	26	...	1,454
	XX.—LEARNED AND ARTISTIC PROFESSIONS	TOTAL ORDER XX.—LEARNED AND ARTISTIC PROFESSIONS.	2,735	1,154	144	26	...	1,437
		TOTAL SUB-ORDER 63	1,632	695	127	14	...	810
		Religion.						
		444. Priests, ministers, etc.	1,541	671	127	14	...	743
		446. Religious mendicants, inmates of monasteries, convents, etc.	8	7	...	...	...	1
		447. Church, temple, burial or burning ground service, pilgrim conductors, undertakers, etc.	67	12	...	...	...	55
		449. Astrologers, diviners, horoscope makers, etc.	16	5	...	...	...	11
		TOTAL SUB-ORDER 64	82	41	...	2	...	41
		Education.						
		452. Principals, professors and teachers	42	16	...	1	...	26
		453. Clerks and servants connected with education	40	25	...	2	...	15
		TOTAL SUB-ORDER 65	66	53	2	...	...	11
		Literature.						
		457. Public scribes and copyists	59	53	...	...	...	[illegible]
		458. Service in libraries and literary institutions	7	1	2	...	...	4

* Excluding police on Railways.

TABLE XV.

Occupation or Means of Livelihood.

JAMMU CITY.

Class.	Order.	Occupation or means of livelihood.	Table for the City. Total workers and dependents.	Actual workers. Total. Males.	Actual workers. Total. Females.	Actual workers. Partially agriculturists. Males.	Actual workers. Partially agriculturists. Females.	Dependents both sexes.
1	2	3	4	5	6	7	8	9
F.—Professions—concld.	XX.—Learned and Artistic Professions—concld.	Total Sub-order 66	**393**	**142**	...	**2**	...	**251**
		Law.						
		459. Barristers, advocates and pleaders	154	36	...	1	...	118
		461. Law agents, mukhtiárs, etc.	40	18	..	...	...	22
		463. Articled clerks and other laywers' clerks	57	26	...	...	...	31
		464. Petition-writers, touts, etc.	117	54	...	1	...	63
		465. Stamp-vendors	25	8	...	...	...	17
		Total Sub-order 67	**175**	**78**	**10**	...	...	**87**
		Medicine.						
		468. Practitioners without diploma	85	41	1	...	...	43
		472. Midwives	9	...	8	..	...	1
		473. Compounders, matrons, nurses and hospital asylum and dispensary service.	81	37	1	...	...	43
		Total Sub-order 68	**67**	**16**	...	**6**	...	**51**
		Engineering and Survey.						
		475. Civil engineers and architects	29	8	...	6	...	31
		477. Draughtsmen and operators in survey offices, overseers, etc.	37	7	..	...	...	30
		478. Clerks, etc., in offices of the above	1	1	...	...	...	...
		Total Sub-order 70	**225**	**92**	...	**1**	...	**133**
		Pictorial of Art and Sculpture.						
		483. Painters, superintendents of schools of art, etc. ...	1	1	...	...	...	...
		484. Sculptors	223	90	...	1	..	133
		485. Photographers	1	1	...	...	...	...
		Total Sub-order 71	**95**	**37**	**5**	..	...	**53**
		Music, Acting, Dancing, etc.						
		487. Music composers and teachers	2	1	...	...	...	1
		488. Band masters and players (not military)	38	16	...	...	...	22
		490. Actors, singers and dancers and their accompanists ...	55	20	5	...	...	30
	XXI.—Sport.	TOTAL ORDER XXI.—SPORT	**30**	**13**	...	...	...	**17**
		Total Sub-order 72	**20**	**7**	...	...	...	**13**
		Sport.						
		491. Race-course services, trainers, book-makers, jockeys, etc.	19	6	...	...	...	13
		493. Huntsmen, whippers-in	1	1	...	...	...	...
		Total Sub-order 73	**10**	**6**	...	...	...	**4**
		Games and Exhibitions.						
		494. Owners and managers of places of public entertainments	5	1	...	...	...	4
		495. Persons engaged in service of places of public entertainments.	1	1	...	...	...	...
		499. Tumblers, acrobats, wrestlers, professional cricketers, etc.	4	4	...	...	...	...
G.—Unskilled Labour, not Agricultural.	XXII.—Earthwork and General Labour.	TOTAL CLASS G.—UNSKILLED LABOUR, NOT AGRICULTURAL	**3,127**	**1,472**	**398**	**28**	...	**1,257**
		TOTAL ORDER XXII.—EARTHWORK AND GENERAL LABOUR.	**3,032**	**1,469**	**315**	**28**	...	**1,248**
		Total Sub-order 74	**53**	**37**	...	...	...	**16**
		Earthwork, etc.						
		502. Road, canal and Railway labour	53	37	...	...	...	16
		Total Sub-order 75	**2,979**	**1,432**	**315**	**28**	...	**1,232**
		General Labour.						
		504. General labour	2,979	1,432	315	28	...	1,232

TABLE XV.

Occupation or Means of Livelihood.

JAMMU CITY.

Class.	Order.	Occupation or means of livelihood.	Table for the city. Total workers and dependents.	Actual workers. Total. Males.	Actual workers. Total. Females.	Actual workers. Partially agriculturists. Males.	Actual workers. Partially agriculturists. Females.	Dependents both sexes.
1	2	3	4	5	6	7	8	9
G.—Unskilled labour, not agricultural—*concld.*	XXIII.—Independent and disreputable occupations.	**TOTAL ORDER XXIII.—INDEPENDENT AND DISREPUTABLE OCCUPATIONS.**	**95**	**3**	**83**	...	...	**9**
		Total Sub-Order 76	**5**	**3**	...	..	...	**2**
		Indefinite.						
		505. Uncertain or not returned	5	3	...	...	...	2
		Total Sub-Order 77	**90**	...	**83**	...	...	**7**
		Disreputable.						
		506. Prostitutes, including saqins and nautchis	90	..	83	...	..	7
H.—Means of subsistence independent of occupation.	XXIV.—Independent.	**TOTAL CLASS H.—MEANS OF SUBSISTENCE INDEPENDENT OF OCCUPATION.**	**1,283**	**687**	**154**	**9**	...	**442**
		TOTAL ORDER XXIV.—INDEPENDENT	**1,283**	**687**	**154**	**9**	...	**443**
		Total Sub-order 78	**740**	**324**	**113**	**1**	...	**303**
		Property and Alms.						
		510. House-rent shares and other property, not being land ..	73	...	38	...	...	35
		512. Educational or other endowments, scholarships, etc. ...	13	3	2	...	...	8
		513. Mendicancy (not in connection with a religious order) ...	654	321	73	1	...	260
		Total Sub-order 79	**543**	**363**	**41**	**8**	...	**139**
		At the State Expense.						
		514. Pension, civil services	47	11	...	2	...	36
		515. Pension, military services	88	14	...	4	...	24
		516. Pension, unspecified	145	42	24	2	...	79
		518. Prisoners, under-trial	14	4	10	...	...	...
		520. Prisoners, convicted or in reformatories, etc.	299	292	7	...	..	...

TABLE XV.

OCCUPATION OR MEANS OF LIVELIHOOD.

SRINAGAR CITY.

Class.	Order.	Occupation or means of livelihood.	TABLE FOR THE CITY.					
			Total workers and dependents.	Actual workers. Total.		Actual workers. Partially agriculturists.		Dependents both sexes.
				Males.	Females.	Males.	Females.	
1	2	3	4	5	6	7	8	9
		TOTAL SRINAGAR CITY	**122,618**	**40,226**	**14,559**	**103**	**3**	**67,838**
A.—GOVERNMENT.		**TOTAL CLASS A.—GOVERNMENT .. ..**	**9,317**	**3,094**	**54**	**42**	...	**6,169**
	I.—ADMINISTRATION.	**TOTAL ORDER I.—ADMINISTRATION ... ...**	**2,936**	**1,029**	**54**	**5**	...	**1,858**
		TOTAL SUB-ORDER 1 A.	**1,678**	**427**	..	**3**	...	**1,251**
		Service of Tabulating State.						
		b. Darbar officials, Inspectors and Deputy Inspectors, of Police.	53	24	...	...	...	29
		c. Tahsildars and Civil Officers	135	47	...	...	...	88
		d. Constables of Police	1,490	356	...	3	..	1,134
		TOTAL SUB-ORDER 2	**775**	**432**	**54**	**2**	...	**289**
		Service of Local and Municipal Bodies.						
		6. Clerical establishment	353	216	..	2	...	115
		7. Menials other than scavengers	442	214	54	...	...	174
		TOTAL SUB-ORDER 3 . ..	**453**	**170**	...	...	...	**313**
		Village Service.						
		10. Watchmen and other village servants	483	170	...	...	..	313
	II.—DEFENCE.	**TOTAL ORDER II.—DEFENCE ... ...**	**1,239**	**662**	...	**14**	...	**557**
		TOTAL SUB-ORDER 4 A	**1,239**	**662**	...	**14**	..	**577**
		Army (Tabulating State).						
		17. Military Officers, Imperial Service Troops	3	2	...	...	...	1
		18. Non-Commissioned Officers and Privates	1,236	660	..	14	...	576
	III.—SERVICE OF NATIVE AND FOREIGN STATES.	**TOTAL ORDER III.—SERVICE OF NATIVE AND FOREIGN STATES**	**5,142**	**1,403**	...	**23**	...	**3,739**
		TOTAL SUB-ORDER 6	**5,142**	**1,403**	...	**23**	...	**3,739**
		Civil Officers						
		21. Clerical Establishment	5,142	1,403	...	23	...	3,739
B.—PASTURE AND AGRICULTURE.		**TOTAL CLASS B.—PASTURE AND AGRICULTURE ...**	**4,547**	**1,574**	**370**	**3**	..	**2,603**
	IV.—PROVISION AND CARE OF ANIMALS.	**TOTAL ORDER IV.—PROVISION AND CARE OF ANIMALS**	**41**	**21**	**2**	...	...	**18**
		TOTAL SUB-ORDER 8	**33**	**18**	**2**	...	...	**13**
		Stock Breeding and Dealing.						
		25. Horse, mule and ass breeders, dealers and attendants ...	31	18	...	..	...	13
		27. Herdsmen	5	...	2	...	...	...
		TOTAL SUB-ORDER 9	**8**	**3**	...	...	...	**5**
		Training and care of animals.						
		33. Veterinary Surgeons, farriers, etc.	3	1	...	..	...	2
		34. Horse and elephant trainers, etc.	5	2	..	..	...	3
	V.—AGRICULTURE.	**TOTAL ORDER V.—AGRICULTURE ... ...**	**4,506**	**1,553**	**368**	**3**	...	**2,585**
		TOTAL SUB-ORDER 10 ..	**2,722**	**1,045**	**213**	...	...	**1,464**
		Landholders and Tenants.						
		36. Rent receivers	123	48	4	...	...	71
		37. „ payers	2,599	997	209	..	...	1,393
		TOTAL SUB-ORDER 12	**1,275**	**350**	**155**	**3**	...	**770**
		Growers of special products.						
		52. Fruit and vegetable growers	1,275	350	155	3	...	770

TABLE XV.

OCCUPATION OR MEANS OF LIVELIHOOD.

SRINAGAR CITY.

Class.	Order.	Occupations or means of livelihood.	Table for the City. Total workers and dependents.	Actual workers. Total. Males.	Actual workers. Total. Females.	Actual workers. Partially agriculturists. Males.	Actual workers. Partially agriculturists. Females.	Dependents both sexes.
1	2	3	4	5	6	7	8	9
B.—PASTURE AND AGRICULTURE.—concld.	V.—AGRICULTURE—concld.	TOTAL SUB-ORDER 13	509	158	...	...	...	351
		Agricultural training and supervision and forests.						
		58. Forest officers	46	35	...	...	...	11
		59. Forest rangers, guards, peons	463	123	...	...	...	340
C.—PERSONAL SERVICES.	VI.—PERSONAL, HOUSEHOLD AND SANITARY SERVICES.	TOTAL CLASS C.—PERSONAL SERVICES	9.039	3.130	346	20	...	5,563
		TOTAL ORDER VI.—PERSONAL, HOUSEHOLD AND SANITARY SERVICES.	9.039	3.130	346	20	...	5,563
		TOTAL SUB-ORDER 14	8.700	3,062	268	20	...	5,370
		Personal and Domestic Services.						
		60. Barbers	1,432	800	...	...	...	632
		61. Cooks	457	190	2	...	...	265
		63. Grooms, coachmen, dog-boys, etc.	102	34	...	...	...	68
		64. Indoor servants	5,289	1,572	128	20	...	3,589
		65. Washermen	695	254	100	...	...	341
		66. Water carriers	725	212	38	...	...	475
		TOTAL SUB-ORDER 16	339	68	78	...	...	193
		Sanitation.						
		74. Sweepers and scavengers	339	68	78	...	...	193
D.—PREPARATION AND SUPPLY OF MATERIAL SUBSTANCES.	VII.—FOOD, DRINK AND STIMULANTS.	TOTAL CLASS D.—PREPARATION AND SUPPLY OF MATERIAL SUBSTANCES.	66.639	21,390	12.726	31	3	32,723
		TOTAL ORDER VII.—FOOD, DRINK AND STIMULANTS.	9.123	3.120	493	6	...	5.510
		TOTAL SUB-ORDER 17	3.558	1.202	290	...	...	2,066
		Provision of Animal Food.						
		78. Cow and buffalo keepers, and milk and butter sellers ...	2,184	774	265	...	...	1,145
		79. Fishermen and fish-curers	109	18	16	...	...	75
		80. Fish dealers	96	39	8	...	...	49
		81. Fowl and egg dealers	26	6	...	...	...	20
		84. Miscellaneous	1,143	365	1	...	...	777
		TOTAL SUB-ORDER 18	4.944	1.650	200	1	..	3.094
		Provision of vegetable food.						
		95. Bakers...	1,471	562	74	...	...	835
		96. Flour grinders	209	30	...	...	...	179
		98. Grain parchers	74	17	...	...	...	57
		100. Oil pressers	408	142	15	...	...	251
		102. Rice pounders and huskers...	434	115	70	...	...	240
		103. Sweetmeat-makers	1,008	276	...	...	...	732
		105. Vegetable and fruit sellers	1.340	508	41	1	...	791
		TOTAL SUB-ORDER 19	621	263	3	5	...	350
		Provision of drink Condiments and Stimulants.						
		112. Distilleries : operatives and other subordinates	1	...	...	...	...	1
		121. Water-works : managers and superior staff	9	9	...	...	...	...
		122. Water-works-workmen and other subordinates	58	12	...	5	...	46
		123. Cardamom, betel leaf and areca nut sellers	1	1	...	...	...	...
		126. Opium, bhang, gánja, etc., sellers	16	7	...	...	...	9
		130. Tobacco and snuff sellers	536	239	3	...	...	296

TABLE XV.

Occupation or Means of Livelihood.

SRINAGAR CITY.

Class.	Order.	Occupation or means of livelihood.	Total workers and dependents.	Actual workers. Total. Males.	Actual workers. Total. Females.	Actual workers. Partially agriculturists. Males.	Actual workers. Partially agriculturists. Females.	Dependents both sexes.
1	2	3	4	5	6	7	8	9
D.—PREPARATION AND SUPPLY OF MATERIAL SUBSTANCES—contd.	VIII.—Light, Firing and Forage.	**TOTAL ORDER VIII.—LIGHT, FIRING AND FORAGE** ...	**1,590**	**404**	**64**	**4**	...	**1,122**
		Total Sub-order 20	**213**	**50**	...	...	...	**163**
		Lighting.						
		145. Match, candle, torch, lamp, lantern makers and sellers, etc.	213	50	...	...	...	163
		Total Sub-order 21	**1,377**	**354**	**64**	**4**	...	**959**
		Fuel and Forage.						
		149. Hay, grass, and fodder sellers	293	86	16	..	...	191
		150. Firewood, charcoal and cow-dung sellers	1,084	268	48	4	...	768
	IX.—Buildings.	**TOTAL ORDER IX.—BUILDINGS**	**1,713**	**371**	**1**	**5**	...	**1,341**
		Total Sub-order 22	**714**	**107**	...	...	...	**607**
		Building Materials.						
		155. Brick and tile makers	684	107	..	...	...	577
		158. Lime, chunam and shell sellers	30	...	...	...	...	30
		Total Sub-order 23	**999**	**264**	**1**	**5**	...	**734**
		Artificers in Buildings.						
		163. Masons and builders	578	216	1	5	...	361
		164. Painters, plumbers and glaziers	421	48	...	...	...	373
	XI.—Supplementary Requirements.	**TOTAL ORDER XI.—SUPPLEMENTARY REQUIREMENTS.**	**2,044**	**732**	**5**	...	...	**1,307**
		Total Sub-order 27	**20**	**1**	...	...	...	**19**
		Paper.						
		181. Paper makers and sellers and palm leaf binders ...	20	1	...	...	...	19
		Total Sub-order 28	**343**	**87**	...	...	...	**256**
		Books and Prints.						
		185. Hand-press: proprietors, lithographers and printers ...	225	47	...	...	...	178
		186. Book binders	82	28	...	...	...	54
		187. Book-sellers, book agents and publishers	36	12	...	..	...	24
		Total Sub-order 29	**40**	**11**	...	..	...	**29**
		Watches, Clocks and Scientific Instruments.						
		190. Watch and clock makers	31	10	...	...	...	21
		191. Watch and clock sellers and opticians	9	1	...	...	..	8
		Total Sub-order 30	**200**	**76**	...	...	...	**124**
		Carving and Engraving.						
		197. Turners and lacquerers	48	3	...	...	...	45
		198. Dye-sinkers and seal, etc., engravers	128	63	...	..	...	65
		200. Mica, flint and talc workers, etc., and sellers	24	10	...	...	...	14
		Total Sub-order 31	**171**	**38**	...	...	...	**133**
		Toys and Curiosities.						
		203. Hukka-stem makers and sellers	90	26	...	...	...	64
		204. Papier-maché workers and sellers	81	12	...	...	...	69

TABLE XV.

Occupation or means of livelihood.

SRINAGAR CITY.

Class.	Order.	Occupations or means of livelihood.	Total workers and dependents.	Actual workers. Total. Males.	Actual workers. Total. Females.	Partially agriculturists. Males.	Partially agriculturists. Females.	Dependants both sexes.
1	2	3	4	5	6	7	8	9
D.—Preparation and supply of material substances—contd.	XI.—Supplementary requirements—concld.	Total Sub-order 33	**172**	**62**	**2**		...	**108**
		Bangles, necklaces, beads, sacred threads, etc.						
		211. Sellers of glass bangles	165	59	2	...	...	104
		215. Rosary, bead, and necklace sellers	7	3	...	...	...	4
		Total Sub-order 35	**1,019**	**402**	**3**	...	..	**614**
		Harness.						
		223. Saddle cloth makers, embroiderers and sellers	465	217	3	...	...	245
		224. Whip, good, and walking stick makers	554	185	..	...	...	369
		Total Sub-order 37	**79**	**55**	...	...	...	**24**
		Arms and Ammunition.						
		243. Gun makers, menders and sellers	72	52	...	...	...	20
		245. Ammunition, gunpowder and firework sellers	4	2	...	...	..	2
		246. Makers of swords, spears and other weapons	3	1	...	...	...	2
	XII.—Textile fabrics and dress.	TOTAL ORDER XII.—TEXTILE FABRICS AND DRESS	**43,552**	**13,535**	**12,073**	**14**	**3**	**17,924**
		Total Sub-order 38	**12,259**	**6,093**	**45**	**11**	...	**6,121**
		Wool and Fur.						
		248. Carpet weavers	3,660	1,022	33	...	...	2,605
		249. Shawl weavers	8,473	5,025	13	11	...	3,435
		250. Felt and pasham workers	126	46	..	...	...	80
		Total Sub-order 39	**1,367**	**564**	**27**	...	...	**776**
		Silk.						
		257. Silk mills: owners, managers and superior staff ...	9	7	...	...	...	2
		258. Silk mills: operatives and other subordinates	723	331	...	...	..	392
		259. Silk worm rearers and cocoon-gatherers	44	15	.	...	...	29
		260. Silk carders, spinners and weavers; makers of silk braid and thread.	591	211	27	...	...	353
		Total Sub-order 40	**14,907**	**870**	**11,769**	**1**	**3**	**2,268**
		Cotton.						
		271. Cotton cleaners, pressers and ginners	228	71	2	...	...	155
		272. Cotton weavers, hand industry	787	338	6	1	...	443
		275. Cotton spinners, sizers and yarn beaters	12,713	75	11,758	...	3	880
		277. Calenderers, fullers and printers	289	123	..	...	.	166
		278. Cotton dyers	392	132	1	...	...	259
		279. Tape-makers	480	131	2	...	...	347
		281. Tent-makers	18	...	...	...	...	18
		Total Sub-order 41	**270**	**38**	**133**	...	...	**99**
		Hemp, Flax, Coir, etc.						
		291. Rope, sacking and net sellers	3	1	...	.	.	2
		292. Fibre matting and bag makers	247	37	183	...	...	97
		Total Sub-order 42	**14,749**	**5,970**	**99**	**2**	..	**8,680**
		Dress.						
		301. Embroiderers and lace and muslin makers	1,057	465	1	1		591
		302. Hat, cap, and turban makers, binders and sellers ...	625	388	5		...	232
		303. Hosiers and haberdashers	306	31	63	...	...	212
		304. Piece-goods dealers	953	330	1	...	..	622
		306. Tailors, milliners, dress-makers and darners	11,805	4,756	29	1	...	7,020

TABLE XV.

Occupation or Means of Livelihood.

SRINAGAR CITY.

Class.	Order.	Occupation or means of livelihood.	Table for the City. Total workers and dependents.	Actual workers. Total. Males.	Actual workers. Total. Females.	Actual workers. Partially agriculturists. Males.	Actual workers. Partially agriculturists. Females.	Dependents both sexes.
1	2	3	4	5	6	7	8	9
D.—Preparation and supply of material substances—contd.	XIII.—Metals and Precious Stones.	**TOTAL ORDER XIII.—METALS AND PRECIOUS STONES**	**3,878**	**1,634**	**8**	...	...	**2,236**
		Total Sub-order 43	**2,472**	**1,127**	**2**	...	...	**1,343**
		Gold, Silver and Precious Stones.						
		314. Electro-platers	1	1	...	..	...	...
		315. Dealers in plate and plate-ware	86	14	...	...	...	72
		316. Gold and silver wire-drawers and braid-makers ...	478	195	...	...	...	283
		317. Workers in gold, silver and precious stones	1,870	908	2	...	...	960
		318. Dealers in gold, silver and precious stones	37	9	...	...	...	28
		Total Sub-order 44	**516**	**178**	...	..	..	**338**
		Brass, Copper and Bell Metal.						
		322. Brass, copper and bell metal-workers	516	178	...	...	...	338
		Total Sub-order 45	**151**	**43**	...	..	...	**108**
		Tin, Zinc, Quicksilver and Lead.						
		324. Workers in tin, zinc, quicksilver and lead	151	43	...	..	...	108
		Total Sub-order 46	**739**	**286**	**6**	...	...	**447**
		Iron and Steel.						
		325. Workers in iron and hardware	739	286	6	...	...	447
	XIV.—Glass, Earthen and Stoneware.	**TOTAL ORDER XIV.—GLASS, EARTHEN AND STONE-WARE.**	**311**	**105**	**20**	...	...	**186**
		Total Sub-order 47	**15**	**3**	...	...	...	**12**
		Glass and Chinaware.						
		333. Sellers of glass and Chinaware other than bangles ...	15	3	...	...	...	12
		Total Sub-order 48	**296**	**102**	**20**	...	..	**174**
		Earthen and Stoneware.						
		336. Potters and pot and pipe-bowl makers	296	102	20	...	...	174
	XV.—Wood, Cane and Leaves, etc.	**TOTAL ORDER XV.—WOOD, CANE AND LEAVES, etc. ...**	**3,113**	**952**	**24**	**2**	...	**2,137**
		Total Sub-order 49	**2,449**	**865**	**2**	**2**	...	**1,582**
		Wood and Bamboos.						
		344. Carpenters	1,688	553	1	...	...	1,134
		346. Wood cutters and sawyers	761	312	1	2	..	448
		Total Sub-order 50	**664**	**87**	**22**	...	...	**555**
		Cane works, matting and leaves, etc.						
		347. Baskets, mats, fans, screens, brooms, etc., makers and sellers.	158	45	22	...	...	91
		348. Comb and tooth stick makers and sellers	64	18	...	..	..	46
		349. Leaf plate makers and sellers	442	24	..	...	...	418
	XVI.—Drugs, Gums, Dyes, etc.	**TOTAL ORDER XVI.—DRUGS, GUMS, DYES, etc. ...**	**425**	**106**	**34**	...	..	**285**
		Total Sub-order 52	**425**	**106**	**34**	..	...	**285**
		Drugs, Dyes and Pigments, etc.						
		364. Soap factories: operatives and other subordinates ...	129	24	34	...	..	69
		369. Chemists and druggists	223	68	...	...	...	155
		373. Antimony preparers and sellers	33	...	...	...	...	33
		374. Madder, saffron and logwood workers and dealers ...	16	5	...	...	...	11
		377. Perfume, incense and sandal wood sellers	24	7	...	...	...	17

TABLE XV.

Occupation or Means of Livelihood.

SRINAGAR CITY.

Class.	Order.	Occupation or means of livelihood.	Total workers and dependents.	Actual workers. Total. Males.	Actual workers. Total. Females.	Actual workers. Partially agriculturists. Males.	Actual workers. Partially agriculturists. Females.	Dependents both sexes.
1	2	3	4	5	6	7	8	9
D.—Preparation and supply of material substances—concld.	XVII.—Leather, etc.	TOTAL ORDER XVII.—LEATHER, etc.	1,090	431	4	...	...	655
		Total Sub-order 53	1,090	431	4	...	..	655
		Leather, Horn and Bones.						
		386. Leather dyers	234	87	1	...	..	146
		387. Shoe, boot and saddle makers	814	338	3	...	...	473
		390. Sellers of hides, horns, bristles and bones	42	6	..	...	...	36
E.—Commerce, Transport, Storage.		TOTAL CLASS E.—COMMERCE, TRANSPORT, STORAGE	14,859	5,151	509	1	...	9,229
	XVIII.—Commerce.	TOTAL ORDER XVIII.—COMMERCE	8,637	2,853	18	...	...	5,766
		Total Sub-order 54	1,012	333	1	...	...	678
		Money and Securities.						
		392. Bankers, money-lenders, etc.	1,012	333	1	...	...	678
		Total Sub-order 55	2,439	635	15	...	...	1,789
		General Merchandise.						
		396 General merchants	2,439	635	15	...	...	1,789
		Total Sub-order 56	4,562	1,736	2	...	...	2,824
		Dealing Unspecified.						
		398. Shop-keepers, otherwise unspecified	4,360	1,626	2	...	...	2,732
		401. Pedlars, hawkers, etc.	202	110	...	...	...	92
		Total Sub-order 57	624	149	...	...	...	475
		Middlemen, Brokers and Agents.						
		402. Brokers and agents	392	79	...	...	...	313
		405. Farmers of liquor, opium, etc.	8	6	...	...	...	2
		407. Contractors, otherwise unspecified	224	64	...	...	...	160
	XIX.—Transport and Storage.	TOTAL ORDER XIX.—TRANSPORT AND STORAGE ...	6,252	2,298	491	1	...	3,463
		Total Sub-order 59	465	137	...	...	...	328
		Road.						
		422. Pack[camel, elephant, mule, etc., owners and drivers ...	465	137	...	...	...	328
		Total Sub-order 60	5,084	2,006	476	1	...	2,602
		Water.						
		429. Boat and barge men	5,061	2,003	476	1	...	2,582
		430. Pilots	23	3	...	..	...	20
		Total Sub-order 61	385	78	...	...	...	307
		Messages.						
		433. Post Office: officers and superior staff	3	1	...	..	...	2
		434. Post Office: clerks, messengers, runners and other subordinates.	329	63	...	...	...	266
		435. Telegraph: officers and superior staff	7	5	...	...	...	2
		436. Telegraph: clerks, signallers, messengers and other subordinates.	46	9	...	...	...	37
		Total Sub-order 62	318	77	15	...	...	226
		Storage and Weighing.						
		441. Porters	261	50	14	...	...	197
		442. Weighmen and measurers	57	27	1	...	...	29

TABLE XV.

OCCUPATION OR MEANS OF LIVELIHOOD.

SRINAGAR CITY.

Class.	Order.	Occupation or means of livelihood.	TABLE FOR THE CITY. Total workers and dependents.	Actual workers. Total. Males.	Actual workers. Total. Females.	Actual workers. Partially agriculturists. Males.	Actual workers. Partially agriculturists. Females.	Dependents both sexes.
1	2	3	4	5	6	7	8	9
F.—PROFESSIONS	XX.—LEARNED AND ARTISTIC PROFESSIONS	TOTAL CLASS F.—PROFESSIONS ...	8,745	2,935	69	2	...	5,741
		TOTAL ORDER XX.—LEARNED AND ARTISTIC PROFESSIONS.	8,574	2,873	65	1		5,636
		TOTAL SUB-ORDER 63 ...	4,404	1,566	31		...	2,807
		Religion.						
		444. Priests, ministers, etc.	2,490	534	25		...	1,629
		445. Catechists, readers, church and mission service, etc. ...	60	2		...	...	58
		446. Religious mendicants, inmates of monasteries, convents, etc.	1,391	569	3	...	...	819
		447. Church, temple, burial or burning ground service, pilgrim conductors, undertakers, etc.	325	132	.	..	...	193
		449. Astrologers, divines, horoscope makers, etc.	138	29	...	...	...	109
		TOTAL SUB-ORDER 64 ...	619	173	6	1	...	440
		Education.						
		452. Principals, Professors and Teachers	83	43	4	1	...	36
		453. Clerks and servants connected with education	536	130	2	...	...	404
		TOTAL SUB-ORDER 65 .	923	229		..	...	694
		Literature.						
		457. Public scribes and copyists	923	229	..	..	...	694
		TOTAL SUB-ORDER 66 ...	343	70	...		...	273
		Law.						
		459. Barristers, advocates and pleaders...	164	34	...	...	...	130
		461. Law agents, mukhtiárs, etc	7	1	...	...	...	6
		462. Kazis	8	..	...	...	...	8
		465. Stamp-vendors	164	35	...	...	...	129
		TOTAL SUB-ORDER 67	763	214	26	2	...	523
		Medicine.						
		467. Practitioners with diploma, license or certificate ..	3	3	...	...	...	...
		468. Practitioners without diploma	520	156	19	...	...	345
		473. Compounders, matrons, nurses and hospital asylum and dispensary service.	240	55	7	...	...	178
		TOTAL SUB-ORDER 68	75	25	...	...	...	50
		Engineering and Survey.						
		475. Civil Engineers and architects	4	2	...	...	...	2
		477. Draughtsmen and operators in survey offices, overseers, etc.	71	23	...	...	...	48
		TOTAL SUB-ORDER 70 . ..	1,218	527	2	...	...	689
		Pictorial Art and Sculpture.						
		483. Painters, Superintendents of Schools of Art, etc. ...	1,173	516	1	...	...	656
		484. Sculptors	84	6	1	...	...	77
		485. Photographers	11	5	...	...	...	6
		TOTAL SUB-ORDER 71	229	69	...	...	...	160
		Music, Acting, Dancing, etc.						
		490. Actors, singers and dancers and their accompanists ...	229	69	...	...	...	160

TABLE XV.

Occupation or Means of Livelihood.

SRINAGAR CITY

Class.	Order.	Occupation or means of livelihood.	Total workers and dependants.	Actual workers. Total. Males.	Actual workers. Total. Females.	Partially agriculturists. Males.	Partially agriculturists. Females.	Dependants both sexes.
1	2	3	4	5	6	7	8	9
F.—Professions—concld.	XXI.—Sport.	TOTAL ORDER XXI.—SPORT ..	171	62	4	1	..	105
		Total Sub-order 72	84	35	3	1	...	48
		Sport.						
		492. Shikaries, falconers, bird-catchers	84	35	3	1	...	46
		Total Sub-order 73	87	27	1	...	...	59
		Games and Exhibitions						
		498. Conjurors, buffoons, reciters, fortune-tellers, etc. ..	87	27	1	...	...	59
G.—Unskilled labour, not agricultural.		TOTAL CLASS G.—UNSKILLED LABOUR, NOT AGRICULTURAL.	5.130	1.712	346	1	...	3.072
	XXII.—Earthwork and General Labour.	TOTAL ORDER XXII.—EARTHWORK AND GENERAL LABOUR.	4.972	1.686	278	1	...	3,008
		Total Sub-order 74	13	3	4	...	...	6
		Earthwork, etc.						
		500. Well-sinkers	13	3	4	..	...	6
		Total Sub-order 75	4,959	1,683	274	1	...	3,002
		General Labour.						
		504. General labour	4,959	1,683	274	1	...	3,002
	XXIII.—Indefinite and Disreputable Occupations.	TOTAL ORDER XXIII.—INDEFINITE AND DISREPUTABLE OCCUPATIONS.	158	26	68	...	...	64
		Total Sub-order 76	29	26	...	...	...	3
		Indefinite						
		505. Uncertain or not returned	29	26	...	...	...	3
		Total Sub-order 77	129	..	68	...	.	61
		Disreputable						
		506. Prostitutes including saqins and nauchis	129	.	68	...	...	61
H.—Means of subsistence independent of occupation.		TOTAL CLASS H.—MEANS OF SUBSISTENCE INDEPENDENT OF OCCUPATION.	4,112	1,240	139	3	...	2,733
	XXIV.—Independent.	TOTAL ORDER XXIV.—INDEPENDENT	4,112	1,240	139	3	...	2,733
		Total Sub-order 78	3.097	953	128	3	...	2,016
		Property and Alms.						
		510. House-rent, shares, and other property not being land ...	1,473	460	20	2	...	993
		511. Allowances from patrons or relatives	20	8	3	...	...	9
		513. Mendicancy (not in connection with a religious order)	1.604	485	105	1	...	1.014
		Total Sub-order 79	1.015	287	11	...	...	717
		At the State Expense.						
		514. Pensions, civil services	200	63	8	...	...	129
		516. Pension, unspecified	671	83	3	...	...	585
		518. Prisoners, under-trial	15	15	...	...	...	...
		520. Prisoners, convicted or in reformatories, etc.	129	127	...	...	...	2

TABLE XVII.

JAMMU AND KASHMIR STATE.

Territorial Distribution of the Christian Population

BY

Sect and Race.

TABLE

JAMMU AND

TERRITORIAL DISTRIBUTION OF THE

DENOMINATION.	TOTAL STATE.									JAMMU PROVINCE.								
	TOTAL RETURNED.			DISTRIBUTION BY RACES.						TOTAL RETURNED.			DISTRIBUTION BY RACES.					
				European and allied races.		*Eurasian.*		*Native.*					*European & allied races.*		*Eurasian.*		*Native.*	
	Persons.	Males.	Females.	Males.	Females.	Males.	Females.	Males.	Females.	Persons.	Males.	Females.	Males.	Females.	Males.	Females.	Males.	Females.
1	2	3	4	5	6	7	8	9	10	11	12	13	14	15	16	17	18	19
ANGLICAN COMMUNION.																		
Church of England ...	152	73	79	60	69	2	6	11	4	10	6	4	3	4	...	...	2	...
" " Ireland ...	3	3	...	3	...	...	...	...	...	...	...	...	...	...	...	...	...	...
Protestant ...	81	43	38	22	8	5	2	16	28	18	10	8	3	1	1	...	6	7
Total Anglican Communion ...	236	119	117	85	77	7	8	27	32	28	16	12	6	5	1	...	9	7
CALVANIST ...	1	1	...	...	...	...	...	1	...	1	1	...	...	...	...	...	1	...
PRESBYTERIAN.																		
Church of Scotland ...	6	6	...	6	...	...	...	...	...	2	2	...	2	...	...	...	...	...
American ...	7	4	3	...	...	...	...	4	3	...	...	...	...	...	...	...	...	...
Scotch Mission ...	27	14	13	...	...	...	...	14	13	27	14	13	...	...	...	...	14	13
Total Presbyterian ...	40	24	16	6	...	...	...	18	16	29	16	13	2	...	...	...	14	13
ROMAN CATHOLIC ...	33	26	7	10	5	2	2	14	...	2	2	...	...	...	...	...	2	...
Denomination not returned ...	112	66	46	5	9	1	3	60	34	85	52	33	...	...	1	3	51	30
GRAND TOTAL ...	422	236	186	106	91	10	13	120	82	145	87	58	8	5	2	3	77	50

KASHMIR STATE.

CHRISTIAN POPULATION BY SECT AND RACE.

Kashmir Province.									Frontier Districts.								
Total returned.			Distribution by races.						Total returned.			Distribution by races.					
			European and allied races.		Eurasian.		Native.					European and allied races.		Eurasian.		Native.	
Persons.	Males.	Females.	Males.	Females.	Males.	Females.	Males.	Females.	Persons.	Males.	Females.	Males.	Females.	Males.	Females.	Males.	Females.
20	21	22	23	24	25	26	27	28	29	30	31	32	33	34	35	36	37
128	60	68	50	58	2	6	8	4	14	7	7	7	7	...	...	...	...
3	3	...	3	...	...	...	...	...	...	...	...	...	...	...	...	...	...
53	25	28	14	5	1	2	10	21	10	8	2	5	2	3	...	...	...
184	**88**	**96**	**67**	**63**	**3**	**8**	**18**	**25**	**24**	**15**	**9**	**12**	**9**	**3**	...	...	...
...	...	...	...	...	...	...	...	...	...	...	...	...	...	...	...	...	...
4	4	...	4	...	...	...	...	...	...	...	...	...	...	...	...	...	...
7	4	3	...	...	...	...	4	3	...	...	...	...	...	...	...	...	...
...	...	...	...	...	...	...	...	...	...	...	...	...	...	...	...	...	...
11	**8**	**3**	**4**	...	...	...	**4**	**3**	...	...	...	...	...	...	...	...	...
23	19	4	7	2	2	2	10	...	8	5	3	2	3	1	...	2	...
26	13	13	4	9	...	...	9	4	1	1	...	1	...		...	...	...
244	**128**	**116**	**82**	**74**	**5**	**10**	**41**	**32**	**33**	**21**	**12**	**15**	**12**	**4**	...	**2**	...

TABLE XVIII.

JAMMU AND KASHMIR STATE.

Europeans and Eurasians by Age.

JAMMU AND

EUROPEANS AND

Civil condition.	Total.			European and Allied — British Subject. All ages.			0 and under 12.		12 and under 15.		15 and under 30.		20 and under 50.		50 and over.		All ages.			0 and under 12.	
	Persons.	Males.	Females.	Persons.	Males.	Females.	Males.	Females.	Males.	Females.	Males.	Females.	Males.	Females.	Males.	Females.	Persons.	Males.	Females.	Males.	Females.
1	2	3	4	5	6	7	8	9	10	11	12	13	14	15	16	17	18	19	20	21	22
JAMMU PROVINCE.																					
Unmarried ..	9	4	5	7	4	3	..	2	..	..	2	1	2		...	.	..	.			...
Married .	6	6	3	6	4	2	..	...	...	...	1	2	3	..	...	...		...	..	...	...
Widowed .	...	...		..		..			.	..	...	..	...	...	.	..		...	...	...	...
Total	**18**	**10**	**8**	**13**	**8**	**5**	..	**2**	..	..	**3**	**3**	**5**	...		...	.	...		...	...
KASHMIR PROVINCE.																					
Unmarried ..	121	65	56	101	55	46	17	15	3	..	17	21	15	8	...	2	6	3	3	1	2
Married ...	70	38	32	67	37	30	...	..	..	..	4	10	21	14	12	6	1	1	...	...	..
Widowed ...	11	3	8	8	1	7	...	..	.	-	.	..	1	2	...	5	1	1	...		...
Total ...	**202**	**106**	**96**	**176**	**93**	**83**	**17**	**15**	**3**	.	**21**	**31**	**45**	**24**	**12**	**13**	**8**	**5**	**3**	**1**	**2**
JAMMU AND KASHMIR STATE.																					
Unmarried ...	130	69	61	108	59	49	17	17	3	..	19	22	20	8	...	2	6	3	3	1	2
Married ...	79	44	35	73	41	32	..	...	...	..	5	12	24	14	12	6	1	1	...	...	...
Widowed ...	11	3	8	8	1	7	.	...	...	...	..	..	1	2	..	5	1	1	...	...	...
Total State ...	**220**	**116**	**104**	**189**	**101**	**88**	**17**	**17**	**3**	.	**24**	**34**	**45**	**24**	**12**	**13**	**8**	**5**	**3**	**1**	**2**

Note.—No Armenians.

KASHMIR STATE.

EURASIANS BY AGE

RACES. Others. 12 and under 15. Males.	Females.	15 and under 30. Males.	Females.	30 and under 50. Males.	Females.	50 and over. Males.	Females.	EURASIANS. All ages. Persons.	Males.	Females.	0 and under 12. Males.	Females.	12 and under 15. Males.	Females.	15 and under 30. Males.	Females.	30 and under 50. Males.	Females.	50 and over. Males.	Females.
23	24	25	26	27	28	29	30	31	32	33	34	35	36	37	38	39	40	41	42	43
...	...	...	...	...	...	...	...	2	...	2	...	2	...	...	...	...	...	...	...	...
...	...	...	...	...	...	...	...	3	2	1	...	...	...	...	...	...	2	1	...	...
...	...	...	...	...	...	...	...	...	...	...	...	...	...	...	...	...	...	...	...	...
...	...	...	...	...	...	...	...	**5**	**2**	**3**	...	**2**	...	...	...	...	**2**	**1**	...	...
...	...	2	1	...	...	...	...	14	7	7	1	...	...	...	4	6	2	1	...	...
...	...	...	...	...	...	1	...	2	...	2	...	...	...	...	...	...	...	2	...	...
...	...	...	...	...	...	1	...	2	1	1	...	...	...	...	...	...	1	1	...	...
...	...	**2**	**1**			**2**	...	**18**	**8**	**10**	**1**	...	...	...	**4**	**6**	**3**	**4**	...	...
...	...	2	1	...	...	...	...	16	7	9	1	2	...	...	4	6	2	1	...	...
...	...	...	...	...	...	1	...	5	2	3	...	...	...	...	...	...	2	3	...	...
...	...	...	...	...	...	1	...	2	1	1	...	...	...	...	...	...	1	1	...	...
...	...	**2**	**1**	...	...	**2**	...	**23**	**10**	**13**	**1**	**2**		...	**4**	**6**	**5**	**5**	...	...

have been censused.

TABLE XVIII.

JAMMU CITY.

Europeans and Eurasians by Age.

TABLE

JAMMU AND

EUROPEANS AND

Civil Condition.	Total.			European and Allied																	
				British Subjects.																	
				All ages.			*0 and under 12*		*12 and under 15.*		*15 and under 30.*		*30 and under 50.*		*50 and over*		*All ages.*			*0 and under 12.*	
	Total.	Males.	Females.	Total.	Males.	Females.	Males.	Females.	Males.	Females.	Males.	Females.	Males.	Females.	Males.	Females.	Total.	Males.	Females.	Males.	Females.
1	2	3	4	5	6	7	8	9	10	11	12	13	14	15	16	17	18	19	20	21	22
JAMMU CITY																					
Unmarried ...	4	2	2	2	2	...	...	...	...	...	...	...	2	...	...	...	...	...	...	...	...
Married ...	6	4	2	4	3	1	...	...	...	...	1	1	2	...	...	...	...	...	...	...	...
Widowed ...	...	...	...	...	...	...	...	...	...	...	...	...	...	...	...	...	...	...	...	...	...
Total ...	10	6	4	6	5	1	...	...	...	...	1	1	4	...	...	...	...	...	...	...	...

Note.—No A[illegible].

KASHMIR STATE.

EURASIANS BY AGE.

RACES.								EURASIANS.												
OTHERS.								*All ages.*			*0 and under 12.*		*12 and under 15.*		*15 and under 30.*		*30 and under 50.*		*50 and over.*	
12 and under 15		*15 and under 30.*		*30 and under 50.*		*50 and over*														
Males.	Females.	Males.	Females.	Males.	Females.	Males.	Females.	Totals.	Males.	Females.	Males.	Females.	Males.	Females.	Males.	Females.	Males.	Females.	Males.	Females.
23	24	25	26	27	28	29	30	31	32	33	34	35	36	37	38	39	40	41	42	43
...	...	...	...	...	...	...	...	2	...	2	...	2	...	...	...	...	...	...	...	...
...	...	...	...	...	...	...	...	2	1	1	...	...	...	...	...	...	1	1	...	...
...	...	...	...	...	...	...	..	...	...	...	...	..	..	...	...	..	..	...	...	...
...	...	...	...	...	..	...	...	4	1	3	..	2	...	...	...	...	1	1	...	...

have been censused.

TABLE XVIII.

SRINAGAR CITY.

Europeans and Eurasians by Age.

TABLE

JAMMU AND

EUROPEANS AND

Civil Condition.	TOTAL			EUROPEAN AND																	
				British Subjects.																	
				All ages.			0 and *under* 12		12 *and under* 15		15 *and under* 30		30 *and under* 50		50 *and over*		*All ages.*			0 *and under* 12	
	Total.	Males.	Females.	Total	Males.	Females.	Males.	Females.	Males.	Females.	Males.	Females.	Males.	Females.	Males.	Females.	Total	Males.	Females.	Males.	Females.
1	2	3	4	5	6	7	8	9	10	11	12	13	14	15	16	17	18	19	20	21	22
SRINAGAR CITY.																					
Unmarried ...	71	33	38	61	29	32	8	9			11	14	10	8	...	1	2	1	1	...	...
Married ...	40	22	18	38	21	17					1	5	10	7	10	5	1	1	...		...
Widowed ...	9	2	7	8	1	7	...	...					1	2	...	5		...	...		...
Total ...	**120**	**57**	**63**	**107**	**51**	**56**	**8**	**9**			**12**	**19**	**21**	**17**	**10**	**11**	**3**	**2**	**1**	**...**	**...**

Note.—No Armenians have

XVIII.

KASHMIR STATE.

EURASIANS BY AGE.

ALLIED RACES. Others.								EURASIANS.												
12 and under 15.		15 and under 30.		30 and under 50		50 and over.		All ages.			0 and under 12		12 and under 15.		15 and under 30.		30 and under 50.		50 and over.	
Males.	Females.	Males	Females	Males	Females	Males	Females	Total	Males.	Females.	Males	Females.	Males.	Females.	Males.	Females	Males.	Females.	Males.	Females.
23	24	25	26	27	28	29	30	31	32	33	34	35	36	37	38	39	40	41	42	43
.		1	1		..			8	3	5	...	..	...		3	4	..	1	..	...
.		..	.		..	1	.	1		1	...	...	..				.	1	..	...
.			.	.				1	1	...	.		.			..	1		..	...
...	...	1	1		..	1	...	10	4	6	..	...		...	3	4	1	2	...	...

[illegible]